Augsburg College
George Sverdrup Library
Minneapolis, Minnesota

WITHDRAWN

Mathematical Models
in International Relations

edited by
**Dina A. Zinnes
John V. Gillespie**

The Praeger Special Studies program—utilizing the most modern and efficient book production techniques and a selective worldwide distribution network—makes available to the academic, government, and business communities significant, timely research in U.S. and international economic, social, and political development.

Mathematical Models
in International Relations

Praeger Publishers   New York   Washington   London

PRAEGER SPECIAL STUDIES IN INTERNATIONAL POLITICS AND GOVERNMENT

Library of Congress Cataloging in Publication Data
Main entry under title:

Mathematical models in international relations.

(Praeger special studies in international politics and government)
Includes bibliographical references.
1. International relations—Mathematical models.
I. Zinnes, Dina A.   II. Gillespie, John V.
JX1291.M38   327'.01'51   75-25000
ISBN 0-275-55870-3

PRAEGER PUBLISHERS
111 Fourth Avenue, New York, N.Y. 10003, U.S.A.

Published in the United States of America in 1976
by Praeger Publishers, Inc.

All rights reserved

© 1976 by Praeger Publishers, Inc.

Printed in the United States of America

PREFACE

A few years ago a volume of this sort would have been a near impossibility in international relations. Today, with the ever-increasing sophistication of young scholars and the retooling by those with years of experience, a volume demonstrating the utility and productivity of mathematical reasoning in international relations research is possible. In fact some may argue that the kind of rigorous analysis presented in this volume is overdue.

Our intent in editing this book is to demonstrate the rich uses to which mathematical reasoning can be put in international relations research. Whether one is interested in clarifying theoretical ideas and principles, constructing and testing models about international processes, or discussing public policy options and implications, mathematics can be used effectively to assist the researcher in reasoning through complicated problems. Although a single volume cannot cover the full range of mathematical techniques and methods that can be employed in international relations research, we hope that, by selecting topics that apply such areas of mathematical reasoning as probability theory, mathematical logic, ordinary differential equations and linear optimization, we have represented some of the more fruitful mathematical tools for international relations research. And yet these tools are only a beginning; as modelers and scholars of international politics we have only begun to see the precision and utility derived from mathematical reasoning. Our purpose is not only to demonstrate the utility of mathematical reasoning but also to build awareness that through such rigorous argumentation, the researcher-scholar can make significant statements about international relations.

In editing this volume several individuals have been generous in their assistance. We especially have benefited from the loyal and careful assistance of Ms. Roslyn L. Simowitz and Ms. Marcia Prins. We also desire to thank the National Science Foundation for their support of our research through grants GS-36806, 74-24186, and SOC 75-04212. Drs. G. R. Boynton and David C. Leege, Program Directors for Political Science at NSF during the tenure of our support have offered constant encouragement and have served as devoted administrators. They both have represented their profession and the National Science Foundation well. We also wish to thank the Ford Foundation for their institutional support grant to the Center for International Policy Studies at Indiana University (grant 750-0514). These monies have enabled us to interact with colleagues through seminars and cooperative projects. Our colleagues have spirited us to think about new things and have given us outstanding advice and criticism.

CONTENTS

	Page
PREFACE	v
LIST OF TABLES	xiv
LIST OF FIGURES	xvi

Chapter

PART I: PERSPECTIVES ON MATHEMATICAL REASONING

1 INTELLECTUAL INDENTITY AND THE STUDY OF INTERNATIONAL RELATIONS, OR COMING TO TERMS WITH MATHEMATICS AS A TOOL OF INQUIRY — 3
James N. Rosenau

2 MATHEMATICAL METHODS IN THEORIES OF INTERNATIONAL RELATIONS: EXPECTATIONS, CAVEATS, AND OPPORTUNITIES — 10
Anatol Rapoport

The Quest for Objectivity	10
The Quest for A Rigorous Theory	11
The Quest for Control	12
The Quantitative Empirical Approach	14
The Mathematical Approach	17
What Are the Obstacles to Mathematization?	19
Are Prediction and Control the Main Goals of Social Science?	26
Ideational Spin-offs	27
The Game-Theoretic Approach	28
Conclusions	32
Notes	36

3 WHY MATHEMATICAL MODELS? — 37
John V. Gillespie

Chapter		Page
	Mathematics as Language	38
	The Language of International Relations	44
	Mathematics as a Language in International Relations	49
	On the Use of Mathematics	55
	Concluding Comments	58
	Notes	59

PART II: PROBABILITY MODELS

4   INTRODUCTION TO PROBABILITY MODELS   65
The Editors

	Assumptions	67
	Analyses of the Models	71
	Conclusion	72

5   MEMBERSHIP IN INTER-NATION ALLIANCES, 1815-1965: AN EXPLORATION UTILIZING MATHEMATICAL PROBABILITY MODELS   74
Brian L. Job

	Membership in Inter-Nation Alliances	75
	An Initial Clarification of Terms	75
	Previous Research on Inter-Nation Alliances	76
	The Distinction Between Alliance Memberships and Dyadic Partnerships	78
	Mathematical Models and Our Research Problem	79
	"One-Way" Process Models	82
	Data on Inter-Nation Alliances, 1815-1965	82
	A Brief Check on Inter-Nation Alliance Activity over Time	83
	An Initial Model of the Acquisition of Alliance Memberships	86
	A Model Involving Contagion Effects	90
	Models of the Acquisition of Dyadic Alliance Ties	95
	"Equilibrium" Models	96
	An Initial Model Involving the Acquisition and Loss of Alliance Membership	97
	A Revised "Equilibrium" Model	98
	Equilibrium Models and the Distribution of Dyadic Alliance Ties	103

Chapter		Page
	Some Final Comments	104
	Notes	106
6	STOCHASTIC MODELS OF INTERNATIONAL ALLIANCE INITIATION, 1885-1965 Randolph M. Siverson and George T. Duncan	110
	The Models	111
	The Poisson Process Model	111
	Alternatives to the Poisson Process: Contagion and Heterogeneity	113
	The Data	116
	Data Analysis	117
	1815-1965	117
	1815-1914	119
	1919-39	120
	1945-65	124
	Conclusion	128
	Notes	129
7	POWER AND DISTANCE IN INTERNATIONAL CONFLICT BEHAVIOR Manus I. Midlarsky	132
	Power as Uncertainty Reduction	134
	The Most Probable Distribution of Power in Relation to Distance	137
	Comparisons Among Theoretical and Observed Distributions	141
	A Model of Conflict Behavior	143
	Applicability to Crisis Situations	147
	Assessing Empirical Validity in the Context of Interventions	150
	Conclusion	153
	Notes	154
8	RICHARDSON'S MODEL AS A MARKOV PROCESS Philip A. Schrodt	156
	The Richardson Arms-Race Model	159
	Stochastic Processes	159
	Richardson's Model as a Markov Chain	162
	Long-Term Properties of a Markov Chain	169

Chapter		Page
	Conclusion	172
	Notes	173

PART III: RICHARDSON-TYPE PROCESS MODELS

9	INTRODUCTION TO RICHARDSON-TYPE PROCESS MODELS The Editors	179
	The Structure of the Models	180
	Relationship to the Arms Literature	185
	Notes	187
10	A REINTERPRETATION OF THE RICHARDSON ARMS-RACE MODEL Dina A. Zinnes, John V. Gillespie, and R. Michael Rubison	189
	The Meaning of Negative Constants	190
	The Concepts of Equilibrium and Stability	192
	Patterns of Stability	199
	Patterns of Instability	212
	Stability in the Rivalry Model	212
	Summary and Conclusion	216
	Notes	216
11	ON THE EFFECTS OF AID TO NATIONS IN ARMS RACES John A. Ferejohn	218
	The Richardson Model	218
	Empirical Quandary of Richardson-type Models	220
	A Graphical Analysis of Military Aid	222
	A Model	229
	Estimation and Analysis	238
	Conclusions	249
	Notes	251
12	THREE MODELS OF ARMS RACES Michael L. Squires	252

Chapter		Page
	Discussion	253
	Economic Constraints	254
	Desired Arms Stocks, Unconditional Viability, and Trust	255
	Alliances	258
	Conventional Weapons and Strategic Weapons	260
	Differential Equations and Difference Equations	261
	Model 1: A Difference Equation Model Convertible into Computer Simulation	262
	Model 2: Addition of Defensive Alliances	267
	Model 3: Defensive Alliances as a Dynamic Component	267
	Stability Conditions for Model 1	270
	Conclusion	272
	Notes	272
13	AN OPERATIONS ANALYSIS MODEL FOR THE STUDY OF NUCLEAR MISSILE SYSTEM POLICIES William H. Baugh	274
	Development of the Model as an Assumption Set	277
	Political Assumptions	277
	Weapons Assumptions	278
	Strategic Doctrine and Usage Assumptions	279
	Development of the Model in Mathematical Form	282
	Structure and Sequence of Action	282
	The General Survivability Function	283
	The Counterforce (First) Strike	286
	The Countervalue (Second) Strike	290
	Kill Probabilities	292
	Summary Expression of the Model in Mathematical Form	293
	Interactive Computation Structure	294
	Sample Applications	295
	The U.S.-Soviet Strategic Balance, Circa 1975	295
	The Vladivostok Accords of 1974	298
	The ABM Contribution	299
	The Accuracy Race	300
	New Avenues for Nuclear-Exchange Model Application and Development	302
	Notes	304

Chapter		Page

PART IV: DECISION-MAKING MODELS

14	INTRODUCTION TO DECISION-MAKING MODELS The Editors	309
	Elements of a Rational Decision-making Model	310
	Additional Assumptions	313
	Uses of Rational Decision Making	314
	Concluding Comment	317
15	BALANCE OF POWER AND THE MAINTENANCE OF "BALANCE": A RATIONAL-CHOICE MODEL WITH LEXICAL PREFERENCES Charles W. Ostrom, Jr.	318
	The Balance-of-Power Model	320
	Maintaining a Balance	326
	Conclusion	329
	Notes	331
16	ALLIANCES AND THE THEORY OF COLLECTIVE GOODS: AN EVALUATION Roslyn L. Simowitz	333
	Logical Notation and Rules of Inference	335
	Logical Notation	335
	Description of the Rules of Inference	335
	Description of the Reductio Ad Absurdum Strategy	336
	The Concept of Collective Good	337
	An Analysis of the Arguments Used to Explain Disproportionate Cost Sharing in Alliances	343
	Implications for International Relations	344
	Notes	346
17	POLICY ZONE: WHERE POLICIES WORK Martin W. Sampson III	348
	Components of the Model	349
	Decision Rules Toward the USSR	350
	Decision Rule Toward Domestic Influence in the United States	352
	Decision Rule Toward Oil Producers	355

Chapter		Page
	Saudi Arabian Decision Rule Toward the United States	357
	Soviet Decision Rule Toward the United States	358
	U.S. Lobby Decision Rule Toward the USSR	358
	Summary of the Decision Rules	359
	Linear Programming and the Model	359
	Linear Programming	360
	A Linear Programming Model of U.S. Policy	363
	Responses to Other Actors	365
	The Policy Zone	366
	Alternative Policies	368
	Other Policy Zones	372
	Conclusion	373
	Notes	373
18	A GAME-THEORY MODEL OF OPEC, OIL CONSUMERS, AND OIL COMPANIES, EMPHASIZING COALITION FORMATIONS Charles Bird and Martin W. Sampson III	376
	Cooperative Game Theory	378
	Characteristic Functions	378
	Solution Concepts	380
	Construction of the Characteristic-Function Game	386
	Further Deductive Outcomes	392
	Notes	396
ABOUT THE CONTRIBUTORS		398

LIST OF TABLES

Table		Page
5.1	National Alliance Memberships, 1815-1965	80
5.2	Total National Dyadic Alliance Ties, Excluding the OAS and OAU, 1815-1965	81
5.3	National Alliance Memberships, All Types of Alliances: The Application of the Poisson and Revised Poisson Models, 1815-99 and 1900-65	88
5.4	National Alliance Memberships, All Types of Alliances: The Application of the Poisson and Revised Poisson Models, 1815-70, 1871-1914, 1919-39, and 1945-65	89
5.5	National Dyadic Alliance Ties, Selected Years: The Application of the Poisson and Revised Poisson Models	99
6.1	Instances of Alliance Activity, 1815-1965	119
6.2	Instances of Alliance Activity, 1815-1914	120
6.3	Instances of Alliance Activity, 1919-39	121
6.4	Time Series of Alliance Activity During the Interwar Years, 1919-39	122
6.5	Instances of Alliance Activity, 1945-65	125
6.6	Non-Cold War Alliance Activity, 1945-65	126
6.7	Cold War Alliance Activity, 1945-65	127
6.8	Time Series of Cold War Alliance Activity, 1945-65	128
7.1	Sample of Crises Since World War II	149
7.2	Observed and Predicted Frequencies of Military Intervention, 1948-67	151
11.1	Proportion of Total Expenditures Used for Military Spending	236

Table		Page
13.1	Summary of Symbols Used in the Nuclear-Exchange Model DETER/YIELD	287
17.1	U.S. Armaments Shipments to Israel and Soviet Armaments Shipments to Egypt, 1967-72	352

LIST OF FIGURES

Figure		Page
5.1	National Alliance Commitments, 1815-1965	84
5.2	National Dyadic Alliance Commitments, 1815-1965	85
5.3	National Defensive Alliance Memberships, 1815-99: The Application of the Poisson and Revised Poisson Models	93
5.4	National Dyadic Alliance Memberships, 1939, Excluding the OAS	102
7.1	The Exercise of Power of a Linear Function of Distance for Two Countries, G and H	133
7.2	Observed and Predicted Lift Capabilities from the Continental United States	135
8.1	"Random Walk" Routes, Illustrating the Stochastic Process	161
10.1	An Illustration of the Dynamics of the Richardson Arms-Race Model: The Stability Case	193
10.2	An Illustration of the Dynamics of the Richardson Arms-Race Model: The Unstable Case	195
10.3	Trajectory of Arms Race in Asymptotically Stable Cases	200
10.4	Trajectory and Barriers in Case 1: (ξ, η) Plane	202
10.5	Trajectory and Barriers in Case 1: (x, y) Plane	203
10.6	Trajectory and Barriers in Case 2, subcase a: (ϕ, ψ) Plane	205
10.7	Trajectory and Barriers in Case 2, subcase b: (x, y) Plane	206
10.8	Trajectory and Barriers in Case 2, subcase b: (ϕ, ψ) Plane	206

Figure		Page
10.9	Trajectory and Barriers in Case 2, subcase b: (x, y) Plane	207
10.10	Trajectory and Barriers in Case 3, subcase a: (x, y) Plane	208
10.11	Trajectory and Barriers in Case 3, subcase b: $p(0)$ and $\omega(0)$ Have Same Sign	209
10.12	Trajectory and barriers in Case 3, subcase b: $p(0)$ and $\omega(0)$ of Different Sign	210
10.13	Trajectory and Barriers in Case 3, subcase b: (x, y) Plane, Positive Slope	210
10.14	Trajectory and Barriers in Case 3, subcase b: (x, y) Plane, Positive Slope	211
10.15	Instability in Case 1	213
10.16	Instability in Case 2, subcase b	213
10.17	Instability in Case 3, subcase a	214
10.18	Instability in Case 3, subcase b	214
10.19	Instability When $D > 0$ and $(ab - \ell K) < 0$	215
11.1	The Decision Maker's Allocation Problem	223
11.2	The Effect of Unrestricted Aid on the Allocation of the Budget	224
11.3	The Effect of Military Aid on the Budget When the Aid Is Received Prior to Budget Formation	225
11.4	The Effect of Military Aid on the Budget	226
11.5	The Effect of Military Aid Given After Budget Formation	227
11.6	The Effect of Increased Military Expenditures to the Other Nations	228

Figure		Page
11.7	One-Shot Aid to Nation 1	235
11.8	Continuing Aid to Nation 1	237
11.9	Residual Plot for Pakiston for Model 1	242
11.10	Residual Plot for India for Model 1	243
11.11	India's Military Expenditures	244
11.12	Pakistan's Military Expenditures	245
11.13	Residuals for the Revised India Equation	246
11.14	One-Shot Aid Policies	247
11.15	Continuing Aid Policies	247
11.16	Estimated Effects of Actual Aid Given to the Two Nations	248
13.1	Schematic Representation and Action Summary for Assumed Missile Exchange	281
13.2	A Representative Case of the Interactive Computer Output from the DETER/YIELD Program, with Key	296
16.1	Sequential Screening Procedure for Decision Making in the Balance-of-Power System	323
17.1	Representation of Objective Function $Z = 2X + 4$	361
17.2	Representation of Constraints $X + Y \leq 6$; $2X - Y \leq 2$; $X, Y \geq 0$	362
17.3	Solution to the Maximization Problem	363

PART

I

**PERSPECTIVES ON
MATHEMATICAL REASONING**

CHAPTER

1

INTELLECTUAL IDENTITY AND THE STUDY OF INTERNATIONAL RELATIONS, OR COMING TO TERMS WITH MATHEMATICS AS A TOOL OF INQUIRY

James N. Rosenau

It may be wondered how a person whose work in the international relations field is not of a mathematical nature can dare to write an introduction to a book of essays applying mathematics to international relations. I do so because I have long pondered various approaches to the field and, in the process, have come to terms with mathematics as a tool of inquiry. One does not have to be skilled at mathematics to appreciate its uses. One can be a consumer as well as a producer of mathematical findings. Choosing the consumer role, however, is not much easier than opting for the producer role. There are a number of obstacles to overcome in making either choice, and it is in regard to these obstacles that perhaps some introductory remarks by a nonmathematical investigator can be useful.

Some insight into the obstacles involved is provided by the experience of a good friend of mine. Forty years old, married with two children, and living on an inadequate professor's salary, he recently decided to go further into debt because he found himself unable to undertake the kind of inquiry into politics that he deemed necessary. Prior to this decision he had acquired considerable skills as a generator and analyst of quantified data, skills that resulted in a number of important studies and a growing reputation as one of the nation's most competent political scientists. Despite the success, however, he concluded that he was ill-equipped to carry on his work, that only by tooling up in mathematics could he begin to address and (hopefully) resolve the questions about the

---

In preparing this essay I received considerable help from Tom Johnson, Edwin P. McClain, and Mary Stave.

underlying dynamics of politics that plagued him. So he took a year's leave of absence from his university, borrowed $9,000 from a credit union, reassured his family that somehow they would make ends meet, and set out to learn mathematics, first at the simple levels presented in high school, then on to the more advanced levels to be found in college and postgraduate curricula.

My friend's choice illustrates two points that need to be appreciated if one is to benefit fully from the essays in this volume. One is that mathematics can be seen as a powerful tool with which to probe the dynamics of international politics. The second is that the availability of mathematical approaches to the study of human affairs can serve as a catalyst for confronting important questions about one's own intellectual identity.

Indeed, the power of mathematical tools can hardly be appreciated unless one has first pondered one's approach to the study of world affairs. This question of intellectual identity has to be confronted because the facts and trends of international relations are not self-evident. They do not simply present themselves for any observer to comprehend. The observer must interpret them, give them coherence so that patterns can be discerned in the welter of events and understanding thereby developed. To interpret is to impose meaning, and to impose meaning is to employ one or another tool of analysis. Since different tools of analysis can yield different interpretations of the same phenomena, one's choice of analytic tools can be deeply personal. At stake is nothing less than one's grasp of, posture toward, and commitment to one's subject, the rigor, skill, and imagination with which one probes the mysteries of the past and the likelihoods of the future.

The availability of mathematical tools highlights the need to establish an intellectual identity with respect to one's subject because such tools are widely felt to be inappropriate to the study of international relations. Hence, normally those who use them must overcome both the inhibitions against mathematics that are frequently instilled early in life and the gaps in training that widen as the inhibitions deepen. Unfortunately, the prejudices against the application of mathematical reasoning appear especially strong in the international relations field. Those who enter the field tend to come out of a tradition of legal or historical scholarship, where the notion of reducing human experience to mathematical formulas and analysis is considered to be misguided and absurd at best and degrading and blasphemous at worst. Claiming that such an approach overlooks, even undermines, the spirit and dignity with which people conduct their affairs, many assert that human feelings and aspirations are too varied and too private to be subject to mathematization. In addition, many of those who enter the field do so less out of intellectual curiosity and more out of a commitment to improving the human condition and lessening the chances of war, a priority that is certainly commendable but that also tends to foster impatience with tools of analysis that subject values to the strict rigors of logic.

There are, in short, many intellectual postures one can take toward the field, each with philosophical assumptions and rules of procedures that set it apart from the others. One cannot say that any of these approaches is superior to the others. Much depends on the types of problems that one seeks to solve, the kinds of knowledge one wants to see cumulate, and the criteria of evidence with which one is most comfortable. Mathematical tools are not suitable to any problem and they do not yield empirical findings to which statistical criteria of evidence can be applied. But, as this book so amply demonstrates, they provide powerful instruments with which to probe certain kinds of problems.

While mathematical tools are not inherently superior to any others, and while their use does not necessarily preclude reliance on other modes of inquiry, they are distinctive. As noted below, they require explicit premises and procedures that clearly differentiate them from historical, case-study, quantitative, and journalistic forms of investigation. This is why their availability tends to pose especially intense personal questions of intellectual identity. To be sure, such questions arise with respect to any approach one may follow, but they seem particularly acute in the case of mathematics because the language and procedures on which it rests are so different. Impelled to seek solutions to immediate problems and trained to approach world affairs inductively, most observers must confront the questions of who they are intellectually and what kind of knowledge they want to uncover before they can commit themselves to the style and language that mathematical analysis requires. By the time they become enamored of the potential of mathematics, moreover, many have become so accustomed to one or another of the forms of inquiry that they feel awe for mathematical formulas and inadequate about their capacity to comprehend them. So, unlike my friend, most conclude it is too late to retool and either fall back on a humanistic rejection of the utility of mathematical applications or rationalize that they never have been able to master the intricacies of algebra and calculus, much less the more advanced mathematical tools.

Much the same can be said about the potential consumers of mathematical analyses. Potential producers may have to make excruciating choices that require the reorientation of careers and the disruption of family life in order to be able to engage in mathematical inquiry, but those who simply want to use and apply the results of such inquiries also have to assess who they are and what they regard as valid knowledge. To pick one's way slowly through articles like those in this book is no easy task if one has had little recent training in mathematics. It requires patience with oneself, respect for alternative ways of generating knowledge, and tolerance for insights that are derived more from logic than from observation. All the biases that inhibit the acquisition of mathematical skills operate even more powerfully on those who might have occasion to employ the findings uncovered through their application. Not choosing to learn the intricacies of advanced mathematics, consumers can, if they are so disposed, readily attempt to compensate for their sense of inadequacy about mathematics by stressing the uniqueness of people and the inviolability of the human spirit. Indeed, it seems entirely plausible that those who are most resistant to the idea of using mathematics in the study of international relations are those who know least about it and who cling fearfully to a narrowly defined intellectual identity they perceive as threatened by an obscure methodology.

Chances are that most readers of this book have puzzled through their intellectual identity to the point where mathematical inquiries are not threatening, else they would not have even gotten beyond the table of contents to these introductory comments. However, lest some who got this far still have open minds in their quest for identity—and in the event that a few plan to read on because they intend, perhaps unknowingly, to cite the book as further proof of the wisdom of their prejudices—it is useful to note why mathematics can serve as a powerful tool for unraveling the mysteries of international life. The key lies in the fact that mathematical analysis proceeds deductively and logically from a set of axioms about a problem of concern to the analyst. The axioms are derived either systematically or impressionistically from observation, but however they are derived, once they are linked together in a model rigorous logic takes over and the ensuing analysis is governed by relationships inherent in the mathematics employed rather than by those perceived to be operating empirically. The power of the tool springs from the dynamics of the problem that are thereby revealed—that is, the way in which the variables subsumed by the axioms logically interrelate as the analyst relaxes one or another original condition or builds in one or another new parameter. Unfolding events in the real world may not conform to the logic inherent in the model (indeed, they are unlikely to be very consistent, since the axioms of the model are not designed to cover all the deviations and exceptions that prevail in the real world), but the underlying tendencies and interrelationships from which particular situations deviate are laid bare by tracing deductively the interaction that logically follows from the conditions treated as axiomatic. Precisely because the welter of cross-currents and exceptions that render the real world complex are excluded, the mathematical analyst can uncover the basic tendencies that are at work. A major source of the power of mathematical tools is their capacity to uncover relationships that might not otherwise be discerned or might be so obscured as to be only dimly perceived.

All of this is the case, of course, only if the axioms and model are sound, creative, and relevant and the analyst knowledgeable and skillful as a mathematician. As in everything else, mathematical analysis is no more cogent than the creativity with which it is used. There can be poor mathematics, just as there can be poor history or poor quantitative interpretation. In addition to mastering the discipline of mathematics, the analysts must have a feel for the substantive problems to which the discipline is applied, if the full power of the mathematical tools is to be realized. To apply mathematics creatively one must creatively grasp one's chosen problem, else the logic derived from the axioms one develops will yield barren results. Insight, imagination, wild hunches, and intuitive formulations are as central to the mathematical analyst as to the humanistic scholar. They differ only in the procedures they employ once their minds creatively delineate their respective problems.

This is not to say, or even to imply subtly, that mathematical tools are a panacea. As Rapoport's chapter in this volume so clearly indicates, such tools do have limits and there are many kinds of problems for which they are unsuited. Most notably, being a deductive rather than an inductive science, mathematical tools cannot be employed to solve empirical problems. They can clarify relationships and point to possible outcomes, but they cannot facilitate analysis of what in fact happened or is happening in a real-world situation. Nor do they allow one to trace the impact or sources of deviant cases. Their scope is general and not specific, and one has to turn to empirical methods whenever specificity is a primary characteristic of the problem under investigation.

But to acknowledge that mathematical tools offer no panacea is not to justify rejecting their use. Some are quick to reject them on these grounds, as if to admit that such tools have some utility is to run the risk that they will be obliged to follow my friend's example and make personal sacrifices in order to establish a new intellectual identity. Admirable as my friend's choice may be, it is not the only one available. For a variety of reasons one can make the choice not to engage in extensive retooling and to remain essentially a consumer of mathematically derived analyses. I myself feel inept in this regard and am quite convinced that no amount of diligence could fully retool me as a skilled producer of mathematical studies of international phenomena. My identity, the result of much soul-searching and realistic attempts to assess my interests and talents, lies in a readiness to entertain and ponder insights into world politics, however they may be derived. Because one is untrained in and insecure about mathematical procedures one need not be suspicious of the results they generate. The test is not whether one can follow the progression from one equation to the next, but rather whether one is impressed with the insights to which the application of mathematical reasoning inexorably gives rise. Despite my skimpy knowledge of mathematics, I am impressed with the variety, importance, and incisiveness of the conclusions that pervade the chapters of this volume. The substantive concerns of the authors are not trivial. They deal with questions of war and peace, with alliances and coalitions, with choices that are rational and those that are not—topics that surely can benefit from further investigation from a multiplicity of perspectives.

For nonspecialists to come to terms with mathematical studies, in short, they need merely give up defensiveness about their own identity and recognize that mathematical inquiries are a supplement and not a threat to their own modes of investigation. To make acceptance of this perspective easier they may find it useful to think of mathematics as they do of foreign languages. Few would dismiss an analysis written in German or Arabic because they lack knowledge of these languages. On the contrary, the tendency is to assume it is sound and valuable (why else would it be available?) and to seek help in getting a translation of its essential thrust. Why should we take any less constructive an attitude toward mathematics! It too is a language, as Gillespie's "Why Mathematical Models?" convincingly demonstrates, and thus it too lends itself to translation. Nonspecialists are likely to find their mathematical colleagues cooperative, even flattered, when they ask for help in translating the central points of a mathematical analysis, so that they need merely be clear on the substantive questions around which they seek to initiate a dialogue with their mathematical colleagues.

There is a quid pro quo for the nonspecialist's tolerance for mathematical analyses. If those who undertake such analyses want to enlarge their capacity to frame sound and creative axioms through dialogues with those of us who develop knowledge about international relations in nonmathematical ways, it is reasonable to expect that they will conclude their analyses with nontechnical summaries of their substantive findings. These need not be "complete translations," which, as Gillespie suggests, are an undue burden and in any event can never be as precise as the mathematical analysis itself. But succinct synopses do seem both feasible and warranted, ones that highlight the general (if not the precise) nature of the relationships derived from the parameters posited as axiomatic at the outset. In each case the summary should also include a notation of how the analysis differs from others developed mathematically, thereby giving us nonspecialists a basis for assessing both the merits of an analysis and its potential acceptability to the community of mathematically inclined investigators. The burden for sustaining a dialogue, in other words, must necessarily fall on those who use mathematical methods. If they want to maximize their contribution to understanding, they will have to maintain and extend their contacts with the much larger community of nonmathematical students of world politics, a task that requires them to recall constantly that their mode of inquiry is a form of language that needs to be translated if their ideas and findings are to circulate widely.

I would argue that this translation burden is one that those who have found their intellectual identity through mathematics should happily shoulder. Since mathematical analyses are no sounder than the understandings of world politics on which they rest, and since the larger international-studies community has a great deal to offer by way of penetrating knowledge on the subject, those who employ mathematics have good reason to initiate and maintain communications with their nonmathematical colleagues. We may often be obstinate and impatient, but we are not lacking in valuable insights and findings that can inform and guide the process of formal model building.

In sum, all concerned have much to gain from a continuous dialogue. There are many roads to knowledge about international relations and those who traverse them need each other's assistance when their paths cross if their shared goal of enlarged understanding is to be realized. This book will surely become an important landmark for those seeking guidance along the way. It offers a number of eye-opening insights into crucial aspects of world politics. It demonstrates the utility of deriving understanding through the application of mathematical forms of analysis. Its several chapters provide nontechnical summaries. It sustains the dialogue. It clarifies a major alternative for those whose intellectual identity is still evolving.

CHAPTER 2

MATHEMATICAL METHODS IN THEORIES OF INTERNATIONAL RELATIONS: EXPECTATIONS, CAVEATS, AND OPPORTUNITIES
Anatol Rapoport

In assessing the potentialities of any comparatively young theoretical approach, it is important to keep in mind the expectations associated with the approach. These are, in turn, rooted in the motivations that have propelled the approach and in the basis of the social support given to its proponents. Accordingly, we shall begin our evaluation of mathematical methods in theories of international relations by examining the motivations for pursuing these methods and the expectations associated with them.

THE QUEST FOR OBJECTIVITY

A description of any state of affairs in terms of measurable quantities is objective in the sense that anyone equipped with all the required instruments of measurement and with knowledge of their use can verify the description. If the description is accurate, there will be a high degree of agreement among independent observers to that effect—which is practically a definition of objectivity. Thus, indexes attached to the various components of a country's economy, of its military establishment or its operations, crude as they may be, at least put discussions concerning the country's "power" or "aggressiveness" into some sort of objective perspective.

The use of indexes reflects attempts to operationalize theories of international relations and so to put them on a more solid theoretical footing.

THE QUEST FOR A RIGOROUS THEORY

Quantification is not yet mathematization, but it is a precursor to it. Traditionally, "theory," as this word is used in the social sciences, usually denotes discourse imbued with definitions of terms, categorizations of social phenomena, and speculations about their causes or consequences. Rigorous theory, on the other hand, exemplified in the exact (that is, mathematized) sciences, involves strict operational, predominantly mathematical, definitions of terms and logically compelling deductions. Here the term "theory" is etymologically accurate: It means a collection of theorems. Arguments about the truth of such a theory can be referred to deduced consequences of its initial assumptions, essentially to predictions (or postdictions) of quantified observations. Thus, attempts to make theories of international relations deductively productive are another source of the motivation to mathematize them.

Mathematical reasoning, besides making the meaning of words of common usage precise (in order to fit them into mathematical discourse), also frequently extends the meanings of these terms and thereby induces insights into scientifically fruitful categorizations of events.

A well-known example from the early history of the exact sciences will suffice. In popular legend, Newton posed the question, "Why does the apple fall?" And he provided an "explanation": "Because it is acted upon by gravity." In this version the "discovery" of the law of gravity appears simply to be giving a name to a presumed cause of what is commonly observed. But the dictum, "because of gravity," is no more enlightening than the vacuous remark in a Molière comedy, "Opium puts you to sleep because of its dormative property." Actually, Newton posed another question: not "Why does the apple fall?" but "Why does the moon not fall?" And the answer was not in terms of differences between apples and planets, but in terms of similarities of their motions. The fact is that the moon does fall. Or, if this answer seems bizarre, one can say that the apple, like the moon, moves in the orbit prescribed for it by the law of universal gravitation. It just so happens that the apple's orbit intersects the surface of the earth, whereas the moon's does not. Here, then, we have an insightful generalization of the term "orbit" or, if you like, of the term "falling."

The powerful theoretical leverage introduced into the physical sciences by mathematical deduction is too well known to need elaboration. A desire to replicate the resulting successes in the context of the social sciences is entirely understandable. To what extent this can be done is a separate question to be discussed below. In the meantime, let us examine the third source of motivation for mathematizing theories of international relations, one that has roots outside the needs or aspirations of scientific cognition as such.

THE QUEST FOR CONTROL

Bacon's slogan, "Knowledge is power," was pronounced at the very beginning of the scientific revolution but did not acquire a literal meaning until after the Industrial Revolution. And it was only considerably later that the image of the scientist as an eccentric with quaint interests (for example, gazing at the stars or collecting beetles) was replaced by that of a wizard in possession of secret "formulas." The more recent image of the scientist as a member of an elite fraternity manning "teams" to tackle "problems" was generated by the organization and institutionalization of science. Science has become a career with well-defined channels of training, job procurement, and advancement. It has also become a sector of the "knowledge industry" or "Ed Biz," to quote from an irreverent remark casually dropped by Tom Lehrer.

This transformation of science from a calling to a career has been accompanied by the usual pressures on its directions and output. Possibly the strongest of these pressures is that of producing publishable investigations. The social function of published research is in our day not so much that of adding to cumulating knowledge as that of preserving the bona fides of the practitioners of a profession—the academe.

Social support for this massive proliferation of published research must be based on a rationale. Such a rationale is provided by the image of science as the fountainhead of progress and the source of power. Social support (in the form of grants, academic credentials, and so forth) accorded the attempts to quantify and mathematize the social sciences can be traced to this rationale.

As has been said, the modern image of the scientist is that of a problem solver. In its problem-solving role, science is most visible as an adjunct of technology. Technological successes enhance the problem-solving mode of thinking. Thus, the prevalent "enlightened" view of social iniquities and social disasters (economic dislocations, wars, and so on) is that of formulating them as "problems." It has become commonplace to assert that whereas man has been spectacularly successful in solving the problem of survival in hostile natural environments and of saddling the laws of nature, directing them toward the fulfillment of his physical needs, he still has to solve the problem of intelligently controlling social environments. This problem is especially acute in the sphere of international relations.

Problems successfully solved are those clearly formulated in terms of goals to be attained and means that can be reasonably expected to lead to the attainment. Industrial and medical technology provide obvious successful models to emulate. Both are firmly rooted in the natural (that is, "hard") sciences, where knowledge of determinate causes and effects confers powers of prediction and control. This knowledge, in turn, stems from the fusion of rigorous theory and experiment (or systematic observation), in which mathematical models have played a decisive role.

This pragmatic motivation, extended to the prospect of developing a rigorous and "positive" (in Comte's sense) theory of international relations actually has two aspects. One has already been mentioned: Science carries the promise of suggesting effective solutions of problems, among which, by way of semantic extension of the word "problem," discrepancies between the realities of global politics and man's needs are now also included. In this view, the hardening of theories of international relations is seen as a necessary condition for a technology directed toward controlling the dynamics of the international system in the interest of furthering human needs, for instance by removing iniquities and by alleviating the scourge of war. The other aspect of the pragmatic motivation reflects the needs of ruling elites. Governments with a stake in political systems of countries within their spheres of influence are interested in techniques of "pacification." Military establishments are becoming increasingly sold on the importance of software and strategic analysis. The latter areas, although not directly subsumed under social science, nevertheless rely heavily on mathematical methods extended beyond the context of physical sciences. Thus, preoccupation with computer-aided simulation and gaming, for example, contributes to an intellectual atmosphere congenial to the idea of mathematizing theories of international relations. Here wishful thinking is involved in supporting the faith that a flourishing "hard" science of international relations and its normative fringes (rigorous decision-making methodologies, cost-benefit analysis, and so forth) can be utilized in the preservation or the extension of power. Witness the support rendered by U.S. governmental agencies, including the military, to the development of the mathematical theory of games (for example, at the Rand Corporation).

The two strands of sanguine expectations, one inspired by a vision of science as the epitome of rationality (the instrument of human survival and the generator of human welfare), the other spurred by power appetites, although ideologically antagonistic, reinforce each other in creating an ideational climate receptive to the hardening of theories of international relations. In this climate mathematical approaches acquire considerable prestige. The degree of acceptance attributed to these approaches is, of course, relative to one's expectations. Some proponents of quantitative and mathematical methods in political science insist that their efforts meet with considerable resistance on the part of the academic establishment. However, the fact that the pros and cons of mathematization continue to be a topic of sometimes heated discussions at conferences and the sheer number of pages bristling with mathematical symbols encountered in writings subsumed under political science (compared with the situation two or three decades ago) are sufficient indication of a definite and accelerating trend in that direction.

In assessing the accomplishments and prospects of quantitative and mathematical methods in theories of international relations, we shall distinguish three approaches, namely, a predominantly empirical (descriptive) quantitative approach, a systemic approach based on dynamic mathematical models, and an approach inspired by normative strategic analysis. The first two continue to reflect a strong influence of Lewis R. Richardson, a pioneer in these sorts of investigations. The third was inspired by game-theoretic formulations of conflict situations. Although the first two approaches were carried far beyond Richardson's formulations, we shall use his works as primary illustrations, because his methodology has remained practically intact in subsequent developments.

THE QUANTITATIVE EMPIRICAL APPROACH

The empiricist (or positivist) orientation looks askance at any "theorizing" that is not supported by hard data. As has been pointed out at the start, the hardest data are quantitative data.* To be sure,

---

*The use of the term "hard data" may prompt the question, "What is the difference between 'hard data' and 'soft data'?" The distinction is one of degree. Data are hardest when they depend minimally on concepts derived from complex culturally conditioned and intuitively digested experiences. Consider the following three assertions
  1. This machine gun can fire 240 rounds per minute.
  2. Austria became a republic in 1918.
  3. Nazi Germany was a totalitarian state.

All three are assertions of verifiable "facts," hence representations of data. However, the data are of different "hardness," because

any investigation that purports to be scientific is grounded in theoretical concepts, whether or not they are recognized as such. There is no such thing as a "bare fact," if only because the selection of data to be collected or processed is guided by notions of what is important. Thus, the very area of investigation is an "area" by virtue of the fact that several events or complexes of events are assumed to be instances of a properly defined class of events. For instance, in investigating trends in electoral politics, the empirically oriented political scientist assumes that each election is an instance of a class of events called "elections." It is difficult to take issue with this assumption, at least in the context of elections on a given level in a given country in a circumscribed time period. In other cases, the categorization of events suggested by their being designated by the same name is not so obviously justifiable. For instance, in studying the phenomenon of war, investigators, following the tradition established by Lewis F. Richardson and Sewell Wright, collect data on "wars"—that is, events designated as wars—over a century or centuries. But it is not obvious that these large complexes of events are instances of the same event in the same way as, say, eclipses of the sun or tornadoes are obviously instances of the same event. The question arises as to how many of these classes of complex events can be subsumed under the same category. Are the wars waged by the Comanchees, by the princes of eighteenth century Europe, by the Crusaders, and by the United States since 1950 simply variants of a well-defined event and so deserving a generic name?

The answer to this question is far from obvious. Admittedly, the investigator who hopes to create or to contribute to a theory of war by collecting data on "wars" cannot afford to be incapacitated just because he cannot give a compelling justification for categorizing a very diverse collection of events as instances of "war." Nevertheless, it is important to keep the question in mind, because the meaningfulness of any theory that may emerge from generalizations based on collected data depends crucially on the legitimacy of the underlying concept. This is because the quantitative empirical approach to social phenomena leans heavily on statistical methods that, in turn, rest on probabilistic assumptions that, in turn, are based on the notion of repeated "identical" events.

A particular categorization is usually suggested by some salient feature common to all the members of a presumed category. For Richardson, a salient feature of war was the number of dead.

---

progressively more preliminary agreements on the concrete meanings of terms are required as we pass from 1 to 3.

Accordingly, he classified some scores of "wars" (again, we repeat, complexes of events so labeled by historians) according to their "magnitudes"—logarithms of recorded fatalities, adding, for good measure, other "deadly quarrels," such as murders, riots, and executions.[1]

Note that this lumping of all events associated with violent deaths was dictated by Richardson's particular theoretical orientation reflected in the concept "deadly quarrel" coupled with the assumption that the volume of fatalities is the most essential feature of these confrontations. The aim of the compilation was to examine the statistical distribution of the magnitudes. Such distributions provide some theoretical leverage in that they allow comparisons with distributions of other events or with indexes singled out for attention. These procedures (correlation analysis, regression analysis, factor analysis, and so on) are the stock-in-trade of the empiricist.

I must once more emphasize that although theory, as a determinant of concepts, is inadvertently included in the empiricist approach, the empiricist can claim a certain freedom from preconceived notions in the sense that once the salient features have been selected, the picture that emerges can be taken to be an objective picture of the state of affairs, at least to the extent of the accuracy of the collected raw data. Richardson's picture of war contains no preconceived notions about causes and effects, motivations, or strategic considerations, in terms of which traditional political histories, in particular histories of wars, are written. The empiricist attempts to wipe the slate clean and to assume the stance of the proverbial man from Mars. He observes and he notes. His inferences are, as a rule, statistical inferences emerging from the data themselves.

If the legitimacy of the statistical tools is granted (note, however, the limitations mentioned above), these tools become powerful aids to observation. They are to the social scientist what microscopes and telescopes are to the natural scientist. Examination of statistical distributions (profiles of collections of events) may disclose differences between them undetectable by the "naked eye" and so may suggest the existence of some underlying cause of these differences (without, however, revealing the nature of that cause). Comparisons between distributions and various selected indexes may suggest a causal connection (in either direction or both) between them, or else an antecedent cause of which the phenomena examined are consequences.

In summary, quantitative methods enter the empiricist approach in the role of "objectivizing" the data, of reducing masses of raw data to a few salient features, permitting an overview of an emerging picture and making the observations more acute. Mathematical deduction plays only a modest part in this approach. It is for the

THE MATHEMATICAL APPROACH

The properly mathematical (rather than quantitatively descriptive) approach is embodied in the so-called mathematical model. Here the direction of inference is reversed. It goes from the theoretical formulation outward, hopefully toward data (sometimes not yet gathered). Ideally, the mathematically deduced consequences of the postulated relations should be translatable into verifiable predictions about observable indexes.

The deductive power of mathematics is the distinctive feature of the model approach. Mathematically deduced consequences may be of the sort that could not have been anticipated. The method is, therefore, theoretically productive. Witness the dramatic predictions of relativity theory, for instance, with regard to the bending of light rays in gravitational fields or the transformations of matter into energy. If the mathematically deduced consequences of a model have already been observed, the model offers logically compelling explanations of the observations: If the assumptions of the model are correct, the observations cannot be other than what they are. The converse is, of course, not logically valid. Still, verification of consequences, especially predictions of observations not yet made, constitute a corroboration of the model and suggest further tests. This is the classical conception of the hypothetico-deducive method as it is described in text books.

Again we turn to Richardson for illustration. He postulated the now well-known model of arms races, a pair of differential equations reflecting the positive feedback between the rates of change of armament levels of two rival powers and the negative feedback of the self-inhibiting effect.[2] This model is widely cited as an illustration of the mathematical model approach in political science. Its deduced consequences were the time courses of the armament budgets of the two rival blocs in the years before World War I. This postdiction was verified almost exactly.

On the face of it, then, Richardson's model of an arms race appears to have been dramatically corroborated and presents itself as a foundation for a mathematical theory of arms races. Given such a foundation, at least one line of investigation in the study of international relations seems to have embarked on the well-beaten path of the exact sciences. On careful examination, however, Richardson's success turns out to be illusory.

The illusion stems from assuming a parallel between Richardson's model and analogous models of physical events. A solution of a system of differential equations predicts (or postdicts) the motion of a planet; a solution of a pair of differential equations fits the course of an arms race. In each case, the test of the model consisted of a comparison between the deduced and the observed values of a specified variable—for example, the position of the planet at some specified moments or the combined arms budgets of two rival blocs in specified years. Nevertheless, this is as far as the parallel can go. Beyond are glaring differences.

1. Corroboration of the model of celestial mechanics is possible at any of an infinite set of moments of time and with respect to any of the observable planets. Corroboration of Richardson's model was observed only at two time intervals. Four intervals were examined in all, but two of them were used to fix two free parameters. In no other arms race examined was the corroboration of the model so clear-cut. The results on the last one (U.S.-Soviet) were inconclusive; Richardson died in 1953.
2. The observable variables involved in the model of celestial mechanics are given by the posed problem itself—namely, the time intervals and the coordinates of position. The indexes involved in an arms race must be chosen, and the choice is guided by intuition as to what is important or relevant. In his model of the 1909-13 arms race Richardson chose armaments budgets and trade volumes expressed in monetary units. The units became less clearly defined after the gold standard was abandoned. The definition of units presented a problem that could have been "solved" in a variety of ways, each possibility leading to different results of observations.
3. In celestial mechanics, the system under consideration is given a priori. It is the set of celestial bodies sufficiently far removed from other bodies so that external gravitational forces can be neglected. In choosing the "system" consisting of the rival blocs engaged in World War I, Richardson included Russia and France on the one side and Germany and Austro-Hungary on the other. There was no compelling reason for excluding Britain, Turkey, or Italy, or, if the last were included, to see her on the one or the other side (Italy's position as an ally of Germany and Austro-Hungary had become ambivalent). Had the choice of participants been different, the observed results may have been different.
4. In celestial mechanics, the origin of the time coordinate is arbitrary. The arms race preceding World War I was postulated to have begun in 1908 or 1909; that preceding World War II, in 1933; that preceding the hypothesized World War III, in 1948.

All these dates were chosen ad hoc, that is, to give the "best fit" of the data to the postulated model.

It may be pointed out that in repeating these well-known criticisms of the notion that an arms race can be represented by a quasi-mechanical model, I am belaboring the obvious. I can also be accused of giving aid and comfort to doctrinaire opponents of mathematical approaches to social science. This is not so. My aim is to distinguish clearly between genesis, function, and value of mathematization in the physical and the social sciences, and to guard against unjustified expectations in order to forestall a reactionary swing in the wake of disappointed hopes.

WHAT ARE THE OBSTACLES TO MATHEMATIZATION?

Much of the controversy about the possibility of creating a mathematized social science centers on the issue of "determinism" vs. "free will" and on the applicability of mathematical models to phenomena as complex as those involving human behavior. Indeed, both deterministic causality, which seems to govern the behavior of nonliving matter, and the simplicity of the systems singled out for study in classical mathematized physical science constitute the foundations of that science. Determinism in human affairs remains a metaphysical assumption without convincing evidence. The indefinitely large number of variables that perforce enter the description of any system with human components precludes the use of tractable mathematical models in deriving the behavior of such systems. In defense of mathematization, the following points are usually made.

1. Even though determinism in human affairs is not demonstrable, neither is the absence of determinism. All scientific theories are based, in the last analysis, on metaphysical assumptions—for example, the assumption about the "objective reality" of the physical world, repeatability of observations, and so forth. Therefore, it is permissible to assume determinism in human affairs if this assumption is necessary in order to proceed with the formulation of theories.
2. Actually, the assumption of determinism is not necessary even in the exact sciences. For instance, the uncertainty principle of quantum mechanics did not cripple the physics of subatomic phenomena; on the contrary, it enriched the conceptual repertoire of that science. Probabilistic theories can be as logically compelling as deterministic ones and so can serve as mathematical

theories of social phenomena where determinism cannot reasonably be assumed.
3. The complexity of phenomena involving human actions is a matter of degree. Some physical phenomena (for instance, the weather) are enormously complex. This does not prevent advances in meteorology generated by the development and refinement of mathematical methods. In fact, computer technology has introduced a new dimension into those methods, making possible mathematical investigations of systems far more complex than those studied with the help of classic analytical tools.

These arguments are reasonable as far as they go, but they do not touch on some more fundamental issues that might be raised in connection with the applicability of mathematical methods in the social sciences.

The question of determinism or indeterminism in human affairs ought not be related to the existence or nonexistence of "free will," a nonresolvable metaphysical question, but rather to the effects of theories or descriptions of social reality on this reality. This is the issue of self-fulfilling or self-negating assumptions in social science.

Also, if one accepts indeterminism in human affairs, the difficulty introduced is not simply bypassed by turning to probabilistic models as the proper tools to deal with indeterminism. This amounts only to shifting the methodological problem to another level, the problem of legitimacy of probabilistic models in contexts where it is difficult or impossible to single out a set of "identical" repeated events.

Finally, the argument that the complexity of systems involving human affairs, compared to that of physical systems, is only a matter of degree bypasses an important qualitative difference. No matter how complex a physical model is, it is solidly rooted in very few physical laws that, for all practical purposes, can be assumed to be immutable. Models of meteorological systems are good examples. The relevant variables are pressures, densities, and temperatures distributed throughout the atmosphere and the hydrosphere; the relevant constants are the specific heats, conductivities, compressibilities, and so on of gases, liquids, and solids. The laws governing the interactions of phases, the flows of matter and energy, and so forth are all well-known laws of aerodynamics, hydrodynamics, and thermodynamics. These laws are, in turn, derived from the more fundamental laws of conservation of matter and energy and the laws of motion. The complexity of the atmospheric system differs only in degree from that of, say, the solar system. This means that although an exact solution or even the formulation of equations governing every particle of the atmosphere is impossible, nevertheless, approximate predictions can be made, and, most importantly, the accuracy of the predictions can be steadily improved as methods of observation improve and as more powerful computational techniques become available. This expectation is justifiable, because there is no question about the relevance of the variables constituting the model or about the underlying laws of their interaction.

The analogy between meteorological phenomena and those involving "massive" human behavior (which, incidentally, was proposed by Richardson, who was himself a meteorologist) fails for two reasons. First, the question of relevant variables cannot be settled definitively. Second, there are no "laws" governing human behavior analogous to physical laws. On the metaphysical level one can, of course, insist that all human actions are, in the last analysis, physical processes, even speech (motions of speech organs) and thought (presumably patterns of neural activity), and that therefore the assumption of determinism, derived from the universal applicability of physical laws, can still be made with regard to human behavior. Needless to say, however, this assumption has no practical significance. No one has yet described the simplest of human actions (for instance, that of saying "hello") in terms of patterns of neural events that determine specific muscular movements, let alone the consequences of this action on the actions of other human beings. Therefore, the appeal to the reductionist thesis, whatever force it may have in a philosophical discussion about "free will," is in no way a contribution to method.

It follows that the construction of mathematical models of human behavior on the basis of physical laws is out of the question. Are there other "laws" on which such models could be based? I know of none. All mathematical models proposed in social sciences are either frankly "trial balloons" or idealized formulations of some common-sense generalizations. They are constructed, not cumulatively like models of complex physical phenomena, but de novo in each context—that is, ad hoc.

The so-called laws of supply and demand of classical mathematical economics are typical examples. It is commonly observed that in a competitive market increased abundance of a commodity depresses its market price, which increases demand, which inflates the market price. Postulated mathematical relations among supply, price, and demand constitutes a model from which, say, a price equilibrium can be deduced. But no specific forms of these mathematical relationships are compelling a priori. They are usually chosen on the basis of their mathematical tractability. The resulting mathematical models are not noted for high prediction power. Their function is heuristic, facilitating the formation of ideas within a certain framework. Predictions can sometimes be improved by modifying the mathematical structure of the models, but these modifications are usually ad hoc rather than systematic. Consequently, improved predictions in one context do not, as a rule, generate improved predictions in another. The characteristic interconnectedness of physical theories, the most important achievement of mathematical physics, is not replicated in the social sphere.

Among the mathematized sectors of social science, mathematical economics is probably the most favorably situated. Here, at least the relevant variables are well defined and fairly well observable. In other areas, even this comparative concreteness and relevance of the variables is difficult to establish. For lack of concreteness at the foundations, I believe it is a mistake to expect of, say, an arms-race model, that successive modifications will lead to a more general and more accurate theory of arms races. On the face of it, such modifications appear to be in the direction of bringing the model closer to reality. For instance, some authors have noted that changes in armaments budgets are made not continuously but rather at discrete moments, say, annually. Therefore, it is argued, not differential equations, but difference equations ought to be the point of departure. Next, in order to generalize the model, the assumption of linearity is sometimes dropped. Quadratic or even higher-order terms are added to the differential (or difference) equations. Also, as noted above, Richardson himself was worried about the proper economic units in terms of which the "index of hostility" is to be defined. Once this question is raised, a whole plethora of indexes suggest themselves.

Given sufficient resources and personnel, all of these modifications could be tried. In principle, the resulting models could be pitted against each other and a sort of natural selection process instituted. This is the textbook method of approaching reality by successive refinements of a theory. However, here is a sobering thought. A crucial component of improvement by successive modifications is the controlled experiment. Ideally, two or more models with distinguishably different consequences are pitted against each other in a so-called crucial experiment designed to eliminate some of the contenders, ideally all but one. Where such experiments are impossible (and it stands to reason that we are not in a position to instigate arms races), selection of cases to observe is a second-best alternative. But how many arms races are available for this purpose? When we further consider that the few arms races that are available for testing models may have been "run" under very different political and economic conditions, we realize that our selection of test cases must be severely limited and in many instances precluded altogether.

Let us now examine the difficulties attending the quantitative-empirical approaches. As pointed out, the central problem of these approaches is that of singling out quantitative indexes, in terms of which to describe social phenomena. If that were the entire problem (that is, if description in terms of such indexes were accepted as the final product of an investigation), then the objectivity of quantitative indexes would be ample justification of quantification. However, objective description is seldom an end in itself. It is usually assumed tacitly or explicitly that inferences of some theoretical significance can be drawn from the descriptions, at least from comparisons of two or more situations. In fact, the bulk of quantitative social science is based on inferences from comparisons, supported by statistical evaluation of the significance of observed differences. Observation of significant differences leads to hypotheses about their possible causes. Correlation analysis, multiple regression, analysis of variance, factor analysis, and so on are all techniques designed to ferret out the possible causes of variations observed in indexes of social phenomena. Even though the direction or even the existence of such causal relations is not thereby established, some theoretical leverage is provided for further investigations.

Now the problem of quantification in the social sciences is beset by difficulties that have long since been eliminated in the physical sciences. We have already mentioned the problem of singling out relevant or important indexes. Once this has been done, there remains the problem of determining the scale appropriate to such indexes. Scales are of various strengths. A scale is the stronger, the smaller the class of transformations to which the measures assigned to the data can be subjected without disturbing consistency with observations. For instance, an ordinal scale, which reflects only the order of magnitudes of a set of quantified observations, permits any positive monotone transformation without disturbing consistency with data. This transformation being quite general, the ordinal scale is a very "weak" scale. The interval scale, which permits only positive linear transformations, is stronger. The ratio scale, which permits only multiplication by a constant, is still stronger. The strength of a scale is of crucial importance, because it determines the range of permissible mathematical operations on the indexes. The stronger the scale, the wider the range of permissible operations. Thus, if quantitative description is to serve as the initial phase of an investigation that involves some mathematical manipulations of the indexes (for example, in data reduction), the question of the appropriate scale is vital.

Now, the strongest possible scale is the absolute scale, which permits only the trivial identity transformation. A probability is expressed on such a scale. It stands to reason, then, that indexes expressed as probabilities are, from the point of view of freedom of mathematical manipulation, the most desirable indexes.

Fortunately, such indexes are often quite suitable for the description of social phenomena, namely those describable in terms of recognizable, classifiable events that could be conceived as the quanta of social phenomena. For examples, X voted Republican; Y moved from Littletown to Megapolis; Z committed suicide. These events are the units of social statistics, the raw data in much of empirical-quantitative social science. Their frequencies are estimates of the probabilities of their occurrence, and the probabilities can be taken as indexes measured on an absolute scale, permitting arbitrary mathematical manipulations.

It would seem then, that the use of frequencies of identifiable events as indexes in quantitative social science is the most promising approach. As already pointed out, however, its legitimacy depends crucially on the appropriateness of considering the events in question as repetitions of the "same" event, assuming, for example, that one move from country to city is like another, that one suicide is like another, and so forth. Such conceptions of classes of equivalent events are easier to justify in some contexts than in others. In the case of wars, as has already been pointed out, inferences based on "frequency of occurrence" may be most difficult to justify if only because the identification of a war as a well-defined "event" is far from straightforward, and the treatment of wars as repeated instances of the "same" event is rather far-fetched.

Nevertheless, the study of the "correlates of war" along the lines charted by Richardson in his Statistics of Deadly Quarrels has gone on apace. The net was thrown far and wide in accordance with the "no preconceived notions" principle of strict empiricism. The yield was for the most part meager. Richardson himself found no significant correlations between the indexes of severity of war and any but a couple of factors. One of these, apparently a "pacifying factor," was the existence of a government with jurisdiction over the potential belligerents (for these were not confined to groups separated by national boundaries). Another, an apparently aggravating factor, was the Spanish language. The first finding could have been expected on common-sense grounds and therefore does not represent a particularly interesting contribution. The second finding might be surprising at first sight, but becomes less so in the light of the fact that South America became, in the nineteenth century, a patchwork of states with Spanish the common language of all but one.

Somewhat more interesting results emerged from the extensive studies of J. David Singer and his collaborators.[3] Among these were the correlations of the incidence of wars with the "degree of polarization" of the alliance structure. A negative correlation was observed during the nineteenth century and a positive one during the twentieth, suggesting that a polarized alliance structure (two opposing blocs of approximately equal "power," appropriately defined) may have been a pacifying influence in the nineteenth century and an opposite one in the twentieth.

The inadequacy of correlation measures as indexes of the direction of causality is, of course, well known. Pursuit of evidence of "what causes what" leads to the analysis of time series and to a host of problems associated with the choice of relevant indexes. Richardson's index of the magnitude of a "deadly quarrel" clearly need not reflect the "amount of hostility" (which Richardson associated with it), if only because the destructive efficacy of war technology is possibly a much more important contributing factor than the psychological state of the combatants. In fact, it might be argued that the lethal efficacy of weapons, by removing the combatants from direct contact, is negatively related to subjectively experienced hostility. Many different indexes of "the amount of war" have been examined in relation to many different independent variables. The whole enterprise amounts to a search by trial and error or, at most, to pursuing educated guesses about what might be relevant. The end product of research on the "correlates of war" is at best a list of possible "candidates" to be considered as positive or negative contributing factors.

Viewed in this way, the correlates of war research bears some methodological resemblance to certain areas of medical research where the central problem is that of clarifying the etiology of a class of diseases, for instance, cancers. The strong evidence pointing to cigarette smoking as a major contributing factor to the incidence of lung cancer was a significant success of this method. Findings linking other factors to other forms of cancer have been less definitive but nevertheless enlightening in various degrees. Again, however, in the interest of guarding against unjustified expectations, the fundamental difference between hard natural science and "hard" social science must be pointed out.

Cancer is a relatively well defined condition. Even though the term is an umbrella for many diseases, possibly with very different etiologies, an unmistakable common feature—uncontrolled proliferation of cells—provides a reasonable basis for the general concept. Next, the refinement of the concept—classification of cancers—is based on clear physiological and histological evidence. Finally, statistical methods of research are amply justified because we have good reasons to suppose that we are dealing with "identical repeated events." None of these conditions is satisfied in the case of wars. Even if wars could be considered as well-defined events, those on which data are available number, perhaps, some hundreds. Any substantive taxonomy of wars (which may point to different etiologies) will reduce the numbers in each class to scores or fewer. In these circumstances, the value of statistical techniques becomes at least questionable.

ARE PREDICTION AND CONTROL THE MAIN GOALS OF SOCIAL SCIENCE?

The above skeptical or pessimistic conclusions may have given the impression that I take a dim view of quantitative and mathematical approaches, at least to the study of wars, and, perhaps by extension, to all social science. I should like to dispel any such impression. My skepticism is directed not at the value of the method as such, but only at the expectations usually associated with it, namely, that by making the social sciences hard, man (or, at any rate, decision makers) can acquire a power of prediction and possibly a control over social phenomena. I tend to dismiss these expectations as unrealistic on grounds to be stated presently. I believe, however, that quantitative and mathematical approaches in the social sciences, including political science and particularly in international relations, are justified on other grounds, more relevant to what I take to be the task of social science.

Assume for the moment that research on the correlates of war has attained a degree of success comparable to that attained by research on the correlates of lung cancer, specifically that a major contributing factor to the incidence or severity of war, has been discovered. Assume (arbitrarily) that this factor can be expressed as an index reflecting, say, the degree of departure from equidistribution of resources, some aspect of the network of alliances, the degree of political influence of military establishments, or a combination of these. The question arises, to what use can such knowledge be put?

At times, knowledge of the etiology of a disease makes possible its eradication. Purification of water supplies prevents typhoid epidemics; mass vaccination prevents smallpox epidemics. In the case of lung cancer, however, even conclusive knowledge of a major contributing factor has not led to a reduction of its incidence. Appeals to voluntary reduction of cigarette smoking have been largely ineffective. Experience with prohibitions (for example, those of alcoholic beverages or addictive drugs) suggest that a prohibition of cigarettes would be a failure even if it were politically feasible. Worse, efforts aimed at maintaining or even increasing the level of cigarette consumption, at least under private enterprise, enjoy continued success, compulsory warnings and a trickle of counterpropaganda notwithstanding.

Thus, even when a major contributing factor to a universally admitted evil is known, the knowledge may be quite ineffective in producing desired results. The problem here is not lack of knowledge of what can be done but lack of an institution to undertake appropriate and effective action. How much more grave, then, is the problem of using knowledge about the correlates of war for reducing the incidence or the severity of wars—which aim is most frequently used as a rationale for pursuing this knowledge. To begin with, in view of the methodological difficulties noted above, this knowledge can be nowhere as conclusive as, say, knowledge of the etiology of diseases. Next, the desirability of eradicating institutionalized warfare is by no means as universally and sincerely agreed upon as the desirability of eradicating horrendous diseases. Finally, even if there were a well-nigh universal consensus on the desirability of eradicating war, the presently unsurmountable political obstacles would remain, preventing the creation of institutions empowered to undertake appropriate action.

Mathematical models of arms races fare no better. They may lead to interesting deduced consequences—for instance, critical values of parameters that, if exceeded, lead to the destabilization of the arms race, precluding the establishment of an equilibrium. However, even if such models were corroborated to the extent of establishing their validity with a high degree of confidence, the problem of utilizing this knowledge would in all likelihood remain unsolved for lack of appropriate institutions. The creation of such institutions would necessitate the abolition of others—for example, autonomous war-making establishments. Resistance against encroachments on entrenched power is as a rule fierce and for the most part successful.

IDEATIONAL SPIN-OFFS

Of what value, then, are quantitative and mathematical approaches to the study of war? Their value, I believe, lies primarily in the ideational spin-offs generated by them. The conceptualization of global politics, suggested by Richardson's models, in the framework of a system governed by internal dynamics of quasi-mechanical nature, is directly antithetical to the rationalist, voluntaristic view of international relations. The issue is not of determining the better model of global politics; it is rather the back action of the adopted model on the ideational climate that in turn influences the evolution of global politics.

As an example, consider a model of arms races suggested by the analysis of arms-race data undertaken by Wagner, Perkins, and

Taagepera.4 In Richardson's model an arms race is propelled by the mutual stimulation exerted by the armament budgets of two rival blocs. In the alternative model self-stimulation is the propelling force. Even if conclusive corroboration of the one or the other model were possible, this would not justify the acceptance of the one or the other as the foundation of a theory of arms races. There have been too few arms races, and their etiologies may all be different. The ideational spin-off, on the other hand (namely, the idea that the burgeoning parasitic death industry may be spurred on by built-in self-reinforcing mechanisms that are independent of external threats), puts the matter into new perspective. To be sure, the idea may have been expressed before, but its mathematical formulation makes it concrete. A quantitative corroboration of the model, while by no means conclusive, makes it credible. Controversies concerning the etiologies of arms races cannot be settled by mathematical models, but they can be directed into intellectually more productive channels, thus affecting the ideational climate with possible long-term consequences.

Recall the fundamental distinction between physical and social theory. What we say or think about physical reality has no influence on that reality. But what we say or think about social reality does have an influence because our ideas about it are part of the reality. Thus, whether a poker game model of international relations is a good or a poor description depends in no small measure on whether this model is accepted or not by people who make foreign policy and by populations who give them political support. If one believes (as I do) that continued acceptance of the realpolitik model of international relations with its emphasis on "strategic rationality" and the struggle for power will lead to ever greater disasters (wars, the pillaging of world resources, and so on), then one can only acclaim any development that undermines the intellectual basis of power-oriented global politics.

THE GAME-THEORETIC APPROACH

An intellectual spin-off of this sort can be seen even more clearly in game-theoretic approaches to international relations. These approaches also represent attempts at mathematizing theories of international relations, but in a direction quite different from that introduced by Richardson. Unlike Richardson's system-theoretic analysis, where quasi-mechanical interactions rather than goal-directed choices are at the center of attention, game-theoretic models are rooted in an assumption of "rationality" attributed to actors in a conflict situation.

In its inception, the theory of games was essentially a normative theory, purporting to discover optimal strategies to be undertaken by a "player"–that is, a participant in a conflict with well-defined rules and correspondences between choices and outcomes. "Optimality" is here defined as maximization of the utilities or expected utilities of outcomes (payoffs) under the constraint that each of the actors is attempting to maximize his own payoffs.

Conceived in this way, game theory appears to be a theory of rational decisions in conflict situations. Now classical theories of rational decision have been concerned with situations involving a single "rational" actor, where the problem of choosing the "best" decision is complicated by the fact that the outcome is determined not by the actor's choice alone, but also by the "state of the world." Definite solutions can be obtained in so-called decisions under risk where probabilities can be assigned to the "states of the world" and costs to procedures aimed at obtaining more information about these probability distributions. Real-life situations of this sort are represented by problems arising in the insurance business, investment policies, inventory programs, and so forth.

Introducing conflicts of interest extends the range of problems to those involved in competitive business enterprise, electoral politics, diplomacy, and war. It is not surprising, therefore, that a lively interest in the theory of games, as an applied normative theory of decision, was aroused in circles of decision makers involved in just such fields of activity. We have already mentioned support given by military agencies to research on the theory of games. Indeed, textbook examples of tactical problems are often cited as applications of the theory.

Turning Clausewitz's dictum around to read "politics is the continuation of war by other means" (which, from the point of view of realpolitik, appears as valid as the original version) suggests the relevance of the mathematical theory of games to political science.

In evaluating the relevance of game theory as a theory with practical applications, some obvious questions arise immediately. How well can the options available both to self and to the opponents be defined? How precisely can the utilities of outcomes accruing both to self and to the other players be specified? In particular, can they be specified on at least an interval scale, as they must be if mixed strategies are to be meaningful? How realistic are the postulated correspondences between the choices of strategies and the listed outcomes? How tractable is the mathematics involved in the solution of the postulated game?

All these questions relate to possible limitations of mathematical models of situations involving human behavior. These are quantitative limitations in the sense that they can be more or less severe.

At any rate, awareness of these limitations permits the selection of situations where they are sufficiently mild to permit at least approximate solutions of the posed problems.

In real human conflicts, however, another class of limitations arises. These cannot be overcome, no matter how precisely the choices and utilities are specified, and no matter how much computational power is applied to the problems. This is because the individually rational strategic decision can be unambiguously defined in only one very special class of conflict situations—namely, those represented by the two-person zerosum games. Once this model of diametrically opposed interests of two players is transcended, any definition of optimal strategy becomes ambivalent. If, for example, the "solutions" of a two-person non-zerosum game are identified with equilibria (as they naturally are in zerosum games), it may happen that a choice of a strategy containing an equilibrium among its outcomes by each of the players results in an outcome that is not an equilibrium, or even if it is an equilibrium, is an outcome that is worse for both players than another available one.

All of these difficulties become conspicuous in the light of even the simplest non-zerosum models of international relations, such as the much-cited Prisoner's Dilemma (as a model of arms control) or Chicken (as a model of the eyeball-to-eyeball confrontation). Suggestive as these models are, they offer no solutions in terms of optimal strategies. On the contrary, they call attention to problems arising in conflict situations other than those of finding optimal strategies, problems of resolving a conflict to the mutual advantage of the players, which is possible only if the players forgo the search for strategies optimal from their individual points of view. Solutions of such problems are proposed in the context of so-called cooperative games. They are based on considerations of equity and collective rationality rather than on the strategic equilibria that characterize solutions of zerosum games.

The military are understandably concerned almost exclusively with the two-person zerosum game; for only in that context can strategic rationality be unequivocally defined. It is not surprising, therefore, that a conference sponsored by NATO was devoted almost entirely to applications of two-person zerosum game models.[5]

In some cases such games can be taken as realistic representations of military problems. Consider an automatic guidance system of an antiballistic missile (ABM). It is designed to intercept an attacking intercontinental ballistic missile (ICBM). The latter, on the other hand, can be equipped with a guidance system designed to evade the ABM. The problem of optimal design, applied to both devices, can be formulated as a game of pursuit and evasion, a special case of so-called differential games with continuous strategy spaces. Solving problems of this sort presents a considerable challenge to the mathematician.

The game of pursuit and evasion can be made arbitrarily complex by building in randomized (that is, mixed) strategies into both missiles. Thereby problems of prodigious complexity can be generated and possibly solved, perhaps conferring temporary advantage now on one side, now on the other. However, the social value of the resulting growing sophistication of death technology would be questionable, in fact, negative, from any point of view except that of military technologists.

This sort of mathematization of a normative theory of conflict can hardly be subsumed under social science. However, the mode of thinking it represents, carried over into the diplomatic or the diplomilitary sphere, is regarded in some circles as a contribution to political science. I am referring to the attempts to extend game theory or game-theoretic concepts to techniques of conducting realpolitik.

In fairness to the proponents of such extensions, it must be admitted that the non-zerosum nature of conflicts of interest in international politics has been recognized by some diplomilitary strategists. For instance, models of such conflicts in terms of games like Prisoner's Dilemma or Chicken are sometimes alluded to in their writings, and the ambivalence of "solutions" of such games played noncooperatively is pointed out.

Cooperative game models of partial conflicts of interest do provide "solutions" based on the assumption of collective rationality and on results of bargaining, in which the relative bargaining advantage of the players or some principles of equity or both are taken into account. Here, then, might be a mathematical basis of a normative theory of conflict resolution (rather than of "rational" strategic choices). In this connection may be mentioned the ideational spin-offs of N-person game theory that have led to some descriptive (not normative) theories of coalition formation.[6] However, this is not the way the infusion of game-theoretic concepts (via the analysis of bargaining techniques) is usually conceived by those who look to game theory for solutions of strategic problems. Rather, those concepts are thought of as a source of ideas in developing effective bargaining strategies with the view of gaining an advantage in the "game" of international politics.[7] Since such strategies are available to either side (or all participants), the end result resembles that of progressive sophistication of weapons systems.

In summary, the expectation that game theory or its extension can be an input into "practical" political science, in the sense of providing tools for wresting stretegic advantages in political, diplomatic, or diplomilitary conflicts, is a product of wishful thinking on the part of the power-oriented, quite as the idea that sufficiently developed mathematical theories of international conflicts will generate means of controlling or managing them is a product of wishful thinking on the part of men of good will. The term "wishful thinking" need not be understood in the pejorative sense. After all, hope of success propels all human endeavor and so is an indispensable component of goal attainment. What must be kept in mind, however, is that wishful thinking determines the direction of effort and so influences thought habits and, in the long run, the ideational climate.

As a matter of fact, the value of game-theoretic models of military tactical problems (for example, the so-called Blotto games) is seen by the more sophisticated military scientists not in terms of practical guide lines to solutions of such problems, but rather in terms of pedagogic devices for training strategists and tacticians to think in a certain mode.

Formulation and analysis of game-theoretic models (particularly of so-called mixed-motive conflicts represented by non-zerosum games) can play an analogous role in providing intellectual ammunition for the opponents of the realpolitik conception of global politics. Similarly, the principal value of the Richardsonian models of arms races as special cases of quasi-deterministic interactions of large systems is not in the opportunity they provide for discovering and therefore ultimately controlling the crucial parameters of such interactions. Rather the principal contribution of these models is in their potential for shifting the focus of attention from day-to-day strategic decisions of foreign policy (which, by perpetuating conventional conceptions of global politics preserve its present character) toward a global conception of system interactions and the dangers inherent in some forms of interaction.

CONCLUSIONS

The contribution of the empiricist-positivist approach is the time-honored one of introducing the sobriety of scientifically oriented inquiry into the sector of political science concerned with international relations. I must admit that in frequent spirited discussions with the proponents of this approach, I often lose sight of this aim, which they pursue with missionary zeal. This is because, having come to the fringes of political science from my original habitat (applications of mathematics outside the physical sciences), I tend to take the positivist attitude for granted. To me the insistence on operational definitions, the advantages of quantifiable data, the necessity of statistical evaluations of results, and so on are old hat. I tend to view arguments supporting the use of hard data in the social sciences somewhat the same way I do arguments to the effect that fossil evidence is more relevant to a theory of the origin of species than the account in <u>Genesis.</u> That is, I underestimate, so they tell me, the tenacity of conventional wisdom and of obscurantism still pervading the field of international relations. If this is so, my critique of the empirical-positivist approach can indeed be interpreted as giving aid and comfort to the enemy. Needless to say, it need be construed in this way no more than a critique of the natural-selection theory of evolution centering on its weak spots and difficulties necessarily implies support for the proponents of Lamarckian or special-creation theories.

I have emphasized ideational spin-offs as the principal positive contribution of quantitative and mathematical approaches to theories of international relations. I should, perhaps, emphasize that "ideational" is a more inclusive term than "ideological." Ideational spin-offs include methodologically valuable insights. Turning once more to the work on the correlates of war, we note that serious investigators in this area by no means confine themselves to processing raw data compiled from almanacs and government publications. A great deal of work is involved in the construction of indexes suggested by at times quite sophisticated theoretical considerations. The index of polarization, to take one example, although constructed from published data, is a theoretical construct. It can be distinguished from the vaguely formulated concepts of "traditional" political science in that the method of its construction is explicit—that is, the index is operationally defined. Only in consequence of this definition does it become possible to make meaningful the question, "Does 'polarization' appear to facilitate or to inhibit the incidence of war?" To be sure, I have expressed grave reservations about the meaningfulness of the concept "incidence of war," not because it was vaguely formulated but, on the contrary, because its operational definition may have carried it outside the historically relevant aspects of the problem of war. But there is no choice. If our notions about "causes of war" are to be put into any kind of sober scientific prospective, operationalization and examination of more or less hard data cannot be dispensed with.

In pointing to the value of ideational spin-offs, I am not forgetting the ideational spin-offs of operationalization itself. Again, take the polarization index that suggests different roles of the "balance of power" in the international systems of the nineteenth and twentieth centuries. Similar results are observed with respect to another index called "alliance aggregation," the average fraction of states in the system with which a state is formally allied. Other indexes, however, show an opposite effect. For instance, "capability concentration" is positively correlated with subsequent international war in the nineteenth century (r = 0.81) and negatively in the twentieth (-0.23). Both indexes are components of what Singer and Bouxsein call "clarity."[8] Several other components of "clarity" are singled out by these authors. Very roughly "clarity" is related to ease of identifying friends and enemies, on the one hand, and to readiness of making decisions (for example, to go or not to go to war), on the other.

Now the question arises whether there is reason to suppose that "clarity" (as defined by a complex of indexes) is positively or negatively correlated with the "amount of war" defined in some way. If war is considered as an "error," a result of "miscalculation," or the like (a conception with wide currency), then it would appear that war should be negatively correlated with "clarity." (Recall that the Korean war has often been blamed on the failure of United States to give emphatic advance warning to "the communists.") On the other hand, if decisions to go to war are prompted by high "subjective probability of victory" by the dominant side, then the opposite should be the case. To a certain extent, observed correlations may serve to support one or the other hypothesis. The extent of the support may be unimpressive, but putting the question in this way is better than remaining in complete ignorance or engaging in fruitless controversies generated by opposite a priori assumption.

Any one familiar with the actual results of these correlation analyses will be impressed with their extreme capriciousness. In attempting to make sense of them, come what may, one is strongly tempted to add one ad hoc qualification after another, something in the manner of proliferating epicycles of the Ptolemaic theory of planetary motions. Some will take this development to be evidence of the awesome complexity of international relations and will call for all-out efforts to come to grips with it by amassing more and more data and performing increasingly more sophisticated analyses. Others will dismiss the entire effort as an empty exercise that can only lead to a dead end.

In emphasizing the value of ideational spin-offs, I am trying to forestall the disappointment engendered by the failure of a Copernicus to appear. (See my arguments above concerning the fundamental difference between international dynamics and celestial mechanics.) At the same time, I categorically reject the counsel of despair. The total effect of the "exercises" is bound to be salubrious. The ideational spin-offs are precisely the concepts generated by the search for indexes. To be sure, the theoretical leverage of these concepts remains for the most part questionable, but at least it is

MATHEMATICAL METHODS 35

testable in each instance, which is more than can be said for the equally rapidly proliferating concepts of traditional political science.

So much for the methodological aspects of the ideational spin-offs of the empirical-quantitative approach. These spin-offs also have ideological aspects, although extreme positivist proponents of the approach will deny this, identifying as they do, empiricism with objectivity and objectivity with neutrality. They will probably agree that the approach may have a salubrious effect of laying to rest many persuasive superstitions pervading conventional wisdom. But this constitutes an attack on ideology, which itself entails some ideological leverage. Witness the following excerpt:

> There are, it seems, several reasons why we understand so much less about social processes and conditions at the global level than we do about comparable processes at lower levels of aggregation. One is, of course, that we are dealing with a larger empirical domain, and one that is apparently more heterogeneous and complex. Another might be that the behaviors of nations—the key factors at this level of aggregation—have been shrouded more in mystery and taboo than that of other classes of social entity. By keeping diplomacy and military strategy in the category of the arcane, elites have inhibited serious inquiry, even if there were those unpatriotic enough to ask. A third and related factor may be the extent to which the national state has been the major source of material and psychic sustenance for the world's people over the past century, or so, and thus not an agency whose external behavior will be questioned or examined closely.[9]

The image of elites shrouding their activities in mystery and imposing taboos on questioning their authority and wisdom is certainly generated by an ideological commitment, without which the very concepts marshalled in the challenge would be meaningless.

And there is more. The "dissection" of war into its observable constituents is probably more conducive to the conceptualization of war as an aberration than as an instrument of foreign policy. Thus, although the methodology of the empirical approach is based on "objectivity," its ideational spin-off need not be "neutral." This points up a fundamental difference between objectivity and neutrality. Any approach claiming scientific status must reflect objectivity— by definition of "scientific." "Neutrality," however, is impossible in the sphere of social science. Attempts to impose it tend to make social science sterile rather than objective.

NOTES

1. Lewis F. Richardson, Statistics of Deadly Quarrels (Chicago: Quadrangle Books, 1960).
2. Lewis F. Richardson, Arms and Insecurity (Chicago: Quadrangle Books, 1960).
3. J. David Singer, "The Correlates of War Project," World Politics 24 (1972): 243-70; J. David Singer and Melvin Small, "Alliance Aggregation and the Onset of War, 1815-1945," in Quantitative International Politics, ed. J. David Singer (New York: The Free Press, 1968), pp. 247-86.
4. David L. Wagner, Ronald T. Perkins, and Rein Taagepera, "Complete Solution of Richardson's Arms Race Equations," Journal of Peace Science 1 (1975): 159-72.
5. Andre Mensch, ed., Theory of Games Techniques and Applications (London: The English Universities Press, 1966).
6. Abram de Swaan, Coalition Theories and Cabinet Formations (Amsterdam: Elsevier, 1973). See also Charles Bird and Martin W. Sampson III, "An Analysis of Coalitions Formation in OPEC," Chapter 18 of this volume.
7. Robert Jervis, The Logic of Images in International Relations (Princeton: Princeton University Press, 1970).
8. J. David Singer and Sandra B. Bouxsein, "Structural Clarity and International War: Some Tentative Findings," in Interdisciplinary Aspects of General Systems Theory, ed. Thomas Murray, papers presented at the Third Annual Meeting of the Society for General Systems Research, Middle-Atlantic Region, College Park, Md., September 1974, pp. 126-35.
9. Ibid., p. 126.

CHAPTER 3

WHY MATHEMATICAL MODELS?

John V. Gillespie

The American physicist Gibbs is reported to have said, "Mathematics is a language." This phrase has been repeated by numerous scholars, but no matter how often it is repeated, its significance cannot be minimized. Any language, be it an ordinary one, such as English, French, or Chinese, or an "artificial" language such as Simula, or Fortran, Amerind sign language, shorthand, or mathematics, has certain properties or characteristics. Certainly, there are differences between languages; as a start, they look different. But all languages have syntactical structure and semantical attributes. Although the actual syntax and semantics differ among languages, the functions performed by syntax and semantics are similar. The syntax and semantics of a language work together to provide a means of communication. Communication in a language takes place between those who share (or "speak") the language and understand the meanings of its terms and sentences (word strings). To understand a language is to know when errors (improper syntactical and semantical uses) are made and to use the language productively for meaningful and purposive activities. Using a linguistic approach, the objective of this chapter is to answer the questions: Why use mathematical models in international relations research? What is gained and what is lost by such an adventurous use of language? What intellectual motivations drive some to employ mathematical reasoning when discussing alliances, wars, international conflict, or other phenomena of international relations?

Support for this research was granted by the National Science Foundation Grant 74-24186. I wish to thank Roslyn Simowitz and Dina A. Zinnes for their helpful critical comments.

Is mathematics necessary for scientific understanding of international relations?

My approach to answering these and related questions is to begin with language and its attributes. Once the characteristics of language are explained, we can begin to answer the questions posed above. To the well-informed reader this chapter may seem trite and to some degree not employing the full richness of modern philosophical understandings of language. However, my purpose here is not to review a vast and complex literature; I am concerned with explaining in general terms what mathematics has to offer the scientist concerned with international relations. The student of symbolic and mathematical logic will quickly see that I have used logical terms in an informal way. The student of the philosophy of language will see with ease that I have overlooked many nuances in the contemporary study of language and have taken an approach without mentioning alternative theories of language. However devastating these omissions may be, some beginning understanding of language does provide a basis for addressing the questions posed. Kenneth J. Arrow argued in 1951 that the justification for the use of mathematics in the social sciences is widely misunderstood.[1] Arrow's observation undoubtedly holds true for much of international relations research today, especially in those areas of inquiry involving international politics. Hopefully, by exploring the use of mathematics as language, some of these misunderstandings can be resolved.

MATHEMATICS AS LANGUAGE

Language is the primary means of communication between people, between people and some machines, such as computers, and even on occasion between machines and yet other machines. The term "language" applies by definition to all communication that can be observed using common human senses. This definition implies that language is observable communication. What we observe in communication are such things as marks on a page or blackboard, utterances and sounds, movements such as in Amerind sign language, signs such as those appearing along a highway, and so on. Language refers to the use of such marks and symbols, utterances and sounds, movements and signs, and so on for communication between people or machines.[2] Language for our purposes only refers to those elementary signs and so on that can be observed. There well may exist other forms of communication that require extrasensory devices for observation. These extralinguistic forms of communication are not languages as defined here because observation and understanding of them require skills beyond those involved in common human sensory observation. It should also be noted that not all human behavior involves language: Only that subset of human behaviors that is purposeful communication involves language. Furthermore, for our purposes language does not involve the physiological and mentalistic sources of an utterance, symbol, and so on. We are not concerned with the process by which a sound is uttered or the cognitive processes leading to an inscription on a page. We are only concerned with the inscription or the heard sound and the relations between such marks and sounds. Also eliminated from our discussion because of our notion of language as observable marks, utterances, and so forth are such topics as the history of marks and utterances and their evolution, the esthetics of linguistic devices, and the study of the formation of sounds and symbols. We shall confine our attention to only linguistic devices that can be observed, and the structuring or sequencing of such devices into strings and sets of strings.

The basic building blocks of languages are words. Words are simply conventional strings of utterances or marks. Words are linguistic conventions in the sense that they are known by their repeated use. There are different kinds of words in a language. Some words in a language serve as referents to objects or experiences in the empirical world. For example, the word "tree" is a referent to the class of objects that grow out of the ground and commonly are tall, have trunks, and so on. The word "pain" serves as a referent to the experiences one encounters when suffering from disease or mental anguish. To an observer, "pain" may refer to the bodily movements of placing one's hand on the forehead and yelling, "ouch." Other words in a language serve as logical connectives. In English such words as "and" and "or" serve at times as logical connectives linking other words together. Still other words are fillers. Fillers help us to communicate parsimoniously. Such symbols as the comma and the period are fillers. Often the words "but," "the," and "an" are fillers. On occasion the otherwise logical terms "and" and "or" serve as fillers.

In mathematics the words that are referents to things we observe or experience are undefined. Mathematics per se does not contain specific referential words. However, the language of mathematics has referential words that refer to whole classes of phenomena. For example, the symbols "x" or "y" may refer in a given use to variables; "k," "ℓ" and "g" may refer to constants. Variables and constants are very general classes of objects and experiences. Mathematics also has words that serve as logical connectives. Such words as the plus sign, the minus sign, and the symbol "$\int$" are logical terms. Similarly, mathematics contains fillers that assist in communication. Symbols such as square brackets and parentheses assist in mathematical communication. They add clarity to uses of the language.[3]

A distinction needs to be made between semantics and syntax. Words, their referents, and the appropriate use of words to make reference to objects and experiences are problems in semantics. To label "alliances" as "coalitions" raises a semantical question. It essentially is a question of isomorphism between references. Whether the labeling of "war" as a variable continuously defined over time using the symbol "x(t)" is correct or incorrect is a semantical question.

Language also has syntax or structure; syntactic questions involve the appropriate use of logical connectives. Using words that serve as logical connectives, well-ordered sentences can be written linking word strings (set of words) to other word strings. The logical connective "if . . ., then" can be used in English in the following sentence: "If you run a mile or two a day, then your life expectancy will be longer than the average person's." Such a sentence employs the "if . . . , then" logical connective to provide a relationship between the word strings "you run a mile or two a day" and "your life expectancy will be longer than the average person's." "Or" is another logical connective; it is used in the above sentence to connect the word strings "a mile" and "two."

Mathematics also has its syntax. The sentence "$y = a + bx$" uses the connectives of the equals sign, the plus sign, and the multiplication sign, implied by the convention of writing the symbols "b" and "x" together. Syntax in mathematics and in any ordinary language like English provides the rules or grammar through which well-ordered sentences are written using words and word strings. Syntax identifies the connections between words or word strings and also provides the hierarchy through which we determine the precedence of logical connectives. Syntax tells us, for example, whether to add before we multiply or to multiply before we add. Likewise, syntax in a well-ordered (syntactically correct) English sentence tells us which phrases modify other phrases. It provides the hierarchy of relationships between word strings so that a sentence can be read correctly.

Syntax also assists us in knowing where a sentence begins and ends by governing the placement of fillers. Appropriately placed fillers inform us about the beginning and end of a sentence. In many ordinary languages the first word in a well-ordered sentence is capitalized. The ending is generally denoted by the symbol the period. The spacing of mathematical expressions on a page generally denotes the beginning and ending of sentences. The correct use of punctuation marks is a syntactical issue. The use of punctuation, whether in mathematics or in an ordinary language, is rule governed. There are laws that dictate correct usage. To summarize, whereas semantics refers to the mapping of words or word strings onto objects or experiences in the empirical world, syntax refers to the correct ordering of words and word strings into sentences.

The user of a language employs syntactical rules and semantical references to communicate with other users. A user may also employ language for the purposes of reasoning or constructing an argument. To construct a sound argument one must correctly employ the syntactical rules of the language. In English, the logical connectives, such as "or" or "and," combined with properties of the semantics of the language, provide means through which sets of well-ordered sentences can be combined so as to deduce other well-ordered sentences. The syllogism is the classical example of a sound argument. Every schoolchild has proven that "all men are blue" or that "Jones is a Martian." Such deductions commonly employ quantifiers or the semantical properties of classes in ordinary language. For example, to prove that Jones is a Martian, one might begin with the well-ordered sentence, "All creatures are Martians." "All" in this case is a universal quantifier. Using the semantical attributes in ordinary language, Jones can be identified as a person, and persons are a subset of creatures. In this example semantics is useful in establishing sets and subsets providing the implied logical properties of inclusion, union, and intersection of sets that are used to obtain the deduction.

Likewise, in mathematics the properties of symbols identified as constants or functions of time-varying variables, provide semantical structures that assist in reasoning. Together with the logical terms and the semantical properties of other terms, one can reason from some sets of well-ordered statements to other expressions. If the statements are coupled together, as in a set of simultaneous equations, new truths can be derived from old truths. As in ordinary language, if the axioms and postulates of a sound argument are true, the conclusion or theorem is also true. Sound arguments are distinguished from unsound arguments by the correct use of the semantical properties and the syntactical rules governing the use of logical terms and the relations between the mathematical statements that compose the axioms and postulates. General schemata for forming sound arguments, generally referred to as rules of inference, have been developed by logicians. Such schemata include the rules of modus ponens, modus tollens, and reductio ad absurdum. Although in our daily uses of logic we rarely realize what rules of inference we are employing, the rules of inference are part of the syntactical reasoning structure in our ordinary language. These same rules have their counterparts in mathematics.

Definitions are simply statements about linguistic conventions.[4] Definitions always involve semantical issues. We often deceive ourselves in thinking that they are components of sound arguments. They are not necessary elements in a sound argument; they are neither true nor false. Definitions only map the elements of one word or set of words onto another word or set of words; they are substitutions of words for other words. Definitions may be enlightening and they are often necessary for removing the vagueness of semantics within a language, but they are "extralogical." Definitions only provide further understanding of the referents of words; they do not directly assist in forming arguments. Indeed, definitions do assist in clarifying terms and hence in providing better communication, and with definitions a sound argument may be better communicated. However, definitions are not necessary for assessing whether a given argument is sound or unsound.

For a given discourse—say, this chapter—some terms need to be defined. Other terms do not require definition. Terms not requiring definition are called primitives. The primitives of a given discourse are terms whose reference and use is understood by all parties in the discourse. Definitions of nonprimitive terms can be reduced by repeated definition to primitive terms. On occasion users of a given language resort to crude languages to define terms. For example, one might point to an object rather than defining it. Likewise, one might imitate a gnu to relay the meaning of "gnu." Strictly speaking, such recourses to pointing and imitation are not definitions; they only provide examples that assist in communication. They use crude forms of communication to convey the meanings of primitive terms.

Discourses in mathematics, as with discourses using ordinary languages, also contain primitive terms. For a given mathematical discourse it is commonly assumed that readers understand such symbols as "$x(t)$" (x is time varying), "$\int$" (integration), "t_0" (initial time), or that readers understand which terms are variables and constants. As with ordinary languages, symbols can be defined in terms of other symbols, and this process of definition can be continued until mathematical primitives are reached. In terms of much contemporary mathematical reasoning, the symbol "T" (true) and "F" (false) are primitives. As with ordinary languages, we often resort to crude languages to convey the meaning of mathematical primitives. Also, in many mathematical discourses the meaning of mathematical primitives are conveyed by using ordinary language. However feeble the attempt may be, we often endeavor to aid communication by providing ordinary language counterparts for mathematical expressions.

What we choose to call something in any discourse is arbitrary. That we label the animal cow as "cow" rather than as "woc" is totally an arbitrary choice of language. Likewise the labeling of variables by the symbols "x," "y," and "z," rather than the symbols "α," "β," and "γ," is arbitrary. What is not arbitrary in a discourse are the distinctions, or the lack thereof, made between objects by use of referential words. A discourse by its very nature groups objects together into classes. In a given discourse, if we refer to the large class of objects containing cows, dogs, pigs, and human beings by the word "animals," we have chosen to ignore observable differences between the objects referred to in other discourses by the words "cows," "dogs," "pigs" and "human beings." The selection of terms for a discourse plays an important part in determining what observable things we are ascribing to all of the objects that make up some class of objects. For a particular discourse ignoring observable differences between cows, dogs, pigs, and human beings may pose no communication difficulty. For other discourses choices of words that are less inclusive than the term "animal" are necessary.

The selection of terms for a discourse, whether in mathematics or ordinary language, is a problem of vagueness of communication. Terms are vague if and only if the objects to which they refer cannot be identified by observation and their use agreed upon by all parties in a discourse. In other words, each participant in a discourse should be able to select the objects of reference from the set of all possible objects in the empirical world. In the discourse of international relations the term "war" is often vague, even when a definition is provided. Participants in the discourse of international relations simply may not understand the objects referred to by the terms in a definition of "war." Vagueness can only be avoided either by all participants sharing the same referential meanings of terms or by defining terms on a shared set of primitive terms. No matter what the language of communication happens to be, if the primitives are not understood, ambiguity results.

Let us summarize. Words are the basic building blocks of language. Words are either referents to objects or experiences in the empirical world, logical connectives, or fillers. Following the semantical characteristics and syntactical rules of a language, words can be combined into well-ordered sentences. Sentences can be arranged into arguments, and with the correct use of rules of inference new truths can be derived from old truths. In this way language provides a means for communication and reasoning. Mathematics as a language shares the same general properties of ordinary languages. As is the case with English, mathematics has syntactical structure and semantical characteristics.

Definitions are not parts of sound arguments. Definitions aid in communication by indicating the objects referred to by the use of a given word. Vagueness in arguments is a product of unshared referents for terms and lack of argument on the objects referred to by linguistic primitives. Vagueness is a property of all languages, but for certain uses some languages are less ambiguous than others.

With this general structure we can now discuss the role of mathematics and mathematical modeling in international relations research. First, we need to examine properties of the "ordinary" language of international relations research. Second, we need to study how mathematics relates to the properties of the "ordinary" language of international relations. Third, given the above examinations, the role of mathematics as a language can be analyzed and evaluated. Next we need to address the limitations on the use of mathematics. And last, some general comments on mathematics in international relations research will be offered.

THE LANGUAGE OF INTERNATIONAL RELATIONS

The language of international relations is very similar to ordinary language; however, there are some important differences. The primary difference between ordinary English and the language of international relations is that some terms are given special meanings. Such terms as "war," "conflict," "coalition," and "alliance," are commonly defined to have narrower meanings and more specific empirical referents than in everyday use. A second difference is that logical connectives play a more important role in the language of international relations than in everyday communication. Since in international relations research the effort is commonly to communicate an argument (theory or set of interrelated hypotheses), logical terms linking sentences together play a more important role than in ordinary English. For these reasons the language of international relations can be seen as a "quasi-ordinary" language. It looks and sounds like ordinary language but contains more restrictive uses of terms.

The problems with the quasi-ordinary language used in most international relations research are both semantic and syntactic. Because the language employed by international relations scholars looks like and shares much in common with ordinary English, it is very tempting to jump back and forth between the ordinary language and the disciplinary language. There are serious problems in making these transitions. In the main the problems associated with a quasi-ordinary language as a disciplinary language of discourse in science are based in the penchant of individuals to use the ordinary language as a substitute for the disciplinary language. The intellectual tendency is to resolve ambiguities and reasoning problems by resorting to the ordinary language. The distinction between the ordinary language and the disciplinary language thus becomes fuzzy, and often the more familiar ordinary language serves as a means for interpreting the less familiar scientific language. This is to say that the special terms used in the disciplinary language, those terms such as "war," "alliance," or "coalition," lose their special meanings through use and become undifferentiable from the ordinary-language words that look the same but generally refer more imprecisely to a larger class of empirical phenomena. Similarly, the formal use of logical connectives begins to give way to the casual use of such words. For example, the exclusive and inclusive uses of "and" become indistinguishable. The cavalier use of the logical implication "if . . . , then" replaces the formal and logical meaning of implication. As a result, the logic through which one reasons from axioms and postulates to conclusions (the logic of modus ponens or modus tollens, for example) becomes lost or obfuscated.

In the common parlance of international relations research terms are often provided "operational definitions." Such definitions convey the sets of empirical observations and experiences to which the defined term refers. Although the degree of precision of such definitions may vary, in general they serve to narrow the number of empirical referents for a term.

Operational definitions are constructed so as to map the terms used in the disciplinary language onto the terms of ordinary language, and consequently, at least in principle, the language of international relations is reducible to ordinary everyday language. However, since the ordinary language and the disciplinary language look the same and are defined by words and terms, at least when totally reduced, that are from the common vocabulary of the ordinary language, the temptation is to forget the rigorous operational definitions and simply to substitute the vague and ambiguous ordinary-language cognates. For example, the term "war" may be defined operationally in the language of international relations to require a certain number of deaths or a certain set of formal governmental decrees for an event or set of events to be considered a war. In ordinary language the term "war" does not denote any such restrictions. In many disciplinary uses of the term "war" the restrictions often will be ignored because the symbol "war" (ordinary language) and "war" (international relations research language) are indistinguishable. The operational definition becomes lost. In losing the definitions, terms in the technical or disciplinary language assume no greater rigor than in the ordinary language.

More significant than the loss of accuracy of definitions are the consequences of such linguistic ambiguity for constructing sound arguments.[5] Arguments present one's reasoning on a given topic; they tell readers or listeners what sentences are being associated with other sentences and the structure of such associations. If language becomes ambiguous and vague, relations between sentences in a language may become ambiguous and vague. Using ambiguous and vague terms in arguments may lead to unwarranted conclusions. Readers and listeners cannot subject the reasoning to careful analysis to assess its correctness because of the multiple meanings of terms that all look alike. Communication of the argument is lost. This implies that such activities as empirical assessment of arguments by collecting data, estimating parameters, and so forth only become meaningful under a given interpretation of the ambiguous argument and do not represent definitive assessments even within the measurement, temporal and spatial boundaries and assumptions made to conduct the empirical test. It also implies that further theorizing or construction of arguments is only valid with respect to given interpretations of the original argument.

The consequences for the accumulation of scientific knowledge are considerable. Arguments in ambiguous languages beget more ambiguous arguments if research builds on previous research.[6] Accumulation of ambiguities is precisely that which the construction of the original quasi-ordinary language was intended to avoid. Some may think that with considerable effort ambiguities can be rooted out and a disciplinary vocabulary that stipulates such conventions as, "War_1 means . . . , war_2 means . . . , war_3 means . . . , and so on," can be developed. However, as with the original fuzzy boundary between the ordinary language and the quasi-ordinary disciplinary language of international relations, the subscripts on the word "war" may well become ignored, and hence the distinctions masked, the sentences ambiguous, and the arguments without the credence and support of logical thought. To put the problem in capsule form, the language of international relations is not sufficiently distinct from ordinary language to provide rigorous communication of scientific ideas.

Quasi-ordinary languages such as those employed in most international relations scholarship share the property of clumsiness with their ordinary language look-alikes. Clumsiness refers to the vagueness of logical connectives in a language. For example the "if . . . , then" statement in English has many meanings and consequently is clumsy. Parsimony refers to the degree of conciseness in the presentation of an argument using logical connectives. For example the mathematical sentence "$y = a + bx$" in English is "y equals b multiplied by x and that product added to a." Obviously the mathematical counterpart to the English sentence is a more parsimonious representation of the idea of a straight line in two-dimensional space. Parsimony is especially important when constructing complex arguments. If the number of steps in an argument is considerable, then it is often easy to become lost in the reasoning. Furthermore, the inconvenience of clumsy language becomes a hazard when constructing complex arguments is attempted. It is a hazard in that steps in the argument can often be misinterpreted when assumptions are made that are not obvious to the one constructing the argument. Furthermore, for readers and listeners the misinterpreted steps are difficult to find.

Nonparsimonious languages also have more complex grammars. To claim that a given argument in a quasi-ordinary language is unreasonable is to say that one does not find the argument convincing. The convincingness of arguments has two components: One is strictly logical; the other is taste. The logical component can be assessed by recourse to logical analysis, which generally involves translating the terms into symbols of a language having a well-defined grammar and putting them to the test of canons of logic. Because of linguistic ambiguities, a number of translations may be required. Depending on the number of translations required, some answer, however inconclusive, can be found. The taste component of convincingness rests on extralogical grounds. It stipulates that for some reasons, beyond logic, the argument is reasonable or unreasonable. The problem with quasi-ordinary languages is that the two components to convincingness can rarely be unpacked: Taste rarely can be separated from logic. Even the word "logic" begins to assume its ordinary linguistic ambiguity of meaning everything from "taste" to "formal logic" to "reasonable." Mathematics separates taste from logic. In mathematical languages tests can be made for the correct use of grammar or syntax irrespective of the tastefulness of the argument. The implications of clumsy grammars that can vary by use as in quasi-ordinary languages are such that we do not often know precisely why arguments are found unreasonable. Unraveling reasons may be more difficult and time consuming than the argument itself merits.

The use of quasi-ordinary languages as disciplinary languages is not all negative. On the positive side is the versatility of quasi-ordinary languages and their greater number of readers and listeners. Both of these positive qualities, however, are two-edged swords. Versatility allows for variety and perhaps the envisioning of relationships that otherwise would be difficult to find. It is also a common source of originality. However, versatility may well produce ambiguity and careless reasoning.

The benefit of large numbers of readers and listeners cannot be overlooked. Certainly, the desire to communicate with large audiences is best enhanced by using a language common to the large audience. Using ordinary language in communicating with large audiences is a necessity if the communication is to be understood, at least to some minimal degree. However, the use of quasi-ordinary languages is very risky in large-audience communication tasks. It is reasonable to assume that one's audience shares a basic ordinary language. However, it is very risky to assume that one's audience shares the quasi-ordinary language. In reality it may well be the case that the quasi-ordinary language is only understood as ordinary language by the audience. The precision of the quasi-ordinary language is lost, and seemingly technical terms are taken to be equivalent to their ordinary language look-alikes. The arguments presented may well be misunderstood.

It has been noted elsewhere that international relations scholars do not even share the same quasi-ordinary language.[7] There are several definitions of "war" floating around in the numerous pages of international relations research. It has been argued that this lack of linguistic consensus is a primary barrier to obtaining fruitful communication and accumulation of scientific knowledge about international relations. Certainly, these arguments are correct. However, to take them a step further, part of the problem is what we are choosing to define and another part is what we are willing to take as being linguistic primitives. Many of the terms of the quasi-ordinary language of international relations involve large constellations of phenomena in the empirical world. For example, the term "war," however defined, refers to such categories of observable phenomena as movements of troops, dispatch of military materiel, battle deaths, governmental decrees and proclamations, and so on. Even these categories are themselves composed of constellations of observations.

The problem is that international relations scholars desire to define terms whose referents are complex. As a result, the terms are rarely well defined (a reader or listener does not know what to select out of all objects in the empirical world as the ones that are being defined). As in contemporary physics, in which complex terms such as "energy" or "light" are not well defined, in contemporary international relations the terms referring to complex constellations of phenomena are not well defined. It is easier to define terms referring to less complex phenomena and build definitions of the more complex terms from the definitions of the less complex. Although this building process does not assure well-defined terms, it does allow for a more cautious and careful approach.

It can also be asserted that international relations scholars do not share a common set of primitive terms. Linguistic primitives are the "base words" in any language, and without a clear set of such primitives, fruitful communication is jeopardized. Primitives for some scholars are for other scholars terms in need of definition. The problem of linguistic primitives, as indeed is the case with many linguistic difficulties, is best resolved through continuous communication. Defining terms that have otherwise been taken as primitives can be accomplished by the persistent questioning, "What does this term refer to?" Only through use can a shared set of primitives be developed. However, developing a shared set of primitives is especially difficult in quasi-ordinary language, since the ordinary language look-alikes obfuscate those terms in need of definition. Meaning can come from two sources: the ordinary language and the quasi-ordinary disciplinary language. Unless the distinction between the two languages can be made clearly and confusion is avoided in use of the languages, there is little hope that a shared set of linguistic primitives in the quasi-ordinary language can be developed.

In this section I have attempted to show some of the hazards and difficulties of employing a quasi-ordinary language as a disciplinary language of science. Mathematics offers remedies to some of these difficulties. But by no means is mathematics a panacea. It too has linguistic difficulties when employed as language of discourse. What I hope to demonstrate, however, is that mathematics as a language of disciplinary communication is to be preferred because while its difficulties, save one, are of the same magnitude as the difficulties of quasi-ordinary language, it does offer resolutions to some of the problems of quasi-ordinary language.

MATHEMATICS AS A LANGUAGE IN INTERNATIONAL RELATIONS

As has been discussed earlier, mathematics is a language whose grammar is very strict. The grammatical rules of mathematics are its major attraction to the modeler; the rules are such that arguments can be easily constructed and assessed for their soundness. Mathematical terms that are defined for a given discourse to have reference to empirical world phenomena are very general (such terms denote objects that are variables, constants, and so forth). As a result, mathematical languages per se do not necessarily tighten the definitional problems of the referential terms in quasi-ordinary languages. However, mathematics does assist in constructing and communicating sound arguments. What I desire to demonstrate in the next few pages is that mathematics offers the advantages of a tight and rigorous rule-governed grammar and that the generality of referential terms in the language poses no greater difficulty than that of the quasi-ordinary languages predominately used in international relations research today. My argument is that the syntax of mathematics is such that it enhances communication and that in use its semantical weaknesses of referential terms are the same as those of quasi-ordinary languages.

Sound arguments, as noted earlier, are what scientists desire to communicate to other scientists. Sound arguments present grammatically correct linkages between sentences. We have discussed the weaknesses and difficulties of employing quasi-ordinary language for the purposes of constructing sound arguments. The problems of quasi-ordinary language are its lack of strict grammatical rules, changes of semantics, especially in the relations between words, lack of parsimony, and openness to multiple interpretations. Correct uses of mathematics remedy these problems of communication.

With its strict grammar, mathematics provides a means through which sound arguments can be constructed by correctly reasoning from axioms and postulates to conclusions. These interrelated sentences of a sound argument can be unambiguously analyzed, and through the application of the grammatical rules of mathematics the reasoning process can be replicated by other readers of the argument. In other words, because the logical terms in the language of mathematics are not subject to the multiple interpretations of ordinary language, the meaning of the logical terms are fixed for a given discourse. The ambiguities that are commonly found in quasi-ordinary language arguments are avoided in mathematical arguments because of the strict grammar. The grammar is strict because it is not subjected to the vagaries of ordinary-language interpretations. The logical terms in mathematical sentences do not have ordinary-language look-alikes, and hence the intellectual tendency to give meaning to logical terms by using their ordinary language counterparts is minimized. The symbol "+" is far more precise than the English language symbol "and." The symbol "=" is far more precise than the symbol "is equal to." The English "and" may denote either the inclusive "and" or the exclusive "and." The English symbol "is equal to" may denote the mathematical cognates "=" or "≡" or ":" (is mapped onto) or mathematical expressions denoting functions. Because of the strictness of the grammar of mathematics, greater precision of interpretation of arguments is assured.

Mathematics is also more parsimonious than quasi-ordinary languages. Parsimony is important for constructing sound arguments. With unparsimonious languages there is a risk of missing steps and making hidden assumptions when constructing arguments.

Parsimonious languages minimize this risk. Missing steps is rather difficult when employing a rigorous grammar. In a mathematical argument, moving from one step to another is possible only if all the necessary information is provided in the previous steps. This is to say that the strictness of the grammar does not allow for new information to enter into an argument in the midst of the orderly process of the argument. If the necessary information is not contained in earlier steps of the argument, then a given sentence cannot be shown to follow from the earlier sentences. In this way hidden or accidental assumptions that enter in the course of an argument are avoided.

As with quasi-ordinary languages, in using mathematics those assumptions necessary for constructing an argument may or may not be explicitly stated at the beginning of an argument. More assumptions may be made, too, than are necessary to derive a given conclusion (theorem). However, these are problems of whatever language one is employing for the purposes of communicating an argument.[8] The advantage that mathematics has over quasi-ordinary languages is that its strict grammar allows other users of the language to ferret out the necessary assumptions or to pare down the assumptions to the smallest necessary set of assumptions. Because of its strict grammar and the avoidance of multiple meanings of logical connectives, mathematics as a language yields the unique capability of correcting or making more parsimonious the arguments of others. Quasi-ordinary languages do not provide sufficient precision of syntax to allow for these capabilities.

Parsimony of a language also allows for complex arguments containing many steps to be neatly packaged. Complex arguments in quasi-ordinary languages often run for many pages. In structuring an argument in quasi-ordinary languages, the problem often encountered is that subtle but significant changes of meaning edge their way into the argument. Because of its strict grammar and because of its fixed assignment of meaning to terms, especially logical terms, such changes of meaning are avoided in mathematical arguments. This attribute of mathematical languages is especially useful when building on the arguments of others. As we noted when discussing quasi-ordinary languages, the difficulty in accumulating knowledge by building on the arguments of others is that a given interpretation of the argument must be taken for the purposes of constructing a more elaborate argument. In mathematical languages this problem is alleviated. Because of the strictness of the syntactical rules, mathematics as a language of discourse offers the benefit of allowing other users to build on the arguments of previous users. Any interpretation of an argument must be derived from that argument following the syntactical rules. Hence, out of the set of all possible interpretations, the set of admissible or correct interpretations can be determined. This lack of ambiguity allows for users of the language to build on the arguments of each other. Building on the arguments of others allows for accumulation of knowledge.

Let us summarize. Mathematics is a language with a strict and well-defined grammar. Its logical connectives have narrower meanings than ordinary language terms that might be used as cognates. The language is more parsimonious than quasi-ordinary language. These attributes give mathematics several desirable features over quasi-ordinary languages. Among these features are precision and lack of ambiguity in communication, ease at constructing unambiguous sound arguments, avoiding hidden assumptions in arguments, detecting unnecessary assumptions in arguments, parsimony of expression, building on the arguments of others, and accumulation of knowledge. We have not as yet considered the semantical properties of referential terms in mathematics as a language of discourse. All the desirable properties listed to this point are more a product of syntax and the semantical properties of logical connective. Indeed, in any empirical science, the referential terms are of major importance.

The referential terms of a language map words onto observations and experiences in the empirical world. The referential terms of quasi-ordinary languages look like the referential terms of ordinary language. The referential terms of mathematics, however, are not ordinary language look-alikes. The mathematical referential terms are variables and constants. Variables and constants are large, gross categories of empirical phenomena; they are not as specific as quasi-ordinary language words such as <u>alliance</u>, <u>war</u>, and, <u>coalition</u>. However, in employing mathematics as a language of discourse, greater specificity is given to variables and constants by mapping them onto quasi-ordinary language words. At the commencement of a mathematical model, the modeler generally provides a lexicon in which symbols to be used in the mathematical model are defined onto quasi-ordinary terms. For example, in Richardson's model of armaments races (equations 1 and 2) the following definitions are employed:

Let:
- $x(t)$: the armaments of nation X
- $y(t)$: the armaments of nation Y
- ℓ : the threat of nation Y's armaments to nation X
- k: the threat of nation X's armaments to nation Y
- α: nation X's economic fatigue and burden of its armaments
- β: nation Y's economic fatigue and burden of its armaments
- g: nation X's grievance toward nation Y
- h: nation Y's grievance toward nation X

(1) $\dot{x} = \ell y(t) - \alpha x(t) + g$

(2) $\dot{y} = kx(t) - \beta y(t) + h$

where $\dot{x}$ and $\dot{y}$ are rates of change in armaments (read dx/dt and dy/dt respectively).[9]

Whereas equations 1 and 2 provide the model, all the mapping done prior to the model tells the reader what the quasi-ordinary-language interpretations are for the symbols. The model (equations 1 and 2) provides the relationships between the terms and the logical connectives to be used. The mappings provide the referents of the variables and constants in the model by using the quasi-ordinary language. When using mathematics as a language for empirical scientific communication, the mappings between the mathematical symbols and quasi-ordinary language are necessary for providing meaning to the referential symbols in the mathematical argument. Because mathematical arguments use quasi-ordinary languages to give meanings to variables and constants, the problems of ambiguity are the same as those found in the quasi-ordinary-language definitions. Mathematical models as a result inherit all the problems as the referential terms in quasi-ordinary scientific languages. On this criterion mathematics and quasi-ordinary disciplinary languages are equally ambiguous as languages of scientific communication.

Referential terms are necessary for scientific communication if that scientific communication is to be about the empirical world. Mathematics does not assist in clarifying referents to the empirical world. However, mathematics does assist in stipulating the logical connections between terms. Equation 1, for example, clearly stipulates the logical connections between the terms "ℓ," "y(t)," "α," "x(t)" and "g." As noted earlier, such logical connectives are often ambiguous in quasi-ordinary scientific language. What the symbol "y(t)" means in terms of the empirical world is dependent on its quasi-ordinary language cognate; it is not provided meaning by equations 1 or 2.

To construct a mathematical model, the modeler is often required to provide additional specification over and above the quasi-ordinary language. In equations 1 and 2, some terms were labeled as constants and others as variables. The constants ℓ, k, α, β, g and h and the variables x(t), y(t), $\dot{x}$, and $\dot{y}$ are all understood as such from their notation. However, in a quasi-ordinary language use of such terms may not be clearly labeled as variables and constants. The additional specification is a product of the modeling process. In this way, for a given use, mathematical modeling may force more precise definitions, ridding the quasi-ordinary language of some ambiguities. However, such additional precision is not necessarily the case; it only occurs when the quasi-ordinary language is excessively vague.[10]

Let us summarize what we have thus far argued. In questions of syntax mathematics is superior to quasi-ordinary language; in questions of the semantics of logical connectives mathematics is superior to quasi-ordinary languages; in questions of the semantics of referential terms neither language is superior. One further question remains and this is the desire to communicate to large audiences. As noted earlier, quasi-ordinary language, because it looks like ordinary language, offers the benefit of some modicum of communication with diverse audiences. Mathematics fails, at least to some degree, on this criterion. Fewer people are familiar with mathematics than with ordinary language. Although the message conveyed may be more precise and the arguments less ambiguous, the potential audience is smaller than that for messages in ordinary language. Even among international relations scholars, the audience equipped to understand and literate in mathematics is composed of a precious few. As a result, modelers are often asked to give complete translations back into quasi-ordinary, and consequently into ordinary language. Such translations are obviously vague and do injustice to the mathematical argument.

However, there are some very real advantages to mathematics as a language for scientific communication. Mathematics is a universal language; its grammar is invariant across cultures and national boundaries. Quasi-ordinary languages that use English ordinary language terms, such as "war," and "alliance," are not universal scientific languages; such languages are culture-bound and must be translated and retranslated into other quasi-ordinary languages for the purposes of international communication. Quasi-ordinary languages when translated encounter very serious problems of ambiguity. The nuances of meaning of referential and logical terms are not only numerous within one language but are multiplied when translation into other languages occurs. As a consequence, precision gives way to even greater ambiguity. Mathematics does not share these problems encountered in translation, especially given its strict grammar. Mathematics does not have to be translated. Only the mapping of the referential terms requires translation; and this translation is of the same magnitude and difficulty as in the translation of quasi-ordinary scientific language. Arguments in mathematics are unencumbered by nuances of the meanings of logical terms. For the sake of clarity of international communication, mathematics is a desirable language. For the breadth of audiences, quasi-ordinary language is preferable.

I have attempted to show that mathematics is a desirable language for scientific communication. I have argued that it is preferable to quasi-ordinary languages on all criteria except for the ambiguity of referential terms and numbers of members of potential audiences. On the criterion of the ambiguity of referential terms both mathematics and quasi-ordinary languages as languages for empirical science suffer the same weaknesses. In terms of the size of the potential audience, quasi-ordinary languages are superior, except when the precision of messages, which is especially frustrated in international communication, is considered. The problem with the size of the potential audience is not an inherent weakness of mathematics as a language. It is a problem of the number of people who are mathematically illiterate.[11] However, if mathematics is so desirable as a language of scientific communication, why has it not been more widely employed? In the next section I will review some of the limitations of mathematics as a disciplinary language.

ON THE USE OF MATHEMATICS

A scenario for the mathematical modeler in international relations research is something like the following. First, the modeler begins with a problem. The problem may be vague and quite ambiguous and in its original state may be simply a question that is of the form, "What are the consequences of some change?" The modeler then searches for clues in answering the question. For example, he may examine an array of international relations literature to assess whether other modelers have provided mathematical structures that may assist in answering the question. The modeler also consults the nonmathematical literature to obtain insights into how the problem may have been posed in quasi-ordinary language.

This searching is essential for the modeling process. One major difficulty is in the writing of a set of expressions that describe the referential empirical world—indeed, when done successfully, this is the creativity of mathematical modeling. Just as the scholar who employs quasi-ordinary language needs to write a set of sentences that describe political processes or international interactions, the modeler needs to write a set of mathematical expressions that describe the empirical phenomena that are relevant for answering his question. To use the jargon of mathematical modeling, the "systems equations" need to be written. The systems equations are those expressions that describe relevant and essential features in the empirical world.[12]

Richardson's arms-race model in equations 1 and 2 is an example of systems equations. Another example is Saaty's model of counterforce and countervalue strategies in the world of nuclear weapons.[13] Olson and Zeckhauser's model of alliances is yet another example.[14] The systems equations are the guts of the mathematical model; they describe the empirical world in mathematical terms.

Writing systems equations is not the total task of mathematical modeling because in the process of writing these equations little mathematics has been employed. No inferences or deductions have been made from the systems equations. The next step for the modeler is to pose his question or problem to the model. For example, Richardson asked of his systems equations the question: What are the conditions necessary to achieve equilibrium and stability in an arms race? Saaty asked of his system equations the question: What are the consequences of MIRVing and constructing ABM installations for the total number of missiles needed to satisfy nuclear weapons strategies? Olson and Zeckhauser asked of their collective goods systems equations: What are the consequences of unequal size of partners in an alliance on the sharing of costs? The questions that modelers ask of their systems equations are restatements of the initial problem that beckoned the curiosity of the modeler. To answer the questions the modeler needs to develop additional mathematical expressions. These expressions, which in the jargon of mathematical modeling are often referred to as "specifications," require the modeler to provide linkages between the systems equations and the questions asked of the equations. For example, Richardson had to specify what stability and equilibrium meant in a system of differential equations. Saaty had to specify the relationships between MIRVed missiles and ABMs and un-MIRVed missiles. Olson and Zeckhauser had to specify the relationships between partners of unequal size in an alliance with respect to collective goods.

With the specifications and the systems equations the modeler then attempts to derive an answer to his question. If the systems equations and specifications are not linked into a well-formed grammatical mathematical structure, a valid conclusion cannot be reached. Likewise, without mathematically linked sets of expressions, a sound argument cannot be made. The problem of linkages between the specifications and systems equations is part of the general problem of "tractability." Linkages are tractable if and only if derivations can be generated from the mathematical model. The problem of tractability is partly a function of the language of mathematics itself and partly a function of the modeler's use of the language. If the modeler has provided a tractable system of equations (both specifications and systems equations), then deductions, hopefully rich in significance, can be drawn.

Unfortunately it is true that, using mathematics, one can formulate interesting and significant problems for which there are no known mathematical solutions.[15] Many purely mathematical problems have not been solved, and consequently some questions asked of mathematical models referring to the empirical world of international relations may not be answerable. In the quest for finding deductions, one may encounter those areas in the language of mathematics in which the grammatical development is insufficient. Although the problem posed by the modeler may be well formed, answers to questions may be impossible to achieve because the necessary sound mathematical methods are nonexistent. Often, when confronted with this problem, one must resort to inferior questions and answers. For example, occasionally one asks questions of a mathematical model for which only sufficient answers can be found. In these instances mathematical methods yielding answers that are both necessary and sufficient have not been developed. The modeler must be satisfied with an answer that does not provide all the information posed by the question. This problem of tractability is one of the very major limitations on the use of mathematics as a language for empirical science. Of course, the tractability difficulty may be in the way the modeler has formulated his problem; it may not be at all a product of the mathematical language.

Another major limitation on the use of mathematics is confirmation. It is difficult to confirm that the systems equations in a mathematical model are an accurate reflection of the empirical world. As with "models" in quasi-ordinary language, empirical evidence is commonly garnered to support the accuracy of the systems equations. The problems of evidence and its reasonability are complex, and there are no pat solutions to these difficulties. Standards of evidence vary, and the quality of data in much of international relations research is in doubt. Without the availability of neat laboratory experimental methods, solid evidence is an even more serious problem.

However, the mathematical modeler is less concerned about evidence concerning his state equations than evidence that can be brought to bear on the deductions from the state equations. A system of empirically naive and incorrect sentences may lead to a deduction that is empirically true. Certainly, one may question, for example, the sentences that Freudian analysts use to describe mental systems. However, many "deductions" from Freudian models of mind have proven to be empirically accurate. Likewise, the modeler may have a set of systems equations that to many are incorrect descriptions of the empirical world as observed and experienced, but the deductions from that set of systems equations may yield empirically correct equations. The maxim of logic that false premises can lead to true conclusions cannot be denied. Following this maxim, modelers are less concerned with the empirical accuracy of their systems equations than with the empirical validity of their deductions. Criticisms to the effect that systems equations do not totally conform to the empirical world because some variables are lacking or because the relationships between variables have been misstated are somewhat irrelevant to the modeler. What is relevant to the modeler is whether or not the deductions from the systems equations provide empirically accurate statements. The modeler desires to answer questions in precise ways. The grammar of mathematics gives the modeler precision. The accuracy of the answers is an empirical concern.[16]

It is precisely the empirical question as to accuracy, however, that causes difficulty. The difficulty is that there are few definitive tests of any hypothesis, whether it is stated in mathematical language or quasi-ordinary terms. Testing hypotheses, whether they are based on rigorous mathematical deductions or on not so rigorous quasi-ordinary propositions, is a problem that equally afflicts both mathematical modelers and those who choose to use quasi-ordinary language. However, the mathematics modeler is often led to hypotheses that might never have been entertained, had all reasoning been constructed using quasi-ordinary languages.

The primary limitation on mathematics as a language for international relations research is that it is insufficiently developed to answer some interesting questions. However, it would be fraudulent to convey that mathematics is a static language. Many mathematical developments in the areas of game theory, especially in differential games, control theory, and information theory, offer promising mathematical methods for solving problems in international relations. Mathematicians do learn from the problems encountered by empirical scientists. They do desire to develop mathematical languages to cope with new problems. Although the development of mathematics may be slow, at least the empirical scientist is assured that such developments will provide precise grammars for solving problems.

CONCLUDING COMMENTS

I have tried to demonstrate the utility of mathematics in international relations research. Although mathematics has its limitations, it does offer a solid language for constructing sound arguments. Its grammars are precise and its structure lessens ambiguity.

Even though mathematics is a useful language for constructing arguments, it is risky to conclude that mathematics should be widely used in international relations. The prescriptive injunction, that mathematics should be used in international relations research, is not the intent of this discussion. My attempt has been to clarify why modelers find mathematics a productive language for reasoning. My endeavor is not to suggest that mathematics must or should be widely employed. To prescribe a language of inquiry is not only presumptive but also requires a far more detailed and rigorous epistemological, if not metaphysical, analysis than presented here.

Many important problems in international relations research can be addressed without mathematics. There is no reason why mathematics is necessary for analyzing problems and obtaining answers. Mathematics is simply a precise tool of communication. However, in principle, there is no logical way to deny that arguments in quasi-ordinary language can be as rigorous as mathematical arguments. Although precise quasi-ordinary language arguments may be unlikely and may be difficult to formulate, there is no reason in principle, especially for simple, noncomplex problems, why they cannot be developed.

Where mathematics has its greatest utility is in addressing complex problems for which answers are not intuitively obvious. It is unnecessary to use mathematics to solve simple reasoning problems, and it is probably preferable to avoid mathematical expression when quasi-ordinary language suffices. Because of quasi-ordinary language's wider audience, many simple problems can be accurately communicated without resorting to the less familiar mathematical language.

Why mathematical models? Because of the precision of the language for handling difficult and complex questions. Why not mathematical models? Because it is a language not shared by many international relations scholars. Perhaps someday, with increasing mathematical training of future cohorts of international relations scholars, the answer to the "why not" question will be moot. However, if the literature and the state of mathematical knowledge among those scientists interested in international relations are convincing evidence, the day of wide communication in mathematical language is far ahead of us.

NOTES

1. Kenneth J. Arrow, "Mathematical Models in the Social Science," in The Policy Sciences, eds. Daniel Lerner and Harold D. Lasswell (Stanford: Stanford University Press, 1951), pp. 129-54.

2. William Alston, Philosophy of Language (Englewood Cliffs, N.J.: Prentice-Hall, 1965); Alfred Tarki, Introduction to Logic and to the Methodology of Deductive Sciences, 3d ed. (New York: Oxford University Press, 1965).

3. Stephan Karner, The Philosophy of Mathematics (New York: Harper & Row, 1960); Raymond L. Wilder, The Foundations of Mathematics (New York: Wiley, 1952).

4. May Brodbeck, "Meaning and Action," Philosophy of Science 30 (1963): 309-24; Ernest Nagel, "Problems of Concept and Theory Formation in the Social Sciences," in Philosophy of the Social Sciences, ed. Maurice Natanson (New York: Random House, 1963), pp. 189-209; Ernest Nagel, "Theory and Observation," in Observation and Theory in Science, eds. Ernest Nagel, Slyvain Bromberger, and Adolf Grunbaum (Baltimore: The Johns Hopkins University Press, 1969), pp. 15-43.

5. May Brodbeck, "Models, Meaning and Theories," in Symposium on Sociological Theory, ed. Llewellyn Gross (New York: Harper & Row, 1959), pp. 373-403.

6. Dina A. Zinnes, "The Problem of Cumulation in the Scientific Study of International Politics," in In Search of Global Patterns, ed. James N. Rosenau (New York: Free Press, 1975), pp. 417-31.

7. Anatol Rapoport, "Mathematical Methods in Theories of International Relations: Expectation, Caveats, and Opportunities," Chapter 2 in the volume.

8. John V. Gillespie and Dina A. Zinnes, "Progressions in Mathematical Models of International Conflict," Synthese 31 (1975): 289-321; John V. Gillespie, "Optimal Control Theory and Comparative Foreign Policy: A Promising Approach for Future Research," in In Search of Global Patterns, ed. James N. Rosenau (New York: Free Press, 1975).

9. Lewis F. Richardson, Arms and Insecurity (Pittsburgh and Chicago: Boxwood and Quadrangle, 1960).

10. Patrick Doreian, Mathematics and the Study of Social Relations (New York: Schocken Books, 1970).

11. Karl W. Deutsch, "Quantitative Approaches to Political Analysis: Some Past Trends and Future Prospects," in Mathematical Approaches to Politics, eds. Hayward R. Alker, Jr., Karl W. Deutsch, and Antoine H. Stoetzel (San Francisco: Jossey-Bass, 1973), pp. 1-62.

12. Anatol Rapoport, "Some Systems Approaches to Political Theory," in Varieties of Political Theory, ed. David Easton (Englewood Cliffs, N.J.: Prentice-Hall, 1966), pp. 129-42; John V. Gillespie, "Some Observations on Dynamic Modeling," in The Shaping of Scientific Research on Politics, ed. David C. Leege (Dordrecht, Holland: forthcoming); Morris P. Fiorina, "Formal Models in Political Science," American Journal of Political Science 19 (1975): 133-59.

13. Thomas L. Saaty, Mathematical Models of Arms Control and Disarmament: Application of Mathematical Structures in Politics (New York: Wiley, 1968).

14. Mancur Olson, Jr., and Richard Zeckhauser, "An Economic Theory of Alliances," Review of Economics and Statistics 48 (1966): 266-79.

15. Gillespie and Zinnes, "Progressions in Mathematical Models."

16. Paul Diesing, Patterns of Discovery in the Social Sciences (Chicago: Aldine-Atherton, 1971).

PART II
PROBABILITY MODELS

CHAPTER

4

INTRODUCTION TO PROBABILITY MODELS
The Editors

Each model presented in this section contains a probabilistic element—when the possible alternatives for an outcome are known, but it is uncertain which outcome will in fact occur. Thus, these models share three unifying ingredients: Each contains (a) a random variable, that is, a variable that specifies all possible values that could occur, (b) assumptions about the probabilities defined on that random variable, and (c) probability distributions for the random variable derived as a consequence of b. It is also the case that there are underlying similarities between the assumptions made about the probabilities. This is not surprising since there are certain basic assumptions about probabilities that allow one to use important facets of probability theory. Given these underlying similarities, the models can be compared along each of the three dimensions: What is the random variable? what assumptions are made about the probabilities? what distributional conclusions are drawn? Such a comparison should highlight both the similarities and differences between these models and, hopefully, shed some light more generally on probabilistic models. In addition, a further comparison between these models will emerge from the discussion: It will be seen that the motivation for constructing a model can be quite different. While this issue is not specific to probabilistic models, the difference between the chapters in this regard provides an interesting contrast that exemplifies the different purposes for which modeling can be used.

Although we do not wish to become unnecessarily bogged down in the terminology of probability theory, an initial clarification of a few basic concepts may be useful in the subsequent discussion. Typically, one begins with an idealized experiment, or more generally some specified procedure. The usual examples are tossing a coin or throwing a die. While we do not know what will occur when we perform the experiment of tossing the coin (it could come up heads or tails), we do know the set of all possible alternatives that might result. These possible alternatives are known as <u>outcomes</u>. When we perform the experiment of throwing a die we have six possible outcomes. However, we may be interested only in odd-numbered outcomes versus even-numbered outcomes. While each possible value of the die is an outcome, the observed odd versus even is termed an <u>event</u>. Events can be equivalent to outcomes, but whereas outcomes represent all possibilities, events are defined subsets of outcomes that the experimenter particularly wishes to observe—for example, odd versus even as opposed to the specific value of the die that results. Finally, then, a <u>random variable</u> is a function that assigns to each event a real number. In the die-tossing example, in which the experimenter is concerned only with odd and even results, the random variable might assign "1" to odd and "2" to even. If the experimenter were in fact interested in all values of the die (the outcomes and events are the same) then the random variable would probably assign "1" to the event 1, "2" to the event 2, and so forth. It should be obvious that the number of events and hence the range of the random variable could be very large, indeed infinite, and that events, and hence the random variable, could be either discrete or continuous. We turn then to a consideration of the "experiment" implicit in these models, the events that are of concern, and most importantly the random variable involved.

Although there are significant similarities between Chapters 5 and 6, it is important to recognize that one major difference between the two chapters lies in the random variable. While both chapters utilize the same data set and hence are considering related phenomena, the experiment and consequently random variable is different in the two cases. For Job the "experiment" is the "tossing," or, more appropriately, the random selection of a nation to see how many alliances it comes up with or how many alliance partners it shows. For this experiment the outcomes, events, and random variables are the same—namely, the number of alliances or alliance partners the randomly selected nation exhibits. The random variable is, of course, finite and discrete: A nation does not belong to half an alliance. In contrast then, the experiment in the chapter by Siverson and Duncan is the random selection of a year to determine the number of alliances initiated. Again, the outcome, event, and random variable are identical: in each case it is the number of alliances enacted in the randomly selected year. Needless to say, this random variable is also both finite and discrete. Thus Job's concern is with the behavior of nations and will aggregate the data over years per nation. Siverson and Duncan, on the other hand, are interested in

INTRODUCTION 67

what might be termed the system—that is, the number of alliances initiated per time period—and consequently will aggregate data over nations per year.

In Chapter 7 Midlarsky derives a model to measure a nation's power vis-à-vis any other nation, primarily as a function of the distance between two nations. In performing the experiment, then, we assume the perspective of a single nation, and the die that is tossed is one whose various faces indicate different distances from the given nation. These distances then become the differing degrees of power our particular nation can exert. In this case the outcomes and events will differ, the outcomes being the actual distance each nation is from our given nation, and the events being the n_i categories into which the nations are placed on the basis of their distances. The random variable is also different and assigns to each n_i category a number based on the number of nations in that category.

Schrodt's analysis in Chapter 8 is concerned with two interacting nations that are stockpiling arms in response to the threats posed by the other—in short, the old Richardson arms-race model. The experiment in this case is a "toss" or random selection of an "international system," where "international system" refers to the joint arms levels of the two arming nations. The outcomes, events, and random variable are once again identical and are the various combinations of arms each side possesses. When nation X has 10 units of arms and Y has 12 units, these two values taken together indicate one possible international system. While this random variable could be treated as discrete, Schrodt gives good reasons for considering it to be continuous. Thus, Schrodt wishes to consider all possible combinations of arms levels of the two countries.

ASSUMPTIONS

In each of these models then we have a random variable (an experiment), of which the outcome is unknown but where the set of alternate possibilities is known. The structure of these models is then determined by the assumptions that are made on the probabilities of the events and the subsequent derivations of the distribution of the random variable based on those assumptions. Thus, the assumptions do not specify the probabilities of a particular event; rather, they specify the properties of the probabilities. From these properties we are then able to say something about the probability distribution of the random variable. Both Chapters 5 and 6 begin with the same model. It is thus not surprising to find that the initial assumptions of the two chapters are identical, although this may not be immediately evident from a comparison of the two sets of assumptions. Assumption 1 is the same in both chapters, but assumption 2 in Job corresponds to 4 in Siverson and Duncan, while assumption 4 in Job does not appear in Siverson and Duncan, and assumption 2 in Siverson and Duncan does not appear in Job. But differences in the wording of the assumptions and differences in the extent to which each author enumerates the assumptions of the model should not obscure the fact that the underlying model in both cases is the same Poisson model.

The assumptions of the Poisson model place constraints on the probabilities. Seen from a different perspective, the assumptions provide information about the probabilities of the random variable. For example, the first assumption in both chapters indicates that the probability that the random variable assumes a certain value will not change as a function of the other values of the random variable. In terms of the die-tossing example, this means that the probability that the die will assume a particular value on one toss has no effect on the value it will assume on the next toss. In Chapter 5 this means that when we randomly select a nation, the number of alliances it joins will have no effect on the number of alliances of the second randomly selected nation. In Chapter 6 it means that each randomly selected year renders values independent of every other randomly selected year. Assumption 2 in Job and 4 in Siverson and Duncan postulates that information about the randomly selected nation or year will not help you predict the value of the random variable; knowing, for example, that the nation is highly developed or that the year contained many crises will not provide any information on what value the randomly selected nation or year will assume. We see that both of these examples are not assumptions about the specific probability distribution of the random variable; that is, we are not told that nations will join two alliances with probability 0.1, but rather are told something about the characteristics of the probabilities and probability distribution—for example, that the probabilities of the random variable do not change from experiment to experiment.

Having stated the assumptions of the Poisson model, both Job and Siverson and Duncan wish to consider related models. Specifically, they propose a consideration of the negative binomial and the Yule-Greenwood models. Whereas the former model results when assumption 1 is changed to allow for "contagion," the latter is the consequence of modifying the Job assumption 2 and Siverson and Duncan assumption 4 to allow for "heterogeneity." Unfortunately, however, while the assumptions of these two new models differ, the distributions that are subsequently derived are indistinguishable. Consequently, while the authors can determine whether either of the

INTRODUCTION

two modified models fit better than the Poisson, they cannot determine which of the two new models is operative. Thus, in both cases the authors search for extramodel ways in which they might eliminate one or the other alternative. We will return to these analyses when we discuss the predictions of the models and the results that were obtained in the analyses.

Finally, it is important to point out that Job proposes two additional models, "equilibrium" or "two-way" interpretations of both the Poisson and the modified-Poisson. These models contain two parameters, one that measures alliance-joining and another that measures alliance-leaving behavior. The previous models contained only the first parameter. However, although these new two-way models contain two parameters, it can be shown that there is a direct relationship between the two new parameters and the one old parameter—that is, $\sigma/\theta = \lambda$, where σ and θ are the new parameters and λ is the old parameter. Consequently, when these models are examined empirically the estimation procedure and the subsequent test of the models become identical to the earlier analyses. The empirical analyses, however, do differ from the earlier analyses with respect to the data used. The assumption that σ and θ be constant leads Job to propose that the analysis be performed on particular years rather than over longer periods of time which might lead to violations of the assumption.

There appear to be two principal assumptions in the first Midlarsky model. The first set of assumptions come from the assumption of the multinominal distribution. Thus it is proposed that (a) the distance attribute of each of the N nations considered is independent of the distance attribute of any other nation, and (b) the distance categories into which the N nations are partitioned—the n_i categories—are mutually exclusive and exhaustive. The second assumption amounts to saying that the sum of the nations in all the n_i categories must equal N or that the sum of the probabilities n_i/N must equal one. The other principal assumption of the model proposes that if each distance category is multiplied by the distance those nations are from the nation being considered (for example, s_i could be the average distance of the nations in category n_i) and all those (category-x distance) results are added, then the sum will equal a constant S. This assumption says in effect that if we were to move a nation from one category to another and redo the multiplication and summing we would obtain the same result S.

Having constructed and analyzed his model empirically, Midlarsky subsequently moves in the last part of his paper to another model, a modification of the first. The principal difference between this model and the first lies in the fact that the power function is normalized. Thus the nation's power vis-à-vis every other nation is expressed as a proportion of that nation's total power with respect to the entire system of nations (see equation 7.14 in Midlarsky). There is also a difference in the focus of the analysis with respect to this second model. Whereas in the first model the question, at least in part, is whether or not the generated distribution fits certain empirical regularities, here the issue is with what might be termed the <u>sensitivity</u> of the function to slight perturbations in the distance variable.

In the Schrodt chapter it is possible to identify three separate sets of assumptions. The first set, consisting of three assumptions, identifies a Markov process. The central Markov assumption specifies that the result of an experiment does depend on the result of the previous experiment, but that it depends on only the results of the previous experiment—that is, it does not depend on what occurred for the last two, three, and so on experiments. We see that the Markov assumption is in direct contrast to the independence assumption of the Poisson model in Job and in Siverson and Duncan. However, this is precisely the assumption that is subsequently modified in both Job and Siverson and Duncan to produce models of contagion. In the negative binomial, subsequently entertained by the latter two papers, a "contagion" parameter is introduced, measuring the "amount of contagion" or degree of dependence. In the Markov model a similar dependence exists but is specified not by a single parameter but by the transition probability function. The Markov model, however, indicates that it was the previous—in a time-ordered sense—experiment that affects the subsequent experiment. In the negative binomial model, while there is an implicit notion of time in that something affects something else, it is the value of the random variable that affects other values. The significance of the Markov assumption lies in the fact that it subsequently allows Schrodt to model a process. In contrast, then, to the previous models, which were all static in character, the Schrodt model will be dynamic. Although Job and Siverson and Duncan wish in their contagion analyses to consider dynamics, the models postulated are stationary. The two additional assumptions needed by Schrodt to identify a Markov process specify that the transition probabilities do not change with time and that the transition probabilities are independent of one another.

The second main assumption of the Schrodt model occurs in the initial theorem proved in the chapter. If we conceive of all the possible "international systems," then we could construct a matrix of essentially infinite size. Technically speaking, we cannot speak of "cells" in this matrix—indeed, we really cannot speak of a matrix—because the rows and columns of the matrix are continuous random variables. Thus, we think of a surface defined over this "continuous

INTRODUCTION 71

matrix," and this surface is a probability-density function. Suppose for the moment, however, that the rows are in fact discrete and that it is possible to select one row. The principal hypothesis of Schrodt's theorem is that the expected value of the probability density function defined over that row is given by a Richardson equation that describes how a nation increases its arms in response to the arms of the opponent—that is, given that the international system is in a particular "state" (that is, both sides have so many arms), the expected value of the transition probabilities is determined by a Richardson process.

The last set of assumptions occur in the second theorem given by Schrodt; these assumptions are sufficient to imply that the Markov process is ergodic. They require that the transition function be continuous, that there be a limited range of possible arms levels, and that all transitions are possible.

ANALYSES OF THE MODELS

We come finally, then, to a consideration of the conclusions derived in each of the models. Here we find an interesting difference in focus between the models of Chapter 5, 6, and 7 and the model presented in Chapter 8. Each of the first three chapters generates a distribution involving the random variable and then assesses the extent to which the empirical world is described by the resulting theoretical distribution. In the Job and Siverson and Duncan cases the resulting distributions are the Poisson and subsequently the negative binomial or Yule-Greenwood. In the Midlarsky chapter the distribution of the particular nation's power is given by equation 7.11 (p. 140). The three papers then examine whether the random variable is empirically described by the resulting distribution: Are the number of alliances or alliance partners over nations Poisson distributed? are the number of alliances by year Poisson distributed? is the power of a nation measured by the equation given in 7.11?

The purpose of the Schrodt chapter is different, however. Although a distribution is in fact generated, it is the expected value of that distribution that is of interest. Furthermore, the purpose of the argument in the Schrodt chapter is not to examine the distribution empirically but to demonstrate that the expected value of the distribution will be equivalent to the solution of the difference equation form of the original Richardson model. Schrodt then goes on to show that if the stochastic process is in fact Markovian, as stipulated by the assumptions, then, provided the process meets several additional properties (which he argues are generally met in arms races), the process will be ergodic; that is, the probability distribution of the random variable will stop changing. The significance of this point lies in the fact that the expected value of the ergodic distribution will be the equilibrium point of the Richardson model. Thus, the Schrodt chapter can be seen as a translation. He begins with a Markov model in which the expected values of transition probability distributions are the Richardson equations and shows that the expected values of the Markov chain are in fact identical to the solution of the Richardson model. He has shown how one model can be translated into another.

Because of the similarity between the chapters by Job and by Siverson and Duncan, it is perhaps important to conclude with a few remarks concerning the results of the two sets of analyses and a comparison of the analysis of the revised Poisson models. Although the random variables in the two chapters are different, both sets of analyses essentially find that the negative binomial or Yule-Greenwood models fit better than the Poisson, regardless of the time period examined. Siverson and Duncan opt for the Poisson over the other models in cases where the difference in degree of fit is not appreciable, arguing that parsimony dictates the adoption of a simpler model when the fits are not dramatically different. However, if one examines the measures of fit, it is clear that the modified models fit better. In trying to assess whether it is the contagion or heterogeneity version of the model that fits, the two sets of analyses are again generally in agreement: They both agree that heterogeneity was probably present in the period 1919-39, while contagion was not; they both agree that it is contagion and not heterogeneity that is responsible for the results in the period 1945-65. There is, however, an interesting difference between the analyses of the two chapters at this juncture. Job applies a single analysis—the correlation analysis suggested by Feller—to determine whether contagion or heterogeneity is present. He presents the argument that if the correlation is high, it indicates heterogeneity, while if the correlation is low, this is taken to mean that contagion exists. Siverson and Duncan on the other hand employ two tests, one for contagion—a run test—and another for heterogeneity—the same Feller correlation analysis used by Job. Presumably, then, under the Siverson and Duncan analysis the results of the two analyses could show that both heterogeneity and contagion are present.

CONCLUSION

The foregoing has attempted to outline certain elements that tend to be fairly standard in probability models: the identification

INTRODUCTION

of a random variable and the subsequent derivation of distributions. We also have seen that a difference exists between the purpose of the modeling enterprise: to produce results that can be empirically examined and to demonstrate correspondences between types of models. The chapters that follow demonstrate that probability modeling can be effectively employed for a variety of research tasks in international relations. Although the articles share common assumptions due to the probabilistic element in each, they clearly demonstrate that probability modeling is a flexible tool for building mathematical models in international relations.

CHAPTER
5

MEMBERSHIP IN INTER-NATION
ALLIANCES, 1815-1965:
AN EXPLORATION UTILIZING
MATHEMATICAL PROBABILITY MODELS
Brian L. Job

The alliance activity of nations has long been a topic of interest to international relations scholars, but until recently little data-based research has been done on the subject. This chapter will present a series of empirical investigations concerning the patterns or networks of nation-state alliance memberships in the international system. The study has two basic goals: (a) to develop and explain how several types of mathematical probability models are applicable to the exploration of inter-nation alliance membership patterns, and (b) to demonstrate that, when the "predictions" of these models are compared to the actual alliance membership patterns exhibited in the international system between 1815 and 1965, it is possible to draw inferences as to processes of inter-nation behavior that gave rise to such observations. Thus, the two key notions to be combined in this research are longitudinal patterns of nation-state alliance behavior—the substantive concern—and mathematical probability modeling—a methodological procedure. Our intent is to extend the application of certain models and techniques, some of which have been previously employed by sociologists to study the distributional properties of interaction networks among humans, to the study of inter-nation alliance behavior. As such, this research is not to be seen as definitive or complete, but instead as part of the growing body of literature that employs stochastic probability models to explore questions and problems in international relations.

There are three major divisions in the following presentation. After clarifying more precisely what is meant by the term "alliance," the remainder of the first section involves a brief review of the literature, theoretical and applied in nature, concerning national alliance memberships. The second section will be devoted to laying some basic groundwork as to mathematical probability models and

the research strategy to be employed in this investigation. In the
following section, the stochastic models are set forth and their
predictions compared to the observed membership patterns. While
the initial formulations will be quite simple, based upon few assumptions and considering only rates of alliance formation, modifications
will be introduced to achieve more sophisticated models, involving
both rates of alliance formation and dissolution and assumptions
concerning equilibrium behavior processes. Some concluding
thoughts will be given appraising the utility of our adopted research
approach and assessing the possibilities for further modeling efforts
in this field.

MEMBERSHIP IN INTER-NATION ALLIANCES

An Initial Clarification of Terms

In order to give focus to the literature review and to avoid later
questions concerning the data presented in the figures and tables
below, the phrase "alliance" must be delineated carefully. Some
scholars utilize the term with reference to virtually any cooperative
undertaking among nation-states; others, myself included, invoke
a much more specialized and restricted connotation in their usage.
Thus, in this study an alliance will refer to a "formal, peacetime
agreement among a subset of sovereign states within the international
system." Consequently international organizations of an economic,
cultural, or social nature; secret pacts or informal agreements;
and pacts in which one or more parties were not full-fledged nation-states will be excluded from consideration.1

These limitations are dictated by both practical reasons, such
as data availability, and theoretical concerns—that is, attention is
focused solely on the networks of peacetime commitments negotiated
by nation-states in response to perceived threats to their military
security. National membership in alliances, therefore, will have
involved explicit commitments but need not have entailed overt
behavioral responses of assistance to others. Nations may have
belonged to more than one peacetime alliance at a time, and their
memberships may have created overlapping or cross-cutting networks
of ties.

A differentiation may be made as to the level or type of commitment undertaken by the members of an alliance. Thus, an alliance
may be either (a) a defense pact, in which states agree to intervention
on behalf of other members, (b) a neutrality agreement that commits
states to remain neutral toward each other's enemies, or (c) an

entente, which calls upon the parties to consult and cooperate on policy matters.[2]

Previous Research on Inter-Nation Alliances

International relations scholars concerned with the alliance activity of nations have tended to focus their efforts on answering three major questions: Why do states join alliances? what are the distinguishing characteristics of the "alliance joiners"? what types of alliance partnerships are most harmonious and durable? Recent surveys of the literature, however, indicate that there is little consensus among the findings of previous writers and only slight evidence of the beginnings of cumulative knowledge, or any "theory" in international alliance behavior.[3]

Thus, in attempting to answer the first question posed above, Hans Morgenthau argues that most nations who enter into alliances do so for one of two reasons: either to add their power to the power of other nations or to withhold the power of nations from their adversaries.[4] These commitments are undertaken with care, because there are both costs and benefits in any alliance situation. On the one hand, an alliance may provide security to a threatened country, enhance the strategic position of a state, or introduce "stability" in the system. On the other hand, an ill-chosen alliance may lead to interference by a dominant "friendly" ally, to an overextension of a state's capabilities, or to a decrease in the "stability" of the system. Even though states may prefer to avoid obligations to, and entanglements with, other states, few can practically afford the luxury of noncommitment or neutrality. This has been particularly true of small states in the system that have possessed scarce resources or occupied crucial geographic positions. Alliances of major and minor powers, while a very frequent occurrence in history, appear to be fraught with pitfalls for both the powerful and weaker participants.[5]

As to which states join alliances, the literature tends to concentrate attention upon two groups of actors: (a) that small number of states who choose to remain nonaligned and (b) that minority of states who are most actively involved in alliances (and international affairs in general). The "nonjoiners" appear to have been either small, developed European nations, such as Switzerland and Sweden, whose policies have been based upon a desire to avoid great-power entanglement or more recently independent countries of the Third World who wished to avoid Cold War involvement and to enhance their own political and economic development.[6] J. David Singer and

Bruce Bueno de Mesquita, when surveying the alliance data collected for the Correlates of War project note that in the last 150 years there have been a few highly committed nations who have on an annual basis participated in more than twice the average number of alliances, and whose total number of alliance ties far exceed those of other nations.[7] These active states are labelled somewhat ambiguously as the "major" or "great powers," whose ranks have included Austria-Hungary, Germany, Russia, France, England, Italy, Japan, the United States, and China.

The majority of states have chosen to join alliances over the years—but on a much more limited basis. However, little research has been done to determine those characteristics or attributes that tend to have been associated with a state's having a relatively greater or lesser number of such commitments. Propositions on the subject abound but few have been "tested"; certainly, there exists no work in this field equivalent to Richardson's investigations concerning the attributes of nations involved in war coalitions.[8] As Holsti, Hopmann, and Sullivan point out, too many "bad examples" may be cited concerning most hypotheses and propositions, thus making it virtually impossible to draw many sound conclusions on this subject.[9] Even the identifying characteristics of the alliance activists, the great powers, are undetermined: It has been posited, for instance, that the pertinent feature of these actors has merely been their longevity as members in the international system.[10]

A similar degree of uncertainty and dispute exists concerning whether or not certain national characteristics or attributes may have significantly affected alliance partnership selection—there exists the question "With whom have nations joined alliances?" Some authors maintain strongly that "balance of power" or questions of political expediency are and were always paramount in alliance formation, thus making any set of bedfellows possible.[11] Others feel that "nonutilitarian strategy preferences," to borrow Russett's phrase, such as ideology or cultural similarity are important.[12] However, all such arguments appear to be based on relatively impressionistic evidence.

Upon surveying this literature two matters become apparent that impinge upon our investigation. The first is that very few studies have been made of the processes or patterns of behavior of nations involved in alliances. The second is that a distinction has to be made between a state's alliance memberships and a state's alliance partnerships.

While the characteristics of alliances, the effects of alliances upon the outbreak of war, and so forth have received much attention, the behavior patterns of the nations involved in founding and maintaining these groups have gone largely unstudied by political scientists.13 Only recently, for instance, did preliminary research begin on exploring whether or not there were trends or patterns in inter-nation alliance initiations in the 1815-1965 time span. These studies are also notable for being among the first to utilize mathematical probability models (stochastic models) in research upon international alliances. Results to date have been interesting and encouraging: Siverson and Duncan, for example, have shown that inter-nation alliance formations occurred in an essentially random manner in the nineteenth century following the Congress of Vienna, but that during the interwar and postwar periods of the twentieth century alliance initiations may be described by more sophisticated process models based upon assumptions of contagion and diffusion.14

Efforts have also been made to study longitudinal patterns of alliance membership in the international system, utilizing quantitative techniques. Healy and Stein and Hart are gaining prominence for their work employing graph theoretic techniques in investigating European alliance configurations during the 1870s and 1880s.15 Stuart Bremer has applied sociometric modeling techniques to attempt to isolate alliance membership patterns, and Michael Wallace has developed computerized clustering routines for the same purpose.16 While these various procedures achieve some degree of success in describing the static or structural characteristics of the network of alliance ties at any moment in the international system, they do not allow inferences to be made as to the processes of inter-state behavior that may have given rise to these observed patterns. This is the matter that is to be explored in the present study; it is a task for which mathematical probability models appear particularly appropriate.

The Distinction Between Alliance Memberships
and Dyadic Partnerships

An important distinction of a substantive nature remains to be explicated before proceeding with the mathematical models. A state's record of alliance activity may be viewed in two different ways. First, it may be seen as a series of decisions or commitments to seek the support of other nations on matters of mutual concern. Thus, over time a state's alliance activity may be characterized by the number of groups it has joined—that is, the total of its alliance memberships. Alternatively, there is a second aspect to such a series of commitments, focusing instead upon the number of alliance partners that have been engaged by each state. Presumably, a listing of allies or partners indicates the groups of nations that at one time or another have collaborated with the state in question as to their collective security. This second perspective is thus somewhat analogous to a cataloguing of an individual's friends; the interesting questions that arise concern both the absolute number of such friends (or alliance partners, to extend the analogy) and the constancy of these friendships.

The above distinction is basic to our analysis. Two sets of data will be collected for each nation, and the mathematical probability models will be applied separately to each series of distributions. Tables 5.1 and 5.2 present an accounting of the total number of alliance memberships and national dyadic alliance ties during the period 1815-1965. The empirical distinction between these two alliance activity perspectives is apparent. For example, while both the United States and Hungary have had ten alliance memberships, these commitments entailed 67 different dyadic partnerships for the United States, but only 17 different national allies for Hungary. The dyadic measure is thus sensitive to the sizes of the alliances joined by each state and does not result in the equation of membership in bilateral pacts with memberships in larger associations.

MATHEMATICAL MODELS AND OUR RESEARCH PROBLEM

As stated earlier, our goal is to construct models, built upon assumptions about the manner in which states interact, that successfully describe the observed distributions of alliance behavior in the international system. Although the premises and details of the various models to be discussed vary, there are two common foundations to all of them. First, nations are regarded as independent individual units or actors within a specific environment, the international system. Second, although there is considerable variation in the interactions of these actors, on the whole there are assumed to be some common patterns, norms, or processes of behavior that can be discovered by an observer.

Once these statements are established our problem can be viewed in a broader context. Nations in alliance may be considered as individual members within a society. Correspondingly, mathematical models that have been used to study the manner in which people choose their friends, disseminate information, or spread disease may be used to analyze the distribution of alliance ties in the international system.[17]

The basic starting point for models of "social" interaction is the concept of the "net" or "network," which represents each actor

TABLE 5.1

National Alliance Memberships, 1815-1965

Number of Memberships	Number of States	States
0	24	Jamaica, Trinidad, Ireland, Switzerland, Papal States, Two Sicilies, Malta, Cyprus, Sweden, Norway, Zanzibar, South Africa, Israel, Korea, Cambodia, Laos, North Vietnam, South Vietnam, Singapore, Indonesia, India, Ceylon, Maldive Islands, Nepal
1	27	Hanover, West Germany, East Germany, Saxony, Hesse Electoral, Hesse Grand Duchy, Mechlenburg-Schwerin, Tuscany, Iceland, Mali, Liberia, Sierra Leone, Nigeria, Congo (K), Uganda, Kenya, Tanzania, Burundi, Somalia, Zambia, Kuwait, Mongolia, Taiwan, South Korea, Burma, Thailand, Malaya
2	53	Canada, Haiti, Dominican Republic, Cuba, Mexico, Guatemala, Honduras, Salvador, Nicaragua, Costa Rica, Panama, Venezuela, Brazil, Paraguay, Chile, Argentina, Uruguay, Holland, Luxembourg, Bavaria, Baden, Wurtembourg, Austria, Modena, Parma, Lithuania, Finland, Denmark, Gambia, Dahomey, Mauritania, Niger, Ivory Coast, Upper Volta, Togo, Cameroons, Gabon, Central African Republic, Chad, Congo (B), Rwanda, Ethiopia, Malawi, Malagasy, Morocco, Algeria, Tunisia, Sudan, Syria, Lebanon, Jordan, North Korea, Philippines
3	10	Colombia, Bolivia, Belgium, Senegal, Libya, Saudi Arabia, Yemen, Pakistan, Australia, New Zealand
4	8	Ecuador, Peru, Portugal, Estonia, Latvia, Guinea, Ghana, UAR
5	3	Albania, Iran, Afghanistan
6-10	7	Spain (6), Iraq (6), Japan (6), China (9), United States (10), Hungary (10), Greece (10).
11-15	3	Poland (11), Bulgaria (12), Czechoslovakia (15)
16-20	2	Austria-Hungary (16), Rumania (18)
20-24	4	Turkey (21), Germany-Prussia (22), Yugoslavia (23), Italy (24)
25+	3	England (25), France (29), Russia (47)

TABLE 5.2

Total National Dyadic Alliances Ties,
Excluding the OAS and OAU, 1815-1965

Number of Memberships	Number of States	States
0	50	Cuba, Haiti, Dominican Republic, Jamaica, Trinidad-Tobago, Mexico, Guatemala, Honduras, Salvador, Nicaragua, Costa Rica, Panama, Venezuela, Brazil, Paraguay, Chile, Argentina, Uruguay, Ireland, Switzerland, Papal States, Two Sicilies, Malta, Cyprus, Sweden, Norway, Liberia, Sierra Leone, Nigeria, Congo (K), Uganda, Tanzania, Zanzibar, Burundi, Somalia, Zambia, Malawi, South Africa, Israel, Korea, India, Ceylon, Maldive Islands, Nepal, Cambodia, Laos, North Vietnam, South Vietnam, Indonesia, Singapore
1	10	Colombia, Bolivia, Gambia, Kenya, Ethiopia, Mongolia, Taiwan, South Korea, Burma, Malaysia
2	6	Ecuador, Peru, Tuscany, Finland, Mali, North Korea
3	4	Austria, Modena, Parma, Lithuania
4	2	Guinea, Ghana
5	2	Estonia, Latvia
7	4	East Germany, Afghanistan, Japan, Thailand
8	1	Philippines
9	6	Hanover, Saxony, Hesse Electoral, Hesse Grand Duchy, Mecklenburg-Schwerin, China
10	7	Spain, Bavaria, Baden, Wurtemburg, Iran, Australia, New Zealand
11-15	26	Albania (11); Morocco, Algeria, Taiwan, Sudan, Kuwait, Pakistan (12); West Germany, Ireland, Dahomey, Mauritania, Niger, Ivory Coast, Upper Volta, Togo, Cameroon, Gabon, Central African Republic, Chad, Congo (B), Rwanda, Malagasy, Libya (13); Canada, Denmark, Senegal (14)
16-20	12	Holland, Luxembourg, Poland, Hungary (17); Belgium, Portugal, Syria, Lebanon, Jordan (18); UAR (19); Saudi Arabia, Yemen (20)
21-30	5	Bulgaria (21), Czechoslovakia (22), United States (27), Iran (28), Greece (29)
31-40	3	Yugoslavia (31), Rumania (32), Austria-Hungary (38)
41-50	3	Italy, Germany-Prussia (45); Turkey (48)
51+	3	England (62), France (59), Russia (63)

as a point or location in the system and shows the relationships, if any, among these actors.[18] Thus, a "net" may take the form of a "spiderweb drawing" or perhaps a matrix where states are assigned to rows and columns and alliance ties among them are noted in the individual cells. (Sociologists would refer to this as a sociogram.[19]) After the investigator has placed the information from the system under study into such a format, he has to decide either to analyze the "structural" properties of the network or to analyze the "distributional" properties of the same net.[20] There are appropriate mathematical models for each task.

However, for a number of reasons, we are more interested in questions of the latter type—that is, the distributional aspects of the alliance membership networks. Models developed in this context dwell less on the analysis of static characteristics of the relationships within a net (that is, a "structural" concern) and more upon the exploration of the possible patterns of interaction that may have produced specified types of membership networks. Thus, in our investigation assumptions will be made concerning the manner in which nations behave; mathematical formulations will be developed that will produce frequency distributions of memberships or partnerships to be expected on the basis of these assumptions; finally, these predictions will be compared to observed distributions of international alliance activity.

The following research strategy will be adopted: Our point of departure will be the concept of the "random net," a network of interaction arising from a system in which the probability of contact between any and all pairs of nation actors is equal. Admittedly, it is unlikely that such a probability model will prove appropriate to describe the observed alliance distributions. Thus, attention will then shift to models based upon "biased nets," where factors such as (a) previous contact or exposure (contagion), (b) geographic or other types of "social" distance (diffusion), or (c) individual popularity or affinity of certain states (heterogeneity) may alter random interaction patterns. (This approach is similar to that employed by Rapoport in his analyses of large sociograms and is not unlike that utilized by Coleman in his investigations of human interaction processes.[21]

"ONE-WAY" PROCESS MODELS

Data on Inter-Nation Alliances, 1815-1965

Data concerning the memberships of all international alliances formed between 1815 and 1965 has been collected and coded by

Singer and Small in conjunction with research on the Correlates of War project.[22] Their listings provide the information necessary for our investigation. Given the care and attention with which Singer and his associates have approached their data-gathering tasks, and given that their interest is similarly directed at studying formal, peacetime alliances, our confidence in the appropriateness, accuracy, and completeness of the data set derived from their work is high.

Tables 5.1 and 5.2 indicate the total number of alliance memberships and the total number of dyadic alliance partnerships acquired by each state that existed for some portion of the 1815-1965 time span. Countries are grouped according to the frequency of their membership activities, serving to highlight a number of points. First, while most states (83 percent) took part in alliances, most limited themselves to only one or two memberships. Second, very few states remained neutral or nonaligned, and those that did appear to be small, well-developed European states; recently independent, weak, and less developed states; or states experiencing considerable domestic and foreign turmoil (for example, the Vietnams). Third, the so-called great powers give ample evidence of having predominated international alliance formations. The most extreme individual case in the distribution is Russia, which joined 47 alliances (thus about one of every four of the total 178 groups). Fourth, the number of dyads involved in two of the alliances, the Organization of American States (OAS), with 35 members, and the Organization of African Unity (OAU), with 21 members, was so large that these regional associations are excluded from consideration in the second table, as well as from most subsequent calculations involving the models.

A Brief Check on Inter-Nation Alliance Activity over Time

Each of the models that follow requires some assumption as to the constancy or stability of the alliance formation process during the duration of the interval being investigated. If there have been wide fluctuations in inter-nation alliance activity, this assumption will be violated, thus calling into question the utility of the model itself. As a preliminary check, therefore, annual data on total national alliance memberships and dyadic partnerships, expressed in both absolute and percentage terms, were plotted for the 1815-1965 period, as seen in Figures 5.1 and 5.2. Taken as a whole, both sets of graphs are marked by extreme variations.

Figure 5.1 indicates that for 120 years after 1815 no more than 20 states were involved in alliances in one year. This pattern,

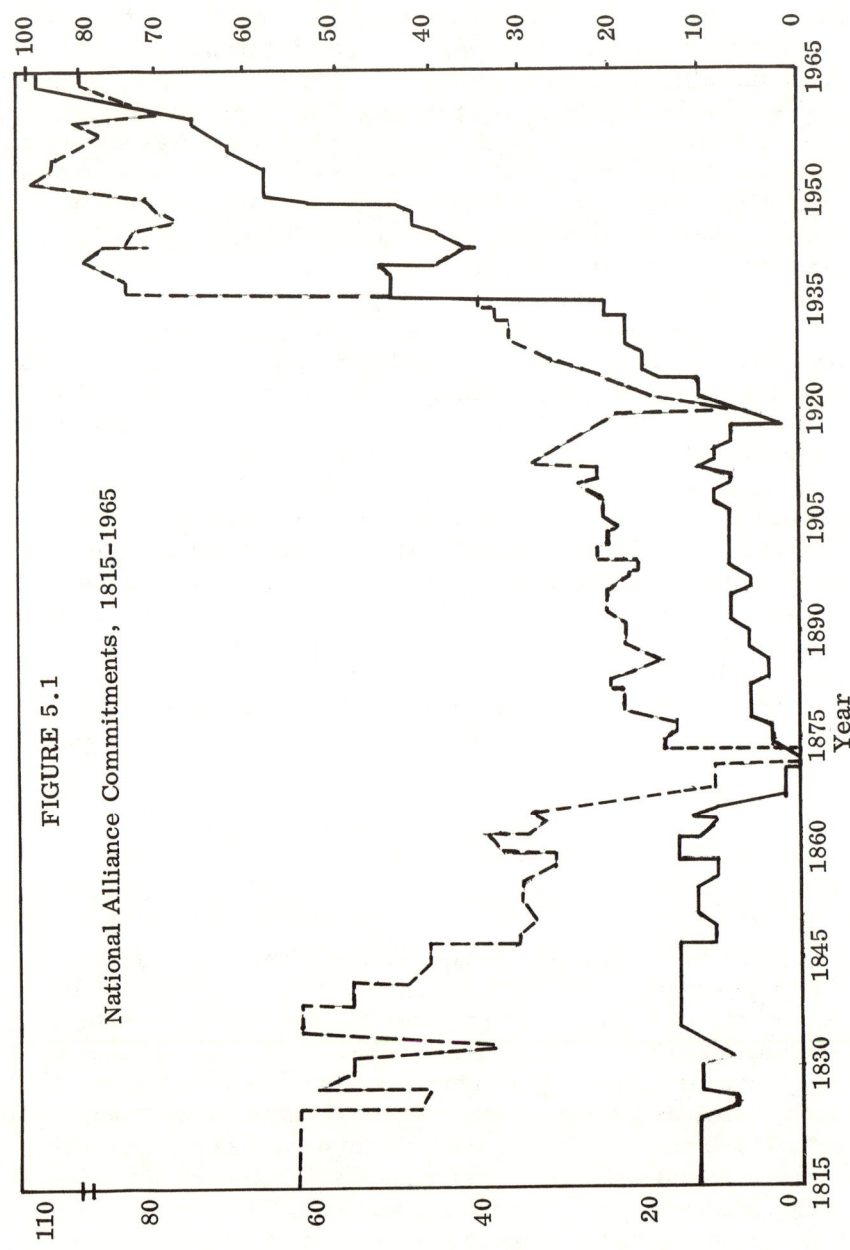

FIGURE 5.1
National Alliance Commitments, 1815–1965

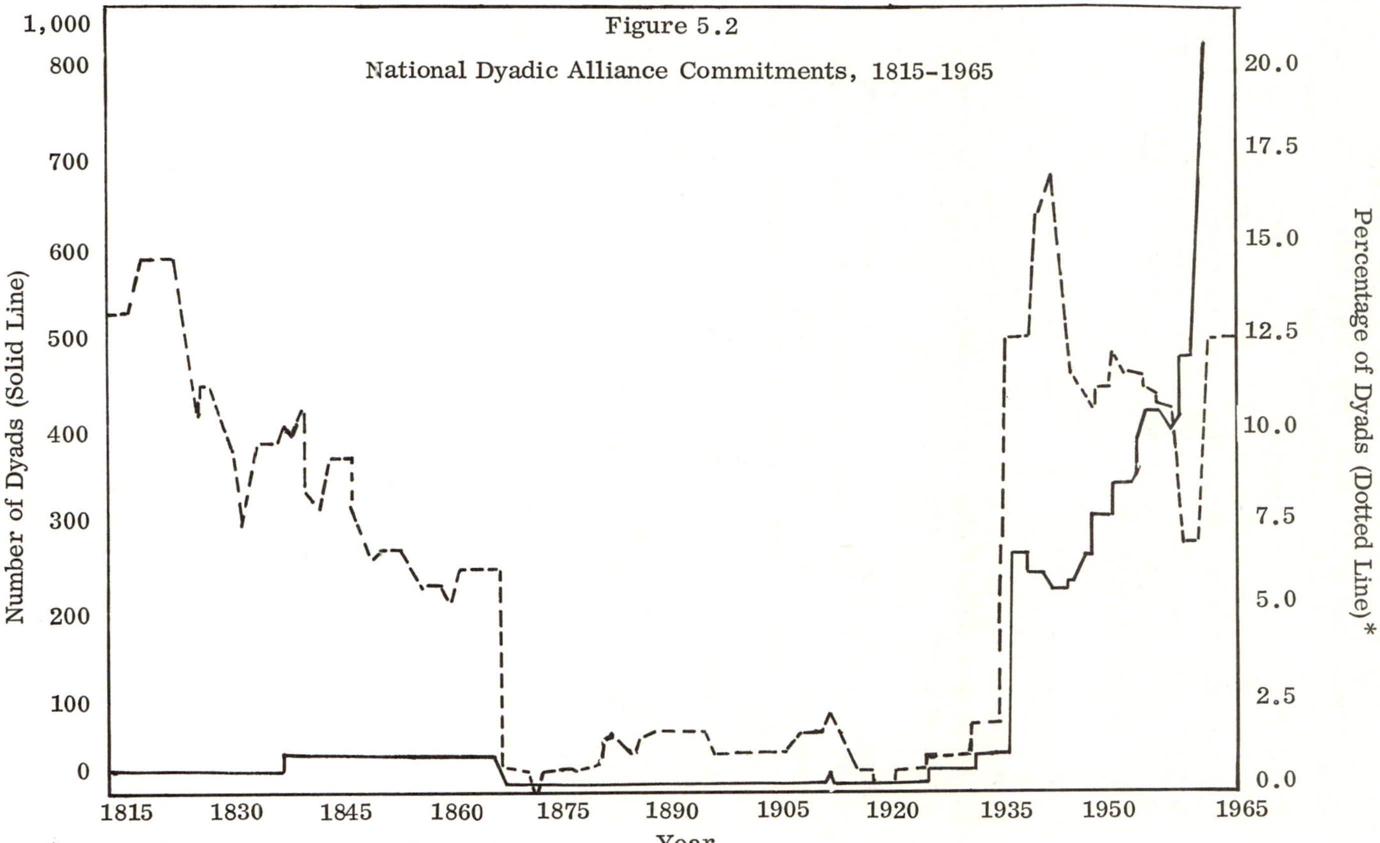

Figure 5.2
National Dyadic Alliance Commitments, 1815–1965

*Note that scale only goes to 20 percent.

representative of the domination of international activity by European nations, was broken in 1936 by the founding of the OAS, and since that time both the geographic scope and number of participants in alliances have risen dramatically. The percentage data further shows that the past three decades have been years of very high proportionate levels of national alliance involvement as well. Figure 5.2, containing dyadic information, exhibits even sharper variation. Severe jumps in the graph are noted for 1936 and 1962, the founding dates of the OAS and OAU, respectively. Note, however, that the proportion of dyadic alliance ties in the system has never risen above 20 percent, and only climbed above 5 percent after 1935.

It is obvious, therefore, that any assumptions as to regularity in alliance activity throughout the 150-year span would be unjustified. In order to have made such an assumption and to have then applied our models to data sets for the entire period we would have had to have found either (a) that the number of states involved had remained relatively constant (and that these were also consistently the same states) or (b) that the proportion of states involved was generally constant, thus compensating for the growing number of countries within the system. Since neither of these conditions holds, it will be necessary to identify relatively stable subsystemic intervals within the larger period and to apply our models separately to correspondingly relevant data sets on alliances. However, the decision as to where to insert such division points is not altogether obvious; presumably, each subsystemic period should be short enough to have been characterized by relatively stable international conditions but at the same time long enough to have experienced a goodly number of alliance formations. For this study we have chosen to work with six different time periods: two being "century" periods (1815-99, 1900-1965), the remaining four being interwar or postwar intervals (1815-70, 1871-1914, 1919-39, 1945-65).[23]

An Initial Model of the Acquisition of Alliance Memberships

Our initial model is designed to explore the notion that states may have joined alliances without any regularity or pattern to the individual behavior of any over time. Borrowing a phrase used by James Coleman, this model will be a "'one-way' process model" in that it involves only the rate of acquisition of alliances by nations and thus requires data only upon the sum of memberships acquired by each nation for its application.[24]

If random processes in fact have operated within the international system for some period of time, then the accumulated distribution of alliance memberships by states will be duplicated by a distribution generated by a Poisson formulation.[25] To be more precise the assumption set of this model will be as follows:

1. The acts of joining alliances by states were a series of independent events. This means that the acceptance of an alliance membership by a state (a) had no effect upon the subsequent membership activity of that state and (b) had no influence upon the joining of alliances by other states.
2. All states behaved similarly with respect to joining alliances. This is not to imply that all states joined (or were "supposed to" have joined) an equal number of alliances, but rather that all states reacted similarly to the opportunities presented them; that is, specific national characteristics did not affect their behavior.
3. The series of alliance formations in the international system was a set of homogeneous events. This implies that the nations did not behave differently when joining alliances of (a) different types or (b) different sizes; that is, the number of partnerships had no effect upon joining.
4. There were no major transformations of conditions in the international system that substantially affected the alliance-membership distributions among states.

If these assumptions were in effect, then the "predicted" distribution of alliance memberships resulting from such a behavior pattern would be a Poisson distribution, given by formula $p_i = (\lambda^i e^{-\lambda})/i!$ with the λ parameter being estimated by the mean number of memberships per state. Comparison of the observed distribution of memberships with the predicted distribution will provide an indication as to whether or not the model accurately describes the behavior within the system.

The Poisson model was applied to each of the six individual subsystems noted above. The observed distributions of alliance memberships among states are presented in Tables 5.3 and 5.4, together with the predicted results based upon the Poisson. These latter figures in each case were obtained by using the mean number of memberships as an estimate for λ, calculating by means of the Poisson formula a series of probabilities of states having different numbers of commitments, and finally by multiplying these probabilities by N, the size of the system, to get predictions of the number of states expected to have had these different alliance memberships.

TABLE 5.3

National Alliance Memberships, All Types of Alliances: The Application of the Poisson and Revised Poisson Models, 1815-99 and 1900-65

Period	Number of Memberships	Observed Number of States	Predicted Poisson	Predicted Revised Model
1815-99				
	0	26	9.3	31.3
	1	11	16.4	7.3
	2	9	14.4	4.0
	3	2	8.4	2.7
	4	0	3.7	1.9
	5	1	1.3	1.4
	6	0	↑	↑
	7	1		
	8	0	0.5	5.4
	9	1		
	10-15	1		
	15+	2	↓	↓
Total		54	54.0	54.0

Poisson: 54 states, $\lambda = 1.759$, $\sigma^2 = 13.20$
Revised Poisson: $\alpha = 0.545$, $\beta = 2.015$, $\chi^2 = 10.99$ $(0.025 < p < 0.05)$, 4 d.f.

Period	Number of Memberships	Observed Number of States	Predicted Poisson	Predicted Revised Model
1900-65				
	0	18	3.6	43.8
	1	21	12.9	19.7
	2	52	23.0	13.0
	3	11	27.2	9.6
	4	5	24.1	7.3
	5	3	17.1	5.8
	6	2	10.1	4.6
	7	0	5.1	3.8
	8	0	2.3	3.1
	9	1	↑	2.6
	10	3		2.1
	11-15	4	1.4	↑
	16-20	3		11.6
	21+	1	↓	↓
Total		127	127	127

Poisson: 127 states, $\lambda = 3.551$, $\sigma^2 = 27.984$
Revised Poisson: $\alpha = 1.0655$, $\beta = 2.064$

TABLE 5.4

National Alliance Memberships, All Types of Alliances: The Application of the Poisson and Revised Poisson Models, 1815-70, 1871-1914, 1919-39, and 1945-65

Period	Number of Memberships	Observed Number of States	Predicted Poisson	Predicted Revised Model
1815-70	0	21	11.8	21.4
	1	10	15.5	9.3
	2	8	10.2	5.2
	3	0	4.5	3.0
	4	0	1.5	1.9
	5	1	↑	1.2
	6	2	0.5	↑
	7	1		2.0
	8	1	↓	↓
Total		44	44.0	44.0

Poisson Model: 44 states, $\lambda = 1.318$, $\sigma^2 = 3.99$
Revised Model: $\alpha = 0.720$, $\beta = 1.11$, $\chi^2 = 8.45$ ($0.05 < p < 0.10$), 4 d.f.

Period	Number of Memberships	Observed Number of States	Predicted Poisson	Predicted Revised Model
1871-1914	0	28	9.8	25.2
	1	7	15.2	7.4
	2	2	11.7	4.1
	3	1	6.0	2.6
	4	1	2.3	1.8
	5	2	↑	1.2
	6	0		↑
	7	3		
	8	0	0.95	3.3
	9	0		
	10	1		
	10+	1	↓	↓
Total		46	46.0	46.0

Poisson Model: 46 states, $\lambda = 1.54$, $\sigma^2 = 8.07$
Revised Model: $\alpha = 0.604$, $\beta = 1.656$, $\chi^2 = 4.03$ ($0.25 < p < 0.50$), 4 d.f.

Period	Number of Memberships	Observed Number of States	Predicted Poisson	Predicted Revised Model
1919-39	0	14	5.4	24.6
	1	30	13.6	12.2
	2	6	17.1	7.9
	3	2	14.4	5.5
	4	5	9.1	4.0
	5	2	4.6	3.0
	6	0	↑	↑
	7	0		
	8	1		
	9	2	2.9	9.8
	10	1		
	11-15	4	↓	↓
Total		67	67.0	67.0

Poisson Model: 67 states, $\lambda = 2.522$, $\sigma^2 = 12.91$
Revised Model: $\alpha = 1.00$, $\beta = 1.632$

Period	Number of Memberships	Observed Number of States	Predicted Poisson	Predicted Revised Model
1945-65	0	20	13.6	34.3
	1	26	30.1	27.9
	2	52	33.2	20.1
	3	10	24.5	13.9
	4	3	13.5	9.4
	5	1	6.0	6.3
	6	2	2.2	4.2
	7	2	↑	2.7
	8	4		1.8
	9	0	0.95	1.2
	10	1		0.8
	10+	2	↓	1.4
Total		124	124.0	124.0

Poisson Model: 124 states, $\lambda = 2.21$, $\sigma^2 = 6.01$
Revised Model: $\alpha = 1.285$, $\beta = 1.001$

(To determine an N for each period, every state that existed during the interval in question was counted, regardless of the length of that existence. This may have significantly exaggerated the size of the system for the 1900-65 period; however, for the other periods the membership in the system was relatively stable.)

In no instance, either with the four short intervals or with the nineteenth- and twentieth-century periods, did the Poisson model provide even minimally satisfactory description of the membership distribution among nations. (Values and probabilities for the chi-square statistic were computed but are not reported as in no instance did p exceed 0.001.[26]) This initial model can be rejected at once.

Note that the decision to analyze the various subsystems separately is vindicated by the wide variations exhibited over time in the average number of memberships per state (λ). For example, the value of λ changed from 1.7 to 3.6 for the pre- and post-1900 periods and varied between 1.3 and 2.5 for the four smaller intervals. To have assumed that there were no transformations of systemic conditions from 1815 to 1965 would not be justified (assumption 4). Given the results of the model, it is clear that allowing for different subsystemic environments alone was not adequate and that state behavior must violate other conditions within the assumption set as well.

Assumption 3, which states that alliance formations constitute a set of "homogeneous events," was also investigated by applying the Poisson model to the subset of defensive alliance memberships during each of the six periods—the assumption now being that states continued to behave as prescribed in premises 1 and 2 but only within one particular "type" of alliance category. There were no instances in which the observed and predicted distribution matched closely. Another condition that would cause assumption 3 to be violated would be the domination of the membership distributions by certain alliances because of the large size of those alliances. We recalculated our membership arrays for the periods within the twentieth century omitting all OAS and OAU commitments, but again the expectations based upon the Poisson probability model were far from correct.

A Model Involving Contagion Effects

A critical look at the pattern of discrepancies found in the above applications indicates that in almost every instance the observed distribution is a quite different shape than that predicted by the model.

There are consistently more states without alliance commitments than are predicted, and there is always a small number of states with very great alliance activity. (Whereas the predicted frequencies form a unimodal distribution about the mean with a longer tail to the right, the observed frequencies are usually in a bimodal pattern—a great number of states grouped in the low values, and a small minority scattered among much higher values. Furthermore, the variances of the observed distributions, denoted by the sumbol σ^2 in the tables, are much higher than should exist if one is to attribute a Poisson process to these interactions.)

The Poisson model is constructed upon the premise (assumption 1) that inter-nation behavior is unaffected by previous alliance commitments; that is, all states are viewed as being equally susceptible to joining additional alliances, regardless of whether they presently belong to zero, three, or six other associations. There are good reasons, however, to suspect that nations do not actually operate in such a fashion; instead, their acquisition of alliances might be viewed as a behavior process characterized by "contagion." That is, the probability of a state gaining additional membership increases with the number of ties previously held. Nations may be reluctant to leave isolation and join their first alliance, but having done so, they become increasingly active and thus are drawn into more and more international commitments. On an intuitive basis, reasoning along these lines could account both for the large number of states who have joined few, if any, alliances (that is, the probability of joining for them is low) and for the small minority of activist states who have assumed a considerable number of such commitments (that is, due to contagion, the probability of their joining becomes increasingly larger).

A modification of the Poisson model, in fact, yields an expected probability distribution of outcomes for a system of actors who interact in a contagious fashion. Referring to the initial Poisson formulation, assumptions 2, 3, and 4 would remain as before. It is the first assumption, however, that is altered, from positing a constant national probability rate of alliance membership, regardless of the experience of the state or of other states, to positing that the probability of membership is (positively) incremented as a state gains alliance commitments. Phrased more explicitly, if the probability of joining a first alliance is $q_{0,1} = \alpha$, then the probability of joining a second is $q_{1,2} = \alpha + \beta$; and a third, $q_{2,3} = \alpha + 2\beta$. Thus, generally, the probability increases in a positive linear manner: $q_{i,i+1} = \alpha + i\beta$, where α represents the initial probability of joining, and β represents the increased likelihood of additional memberships due to contagion. The formula for this "contagious Poisson" is given by the following expression (which is also identified as the formula of the negative binomial distribution)[27]: $\{\alpha(\alpha+\beta)\ldots(\alpha+[i-1]\beta)e^{-\alpha}(1-e^{-\beta})i\}/i!\,\beta^i$. Estimation of the α and β parameters is based upon the mean and variance of the observed distributions: $\alpha = \mu^2\beta/(\sigma^2 - \mu)$ and $\beta = \ln(\sigma^2/\mu)$, where μ = the mean of the observed distribution and ln refers to the natural logarithm.[28]

The predictions of this model—the revised Poisson as it is termed in Tables 5.3 and 5.4—are seen to be considerably closed to the observed membership frequencies. Commitment patterns of the nineteenth century are described quite well by the model (although the chi-square probability values are not exceptionally high), but the results are less satisfactory for the twentieth-century alliances. In the later periods, the model predicts more states to be without memberships and fewer states to have one or two commitments than is observed. This suggests a somewhat different variety of behavior than is described in our revised model.

The relative values of α and β may be compared to provide an indication of the effect of contagion in relation to the initial probability rate of joining an alliance.[29] Contagion effects, therefore, appear to have been most pronounced during the nineteenth century, particularly between 1871 and 1914, and also during the interwar years (that is, 1919-39) of the twentieth century.

Of course, assumption 3 may be modified as well, restricting application of the model to specified alliance subpopulations. For example, Figure 5.3 indicates that the revised Poisson with its contagion assumptions provides a good description ($\chi^2 = 2.06$, $0.50 < p < 0.75$, 3 d.f.) of the distribution of inter-nation defensive alliance memberships during the 1900s. When applied to the defensive alliances of the 1815-70 and 1871-1914 periods, the fit of the model was slightly less satisfactory, perhaps because such an unusually high number of states (21/44 and 30/46 respectively) stayed out of alliances altogether. Little success was achieved concerning the defensive commitments of the twentieth century: The model continued to underestimate the proportion of nations who had one or two memberships. However, when the OAS and the OAU were eliminated from the distributions and the model was reapplied, the adjustment was sufficient for the model to provide a "good" description of the observed frequencies during the 1919-39 period ($\chi^2 = 3.26$, $0.50 < p < 0.75$, 4 d.f.).

All in all, the contagion model met with some measure of success, providing a better approximation in all instances and a very close fit to the actual national membership distributions during the nineteenth century and selected aspects of the twentieth century. However, a point of caution must be interjected because the formula for the "contagious Poisson" is identical to the formula for the

FIGURE 5.3

National Defensive Alliance Memberships, 1815-99: The Application of the
Poisson and Revised Poisson Models

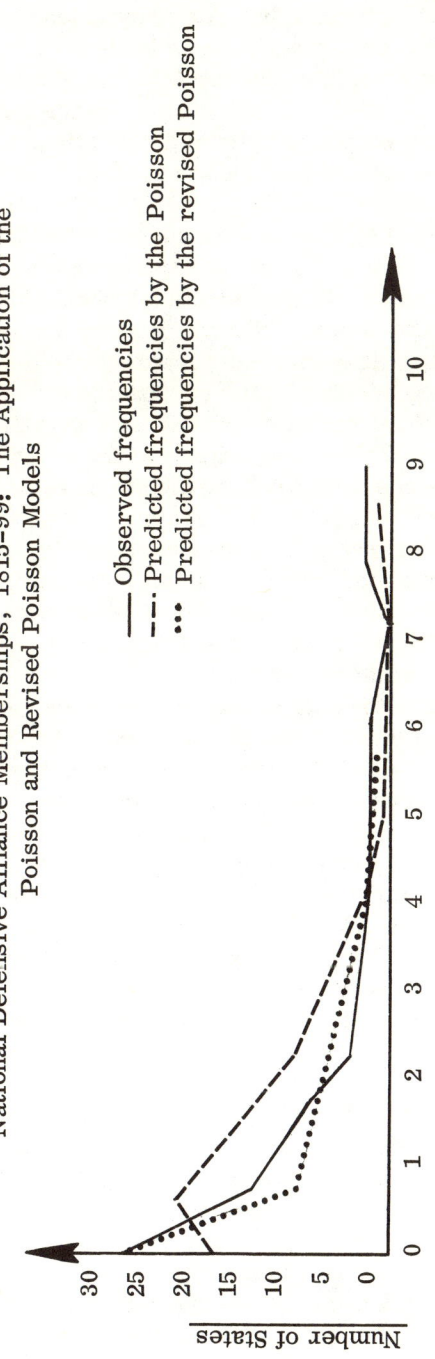

$N = 54$ states, $\lambda = 1.222$, $\sigma^2 = 3.765$
$\alpha = 0.6607$, $\beta = 3.765$, $\chi^2 = 2.06$ ($0.50 < p < 0.75$), 3 d.f.

Number of memberships	0	1	2	3	4	5	6	7	8	9	
Observed number of states	27	12	8	2	1	1	1	0	1	1	54
Predicted number of states: Poisson	15.9	19.4	11.9	4.8	1.5			0.5			54.0
Predicted number of states: revised Poisson	27.9	11.1	5.9	3.5	2.1			3.5			54.0

so-called Yule-Greenwood distribution. This latter mathematical model is constructed on assumptions of heterogeneity among the units in a system, rather than on contagion in the behavior processes; that is, the Yule-Greenwood version would posit that all states have unique and varying "propensities" to join alliances. On the basis of the comparison between observed and predicted distributions alone, there is no way of distinguishing which of these two models is actually correct.[30]

In our situation, we cannot tell whether assumption 1 should be changed to allow for contagion in membership acquisition (the contagious Poisson model), or whether assumption 2 should be changed to suggest that all states have different "joining" tendencies (the Yule-Greenwood model). However, a separate test for heterogeneity has been suggested by William Feller.[31] It involves computing the correlation between the frequencies of behaviors or events experienced by each actor in two different adjacent time intervals. The value of the correlation coefficient will be high when each individual maintains his level of activity, either high or low, from one period to the next, thus indicating heterogeneity (that is, unique, unchanging propensities associated with each actor). If contagion exists, the simple correlation should be low, because states would be likely to acquire more and more commitments as time progressed—thus providing two quite disparate values for adjacent time intervals.

This "test" was applied to the data on national-alliance membership in the following manner: Each of the periods, 1871-1914, 1919-39, and 1945-65, was divided in half, and the correlation between the number of memberships acquired by each state in each of the two half-periods was computed.* Sharply contrasting results were obtained for the twentieth century; for the years 1919-39, $r = 0.73$ ($N = 64$, $p = 0.001$); for the years 1945-65, $r = 0.03$ ($N = 83$, $p = 0.4$). These values are altered only slightly if the OAS and OAU are omitted, or if calculations are confined to those states that joined at least one alliance—that is, the active states. Evidence is provided, therefore, that the interwar alliance activity was carried out by a heterogeneous group of nations, instead of there being a contagious interaction process in operation in the system. This conclusion is supported by examining the membership lists of the alliances during this period: Activity was dominated by a group of European nations who formed numerous associations immediately

---

*A state was included in the calculations only if it existed for at least five years during each of the halves of each period. As there were only 19 alliances formed between 1815 and 1870, involving only a few states, this interval was not analyzed.

following World War I but then constantly dissolved and regrouped up until World War II. An alternate interpretation is required for the 1945-65 span. Although the r is very low, it is difficult to attribute this to the contagion process formulated in our model, given that the predictions do not fit at all well. Perhaps contagious membership behavior was exhibited—but of a more specialized nature.[32]

The results for the 1871-1914 period are not so clear-cut: $r = 0.36$ ($N = 37$, $p = 0.001$), which is a significant value but not high. However, when calculations are restricted to the active states only, $r = 0.07$ ($N = 16$, $p = 0.4$). This, plus a look at the membership lists, suggests a rather curious possibility—that is, of a contagious process operating among a few active states within a larger "heterogenous" system. Thus, while the majority of states (21/37) remained totally uninvolved, states such as England, France, and Japan became increasingly active in an alliance system in which Russia, Italy, Austria, and Germany were already involved.

Models of the Acquisition of Dyadic Alliance Ties

One-way process models could also be applied to the question of the acquisition of dyadic alliance partnerships by nations over time. The formulations employed would be basically the same as those used above. In the Poisson and contagious Poisson models, the parameters would simply refer to the rate of acquisition of dyadic alliance ties, rather than to the acquisition of alliance memberships as before.

However, for both practical and theoretical reasons, it was decided not to extend our examination of the one-way process models to this second topic. From a practical point of view, calculation of numerous distributions of accumulated dyadic alliance ties over long time periods is a complicated and cumbersome procedure, even utilizing computers. Such effort, nonetheless, would be justified if there were any reason to expect that these applications would have revealed much that was new or interesting. This is not the case, however. The distributions of dyadic partnerships would be characterized by greater variance and extremes than that of the previously studied membership distributions, and consequently the "fit" of the models would be generally unsatisfactory. Furthermore, a minority of very large alliances would have a very exaggerated effect upon the dyadic arrays, and steps would have to be taken to discount them. Consideration of networks of dyadic commitments among nations becomes more manageable and theoretically relevant when studied in the context of "equilibrium models" described in the following section.

"EQUILIBRIUM" MODELS

Up until now the models utilized have reflected "one-way" behavior processes and were aimed at describing only the manner in which states acquired commitments over time. It may be objected that they have in effect considered only a single aspect, or "one-way," of what is really a process of both acquisition and loss of alliance ties by nations (that is, a "two-way" process). Models that capture both of these complementary patterns of inter-nation activity would require assumptions concerning two probability rates: a national rate of acquisition of alliance memberships, and a national rate of loss of alliance memberships. Construction of such models requires the adoption of assumptions and techniques such as those outlined by Coleman in his treatment of "equilibrium" models.[33]

Two basic modifications of former procedures are necessitated. First, before setting out our assumptions as to the acquisition rate and the loss rate of alliance memberships, an initial assumption must be made as to the "equilibrium" of the system in question. This means it must be assumed that throughout a specified time period alliance activity has remained "stable," such that the fractions of nationstates with 0, 1, . . . , i alliance commitments have remained constant. Thus, while individual nations may have acquired and lost memberships, the presumption is that the losses from any category are compensated for by gains and losses from other categories. This rather sweeping assumption is necessary in order to assure the mathematical tractability of the construction and testing of a two-way process model.

Second, the data distributions required to "test" this type of model are also quite different. Rather than employing information about the number of memberships accumulated over a number of years, we are to compare the equilibrium-model predictions to a distribution indicating the dispersion of alliance memberships at individual specified observation points—that is, single years only, such as 1870 or 1929. The fact that a less "general" data set may be used to test the two-way models is brought about by the equilibrium assumption. For if conditions of equilibrium are in effect in a system, then we can, at any chosen point in time, observe the proportions of actors in each different state, and this is all the information required to test the model.

The question then arises as to which annual data distributions are to be used in our analyses. If the idealized conditions of equilibrium were indeed in effect, one would need to select the alliance data of only one year between 1815 and 1965 to provide an adequate "test" for the two-way process models. But, obviously, equilibrium has not existed throughout the 150-year period, and some compromise and discretion is necessary. In fact, the period has already been broken into four distinct subsystems in previous model applications. After some thought the final and median years within the four intervals were chosen for analysis: 1843, 1870, 1892, 1914, 1929, 1939, 1956, and 1965. The beginnings of these eras were not included because 1815, 1871, 1919, and 1945 each marked occasions immediately following major upheavals in the international system. Figure 5.1 indicates that during two of these periods, 1871-1914 and 1945-65, the proportion of states without alliance ties remained relatively unchanged, thus satisfying in a most minimal way the requirements of an environment in equilibrium. On the other hand, there is considerable variation in the activity between 1815 and 1870 and between 1919 and 1939, and here assumptions of equilibrium remain a bit tenuous.

An Initial Model Involving the Acquisition and Loss of Alliance Memberships

Following the pattern of previous investigations, an initial probability model is constructed to produce a predicted distribution of outcomes consistent with the outcomes of a random behavior process within the system. The assumption set will be as follows:

1. The international system from which the annual data is chosen is in "equilibrium" concerning national alliance membership behavior.
2. Alliance formations constitute a set of homogenous events in the international system.
3. All states behaved similarly with respect to their joining and leaving alliances. Again, this does not imply that equal commitments are expected of everyone; rather it implies that states reacted similarly to the opportunities presented them, without being affected by idiosyncratic national attributes.
4. The joining into alliances by states was a series of independent events. Factors of contagion and diffusion that might affect subsequent behaviors of the joining state, or the contemporaneous behavior of other states, did not exist. Then (a) the

probability rate of acquisition of alliance memberships, δ, is assumed to be constant regardless of the number of memberships possessed by that state, and (b) the probability rate of loss of alliance memberships, θ, is assumed to be a constant loss coefficient per membership held. Thus, national rate of loss will be dependent upon the number of memberships held by that state.

We have envisaged a system in which states are all alike in their "willingness" to acquire new commitments. However, states are also all alike in their ability to maintain these commitments. A constant loss probability for each commitment translates into a transition rate dependent upon the number of memberships each state has. The probability formula for such a model may be given by $p_i = e^{-(\delta/\theta)}(\delta/\theta)^i/i!$, which the reader will recognize as the formula for the Poisson distribution if $(\delta/\theta) = \lambda'$, that is, $p_i = (e^{-\lambda'}\lambda'^i)/i!$. Thus, as Coleman has demonstrated, the same mathematical distribution may reflect either a one-way or a two-way process model—depending upon the assumptions made.[34]

However, the application of this model to the observed alliance commitment data in all of the eight chosen years proves unsatisfactory, as seen in Table 5.5. Modifying assumption 3 and dealing only with data on defensive pacts or with distributions that omitted the large regional alliances (the OAS and the OAU) still did not yield any evidence that the model adequately reflected national behaviors. Something other than the straightforward processes assumed above was in effect. It is necessary to reexamine assumptions 1 and 2 as well.

A Revised "Equilibrium" Model

Previous experience with the one-way models of membership behavior suggests that contagion may be a possible explanation for the manner in which alliance commitments are distributed. Therefore, a two-way equilibrium model analogous to the "contagious Poisson" model may be an appropriate alternative to our initial model. Construction of such a formulation entails maintaining previous assumptions 1, 2, and 3 and changing the fourth assumption to reflect the contagious acquisition of memberships. With these revisions the transition rates posited in assumption 4 for the two-way process can now be described as follows:

A. θ, the probability rate of a state's losing or leaving an alliance. Because we are only discussing "contagious" acquisitions of

TABLE 5.5

National Dyadic Alliance Ties, Selected Years:
The Application of the Poisson and Revised
Poisson Models

Number of Memberships	Observed Number of States	Predicted Poisson	Predicted Revised Model
1843			
0	20	*	*
1	14	—	—
2	1	—	—

Poisson: 35 states

1870			
0	30	28.5	29.9
1	3	5.0	2.9
2	0	0.4	0.8
3	1	>2/0.03	>2/0.4

Poisson: 34 states, $\lambda' = 0.177$, $\sigma^2 = 0.322$, $\chi^2 = 1.86$, 1 d.f., $0.25 < p < 0.1$
Revised Model: $\alpha = 0.129$, $\beta = 0.601$, $\chi^2 = 1.60$, 1 d.f., $0.25 < p < 0.1$

1892			
0	29	24.3	29.0
1	6	10.9	5.1
2	1	2.4	2.0
3	0	>2/0.4	0.9
4	1		>3/1.0
5	1		

Poisson: 38 states, $\lambda' = 0.447$, $\sigma^2 = 1.142$
Revised Model: $\alpha = 0.270$, $\beta = 0.938$, $\chi^2 = 1.08$, 2 d.f., $0.50 < p < 0.25$

1914			
0	33	24.1	31.68
1	4	15.0	6.88
2	3	4.7	2.98
3	0	>2/1.2	1.51
4	2		>3/1.95
5	2		

Poisson: 45 states, $\lambda' = 0.622$, $\sigma^2 = 1.782$
Revised Model: $\alpha = 0.351$, $\beta = 1.052$

1929			
0	45	28.26	41.86
1	9	23.97	11.38
2	3	10.16	5.41
3	3	2.87	2.94
4	1	0.61	1.70

(continued)

Table 5.5 Continued

Number of Memberships	Observed Number of States	Predicted Poisson	Predicted Revised Model
5	2	>4/0.12	1.02
6	3		>5/1.68

Poisson: 66 states, $\lambda' = 0.848$, $\sigma^2 = 2.64$
Revised Model: $\alpha = 0.455$, $\beta = 1.37$, $\chi^2 = 4.075$, 4 d.f., $0.50 < p < 0.25$

1939

0	17	12.35	26.30
1	32	21.07	15.30
2	5	17.97	9.49
3	4	10.22	6.01
4	3	4.36	3.85
5	2	1.49	2.47
6	1	>5/0.55	1.60
7	3		1.04
8	0		>7/1.93
9	0		
10	0		
>10	1		

Poisson: 68 states, $\lambda' = 1.076$, $\sigma^2 = 5.002$
Revised Model: $\alpha = 0.950$, $\beta = 1.076$

1956

0	21	28.22	32.27
1	50	31.77	28.33
2	11	17.89	15.56
3	0	6.71	6.84
4	2	1.89	2.63
5	1	>4/0.52	0.95
6	1		>5/0.44
7	1		

Poisson: 87 states, $\lambda' = 1.126$, $\sigma^2 = 1.444$

1965

0	25	38.52	†
1	71	45.03	
2	21	26.32	
3	2	10.26	
4	1	3.00	
5	3	>4/0.86	
6	0		
7	1		

Poisson: 124 states, $\lambda' = 1.169$, $\sigma^2 = 1.157$

*The distribution has too few values to compute the models.
†Revised model cannot be computed as the ratio of variance/mean is less than 1.0.

memberships, and because there is no reason to expect that the loss rate of memberships will have changed, this transition rate remains as before. That is, a state is presumed to abandon commitments at a rate proportional to this level of involvement.
B. τ, the probability rate of a state's joining an additional association. We shall assume that contagion is exhibited by a linearly increasing probability rate, a constant increment being added with each additional new membership. Thus, if $\tau_{0,1} = \delta$, then $\tau_{1,2} = \delta+\rho$ (where ρ represents the additional likelihood due to contagion), and the acquisition rate could be generally noted as $\tau_{i,i+1} = \delta+(i-1)\rho$.[35]

After considerable mathematical manipulation, Coleman and others have derived the formula that may be used to generate the predicted probability distribution of this model. Setting $a = \rho/\theta$ and $b = \delta/\rho$,

$$p_i = \{a(a+b) \ldots (a+[i-1]b)e^{-a}(1-e^{-b})^i\}/i! \, b^i$$

which is the representation of the negative binomial, or the "contagious Poisson" described before. Once again we see that it is possible to use one basic mathematical form for either a one-way or a two-way process model. (Note that although a and b may be estimated from the observed data in the same way as α and β, these parameters may not be given analogous interpretations. In the present model δ and θ are positive and negative transition rates, and ρ is the indicator of the contagion in the acquisition process. The two terms "a" and "b" are merely shorthand forms for ratios of these various factors, not the coefficients themselves.[36])

Better, although mixed, results are achieved by this revised two-way model when its predictions are compared to the eight annual data sets in Table 5.5. There is some evidence of a contagion process operating around 1892 and 1929, that is, the middle years of the second and third subsystems (although the X^2 probability values are not impressive: $0.25 < p < 0.50$). When applied only to defensive alliance memberships, the results are the same for 1929 and slightly less significant for 1870, 1892, and 1939. Elimination of the OAU and the OAS gives rise to an almost perfect correspondence between the observed and predicted distributions in 1939. As Figure 5.4 indicates, this is by far the best fit achieved by this revised model, and as the 1929 data was also relatively well-described, there are some suggestive findings of an equilibrium process operating during this subsystemic period.

The distribution of alliance commitments in 1956 and 1965 are very unusual: Even though there were a great number of states in

FIGURE 5.4

National Dyadic Alliance Memberships, 1939, Excluding the OAS

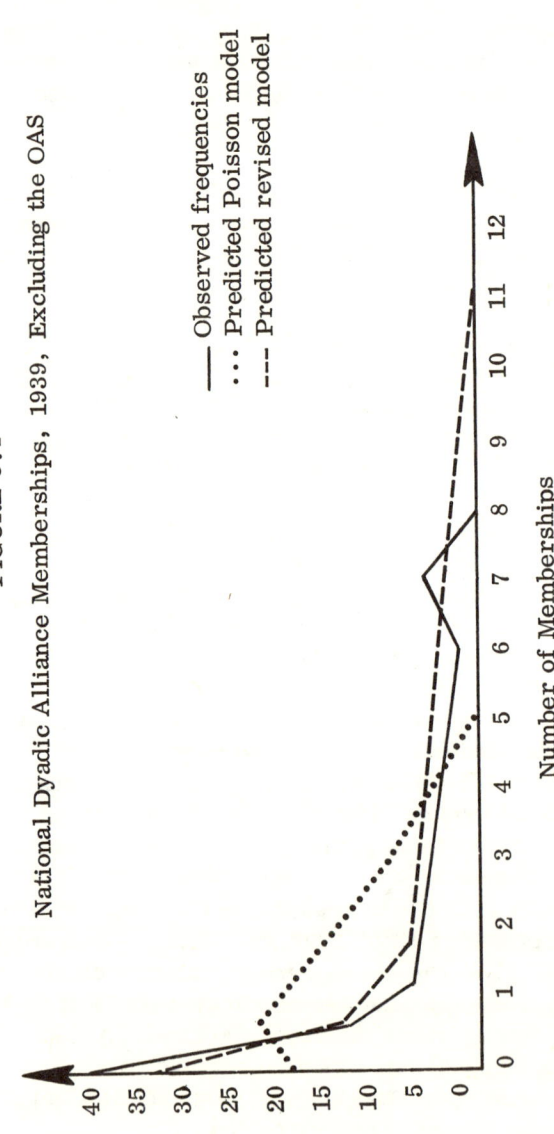

Number of Memberships

$N = 68$, $\lambda' = 1.397$, $\sigma^2 = 5.65$
$a = .641$, $b = 1.398$, $\chi^2 = 1.175$ ($0.75 < p < 0.90$), 5 d.f.

Memberships	0	1	2	3	4	5	6	7	8	9	10	10+
Observed number of states	38	11	5	4	3	2	1	3	0	0	0	1
Predicted number of states: Poisson	16.8	23.5	16.4	7.6	2.7	0.7	>6/0.3					
Predicted number of states: revised Poisson	35.8	12.4	6.8	4.2	2.7	1.8	1.3	>6/3.0				

the system, there is very little variance in the membership data for these years as almost every state belonged to one, two, or perhaps no international associations. This might lead to the mistaken impression that there was little international activity or variety of behaviors in the 1950s and 1960s but Figure 5.1 clearly shows this to be false. One of the problems is that the membership distributions do not account for the <u>sizes</u> of the alliances that the nations have joined. Since the size and character of alliances have changed radically since World War II, it is not surprising that the above models were least applicable to the 1956 and 1965 distributions.

Equilibrium Models and the Distribution of Dyadic Alliance Ties

Looking at the frequencies of alliance partnerships (dyadic alliance ties) instead of membership distributions may help to avoid the above problem, because the dyadic cumulations reflect the number of partners in each alliance. The remainder of this short section, therefore, will detail our attempts to apply the two-way Poisson and two-way contagious Poisson models to the dyadic alliance-partnership frequency arrays.

Annual data distributions were calculated for the same eight years as selected above. A connection between two nations was recorded only once, thus avoiding double counting for pairs of states who belonged to more than one alliance together. The two large regional alliances, the OAS and the OAU, presented difficulties because they tended to inflate the frequency counts a great deal. Thus, most computations were performed twice: the first time including these groups, the second time without them.

Application of the initial model can be seen as a "test" to determine whether the interconnections among nations assumed some sort of random "net." The assumptions involved are identical to those of the two-way Poisson discussed above, except that the events are now the acceptance and rejection of alliance ties by states, rather than the joining and leaving of the groups themselves. The transition rates refer to the manner in which states gain and lose their partnerships: The rate of acquisition is assumed constant despite the number of previous ties, and the rate of loss is assumed proportional to the level of such engagements. The method of calculating the values of the predicted distribution remained unchanged. However, the results indicated very clearly that there was no support for notions of random processes or networks being used to describe national dyadic alliance ties. In every year, regardless of whether or not the two large alliances were omitted, the model predicted too few nonaligned states, too many states with low levels of activity, and too few states with large numbers of associates. The observed distributions were simply too varied and discontinuous to be approximated by the model.

To explore the possibility that inter-nation activity may have been characterized by contagion, a two-way equilibrium model like the second one in the subsection above was developed and applied. The assumptions of this model do not require repeating; assumptions 1, 2, and 3 would remain the same, while the final premise, concerning the transition rates, need only be revised to speak of positive and negative probability rates of acquiring dyadic alliance ties.

Two points became clear when the results of this contagious model were compared to the observed frequency distributions. Generally speaking, the reviewed formulations were somewhat closer to the actual dyadic distribution values than were those of the previous model. In fact in some of the intermediate years, such as 1892 and 1929, the model provided a quite satisfactory fit to the data. However, for the earliest point, 1843, and for the latest years, 1956 and 1965, the model could not accommodate the extreme separations in the data between the nonactive and the very active nations. If a contagious process of some kind is operating among states, then it must involve step changes or transformations in the transition rates that are less continuous and gradual than those involved in our formulation.

SOME FINAL COMMENTS

The probability models in this work were designed to analyze and describe the behavior patterns of nations in their acceptance and rejection of alliance commitments. A variety of applications were demonstrated for two basic mathematical formulations, the Poisson distribution and the negative binomial distribution (under various names). Our success was varied. We realized in advance that inter-nation alliance activities fluctuated widely between 1815 and 1965. Therefore, most analyses were performed upon four subsystemic periods or upon selected years from within these intervals. Still, the alliance behaviors of the final period, 1945-65, and to a lesser degree of the initial era, 1815-70, largely resisted attempts at regularization and characterization.

On the other hand, the "revised" models provided relatively satisfactory descriptions of the observed outcomes from 1871 to

1914 and from 1919 to 1939. Further analysis suggested that while a contagious process may have been in operation prior to World War I, the alliance distributions of the interwar era were probably influenced by the heterogeneity of the nation-states themselves. When combined with the results of our "equilibrium" models of these intervals, which provided good descriptions of the midyears 1892 and 1929, and with the results of others, such as Siverson and Duncan, who studied the pattern of alliance formation during these periods and also found evidence of contagion and heterogeneity, respectively, a confirmed pattern begins to emerge. Further detailed analysis of the 1871-1914 and 1919-39 periods, including detailed examination of the membership lists, may provide additional clues as to the development of more complete and sophisticated process models.

There may be a central reason for our general pattern of results. Our basic premise throughout this chapter has been that all nations may be regarded as actors within a "system," and that their behavior assumed some type of pattern or regularity. It now seems that perhaps we "case our net too broadly" in making such an assumption. Our model may have "worked" for the 1871-1939 periods because the international "system" did in fact include all nations in its activity patterns, even if inter-nation affairs were dominated by Western European states. During both of the other periods, however, proportionally large numbers of units existed in the international environment but were not effectively in the "system." Thus, our models could not account for the high concentration of activity among the Great Powers during the Concert of Europe era, nor could they accommodate the last two decades, 1945-65, in which the nature and size of alliances has undergone fundamental change and in which large numbers of states maintained nominal alliance commitments but essentially were not committed to activity in an international sense.

This leaves us with several thoughts as to new possibilities and revised modeling strategies for studying alliances in three different eras. The interesting questions about post-Napoleonic Europe center on the maneuvers and strategies of a select group of states supposedly attempting to maintain a "balance-of-power" system. Perhaps the most suitable models to be employed here are those tailored to the analysis of small groups—particularly "graph theory" techniques that facilitate understanding of the notion of "balance." During the 1871-1939 periods a great deal of international alliance activity occurred, interrupted twice by major world wars. We have in this research discovered several models that could quite successfully describe the observed distributions of national behaviors within this "system." Additional work needs to be done to explore the nature of the processes underlying these aggregated distributions, particularly concerning systemic "biases" such as contagion and diffusion, and the possibility of some type of systemic equilibrium.

As for recent international alliance formation, the scope of the system and the range of behaviors seems too broad to be captured by the models suggested above. Perhaps the best tack here is to isolate specific subsets of alliances and concentrate on specifying the influence patterns or structures within these groups. As an alternative approach the modeler might focus on particular unusual series of events, such as alliance proliferation immediately following World War II, possibly studying this behavior in the context of "biological" or medical models of epidemic, information transfer, or diffusion processes.[37] After numerous such smaller modeling approaches, we may obtain enough information to be able to discern those constant patterns and structures that could form the bases for the assumptions and construction of a more comprehensive international model.

NOTES

1. While the phrasing of this definition of alliance follows that of Edwin Fedder, "The Concept of Alliance," International Studies Quarterly 12 (1968): 65-86, the substantive meaning is similar to the notion of alliance adopted by Singer and Small, Liska, Morgenthau, Holsti, and others. See J. David Singer and Melvin Small, "Formal Alliances, 1815-1939: A Quantitative Description," Journal of Peace Research 3 (1966): 1-32; George Liska, Nations in Alliance: The Limits of Interdependence (Baltimore: Johns Hopkins University Press, 1962); Hans Morgenthau, Politics Among Nations, 5th ed. (New York: Knopf, 1973); Kal J. Holsti, International Politics (Englewood Cliffs, N.J.: Prentice-Hall, 1972).

2. The separation of alliances according to these three commitment levels follows Singer and Small, "Formal Alliances, 1815-1939."

3. There exist a number of propositional inventories that attempt to summarize the literature on alliances. The following three sets of authors all concur as to the "noncummulative" nature of previous research efforts: Phillip Burgess and David Moore, "Inter-Nation Alliances: An Inventory and Appraisal of Propositions," in Political Science Annual, vol. 3, ed. James A. Robinson (Indianapolis: Bobbs-Merrill, 1972), pp. 339-84; Ole Holsti, P. Terrence Hopmann, and John Sullivan, Unity and Disintegration in International Alliances (New York: Wiley, 1973); J. David Singer and Bruce Bueno de Mesquita, "Alliance, Capabilities and War:

A Review and Synthesis," in Political Science Annual, vol. 4, ed. Cornelius Cotter (Indianapolis: Bobbs-Merrill, 1973), pp. 237-80.

4. Morgenthau, Politics Among Nations, p. 181.

5. For a most interesting and detailed analysis of the strategies and motivations involved in alliance formation, see Robert L. Rothstein, Alliances and Small Powers (New York: Columbia University Press, 1968), Ch. 2.

6. See on this topic the following: Robert L. Rothstein, "Alignment, Nonalignment, and Small Powers: 1945-1965," International Organization 20 (1966): 397-418; Samir Anabtawi, "Neutralists and Neutralism," The Journal of Politics 27 (1965): 351-61.

7. Singer and Bueno de Mesquita, "Alliance, Capabilities and War."

8. Lewis F. Richardson, Statistics of Deadly Quarrels (Pittsburgh: Boxwood Press, 1960).

9. Holsti, Hoppmann, and Sullivan, Unity and Disintegration, p. 12.

10. J. David Singer and Melvin Small, "National Alliance Commitments and War Involvements," Papers, Peace Research Society (International), vol. 4 (1967), p. 138.

11. See for example, Morgenthau, Politics Among Nations, or Rothstein, Alliances and Small Powers.

12. Bruce Russett, "Components of an Operational Theory of International Alliance Formation," Journal of Conflict Resolution 12 (1968): 285-301.

13. Much of the recent empirical research on alliances has been carried out in conjunction with the Correlates of War project directed by J. David Singer. For example, the relationship between national alliance activity and war involvement was explored in Singer and Small, "National Alliance Commitments," and the relationship between systemic alliance activity and war was explored in J. David Singer and Melvin Small, "Alliance Aggregation and the Onset of War," in Quantitative International Politics, ed. J. David Singer (New York: Free Press, 1968), pp. 274-86.

14. Randolph M. Siverson and George T. Duncan, "Stochastic Models of International Alliance Initiation, 1815-1965," Chapter 6 of this volume. Other works on this topic that employ probability models include Brian L. Job, "Alliance Formation in the International System," paper prepared for delivery at the 1973 Annual Meeting of the International Studies Association; Patrick McGowan and Robert Rood, "Alliance Behavior in Balance of Power Systems," American Political Science Review, forthcoming.

15. Brian Healy and Arthur Stein, "The Balance of Power in International History," Journal of Conflict Resolution 17 (1973):

31-61; Jeff Hart, "Symmetry and Polarization in the European International System, 1870-1879," *Journal of Peace Research* 11 (1974): 229-44.

16. Stuart Bremer, "Formal Alliance Clusters in the Interstate System," paper prepared for delivery at the 1972 American Political Science Association Annual Meetings; Michael Wallace, "Clusters of Nations in the Global System, 1865-1964: Some Preliminary Evidence," *International Studies Quarterly* 19 (1975): 67-110.

17. For general introductions to the various types and uses of models in social science the reader is referred to James Coleman, *Introduction to Mathematical Sociology* (New York: Free Press, 1962); Thomas Fararo, *Mathematical Sociology* (New York: Wiley, 1973); Ottamar Bartos, *Simple Models of Group Behavior* (New York: Columbia University Press, 1967); David J. Bartholemew, *Stochastic Models for Social Processes* (New York: Wiley, 1967); Anatol Rapoport, "Mathematical Models of Social Interaction," in *Handbook of Mathematical Psychology*, vol. 2, ed. Robert Luce et al. (New York: Wiley, 1967), pp. 494-597; Edward Rogers and F. Floyd Shoemaker, *Communication of Innovations: A Cross-Cultural Approach*, 2d ed. (New York: Free Press, 1971).

18. Rapoport, "Mathematical Models."

19. For a more rigorous definition of a *sociogram*, the reader is referred to Anatol Rapoport and William Horvath, "A Study of a Large Sociogram," *Behavioral Science* 6 (1961): 279.

20. Ibid.

21. Ibid.; Coleman, *Introduction*; Caxton Foster, Anatol Rapoport, and Carol Orwant, "The Study of a Large Sociogram II: Elimination of Free Parameters," *Behavioral Science* 8 (1963): 56-65.

22. J. David Singer and Melvin Small listed all formal alliances established between 1815 and 1965 in two articles: Singer and Small, "Formal Alliances, 1815-1939"; J. David Singer and Melvin Small, "Formal Alliances, 1816-1965: An Extension of the Basic Data," *Journal of Peace Research* 6 (1969): 257-82. The data for this research were abstracted from these listings. For a detailed description of the coding and selection procedures, the reader is referred to Brian L. Job, "The Alliance Formation Behavior of Nations in the International System," Ph.D. dissertation, Indiana University, 1974.

23. The division of 1815-1965 into the two "century" periods follows the procedures adopted by Singer and Small in much of their research on alliances. See for example Singer and Small, "Alliance Aggregation." The use of the four interwar periods involves a consolidation of the seven time periods that is employed by Richard Rosecrance, *Action and Reaction in World Politics: International Systems in Perspective* (Boston: Little, Brown, 1963).

24. Coleman, Introduction, pp. 315-16.

25. A discussion and derivation of the Poisson formula may be found in many statistics texts. This function and examples of its applications are discussed in William Feller, An Introduction to Probability Theory and Its Applications, 2d ed., vol. 1 (New York: Wiley, 1957). Coleman, Introduction, pp. 288-90, gives a slightly different derivation of the formula. For examples of the application of the Poisson to the study of international politics, the reader is referred to Manus Midlarsky, "Mathematical Models of Instability and a Theory of Diffusion," International Studies Quarterly 14 (1970): 60-84; Siverson and Duncan, "Stochastic Models"; McGowan and Rood, "Alliance Behavior"; Job, The Alliance Formation Behavior.

26. The use of the chi-square statistic to assess the significance of the deviations from the Poisson predictions is common in the literature. See Frank A. Haight, Handbook of the Poisson Distribution (New York: Wiley, 1967), where additional references are also given.

27. Coleman, Introduction, Ch. 10.

28. Ibid., p. 300.

29. Ibid., p. 305.

30. Rapoport and Horvath, "A Study," p. 282; Coleman, Introduction, p. 301; Feller, An Introduction, p. 111.

31. William Feller, "On a General Class of Contagious Distributions," Annals of Mathematical Statistics 14 (1943): 389-400. See also Midlarsky, "Mathematical Models," p. 72; Siverson and Duncan, "Stochastic Models."

32. Siverson and Duncan in "Stochastic Models" explore the possibility of a contagious process operating among nations involved in the Cold War.

33. Coleman, Introduction, Ch. 11.

34. Ibid., pp. 316-19.

35. Ibid., pp. 326-32.

36. Ibid., p. 329.

37. See, for example, ibid.; Bartholemew, Stochastic Models; Fararo, Mathematical Sociology; Bartos, Simple Models; D. R. Cox and P. A. W. Lewis, The Statistical Analysis of Series of Events (New York: Wiley, 1966).

CHAPTER

6

STOCHASTIC MODELS OF INTERNATIONAL ALLIANCE INITIATION, 1885-1965

Randolph M. Siverson
George T. Duncan

Alliances among nations in the international system appear as important and ubiquitous phenomena, basic and seemingly essential to the interactive character of the system. A property of alliances that has received substantial scholarly attention is their structural nature. We find, for example, that many analyses of the international system as it existed in the nineteenth century are organized around the idea of the "balance of power," while in analyzing the twentieth-century system (particularly the period 1947-65) substantial attention has been devoted to bipolarity and several of its variants.[1] Frequently, students of international politics have suggested that the structural properties of alliances in the international system have profound consequences for the processes of the system.[2] But in focusing upon the structure of alliances, investigators have generally tended to ignore the dynamics of alliance initiation and, in particular, have neglected the temporal dimension of alliance initiation. Certainly, at this point there exists no general model to account for the distribution of alliance initiation in time or for the occurrence of particular patterns of alliance initiation within a time framework. Since this aspect of alliances has not been pre-

---

Since this research was the result of a truly collaborative effort, the listing of the authors was determined through the use of a table of random numbers. The authors gratefully acknowledge the comments of Patricia M. E. Altham, Dina A. Zinnes, Ole R. Holsti, J. David Singer, and Michael P. Sullivan on an earlier version of this paper. The work of George T. Duncan was partially supported under Grants N00014-67-A-0314-0022 from the Office of Naval Research and GS-32514 from the National Science Foundation.

viously examined, it may provide a new perspective for those interested in the theory of international alliances. (However, in recent papers Job and McGowan and Rood do pursue this line of inquiry.[3] Their research differs from the present inquiry in several respects. McGowan and Rood limit their study to the period 1815-1914 and consider only the Poisson model. Job also uses only the Poisson, but he uses data from the period 1815-1965. There are also differences among the types of alliances included in the data sets. In earlier research Horvath and Foster developed equilibrium models of the size of wartime alliances.[4])

This chapter attempts to examine the temporal dimension of alliance initiation by evaluating probabilistic models for the instances of alliance initiation that are compatible with available empirical evidence. Specifically, after outlining a basic model and its alternatives, this chapter will evaluate the models against data drawn from Singer's Correlates of War project, explore the various models from a historical perspective, and conclude with a brief discussion of the findings.

THE MODELS

The Poisson Process Model

The basic model used in this research is the Poisson process. This has been found adequate to describe a wide variety of probabilistic phenomena, including von Bortkiewicz's study of deaths from the kick of a horse[5] and, more pertinently, the distribution of wars in time.[6] Coleman offers an extensive discussion of its application to social phenomena.[7] (Most stochastic—that is, probabilistic—models have been developed in the physical or biological sciences. The Poisson model, although widely used in these sciences, was developed, however, to account for the distribution of various types of judicial activity.[8])

The basic units of the international system capable of alliance activity are the various subsets of nation-states recognized at a particular time. Since alliances nominally exist by mutual agreement, these units are at least dyadic, and include all the possible triads and larger alliances.* We shall particularly be concerned

---

*The fact that the number of nations in the international system varied (basically increased) in the years following 1815 does not prohibit use of the Poisson process model in this context. Arguing

with whether these units display essentially independent and identical probabilistic behavior in initiating alliances. The alternatives will be that contagious behavior is evident or that probabilistic heterogeneity is present among the units. Contagion and heterogeneity are not mutually exclusive phenomena as their definitions later in this chapter will make clear. A system may display both contagion and heterogeneity, in which case assessing the predominant character may be of interest.

A basic set of assumptions, given below, lead to the Poisson process as a necessary consequence. Precisely because certain substantive assumptions imply that the data should be in accord with the Poisson process, it is possible to investigate statistically the validity of the assumptions. We record the instant of time when an alliance is initiated by any subset of nation-states. Our concern is with the superposed process formed by pooling the instances for all relevant nation-states.[9] The following assumptions will imply that the superposed process will be essentially Poisson:

1. The instance of alliance initiation in one time period is a random variable independent of the random number of alliances initiated in another nonoverlapping time period.
2. In a sufficiently short time period, the probability of two or more instances of alliance activity is negligible.
3. For sufficiently short time periods, the probability that an alliance will be initiated is proportional to the length of the time period.
4. Alliance-forming units of each type (dyadic, triadic, and so on) have identical probabilistic behavior.

These assumptions lead to the following mathematical model for the probability of $k(k = 0, 1, 2, \ldots)$ instances of alliance activity in the time period from t_0 to t_1:

$$e^{-\lambda(t_1 - t_0)}[\lambda(t_1 - t_0)]^k/k!$$

---

rather heuristically, a large number of potential alliance-forming units consummating alliances independently and with small probability would be expected to manifest essentially Poisson behavior. The variable number of nations might cause the rate at which alliances are initiated over time to increase, but it would have little influence on the other implications of the Poisson model.

where e is the base of the natural logarithm. The parameter λ is the mean number of instances of alliance initiation in a time period of unit length.

One consequence of assumption 3 is that the rate λ at which alliances are being initiated does not change over time. This cannot be strictly true, but this fact does not necessarily obviate the utility of the Poisson process in describing the statistical process of alliance initiation. Richardson was satisfied in using the Poisson process model for the distribution of wars in time, even though with regard to an assumption similar to assumption 3 he stated: "For the wars that is not quite suitable, because there is a seasonal effect: Wars in the north temperate zone have ordinarily begun in spring or summer. . . ."[10] Minor unsystematic variation in the rate λ of alliance initiation is tolerable in using a Poisson process description, but major changes will make it distort the actual process that is at work. Adjustments are also possible to make the Poisson process applicable. For example, if a change in rate from λ to μ≠λ occurs at time t, the system can be analyzed as two separate Poisson processes: The first (with rate λ) is truncated at time t, while the second has rate μ and is initiated at time t.

Assumption 2 is grossly violated when simultaneous occurrence of the initiation of two or more alliances is possible. Thus, one would not want to model the number of countries initiating alliances using the Poisson process, since any initiation, necessarily at least dyadic, would violate the assumption.

Assumption 1 is inconsistent with "carry-over" or contagion effects, whether excitatory or inhibitory. Consider Richardson's data on wars. It is an unhappy fact that an unusually large number of wars in a given year does not seem to produce a significant aversion to war in succeeding years. If such an aversion were to be produced, the Poisson process model would be invalidated through an inhibitory contagious effect. The possibility of violation of assumption 1 suggests a more complex model alternative to the Poisson process, called the contagious or negative binomial process.

Alternatives to the Poisson Process: Contagion and Heterogeneity

Contagion

A reasonable alternative to the essentially random occurrence of alliance initiation implied as a consequence of the Poisson process would allow for an excitatory contagious effect of estimable degree. This would drop the simplifying assumption 1 of the Poisson process. A model with this feature is appropriate to examine the hypothesis that alliance activity among a group of nations provokes other nations to form alliances. As Coleman observes:

> One reason that the Poisson distribution is not more applicable to much social data is the fact that when one person takes an action, then the probability of a second person's taking the action is changed. Often it is increased (a positive "contagion" of the action); sometimes it is decreased (a negative contagion, or aversion).[11]

This process has been found in a variety of social phenomena. Midlarsky, for example, found contagious processes to have occurred in Latin American military coups between 1935 and 1949.[12]

It is possible that this process may occur in alliance initiation. Indeed, throughout the descriptive literature on alliance behavior, it frequently appears that there are implicit descriptions of "contagious" alliance behavior. For example, in A. J. P. Taylor's <u>The Struggle for Mastery in Europe, 1848-1918</u> or William Langer's <u>European Alliances and Alignments</u>, sequences of alliance formation may be readily observed in which one nation's alliance initiation appears to stimulate other nations into alliances, alignments, or coalitions.[13] On a theoretical level Scott offers the following proposition: "The formation of one alliance may serve as a stimulus precipitating the formation of one or more additional alliances."[14]

In an even more general sense one might reasonably argue that contagious alliance behavior is consistent with many of the stimulus-response or action-reaction models of international interaction. While these models are almost always operationalized in terms of a series of interrelated events, usually in a situation of conflict escalation or abatement, there is no reason why this notion may not be conceptualized in terms of processes on a larger scale, such as alliance initiation. In fact, this notion is explicitly set forth by Triska and Finley in their discussion of the alliance behavior of the United States and the Soviet Union, and by Scott in his conceptualization of the balance of power as a challenge and response system.[15]

A simple model providing for contagion is the Polya, or negative binomial process.* Aside from the time parameter, this process

---

*The Polya model is a limiting case of a specific type of urn model. An urn is filled with balls of two colors, and rather than simply drawing with or without replacement, additional balls of the same color drawn are added to the urn. Thus, a positive contagious effect is achieved, since successive drawings of one color increase the probability that the same color ball will be drawn again.

has two parameters, say, α and β. The parameter β is intended to measure the extent of contagion, with larger values of β reflecting more contagion in the system. The negative binomial process has the following mathematical expression for the probability of $k(k = 0, 1, 2, \ldots)$ instances of alliance initiation during the time period t_0 to t_1:

$$[\alpha(\alpha+\beta) \ldots (\alpha + [k-1]\beta)e^{-\alpha(t_1-t_0)}(1-e^{-\beta(t_1-t_0)})k]/[k!\,\beta^k]$$

where e is the base of the natural logarithm.[16]

From this expression it can be shown that the Poisson model exists as a limiting case when β goes to zero. Therefore, since the Poisson probabilities can be approximated with arbitrary precision with small positive β values, this model is essentially more general than the Poisson.

Heterogeneity

Contagion was introduced by dropping assumption 1 of the Poisson process; heterogeneity is introduced instead by dropping the simplifying assumption 4 that led to the Poisson process. This essentially means that the superposed process that is observed is composed of Poisson processes with different rate parameters. According to this model, the individual nations in the system may have different rates of participation, whereas the Poisson process requires the rates to be identical. If in fact the Poisson parameters are assumed to vary according to a gamma distribution,* the model is known as the Yule-Greenwood model. The Yule-Greenwood model, while specifically introducing the possibility of heterogeneity, leads to exactly the same distribution for instances of alliance initiation during a given time period as the contagion model.

Since rival assumptions of either contagion or heterogeneity imply the same distribution in a time period but suggest quite different processes of alliance initiation, a problem emerges. This problem of contagion versus heterogeneity is examined in the accident statistic context by Bates and Neyman and by Bates.[17]

---

*The gamma distribution specifies a positive random variable, say, x, whose probability density function is proportional to $x^{a-1}e^{-x/b}$ where a and b are positive parameters and e is the base of the natural logarithms. Again, the Poisson process will appear as a limiting case: This time, when a goes to infinity, b goes to zero, in such a way that $a \cdot b$ remains constant at λ.

They develop general probability theory for occurrences over several time periods, but do not explicitly develop a statistical test for comparing heterogeneity assumptions against contagious assumptions. Midlarsky's 1970 study of military coups, however, applies a method for making judgments as to whether heterogeneity is operative in the process.[18] Where appropriate we shall apply his methods to the alliance data. Two further methods will also be used in attempting to assess these alternative models: (a) a nonparametric test for runs above and below the median and (b) nonparametric tests for first order autocorrelation. These methods will be explained in more detail in the data analysis section where they are applied.

THE DATA

Singer's Correlates of War project has furnished an extensive listing of interstate alliances between 1815 and 1965. This list furnishes the data base for an examination of the distribution of alliance activity in time.*

Our use of these data involved enumerating the years 1815-1965, inclusive, and recording the instances of alliance initiation in each year. Some years have had no alliance initiation (for example, 1862), while others contain substantial amounts (for example, six in 1921). Since our interest is in alliance initiation, we recorded not only the creation of a wholly new alliance but also those instances in which (a) a nation joined an already existing alliance, (b) nations

---

*There are several aspects of this enumeration that perhaps deserve mention. Basically, the alliances contained within it are those between political entities that qualified as nations and that were of three types: military cooperation agreements in the event of certain contingencies, neutrality agreements, and agreements of entente. Certain alliances were not included; for example, among the alliances not included are those that were "consummated during, or less than three months before, a war in which any of the signatories participated, unless the alliance endured beyond the formal treaty of peace." (Singer and Small, "Alliance Aggregation.")[19] Since Singer and Small are interested in the relationship between alliance aggregation and war, they reason that the inclusion of alliances formed either during a war or just before it would probably contaminate the results. Since our long-run interest is also in examining the impact of alliance activity on the probability of war, it does not seem unreasonable to accept their criteria.

STOCHASTIC MODELS 117

already party to an alliance negotiated a new alliance of another type (say, from neutrality agreement to entente), or (c) several bilateral alliances merged into a larger grouping. For the years 1815-1965, inclusive, this data-selection process produced 204 instances of alliance initiation.

However, it must be pointed out and emphasized that this listing covers only formal alliance initiation; informal alignments and coalitions are beyond the purview of this research. This omission of informal alignments and coalitions from the data base is not occasioned by any lack of interest on our part or by a belief that they are unimportant; it rests on the fact that the investigator is often hard pressed when it comes to determining the actual attributes of many of the alignments and coalitions. For example, because of their informal character, it is frequently difficult to determine exactly when the alignment or coalition came into existence, or even, in some cases, whether it actually existed. The use of formal alliances, however, eliminates the elusive character that the data might otherwise have. Naturally, it limits the breadth of the conclusions that may be drawn.

DATA ANALYSIS

This section will report the application of the Poisson process model and its alternatives to the alliance data discussed in the previous section. Initially, the distribution of alliance initiation for the entire period 1815-1965 will be presented, but since this long time period may contain fluctuations in behavior, the distribution within several subperiods commonly thought of as significant will also be presented.

1815-1965

Table 6.1 reports the distribution of alliance activity by the number of years having a specified number of instances for the period 1815-1965. The table indicates that for this period there were 69 years with no alliance activity, 36 with one instance of alliance activity, 19 with two, 7 with three, 8 with four, 4 with five, 4 with six, 3 with seven, and 1 with twelve. The Poisson and negative binomial models were fitted to this data using the method of moments programmed for the Burroughs 6700 computer. The Poisson parameter λ is estimated by the sample mean $\bar{x}$ while

β is estimated by the natural logarithm of $s^2/\bar{x}$, and α is estimated by the product of $\bar{x}^2/(s^2 - \bar{x})$ and the estimator of β. Note that this method is valid only if s^2 is larger than $\bar{x}$; otherwise, the data suggest that the negative binomial process is inappropriate. A comparison of the observed distribution with the two expected distributions indicates that the Poisson distribution does not give a good fit to the observed data ($\chi^2 = 63.22$, d.f. = 3, $p < 0.001$), but that the contagious-heterogeneous version of the Poisson does ($\chi^2 = 5.14$, d.f. = 6, $p = 0.47$). In a Poisson distribution the mean and variance are equal. If the sample ratio $s^2/\bar{x}$ is large, the data suggest a departure from Poisson behavior and provide support for the negative binomial model. Under the hypothesis of Poisson sampling, $(n - 1)s^2/\bar{x}$ has approximately a chi-square distribution with $n - 1$ degrees of freedom. Hypothesis tests based on this fact are given in Tables 6.1 to 6.3 and 6.5 to 6.7, with one or two asterisks indicating statistical significance at the $\alpha = 0.05$ or $\alpha = 0.01$ levels, respectively. In Table 6.1 the value of $s^2/\bar{x} = 2.76$ is significant at $\alpha = 0.01$. These results are consistent with the proposition that some combination of contagion or heterogeneity existed in alliance activity between 1815 and 1965. However, the failure of the Poisson model over the entire time period from 1815 to 1965 may well be due to dramatic shifts in the rate of alliance initiation over time.

A potentially more interesting approach is to divide the time period 1815-1965 into shorter periods of greater theoretical interest and more nearly constant rates of alliance initiation. There are, of course, a number of potential time periods that could be examined. One division that seems plausible in view of the writings of political scientists and diplomatic historians, focuses upon the balance-of-power system (1815-1914), the interwar years (1919-39), and the post-World War II years (1945-65).* For the period 1815-1914 the mean rate of instances of alliance initiation per year was a low 0.56, while for the interwar years of 1919-39 it increased to 3.29, and then further jumped in the post World War II years of 1945-65 to 4.48. This suggests that it is inappropriate to analyze the entire time period from 1815 to 1965 in terms of the models considered here—models that assume a constant rate of alliance initiation. We

---

*It may be noted that in making these divisions, the years during World Wars I and II have been omitted. These years were dropped from the analysis since Singer and Small did not collect alliance data from them. For the entire period 1815-1965 their inclusion does not make an appreciable difference, but for the shorter periods it might.

TABLE 6.1

Instances of Alliance Activity, 1815-1965

Number of Instances of Alliance Activity (i)	Number of Years (n_i)	Contagious-Heterogeneous Expected	Poisson Expected
0	69	69.23	39.11
1	36	33.93	52.83
2	19	19.12	35.69
3	7	11.25	16.07
4	8	6.75	5.43
5	4	4.11	1.47
6	4	2.52	0.33
7	3	1.55	0.06
8	0	0.96	0.01
9	0	0.90	0.00
10	0	0.37	0.00
11	0	0.23	0.00
12	1	0.14	0.00
$\bar{x} = 1.35$, $s^2 = 3.72$, $s^2/\bar{x} = 2.76$**		$\chi^2 = 5.14$ d.f. = 6 $\alpha = 0.780$ $\beta = 1.014$	$\chi^2 = 63.22$** d.f. = 3

**Significant at $p \leq .01$.

will now examine these three more theoretically relevant time periods in more detail.

1815-1914

Table 6.2 reports the distribution of alliance initiation for the balance-of-power system of 1815-1914. This table indicates that the Poisson process model ($\chi^2 = 0.76$, d.f. = 1, p = 0.40) may be accepted as fitting observed data. Naturally, since the contagious-heterogeneous model is essentially more general (involving a fit of two parameters instead of one), it also will provide an acceptable fit to the data—in fact, nearly perfect ($\chi^2 = 0.00$, d.f. = 1, p > 0.99). However, because parsimony is one of the major criteria for selecting alternative models, we conclude that the Poisson model, with its less complicated assumption set, offers the better description.

TABLE 6.2

Instances of Alliance Activity, 1815-1914

Number of Instances of Alliance Activity (i)	Number of Years (n_i)	Contagious-Heterogeneous Expected	Poisson Expected
0	60	59.89	57.12
1	28	28.18	31.99
2	9	8.88	8.96
3	2	2.34	1.67
4	1	0.56	0.23
5	0	0.12	0.03
$\bar{x} = 0.56$		$\chi^2 = 0.00$	$\chi^2 = 0.76$
$s^2 = 0.666$		d.f. = 1	d.f. = 1
$s^2/\bar{x} = 1.19$		$\alpha = 0.513$	
		$\beta = 0.174$	

1919-39

Table 6.3, describing the distributions of alliance initiation for the interwar years, 1919-39, has different characteristics. Here, there is a suggestion that the contagious-heterogeneous model ($\chi^2 = 7.38$, d.f. = 4, p = 0.12) offers a better fit than the Poisson model ($\chi^2 = 11.92$, d.f. = 5, p = 0.04). For the interwar years, therefore, we conclude that the observed distribution of alliance initiation is better fit with the negative binomial model. The value $s^2/\bar{x} = 1.37$ is nearly significant at $\alpha = 0.05$. Overall, the results are not inconsistent with contagion or heterogeneity. We shall now examine the implications of assumptions of both contagion and heterogeneity in the light of the data. The frequency of alliance activity by year is given in Table 6.4.

If the process is contagious, a high level of alliance activity during a particular year would tend to provoke alliance activity during the following year. Conversely, a low level of alliance activity would tend to be associated with little initiation in the following year. Thus, for the alliance data of 1918-39 we would expect that a contagious process would produce fewer runs above and below the median number of alliances initiated in each year. This median number for the given time period is 3. Applying the test for runs above and below the median given in Walsh[20] to the data in Table 6.4, we find a p-value of 0.13, which does not support the hypothesis of contagion.

To focus specifically on the alternative of positive dependence between the number of instances of alliance initiation in successive years, X_t and X_{t+1}, we compute the value of Kendall's tau and Spearman's rho for the time series in Table 6.4. A nonparametric test for first-order autocorrelation is then available.[21] The computed value of Kendall's tau is $\tau = 0.079$, which for the one-tailed test of the null hypothesis of independence against an alternative of positive τ gives a p-value of 0.33. The calculated value of Spearman's rho is $r_s = 0.10$, which for the analogous test of independence against positive ρ_s gives a p-value of approximately 0.45. This then further confirms the conclusion that there is no statistical evidence in favor of contagion for the time period 1918-39.

Feller has suggested that heterogeneity may be detected by determining the correlation between the rates of the units across two adjacent but nonoverlapping time periods.[22] A strong correlation will imply that individual units are maintaining rates of alliance

TABLE 6.3

Instances of Alliance Activity, 1919-39

Number of Instances of Alliance Activity (i)	Number of Years (n_i)	Contagious- Heterogeneous Expected	Poisson Expected
0	3	1.28	0.79
1	1	3.07	2.58
2	5	4.11	4.24
3	3	4.02	4.65
4	1	3.23	3.82
5	4	2.25	2.51
6	3	1.40	1.37
7	1	0.80	0.64
8	0	0.43	0.26
$\bar{x} = 3.286$		$\chi^2 = 7.38$	$\chi^2 = 11.92$*
$s^2 = 4.490$		d.f. = 4	d.f. = 5
$s^2/\bar{x} = 1.37$		$\alpha = 2.799$	
		$\beta = 0.312$	

*Significant at $p \leq .05$.

TABLE 6.4

Time Series of Alliance Activity During the Interwar Years, 1919-39

Year	Instances	Year	Instances
1919	0	1930	2
1920	2	1931	0
1921	6	1932	6
1922	0	1933	5
1923	1	1934	4
1924	3	1935	3
1925	2	1936	6
1926	7	1937	5
1927	5	1938	2
1928	3	1939	3
1929	2		

initiation, which for each nation is relatively constant but is different across nations. Among nations such differences in rates are incompatible with the assumptions of the Poisson process but are basic to the Yule-Greenwood model from which heterogeneity is derived. (Midlarsky applied this method to determine whether the distribution of military coups in Latin America between 1935 and 1949 was related to contagion or heterogeneity.[23])

If one divides the period 1919-39 into the two periods, 1919-32 and 1933-39, roughly half the alliance activity by nation falls into each of these periods. The Pearson product-moment sample correlation coefficient between the rates of each nation's alliance initiation in these periods is $r = 0.67$ ($n = 52$). This correlation is strong enough to suggest that a substantial amount of alliance initiation during this period is due to heterogeneity. Thus, it appears that a number of nations had substantially different but relatively constant probability of alliance during this interwar period.

This leads to an interesting question. If we accept the notion that the Poisson process is a good description of alliance initiation prior to 1914, what is it that creates the heterogeneity that changed the character of the system? One suggestion as to an answer to this question may be found by noting that of the 164 individual instances of alliance initiation during 1919-39 three nations contributed to 43 of those instances (and were the leaders in participation): Turkey (13 instances), Italy (15 instances), the Soviet Union (15 instances). What is interesting is that to one degree or another these represent "revolutionary" states. In 1917 the revolution brought about a communist government in Russia; in 1922 a coup ushered Mussolini and a fascist government into control in Italy; between 1920 and 1922 the nationalists gained control of the Turkish government in what amounted to a revolution. From this observation one might argue that the heterogeneity in the system in the interwar years could have been related to the high rates of alliance activity on the part of "revolutionary" governments.

If one examines the period 1894-1914, one may observe that alliance initiation on the part of Italy (one instance) and Turkey (no instances) is notably absent. However, Russia and France are tied as the highest participants, with seven apiece. Revolutionary change may have made a difference for Italy's and Turkey's alliance behavior, but it apparently only increased the already high rate of participation by the Soviet Union. (With regard to the Soviet Union, it might be pointed out that as the largest nation in Eurasia it had frontier contact with more nations than any other nation. It may be that alliance behavior, at least before World War II, was in part a function of the extensity of frontier contacts. A similar process has been discerned with regard to participation in warfare.[24])

One additional point with regard to the "revolutionary" governments deserves mention. Between 1919 and 1932 republican Germany participated in only one instance of alliance initiation, but following the Nazi capture of power in 1933 (again, with subsequent changes that were revolutionary), Germany participated in seven instances of alliance initiation before the outbreak of World War II in 1939. In fact, between 1933 and 1939 Germany had the highest rate of alliance initiation.

There are several possible explanations for the fact that the "revolutionary" states have engaged in such high levels of alliance initiation. First, the alliance initiation could well have been motivated by a search for security. New governments or regimes may find that their internal characteristics are not approved by some other members of the international system, including, perhaps, former allies. In order to insure their national security, they may seek new alliance partners. Second, questions of legitimacy frequently plague revolutionary governments. It is frequently questioned whether they are the true representatives of the nation. One way of indicating both to their own citizenry and to unaccepting members of the international system that the government is, in fact, legitimate, is to enter into formal treaties with other established governments. The signing of a treaty with another nation may be seen in one sense as an act of legitimacy. Finally, since revolutionary regimes may have revisionist attitudes toward the distribution of power and resources in the international system or may wish to alter the internal organization of other states, they may require allies to achieve these goals.

The above explanations are each plausible. An inquiry into the extent that they actually did operate would require an analysis of the foreign policies of the various nations, which is a task beyond the scope of this chapter. However, it should be noted that they may have operated in combinations as well as singularly to contribute to the observed distribution of alliance initiation during this period.

1945-65

Turning to the postwar years, 1945-65, we find in Table 6.5 the data describing the distribution of alliance initiation. Again, as in the balance-of-power system, both the Poisson model ($\chi^2 = 7.28$, d.f. = 5, p = 0.20) and the contagious-heterogeneous model ($\chi^2 = 7.38$, d.f. = 5, p = 0.19) give fits to the data that cannot be rejected. Since neither model can be rejected, a decision must be made as to which model gives the better description. As we noted previously, when confronted with a choice between the two models, it is appropriate to choose the one with the fewer assumptions. Hence, parsimony suggests the choice of the Poisson process.

However, it may be profitable to look at the data for this period more closely from another perspective, especially since the value $s^2/\bar{x} = 2.04$ is statistically significant at $\alpha = 0.01$. In the years following the end of World War II, as the Cold War developed, two hostile blocs of nations emerged. Later, as numerous new nations entered the system, a different grouping developed. Some of these nations became allied with one or the other major bloc in the Cold War, while others did not. Making this distinction between nations that participated in Cold War alignments and those that did not, it becomes possible to examine, separately, the probabilistic behavior of these two groups within the area of alliance initiation.*

---

*The division of alliance activity into Cold War and non-Cold War categories was based on the following criteria: Cold War alliance activity was defined as that between (a) either of the bloc leaders and any other nation (for example, USSR-Hungary, 1948; (b) any two members of a bloc (for example, England-France, 1947); (c) any member of a bloc and a nation with whom they had a traditional role of patron (for example, England-Jordan, 1946). All other activity formed the residual category of non-Cold War. China's alliance activity was somewhat troublesome, since after the late 1950s it

TABLE 6.5

Instances of Alliance Activity, 1945-65

Number of Instances of Alliance Activity (i)	Number of Years (n_i)	Contagious-Heterogeneous Expected	Poisson Expected
0	1	1.88	0.62
1	4	3.24	2.18
2	4	3.62	3.84
3	2	3.32	4.52
4	6	2.70	3.98
5	0	2.03	2.80
6	1	1.45	1.65
7	2	0.99	0.83
8	0	0.66	0.37
9	0	0.42	0.14
10	0	0.27	0.05
11	0	0.17	0.02
12	1	0.10	0.00
13	0	0.06	0.00
$\bar{x} = 3.524$		$\chi^2 = 7.38$	$\chi^2 = 7.28$
$s^2 = 7.202$		d.f. = 5	d.f. = 5
$s^2/\bar{x} = 2.04**$		$\alpha = 2.413$	
		$\beta = 0.715$	

**Significant at $p \leq .01$.

Table 6.6 reports the data for the alliance initiation of the non-Cold War nations between 1945 and 1965. Again, as in the case of the entire system for the same dates, both the Poisson ($\chi^2 = 1.47$, d.f. = 2, p = 0.48) and the contagious-heterogeneous ($\chi^2 = 0.88$, d.f. = 2, p = 0.65) models may not be rejected. Again, on the ground of parsimony, we accept the Poisson as the appropriate model for the data.

---

was pursuing an independent line of policy. Since most of China's alliances after 1959 have been with Third World nations, we have placed it within the residual category after that date and in the Cold War category prior to 1959.

However, the results for the Cold War system, given in Table 6.7, are quite different. In the instance of the alliance initiation of these nations, the Poisson model is clearly rejected (χ^2 = 25.61, d.f. = 3, p < 0.001). The contagious-heterogeneous model may not be rejected (χ^2 = 3.79, d.f. = 4, p = 0.45).

As in the case of the years 1919-39, it is necessary to determine whether the process operating in the Cold War system is contagious or heterogeneous. Employing the methods used in the case of the interwar period, we find that the correlation between each nation's rate of alliance activity is r = 0.14 (p = 0.44). The low magnitude of this correlation indicates that probabilistic heterogeneity is not present in the data to any substantial degree.

The hypothesis of contagion, it may be recalled from the previous discussion, is most fruitfully explored by examining the data for first-order autocorrelation. If contagion is present, a high rate of alliance initiation in one year should provoke a high level of alliance initiation in the following period. For the data in Table 6.8 the value of Kendall's tau is τ = 0.30, which for the one-tailed test of significance against the null hypothesis of independence gives p = 0.032. Spearman's rank-order correlation yields a sample

TABLE 6.6

Non-Cold War Alliance Activity, 1945-65

Number of Instances of Alliance Activity (i)	Number of Years (n_i)	Contagious-Heterogeneous Expected	Poisson Expected
0	7	6.90	4.80
1	6	5.93	7.08
2	4	3.29	5.23
3	1	2.14	2.57
4	2	1.13	0.95
5	0	0.57	0.28
6	1	0.28	0.07
$\bar{x}$ = 1.476 s^2 = 2.535 $s^2/\bar{x}$ = 1.72*		χ^2 = 0.88 d.f. = 2 α = 1.113 β = 0.541	χ^2 = 1.47 d.f. = 2

*Significant at p $\leq$ .05.

TABLE 6.7

Cold War Alliance Activity, 1945-65

Number of Instances of Alliance Activity (i)	Number of Years (n_i)	Contagious-Heterogeneous Expected	Poisson Expected
0	9	7.51	2.24
1	3	4.16	5.01
2	1	2.72	5.61
3	3	1.87	4.19
4	2	1.31	2.34
5	0	0.93	1.05
6	1	0.67	0.39
7	1	0.49	0.13
8	0	0.35	0.03
9	0	0.26	0.01
10	0	0.19	0.00
11	0	0.14	0.00
12	1	0.10	0.00
$\bar{x} = 2.238$		$\chi^2 = 3.79$	$\chi^2 = 25.61$**
$s^2 = 9.039$		d.f. = 4	d.f. = 3
$s^2/\bar{x} = 4.04$**		$\alpha = 1.028$	
		$\beta = 1.396$	

**Significant at $p \leq .0$.

value of $r_s = 0.55$, which for the analagous test of independence against a positive ρ_s gives a p-value of $p = 0.005$. Both measures of correlation support the hypothesis of contagion against the alternative hypothesis of independence.

This finding directly supports the contention of Triska and Finley, that of Brzezinski, and that of Scott, that the alliance activities of the Western and Eastern blocs were not independent of each other.[25] In a more general sense it also serves to support the notion that action-reaction processes in international conflict are not limited to military budgets or to the flow of events between nations.

In summary, the analysis above leads us to conclude that over the time period 1815-1965 alliance initiation was characterized by several different processes. For the period 1815-1914 the alliance

TABLE 6.8

Time Series of Cold War Alliance Activity, 1945-65

Year	Instances	Year	Instances
1945	3	1956	0
1946	4	1957	1
1947	7	1958	0
1948	12	1959	0
1949	3	1960	0
1950	1	1961	1
1951	4	1962	0
1952	0	1963	0
1953	2	1964	0
1954	3	1965	0
1955	6		

initiation was random with respect to time. Between 1919 and 1939 the pattern of alliance activity was characterized by probabilistic heterogeneity. Finally, for the post World War II years (1945-65) the non-Cold War nations followed a random pattern of alliances initiated, while those nations within the Cold War system appear to have been influenced by the alliance behavior of other nations, and instances of alliance initiation in one period increased the probability of further initiation in a subsequent period.

CONCLUSION

This research has developed a largely descriptive model for the initiation of alliances during the period 1815-1965. The focus has been on the stochastic nature of the process in an attempt to explore aspects of randomness, contagion, and heterogeneity as characteristic factors of this period.

From the findings presented above, it is evident that the dynamics of alliance initiation have not been constant over time; rather, they have been characterized by several very different processes. This is interesting in at least two respects. First, the contagion of alliance activity is by no means a widespread phenomenon in the international system. Scott's suggestion that contagious processes were present in the balance-of-power system is not supported with these data.[26] To the extent that contagion has operated, the process is apparently quite limited except for the Cold War system between 1945 and 1965. However, since our data are confined to formal alliances, it remains quite possible that a data set drawn from informal alignments and coalitions might reveal contagion patterns. This methodologically difficult question remains to be investigated.

Second, the differences in the patterns of alliance initiation lend support to those who suggest that the international system has functioned differentially through time.[27] In this regard we might speculate that temporal patterns of alliance initiation may be an important variable in some international processes. For example, Singer and Small report that in the nineteenth century the amount of alliance aggregation is negatively related to war, while in the first half of the twentieth century (1900-45) there is a positive relationship.[28] There are, of course, a number of possible explanations of why this is the case. However, on the basis of the research presented above it might be speculated that the type of alliance activity through which aggregation takes place is an intervening variable, with random (or Poisson) behavior associated with the absence of war and contagious-heterogeneous behavior associated with its presence. This may be worthy of further research.

The research presented above, like so much research on new topics, raises further questions. Which factors are responsible for the changing patterns in the dynamics of alliance initiation? In future research we will focus upon this question and attempt to link these changes to a variety of development processes in the international system.

NOTES

1. For analyses of the nineteenth century, see Edward V. Gulick, Europe's Classical Balance of Power (Ithaca, N.Y.: Cornell University Press, 1955); Inis L. Claude, Jr., Power and International Relations (New York: Random House, 1962); A. F. K. Organski, World Politics (New York: Knopf, 1958). For analyses of the twentieth century, see Karl W. Deutsch and J. David Singer, "Multipolar Power Systems and International Stability," World Politics 16 (1964): 390-406; Richard N. Rosecrance, "Bipolarity, Multipolarity and the Future," Journal of Conflict Resolution 10 (1966): 314-27; Kenneth N. Waltz, "The Stability of a Bipolar World," Daedalus 93 (1964): 881-909.

2. Morton A. Kaplan, System and Process in International Politics (New York: Wiley, 1957).

3. Brian L. Job, "Alliance Formation in the International System: The Application of the Poisson Model," paper prepared for delivery at the 1973 Annual Meeting of the International Studies Association, New York, March 13-17, 1973; Patrick McGowan and Robert Rood, "Alliance Behavior in Balance of Power Systems: Applying the Poisson Model to 19th Century Europe," The American Political Science Review, forthcoming, 1976.

4. William J. Horvath and Caxton C. Foster, "Stochastic Models of War Alliances," Journal of Conflict Resolution 7 (1963): 110-16.

5. G. Udny Yule and M. G. Kendall, An Introduction to the Theory of Statistics (London: Griffin, 1950).

6. Lewis F. Richardson, The Statistics of Deadly Quarrels (Chicago: Quadrangle Books, 1960).

7. James S. Coleman, Introduction to Mathematical Sociology (New York: Free Press, 1964).

8. Simeon D. Poisson, Recherches sur la probabilites des jugements en maitiere criminelle et en maitiere civile (Paris: Bachelier, 1837). See also Alan E. Gelford and Herbert Solomon, "A Study of Poisson's Models for Jury Verdicts in Criminal and Civil Trials," Journal of the American Statistical Association 68 (1973): 271-78.

9. D. R. Cox and P. A. W. Lewis, The Statistical Analysis of a Series of Events (New York: Wiley, 1966).

10. Richardson, Statistics of Deadly Quarrels, p. 129.

11. Coleman, Introduction, p. 299.

12. Manus I. Midlarsky, "Mathematical Models of Instability and a Theory of Diffusion," International Studies Quarterly 14 (1970): 60-84.

13. A. J. P. Taylor, The Struggle for Mastery in Europe, 1848-1918 (Oxford, Eng.: Oxford University Press, 1954); William Langer, European Alliances and Alignments (New York: Vintage Books, 1950).

14. Andrew M. Scott, The Functioning of the International System (New York: Macmillan, 1967).

15. Jan F. Triska and David D. Finley, Soviet Foreign Policy (New York: Macmillan, 1968); Andrew M. Scott, "Challenge and Response: A Tool for the Analysis of International Affairs," The Review of Politics 18 (1956): 207-26.

16. Coleman, Introduction, p. 300.

17. Grace E. Bates and Jerzy Neyman, "Contributions to the Theory of Accident Proneness," University of California Publications in Statistics 1 (1952): 215-75; Grace E. Bates, "Joint Distributions of Time Intervals for the Occurrence of Successive Accidents in a Generalized Polya Scheme," Annals of Mathematical Statistics 26 (1955): 705-20.

18. Midlarsky, "Mathematical Models of Instability."
19. J. David Singer and Melvin Small, "Alliance Aggregation and the Onset of War, 1815-1945," in Quantitative International Politics, ed. J. David Singer (New York: Free Press, 1968), pp. 247-86; Melvin Small and J. David Singer, "Formal Alliances, 1816-1965: An Extension of the Basic Data," Journal of Peace Research 3 (1969): 275-82.
20. John E. Walsh, Handbook of Nonparametric Statistics, vol. 1 (Princeton, N.J.: Van Nostrand, 1962).
21. Cox and Lewis, Statistical Analysis of a Series of Events, p. 166.
22. William Feller, "On a General Class of 'Contagious' Distributions," Annals of Mathematical Statistics 14 (1943): 389-400.
23. Midlarsky, "Mathematical Models of Instability."
24. Richardson, Statistics of Deadly Quarrels; James P. Wesley, "Frequency of Wars and Geographical Opportunity," Journal of Conflict Resolution 6 (1962): 387-89.
25. Triska and Finley, Soviet Foreign Policy; Zbigniew K. Brzezinski, The Soviet Bloc: Unity and Conflict (Cambridge, Mass.: Harvard University Press, 1967); Scott, "Challenge and Response."
26. Scott, "Challenge and Response."
27. See Richard N. Rosecrance, Action and Reaction in World Politics (Boston: Little Brown, 1962).
28. Singer and Small, "Alliance Aggregation."

CHAPTER 7

POWER AND DISTANCE IN INTERNATIONAL CONFLICT BEHAVIOR
Manus I. Midlarsky

This study explores certain relationships between power and distance as they bear impact on international conflict behavior. Military interventions, crises, and certainly wars are dependent on the power or capabilities of the several actors involved, as well as on their respective distances from the conflict arena. Larger countries with greater power capabilities may be able to transport troops or materiel over longer distances, while smaller countries may be more limited in their scope of activity. Not only large-scale conventional wars but the conduct of more limited ones, such as Vietnam, may also be governed by such factors. As a result, these variables may be critical in understanding the onset and protraction of certain forms of conflict behavior.

Specifically, one can ask how the exercise of power varies with distance from the actor. Is the ability to exercise power distributed evenly over some distance from home, or does it decrease in some linear or curvilinear fashion? As an illustration, can the United States exercise power equally well in Southeast Asia and in Central America, or is it more likely that the exercise of power in more remote regions will lead to serious crises or interventions? Boulding has introduced an exact treatment of this general problem and therefore provides a useful point of departure for the present analysis.[1] A modification suggested by Wohlstetter also will be considered.[2]

Boulding analyzes two powers, G and H, with home bases located at g and h as shown in Figure 7.1. For purposes of conve-

---

This study was supported by a grant of the National Science Foundation, GS-40319.

FIGURE 7.1

The Exercise of Power as a Linear Function
of Distance for Two Countries, G and H

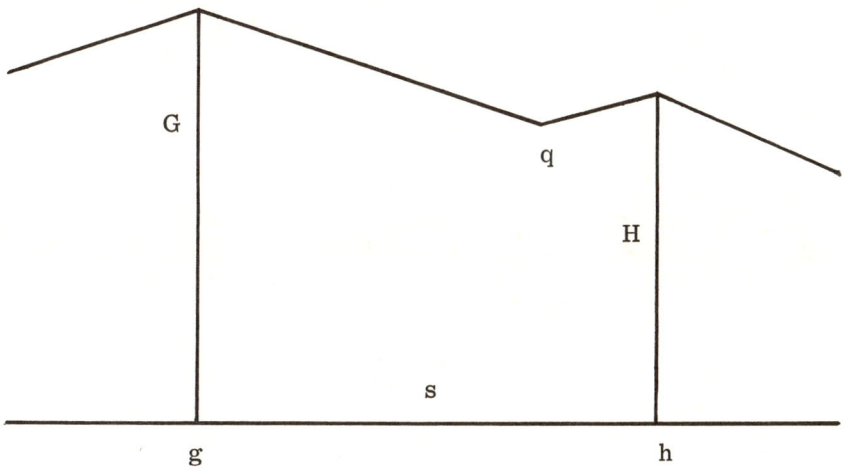

Source: Kenneth E. Boulding, <u>Conflict and Defense</u> (New York: Harper & Row, 1962), pp. 230-32.

nience, they are treated as points but can easily be expanded to cover a given area. Consider the power of both G and H, measured vertically, in relation to the distance, s, between them. (Boulding uses the term <u>strength</u>, and for purposes of the analysis here, the terms "power," "capability," and "strength," will be considered synonymous.) The power of each is at a maximum at g and h, respectively, or when the distance from each is zero and then decreases linearly as the distance increases from the home base. The country G is postulated to be somewhat more powerful than H. The point of intersection, q, is the point at which each can exercise equal capability, and, given Boulding's arguments covering the tendency for each country to expand its power at a point of maximum distance, q is also a point of maximum potential conflict. Note that q is somewhat closer to H than to G because of the initial power advantage that G enjoys, and the linear decrease of this power as distance from home increases.

Wohlstetter comments that the relationship between power and distance is not linear, but curvilinear and with discontinuities. He constructs a plot of lift capability versus distance from the continental United States that, when inspected, is seen to approximate a decreasing curvilinear function with a discontinuity at the upper end of the distance axis.[3] This plot is reproduced in Figure 7.2 (solid-line portion). The plot is data based and, in particular, the discontinuous portion represents the difficulties in reaching remote regions, such as the China-India border or other points in East Asia.

Despite these arguments and their geometric representations by Boulding and Wohlstetter, they have not been incorporated into a formal mathematical model that directly analyzes conflict as a function of power and distance. When such a model has been constructed, certain of the less obvious properties of these relationships may become evident and, in addition, it will be possible to carry out empirical tests to examine the validity of the model. In order to do so, we must first consider certain analytic properties of a formal definition of "power" in terms of uncertainty reduction.

Given the need to reduce environmental uncertainty in order to exercise power over some distance, we ask about the most likely or most probable uncertainty conditions that the actors will be facing. A theoretical distribution of power in relation to distance is then derived from these considerations, followed by the examination of a second theoretical distribution with similar properties to the first. Both are compared with the observed Wohlstetter distribution and are found to have some empirical validity.

These distributions are then used to derive two variants of a model relating power, distance, and international conflict behavior. With the increase in the probability of conflict as international uncertainty increases, the model is developed by examining changes in international uncertainty with changes in power and distance. The two variants of the model are then tested for their respective validities in the contexts of international crises and interventions.

POWER AS UNCERTAINTY REDUCTION

It has been found, upon a review of various treatments of power, that an important analytic strain in the literature is that of power defined as the ability to reduce environmental uncertainty and the exercise of power as the actual reduction of that uncertainty.[4] Beginning with Dahl's formulation of a change in probabilities in B's behavior as the result of A's intervention, through March's definition in terms of constraints on possible outcomes or Deutsch's changes in probabilities of outcomes, all suggest an uncertainty reduction as the result of a power exercise by a given actor.[5] The

FIGURE 7.2

Observed and Predicted Lift Capabilities
from the Continental United States

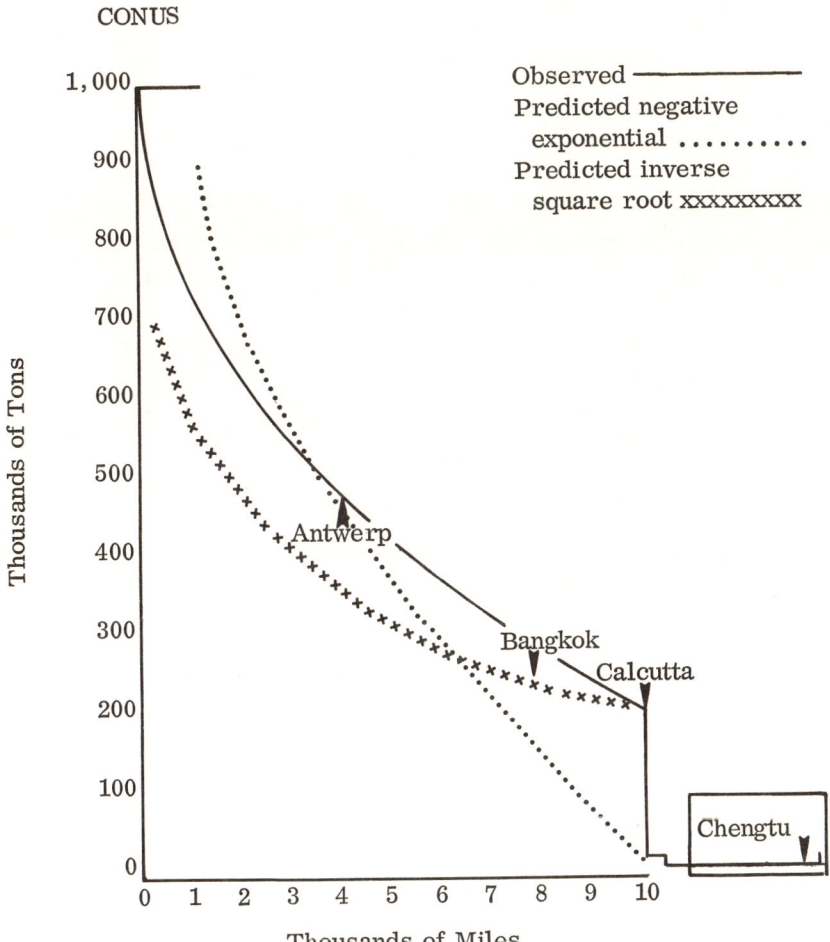

Source: Albert Wohlstetter, "Theory and Opposed-Systems Design," in New Approaches to International Relations, ed. Morton A. Kaplan (New York: St. Martin's Press, 1968), p. 43.

uncertainty at a later point in time, after the intervention by an actor, should be less than the corresponding state of uncertainty prior to the intervention. This has been formalized for the discrete case as an inequality of the form

$$U(X)_{kt_{j+1}} < U(X)_{kt_j} \qquad (7.1)$$

or

$$U(X)_{kt_{j+1}} - U(X)_{kt_j} < 0 \qquad (7.2)$$

where $U(X)_{kt_j}$ is the uncertainty facing actor k at time t_j with regard to the set of outcomes X, and $U(X)_{kt_{j+1}}$ is the uncertainty facing actor k at a later time, t_{j+1}, with regard to the same outcomes.[6] The difference between the two uncertainty values must be negative, thus indicating an uncertainty reduction over time. According to the definition, power is exercised when such a reduction has taken place.*

In general, the uncertainty $U(X)$ in the inequalities 7.1 and 7.2, for any actor k at time t, is given by

$$U(X) = -\sum_{i=1}^{N} p(x_i) \log_b p(x_i) \qquad (7.3)$$

where $p(x_i)$ is the probability of the occurrence of the ith outcome, x_i, and the logarithm is taken to an arbitrary base, $b > 1$, which will here be set equal to e for purposes of calculating the natural

---

*For the continuous case, an analogous treatment exists and, although the discrete case will be used throughout, it is offered here for the sake of completeness. A reduction of uncertainty can be said to exist when

$$\partial/\partial t \left[-\int_{-\infty}^{+\infty} f_k(x/t) \log f_k(x/t) dx \right] < 0$$

where $f_k(x/t)$ is the probability density function that defines the distribution of outcomes, x, facing actor k over the range of the temporal variable, t. This is a continuous version of the inequalities 7.1 and 7.2, with $f_k(x/t)$ the continuous analogue of the discrete distribution $p(x_i)$, and it states that the rate of change of the uncertainty associated with the function $f_k(x/t)$ is negative, meaning that a reduction of uncertainty has occurred over time.

or Naperian logarithm. This is the expression for uncertainty generally used in information theory as developed by original work by Shannon and Weaver in this area.[7] It will be particularly useful later when the outcomes are treated as nations ordered in a particular way in regard to distance from a geographical locus.

The Most Probable Distribution of Power in Relation to Distance

The question now is the most likely distribution of power in relation to distance that the various international actors will be facing. This distribution is also one of maximum uncertainty (greatest number of possibilities) and will be the one acted upon for the exercise of power as uncertainty reduction over the various distances, s_i, from home base for the several actors. Although there are many possible states of uncertainty, we should choose the one that is most probable, or the one that is most likely to occur. Fortunately, this problem has been worked out in detail for several different settings and can be applied directly to the problem of the most probable state facing the actors in an international setting.[8] One can begin by maximizing the uncertainty $U(X)$ in equation 7.3, but it is more instructive to start at a more basic point and see later how this process relates to the maximization of 7.3.

In order to exercise power over some distance, we require a unit that can be aggregated over a distance s_i. This unit could be tons of materiel that can be delivered effectively over that distance as will be seen later in an empirical examination of Wohlstetter's data. However, for our purposes we require a more generalizable unit that is not tied to a given metric. This unit is chosen to be a cell of arbitrary area, which can be made as small or as large as we please for any given analysis but which, once chosen, is constant for that analysis. Both Richardson and Wesley used cells of this type as country analogues in their derivations of models of international warfare, and both later relaxed this restriction in order to deal with the countries themselves.[9]

For convenience, let a single cell be a unit square (one centimeter, inch, or other unit of measurement on a side) that represents a particular area over which power can be exercised. Imagine a uniform grid containing many of these cells to be partitioned and distributed over the geographical area of the world. Let us now construct a hypothetical frequency distribution of these cells according to their distance from an international actor.

The number of cells would likely be greatest in categories of distance close to the actor, with smaller numbers of cells in categories of distance farther from the actor. Essentially, a histogram would be constructed in which the number of cells is measured on the vertical axis and geographical distance from the actor is measured on the horizontal. Such a histogram would provide a measure of the power of an actor measured in cell units, in relation to geographical distance from its borders. The greater the number of cells in the various distance categories, the greater the power of the actor over a given geographical distance; countries with less power would have fewer cells in each of the distance categories. Each international actor would have one such curve describing its power in relation to distance. As a result, a family of curves would be constructed, one curve for each actor, all having the same functional form, but with different parameters specifying the power or capability of each actor at varying distances from home. One plot among such a family of curves could be given by the solid line portion of Figure 7.2.

At this point, we do not know the precise functional form of this family of distributions. Given our state of ignorance, we should find the most probable distribution of these cells—the one that is most likely to occur.

Consider, then, a population of N unit squares or cells to be distributed among r categories of distance from a given actor. In order to find the most probable distribution of the N units, we must maximize the number of possible arrangements of these cells subject to whatever constraints exist. This yields the most probable distribution—the one that is most likely to be found at any given time and is the distribution that provides the greatest number of possible ways of organizing the N cells into the r distance categories. In the case of flipping an honest coin a large number of times, for example, the most probable (binomial) distribution would be 0.50 heads and 0.50 tails. Aside from obvious intuitive considerations, this result also can be found by maximizing the probability distribution of the outcomes, heads and tails. For several coins flipped simultaneously, as in the distribution of several cells, we can no longer use the binomial distribution, but must use the multinomial distribution given by

$$M = N!/n_1! n_2! \ldots \tag{7.4}$$

where M is the number of possible ways of arranging N objects into $1, 2, \ldots, r$ categories with n_r in the rth category. A constraint of the analysis is then given by

$$\sum_{i=1}^{r} n_i = N$$

In order to maximize the number of possible arrangements of the N cells, the value of M must be maximized. This maximization process will lead to a distribution given by equation 7.11. The derivation of 7.11 is not essential for the understanding of the later analyses of power, distance, and conflict, but for those who would be interested in the complete development, it is provided in the next several paragraphs. Readers who would be less interested in the derivation itself can proceed to equation 7.11 and the subsequent analyses.

Since maximizing the logarithm of a variable is equivalent to maximizing the variable itself, we can take logarithms of both sides of equation 7.4 and

$$\log M = \log N! - \sum_{i=1}^{r} \log (n_i!) \qquad (7.5)$$

The value of $\log (n_i!)$ is extremely difficult to evaluate without using Stirling's approximation in which

$$n_i! \simeq (2\pi n_i)^{\frac{1}{2}} (n_i/e)^{n_i}$$

and

$$\log (n_i!) \simeq n_i \log n_i - n_i + \log (2\pi n_i)^{\frac{1}{2}} \qquad (7.6)$$

The variation of log M at its maximum should be zero, and substituting the approximation for $\log (n_i!)$ in equation 7.5, we have

$$0 = \partial/\partial n_j (\log M) = -\sum_{i=1}^{r} \partial/\partial n_j (\log n_i!) =$$
$$-\sum_{i=1}^{r} [\log n_i + 1/(2n_i)] \, \partial n_i/\partial n_j \qquad (7.7)$$

where $j = 1, 2, \ldots, r$. The variation of log N! is zero because of its being constant in any given setting.

Now, the overall distance, S, is partitioned among the distance categories so that

$$\sum_{i=1}^{r} n_i s_i = S = \text{constant}$$

and as a result,

$$\partial/\partial n_j (S) = \sum_{i=1}^{r} s_i (\partial n_i/\partial n_j) = 0, \; j = 1, 2, \ldots, r \quad (7.8)$$

There is an additional constraint that the total number of cells, N, is constant so that

$$\partial/\partial n_j (N) = \sum_{i=1}^{r} (\partial n_i/\partial n_j) = 0 \quad (7.9)$$

Using Lagrange's method of undetermined multipliers, the last two equations, 7.8 and 7.9, are respectively multiplied by the constants K and L and added to equation 7.7. When the small term $1/(2n_i)$ is dropped, we have

$$\sum_{i=1}^{r} (\log n_i + L + K s_i) \, \partial n_i/\partial n_j = 0 \quad (7.10)$$

For any value of i, this becomes

$$\log n_i + L + K s_i = 0$$

and as a result

$$n_i = A' e^{-K s_i}$$

where A' and K are constants, and A' is equal to e^{-L}. Dividing through by the total number of cells, N, we have an expression in probabilistic terms

$$P_i = A e^{-K s_i} \quad (7.11)$$

where $A = A'/N$.

The constant A can be interpreted as a measure of power for that country that has a distribution of unit squares or cells (country analogues) at varying distances, s_i, from its borders. The greater the number of such units in the various distance categories, the greater the power of the actor. Each country would have a different value of A representing a given power distribution within a family of negative exponential curves along lines suggested by a collection of dotted-line portions of Figure 7.2.

This distribution of power in relation to distance from a given international actor is the most probable one—the one most likely to occur. Its derivation also can be understood from a somewhat different perspective. Because the small term $1/(2n_i)$ is dropped from equation 7.7, the first two terms on the right side of equation 7.6 are the only ones that contribute to the maximization procedure. (The variation of log $[2\pi n_i]^{\frac{1}{2}}$ with respect to n_j in 7.6 is equal to $\{1/[2n_i]\} \, \partial n_i / \partial n_j$.) When summed and translated into probabilistic format by dividing through by the total number N, these terms become the mathematical expression for uncertainty,

$$U = \sum_{i=1}^{N} p_i \log p_i \qquad (7.12)$$

In information theoretic terms, the greater the uncertainty, the greater the amount of information conveyed by a given message.[10] If there is a high degree of uncertainty, then the surprisal or information value of the message would be greater than if there were a low degree of uncertainty (high certainty) about an outcome, and the message then conveys little surprise value or information.

Thus, the information content of the particular state of affairs concerning power in relation to distance is maximized by this procedure and is expressed by the distribution 7.11. What this means in a broader sense is that whatever our state of knowledge or ignorance about the manner in which nations order their power relations with other nations based on distance, this is a "best guess" (most probable) estimate of the distribution that is most likely to occur, and it is one that maximizes our information in regard to relations between power and distance.[11] It can also be shown that for a given amount of information the distribution 7.11 also "conserves" distance or is least costly with regard to distance that has to be traversed in order to exercise power.[12]

Comparisons Among Theoretical and Observed Distributions

Now that we have obtained a theoretically derived distribution given by equation 7.11, it will be useful to compare it with the actual exercise of power by countries across geographical distance given by Wohlstetter. In addition, a second theoretical distribution with similar properties to 7.11 will also be compared with the observed data.

Wohlstetter has provided a plot of lift capability versus distance from the continental United States shown in Figure 7.2.[13] If we take this as simply indicating one measure of power or strength, then we can evaluate equation 7.11 as to its empirical adequacy. The values of A and K were calculated for a best estimate of the Wohlstetter distribution shown in Figure 7.2, with K calculated as the reciprocal of the mean of the observed distribution equal to 0.2963, and A as a normalizing constant so that the sum of the probabilities would equal unity. The value of A is equal to 0.3636. This theoretical distribution is plotted in Figure 7.2 as the dotted line over the solid line of the data collected by Wohlstetter.

The values of lift capability for shorter distances are overpredicted by the negative exponential distribution, but they are then underpredicted as one moves along the horizontal axis to longer distances. However, if one considers the discontinuous portion of the curve after 10,000 miles, the steeper descent of the exponential curve provides a useful continuous approximation to an average between the smooth and jagged portions of the curve. Given the comment by Wohlstetter that one must somehow account for deviations from linear prediction, then the approximation offered by the exponential may be appropriate.

However, as we saw, the distribution 7.11 was based on a "best guess" or most likely distribution predicated on our state of knowledge or ignorance about the real world. Given the data provided by Wohlstetter, there are several related distributions that are similar in form to the negative exponential and that may provide a better fit to these data. One such possibility is the family of inverse power functions of distance of the form

$$p_i = Cs_i^{-\kappa} \tag{7.13}$$

where C is some constant and a measure of power or capability, and κ is the exponent. As in the examination of the distribution 7.11, the parameters of this distribution were also computed. The value of κ was estimated as one-half and C was found to be equal to 0.1992. This theoretical curve was plotted as the line of x's in Figure 7.2. It provides a better approximation to the smooth portion of the curve; however, it all but ignores the discontinuous portion that may be critical for logistical operations in remote regions. Because the negative exponential more nearly approaches the discontinuous portion but the inverse power function more closely approximates the smooth portion of the curve, both will be considered in the following analysis of uncertainty and distance.

A MODEL OF CONFLICT BEHAVIOR

Until now, we have developed two theoretical distributions to compare with the observed Wohlstetter data. Given the definition of power exercise as the reduction of environmental uncertainty, a theoretical distribution of power in relation to distance was derived in equation 7.11 and a second related distribution was provided in equation 7.13. Both the negative exponential 7.11 and the inverse power function 7.13 have been compared with the Wohlstetter data and have shown some empirical validity, although in different areas. However, although we have found two distributions of power in relation to distance, we have not yet asked how these distributions bear on the problem of international conflict as found in the original Boulding formulation.

It will be recalled that when the exercise of power is roughly equal at a particular geographic locus, as at the point q in Figure 7.1, this is the point of maximum potential conflict.[14] Each of the actors tends to expand its influence at the point of equal power exercise, and overt conflict is more likely here than at points closer to the home borders. As such, there will be a greater degree of uncertainty as to eventual outcomes. Further, McClelland has shown that a greater degree of uncertainty appears in international crises than in relatively normal times.[15] An equiprobability (maximum uncertainty) of events occurs, and a threat, demand, conciliation, or promise is just as likely as a mobilization or troop intervention. McClelland's measures of both absolute and relative uncertainty increased substantially for both Berlin Crises (1948 and 1961), as well as the Taiwan Straits Crisis of 1958. This state of uncertainty among the actors might explode into violence at some point in time. Thus, an increase in uncertainty will likely portend the coming of some major form of conflict behavior, and the more rapid the rate of increase in areas of relatively high uncertainty, the greater the likelihood of intense conflict.

In another sense, the situation of high uncertainty may be a consequence of power competition among international actors, whereby the high state of uncertainty indicates the lack of capability of any single actor or alliance system of reducing the uncertainty in a desired direction.[16] This reduction of uncertainty, of course, is the definition of power exercise given in the inequalities 7.1 and 7.2. Still another related view is that of a steadily increasing uncertainty as an indicator of a growing power vacuum in which power is being exercised by no single agent, as a consequence of the relative equality of power at the locus of conflict. In any event, all of these perspectives suggest that international conflict of some variety would be expected at the locus of an uncertainty increase involving two or more international actors, as at the point q in Figure 7.1.

To examine the uncertainty increase associated with each of the two distributions, 7.11 and 7.13, we must first look to equation 7.11, which was originally derived for the distribution of power in relation to distance from a single actor. Now, in order to examine the uncertainty increase for two or more international actors contending at some geographical crisis point we must modify equation 7.11 to account directly for the presence of many actors, each having some distribution of power in relation to distance from its borders. Actor 1 would have one such distribution, actor 2 would have a second, and, in general, the ith country would have a distribution of the form 7.11, but with the probabilities explicitly normalized in the denominator to account for the total number of N cells or countries. In this instance, without much loss of generality, we can set N equal to the total number of countries rather than country analogues as in the previous section. Each of the countries would have a constant, A_i, as a measure of its power or capability at a distance s_i from its borders. Thus,

$$P_i(s_1, s_2, \ldots, s_N) = A_i e^{-Ks_i} / \sum_{j=1}^{N} A_j e^{-Ks_j} \qquad (7.14)$$
$$i = 1, 2, \ldots, N$$

where P_i is the proportion of power or influence exercised by the ith actor at a distance s_i from home. The index j is introduced to allow for the summation over all countries, including the ith power.

We want to know how the uncertainty varies upon some change in the distance. As one moves farther away from some geographical point, what is the impact on the uncertainty U? For example, if we begin at a location with a certain set of distances from the N countries and a particular uncertainty value U, what is the effect on the uncertainty when we arrive at some new location with a new set of distances from these countries? A similar problem in econometric theory has been solved by Theil,[17] and the answer is first provided by differentiating equation 7.3 (in its simpler form, as in equation 7.12) with respect to distance. Again, as in the earlier derivation, those not interested in the mathematics per se can proceed directly to equation 7.17. Thus,

$$\partial U/\partial s_j = \partial/\partial s_j \left[-\sum_{i=1}^{N} P_i \log P_i \right] = -\sum_{i=1}^{N} [\partial P_i/\partial s_j + \log P_i (\partial P_i/\partial s_j)]$$

$$= -\sum_{i=1}^{N} (1 + \log P_i) \partial P_i/\partial s_j \qquad (7.15)$$

In order to evaluate $\partial P_i/\partial s_j$, equation 7.14 is differentiated by parts, and

$$\partial P_i/\partial s_j = \partial/\partial s_j \left[A_i e^{-Ks_i} / \sum_{j=1}^{N} A_j e^{-Ks_j} \right] = -KP_i(1-P_i) \quad \text{for } i=j$$

$$= KP_i P_j \quad \text{for } i \neq j$$

Substituting in equation 7.15, we have

$$\partial U/\partial s_j = -\left[\sum_{i \neq j} (1 + \log P_i) KP_i P_j - (1 + \log P_j) KP_j (1-P_j) \right]$$

$$= -\left\{ KP_j \left[\sum_{i=1}^{N} (1 + \log P_i) P_i - 1 - \log P_j \right] \right\}$$

$$= KP_j (U + \log P_j) \qquad j = 1, 2, \ldots, N \qquad (7.16)$$

Since the uncertainty is an additive quantity and we want to know how all of the distances from the N countries contribute to the new value, we can sum the individual changes in uncertainty for all of the $j = 1, 2, \ldots, N$ countries, and translating the differentials into difference terms, the total change in uncertainty, ΔU, is approximated as

$$\Delta U \simeq K \sum_{j=1}^{N} P_j (U + \log P_j) \Delta s_j \qquad (7.17)$$

The increase in uncertainty is proportional to the increase in distance from its home territory for the jth power (or the ith, since both indexes run from 1 to N) and simultaneously, in the sense of a covariance, also is proportional to the sum of the uncertainty U and log P_j. For large values of P_j this sum would be large, and, as a result, the increase in uncertainty would be greater when countries with greater amounts of power or capability are a longer distance from home. Conversely, countries that have less power or influence will have less of an impact on this uncertainty increase.

Let us consider now the inverse power function, expressed by equation 7.13, which also approximated the observed distribution in Figure 7.2, but in a somewhat different manner. By constructing an analogous expression for the increase in uncertainty, we will be able to compare the two in regard to differences introduced by the use of the two separate functions.

In this case, we have

$$P_i(s_1, s_2, \ldots, s_N) = C_i s_i^{-\kappa} / \sum_{j=1}^{N} C_j s_j^{-\kappa} \qquad i = 1, 2, \ldots, N \qquad (7.18)$$

where, as before, C_i is a measure of power for the ith country, s_i is the distance to the point of conflict, and P_i is the proportion of power or influence exerted by the ith country. Differentiating by parts once again to obtain an expression for $\partial P_i / \partial s_j$ to substitute in equation 7.15, we have

$$\partial P_i / \partial s_j = \partial / \partial s_j \left[C_i s_i^{-\kappa} / \sum_{j=1}^{N} C_j s_j^{-\kappa} \right] = -\kappa P_i (1 - P_i) / s_j \quad \text{for } i=j$$

$$= \kappa P_i P_j / s_j \quad \text{for } i \neq j$$

The difference now between the use of the expression 7.18 and the negative exponential function 7.14 is the presence of s_j in the denominator. This translates into a modification of the form of equation 7.16 to be

$$(\partial U / \partial s_j) s_j = \kappa P_j (U + \log P_j) \qquad j = 1, 2, \ldots, N \qquad (7.19)$$

Upon noting that $\partial (\log s_j) / \partial s_j = 1/s_j$, summing over all of the individual changes in uncertainty, and putting the equation in difference terms, we have, approximately,

$$\Delta U \simeq \kappa \sum_{j=1}^{N} P_j (U + \log P_j) \Delta(\log s_j) \qquad (7.20)$$

Thus, the difference between using the inverse power function and the negative exponential is to be found in the variation of changes in uncertainty with changes in the logarithm of distance, rather than with simple linear distance as in equation 7.17. The greater uncertainty increase when larger powers are a longer distance from home is, of course, also a property of equation 7.20.

Applicability to Crisis Situations

In order to assess at least the face validity of equations 7.17 and 7.20, we consider two or more powers interacting at some distance from the home territory of each. Both equations 7.17 and 7.20 suggest that the greater increases in uncertainty will occur when larger powers are at longer distances from their home territory, or point of maximum power. With the proportion of power, P_j, large in equations 7.17 and 7.20, the value of log P_j is large, and the uncertainty increase therefore is high. Similarly, for Δs_j large, both the linear value of Δs_j itself and the logarithmic variant of $\Delta(\log s_j)$ will increase the uncertainty in both equations.

These equations imply that there are essentially two means of increasing the uncertainty values above the level specified by the value of U already existing in some location. The first is that of a small number of very large powers (for example, two) competing at long distances, while the second is by means of a larger number of smaller powers in a state of conflict over shorter distances. Clearly, the two processes are not mutually exclusive, since a larger number of great powers may compete at longer distances. The summation signs in equations 7.17 and 7.20 allow for any or all of the N countries to contribute to the uncertainty increase associated with the onset of the crisis. However, in practice, historically, these seem to be somewhat different avenues to intense conflict, with the former pattern of two competing superpowers tending to predominate in the post World War II period.

Suppose a number of crises are examined as forms of intense conflict to assess the face validity of equations 7.17 and 7.20. A list of such crises is found in Table 7.1. First, one observes that virtually all of these, especially the earlier ones, occurred around the periphery of one of the superpowers—in this case, the Soviet Union or one of its allies. Beginning with Iran in 1946 or the Berlin Crisis of 1948, a pattern of crisis activity occurred around the perimeter of the communist nations, with the Taiwan Straits Crisis of course having occurred in close proximity to the People's Republic of China. When we consider that the United States had preponderant nuclear power well into the 1960s, and in addition, the magnitude of its GNP was by far the largest in the world, the Soviets and Chinese were at a distinct power disadvantage. Given this power disparity, one would expect that the United States would be competing very close to the borders of the communist nations. With the exception of Cuba, which is treated shortly, no crisis occurred in close proximity to the United States. The Suez Crisis or that surrounding Cyprus would also have the property of some proximity to the Soviet Union, although here the presence of other actors with at least an equal degree of involvement, such as Britain or France, would make these instances perhaps conform better to the second variant, specified above, of the additional contribution of several smaller powers interacting at shorter distances from home territory. In any event, there appears to be some face validity to the power-distance covariation specified in equations 7.17 and 7.20.

The implications of these equations appear to be consistent with the historical record. However, the Cuban Missile Crisis is somewhat anomalous: A power disparity still existed in favor of the United States, although it was changing in the direction of the Soviets, and yet the crisis occurred close to U.S. borders. On the one hand, this could be viewed as an exception that violates the rule, and perhaps even invalidates it. On the other hand, perhaps it is this departure from a seeming regularity that demonstrates rather clearly the Soviet risk taking or gambling behavior by Khrushchev (coincident with his internal risk taking in the "virgin lands" episode in Siberia), and that largely predetermined its outcome. Given the power disadvantage at such great distances and only partial accuracy of Soviet missiles, the Soviets very likely would back down when confronted strongly. Consequently, this episode may have been an exception for the Soviet Union, whose expansionist or risk-taking tendencies have been characterized as only moderately aggressive since the end of World War II.[18]

The pattern of relative Soviet weakness shown in the earlier crises in Table 7.1 is not exhibited in later crises, such as the one that occurred at the end of the 1973 Arab-Israeli War. Here, the confrontation took place at a greater distance from Soviet borders, and in a manner that contrasts with the events of 1967. Whereas in the former Middle East War the Soviets were not in a position to challenge directly the potential victory of an opponent's client state, in 1973 they were able to do so successfully by virtue of an increased military capability in that area. Indeed, this new ability to bring power to bear at greater distances from its borders is suggestive of a substantial increase in Soviet power relative to the United States in recent years. Future crises between the United States and Soviet Union may occur in the vicinity of those trouble

TABLE 7.1

Sample of Crises Since World War II

Crisis	Year	Major Participants
Iran	1946	Great Britain, Soviet Union, United States, Iran
Berlin	1948	United States, Soviet Union, Great Britain, France
Korea	1950	United States, Soviet Union, North Korea, South Korea
Hungary	1956	Soviet Union, Hungary, United States
Suez	1956	Great Britain, France, United States, Soviet Union, Israel, Egypt
Lebanon	1958	United States, Soviet Union, Lebanon
Taiwan Straits	1958	United States, China
Berlin	1961	United States, Soviet Union
Cuban Missile	1962	United States, Soviet Union
Tonkin Gulf	1964	United States, North Vietnam, China
Cyprus	1964	Great Britain, Greece, Turkey, United States, Soviet Union
Ussuri River	1965	Soviet Union, China
Czechoslovakia	1968	Soviet Union, Czechoslovakia, United States
Mideast	1973	Soviet Union, United States, Israel, Egypt

areas (high uncertainty, $\cup$, in equations 7.17 and 7.20 where a slight increase in uncertainty may bring on an intense conflict situation or crisis at distances further removed from Soviet borders.

Thus far, we have largely pursued the first alternative of conflict between two great powers at long distances. But what of the second avenue, or the n-adic case of many actors at shorter distances experiencing a crisis situation as in 1914? Here, a relatively large number of somewhat smaller powers were in a state of conflict at a geographical location that was not particularly remote from any of them. The increase in uncertainty in this case can still be large as the result of summing over a larger number of actors in equations 7.17 and 7.20. The role of alliances is evident here, where a larger number of powers will be involved as the result of a crisis experienced by any single ally and the summation effect on $\triangle \cup$ can be pronounced. It is possible, then, that equally high values of increases in uncertainty may be reached in both bipolar (two large powers, long distances) and multipolar (many smaller powers, shorter distances) systems, but each differs from the other in the manner in which it is achieved.

Assessing Empirical Validity in the Context of Interventions

Although we have ascertained that there is at least a face validity to the increases in uncertainty indicated by equations 7.17 and 7.20, we have not yet suggested any empirical differentiation between the two equations. The two models agree on the covariation of power and distance with increases in uncertainty, but whereas equation 7.17 suggests that the covariation proceeds linearly with distance, equation 7.20 indicates a logarithmic relationship. It is possible to provide an empirical basis for assessing the adequacy of each. If P_j, the proportion of power or influence, is held constant in both equations, then the increase in uncertainty leading to conflict should vary linearly or logarithmically, depending on which equation has greater empirical validity. Thus, if a particular conflict form is chosen, it can be examined for linear or logarithmic covariation with distance. Intervention is a particularly serious form of violence short of international warfare and, in fact, several of the crises listed in Table 7.1 such as that of Hungary, Suez, Iran, or the Middle East in 1973 either were initiated by interventions or involved the presence of foreign troops on the territory of a threatened nation.

Data exist in which interventions are listed according to the power categories of the actors.[19] There are six such categories, established by Pearson, and he finds that the greater the power, the greater the distance at which the interventions take place. Whereas countries the size of Greece or North Korea will tend to intervene primarily at distances less than 500 miles from their borders, larger powers, such as the United States, Soviet Union, or China, will intervene at distances exceeding 3,000 miles from home. In one sense at least these data suggest that equations 7.17 and 7.20 are empirically valid. Larger powers tend to intervene at longer distances, while smaller ones intervene at shorter distances.

Given the categorization according to power in this data set, it can be held relatively constant, and the functional form of intervention with distance can be examined for the extent to which it is linear (equation 7.17) or logarithmic (equation 7.20), thus differentiating between the two equations. The first two power categories in

Pearson's analysis are combined in order to increase variation across all of the distance categories shown in Table 7.2. This category now consists of the United States, Soviet Union, Great Britain, France, and the People's Republic of China. These countries are the principal actors in the crises listed in Table 7.1. Furthermore, they together comprise the entire nuclear club with its attendant threat value until the close of the data period in 1967, the interventions having been examined in the period 1948-67.

The midpoint of each of the distance categories listed by Pearson was used to calculate the theoretical linear or logarithmic predicted interventions. In the first distance category, which was open-ended in Pearson's treatment, the maximum limit for distance set by Wohlstetter in Figure 7.2 (12,000 miles) was used to calculate the midpoint. The linear equation was calculated according to

$$l_i = 0.4129 \, s_i + C \qquad C = 0$$

where l_i is the number of interventions in the ith distance category, s_i, and the vertical intercept was effectively set equal to zero to conform to equation 7.17 in which the increase in uncertainty is zero at zero increase in distance. The predicted values are seen in the third column, with a chi-square "goodness of fit" value calculated between the predicted and observed values. This value is significant at $p < 0.01$, and indicates a considerable divergence between the theoretical and observed values.

The predicted values which are based on a logarithmic relationship between interventions and distance holding power constant are found in the fourth column according to the equation

$$l_i = 4.5030 \, \log_e s_i$$

with the variables defined in the same fashion. Here, the vertical intercept is zero because of the requirement that the logarithm of unity be equal to zero. The fit is considerably better in this instance, with a chi-square value having a probability range of $0.10 < p < 0.20$. Thus, the logarithmic relationship between interventions and distance deriving from equation 7.20 appears to provide a better fit to the data than does the linear relationship suggested by equation 7.17. However, the divergence between the actual and predicted values even in the logarithmic case, although nonsignificant, suggests that perhaps some additional linear or curvilinear component also is present. In any event, the logarithmic form expressed in equation 7.20 provides a usable theoretical statement which presents a reasonably good fit to the data.

There is an additional consideration having to do with the form of the function for both the linear and logarithmic cases. Both

TABLE 7.2

Observed and Predicted Frequencies of
Military Intervention, 1948-67

Distance[a] (Miles × 10^{-2})	Observed Number of Interventions[b]	Predicted Number of Interventions (Linear)	Predicted Number of Interventions (Logarithmic)
2.50	1	1.03	4.13
10.00	11	4.13	10.37
17.50	8	7.23	12.89
40.00	18	16.52	16.61
85.00	26	35.10	20.01
		$\chi^2 = 14.009$	$\chi^2 = 6.174$
		$p < 0.01$	$0.10 < p < 0.20$

[a] Midpoint of distance categories given in the data source.
[b] Interventions are for the United States, Soviet Union, Great Britain, France, and People's Republic of China.

Source: Frederic S. Pearson, "Geographic Proximity and Foreign Military Intervention," Journal of Conflict Resolution 18 (1974): 446.

forms suggest that the increase in uncertainty will be greater when larger powers are competing at longer distances, and with a greater increase of uncertainty, the greater the likelihood of the occurrence of an intense conflict. However, aside from the differences in linear or logarithmic variation, there is an additional distinction pertaining to the likelihood of conflict directly at the border. When $s_i = 0$ in the negative exponential (equation 7.14), the value of P_i is always equal to some quantity greater than zero but less than one, and is

$$P_i = A_i / \sum_{j=1}^{N} A_j e^{-Ks_j}$$

As a result, the uncertainty at the border is always some value greater than zero. On the other hand, it can be shown that $P_i \to 1$ as $s_i \to 0$ in the inverse power function (equation 7.18) and, as a result, the uncertainty is absolutely equal to zero at the border (see equation 7.3 or equation 7.12).

The former alternative of an uncertainty value greater than zero is somewhat more realistic in that it allows for a small probability of some conflict at the border of a great power. The Sino-Soviet confrontation of March-August 1969 along the Ussuri River is a case in point. To this extent, the negative exponential form, equation 7.14, is intuitively more satisfactory despite its inferior predictive power in comparison with equation 7.18. However, despite the small probability of a crisis occurring directly at a border, in practice, the vast majority of them occur at some distance, however small, from the borders of the great power. All that needs to be done in order to have $s_i \neq 0$ in equation 7.18 is to set $s_i = \varepsilon_i$, an infinitesimally small quantity, so that even if a crisis occurs virtually at the border, it still is understood to be a very small distance away. This, in fact, is the case for all practical purposes. Thus, equation 7.18 and its consequence, equation 7.20, are viable alternatives, especially in light of the better predictive power as demonstrated in Table 7.2.

CONCLUSION

The Boulding model of power and distance in relation to international conflict behavior has been put in mathematical form with the Wohlstetter modification incorporated in the model. Two versions of the model are developed. Initially defining the exercise of power as uncertainty reduction, a "best guess" or most probable theoretical distribution of power in relation to distance is derived; in addition a related empirical distribution is found to be applicable. The two variants of this model of conflict behavior are derived, based on the two distributions, and both suggest the covariation of uncertainty increase with power and distance, although one indicates a linear relationship with distance while the other is logarithmic.

When international crises are examined, the overall relationship between power, distance, and international conflict behavior suggested by both versions is shown to have face validity. The greater the power of the international actors and the longer the distances from one or more of the participants, the greater the uncertainty increase as an indicator of crisis formation. In addition, interventions as a form of international conflict behavior demonstrate a logarithmic variation with distance when power is held constant, thus suggesting the greater applicability of one of the two varieties of the model. The discontinuity found by Wohlstetter and shown in

Figure 7.2 apparently does not pose a serious limitation on the propensity of great powers to intervene at long distances expressed in logarithmic terms. All of this, of course, is based initially on the definition of power exercise as uncertainty reduction, and given other definitions of power, additional models relating power to distance and international conflict behavior could be derived.

Future tests of this model should systematically vary the remaining parameters and also assess the extent of applicability to other forms of conflict behavior. In this fashion, the mathematical expression for power and distance in relation to international conflict behavior can be tested in several different ways and in a variety of empirical settings.

NOTES

1. Kenneth E. Boulding, Conflict and Defense: A General Theory (New York: Harper & Row, 1962), pp. 230-32.
2. Albert Wohlstetter, "Theory and Opposed-Systems Design," in New Approaches to International Relations, ed. Morton A. Kaplan (New York: St. Martin's Press, 1968), pp. 19-53.
3. Ibid., p. 43. There is a second plot of lift capability versus distance provided by Wohlstetter on p. 44, but its reproduction here would constitute an unnecessary duplication.
4. Manus I. Midlarsky, "Power, Uncertainty, and the Onset of International Violence," Journal of Conflict Resolution 18 (1974): 395-431.
5. Robert A. Dahl, "The Concept of Power," Behavioral Science 2 (1957): 201-15; James G. March, "Measurement Concepts in the Theory of Influence," Journal of Politics 19 (1957): 202-26; Karl W. Deutsch, The Analysis of International Relations (Englewood Cliffs, N.J.: Prentice-Hall, 1968), p. 24.
6. Midlarsky, "Power, Uncertainty, and Violence," pp. 405-07.
7. Claude E. Shannon and Warren Weaver, The Mathematical Theory of Communication (Urbana, Ill.: University of Illinois Press, 1964).
8. Among the many treatments of problems of this form in the literature of statistical physics, one of the most straightforward introductory analyses is found in Earle H. Kennard, Kinetic Theory of Gases: With an Introduction to Statistical Mechanics (New York: McGraw-Hill, 1938), pp. 351-54.
9. Lewis F. Richardson, Statistics of Deadly Quarrels (Pittsburgh: Boxwood Press, 1960), pp. 290-91; James Paul Wesley, "Frequency of Wars and Geographical Opportunity," Journal of Conflict Resolution 6 (1962): 387-89.

10. The major exposition of this information-theoretic perspective is found in Shannon and Weaver, Mathematical Theory of Communication.

11. The interpretation that the distribution of the form 7.11 is one that makes maximum use of our knowledge about a given state of affairs is found in E. T. Jaynes, "Information Theory and Statistical Mechanics," Physical Review 106 (1957): 620-30.

12. This argument as it relates to "costliness" of words is found in Benoit Mandelbrot, "Simple Games of Strategy Occurring in Communication Through Natural Languages," Transactions of the IRE: Professional Group on Information Theory (March 1954): 124-37.

13. Wohlstetter, "Theory and Design," p. 43.

14. Boulding, Conflict and Defense, pp. 230-32. Also see A. F. K. Organski, World Politics, 2d ed. (New York: Knopf, 1968), passim.

15. Charles A. McClelland, "Access to Berlin: The Quantity and Variety of Events, 1948-1963," in Quantitative International Politics: Insights and Evidence, ed. J. David Singer (New York: Free Press, 1968), pp. 159-86. Also see Charles A. McClelland, "The Beginning, Duration, and Abatement of International Crises: Comparisons in Two Conflict Arenas," in International Crises: Insights from Behavioral Research, ed. Charles F. Hermann (New York: Free Press, 1972), pp. 83-105.

16. Manus I. Midlarsky, On War: Political Violence in the International System (New York: Free Press, 1975), pp. 60-93.

17. Henri Theil, Statistical Decomposition Analysis: With Applications in the Social and Administrative Sciences (Amsterdam: North-Holland, 1972), pp. 43-45.

18. William Welch, "Soviet Expansionism and Its Assessment," Journal of Conflict Resolution 15 (1971): 317-27.

19. Frederic S. Pearson, "Geographic Proximity and Foreign Military Intervention," Journal of Conflict Resolution 18 (1974): 432-60.

CHAPTER 8

RICHARDSON'S MODEL AS A MARKOV PROCESS
Philip A. Schrodt

To the reader accustomed to the traditional view of history and international politics as the product of the interaction of virtually countless individual factors, many of them unique to each situation, perhaps the most unsettling feature of most mathematical models of arms races is their determinism. Lewis F. Richardson, formulating the first arms-race model, anticipates this criticism as he has the "Critic" in <u>Arms and Insecurity</u> ask, "But why equations? History is not mechanical."[1]

In the earliest discussion of Richardson in modern political science literature, Rapoport is also sensitive to the deterministic nature of the models.[2] He goes into considerable detail distinguishing between the "mathematical history" of Richardson and Rashevsky and the mystical determinism of Hegel or the "semi-mystical rationale" of Marx and Toynbee. The deterministic processes of Richardson are "models which are the simplest to handle mathematically and which have only the barest resemblance to some intuitive notions about what <u>may</u> be happening. . . ."

While Richardson has a somewhat different justification for the deterministic process than Rapoport, it is still hardly an argument that inspires confidence in his model: "The process is what would occur if instinct and tradition were allowed to act uncontrolled. In this respect the equations have some analogy to a dream."[3] Since instinct and tradition do not act uncontrolled in contemporary international relations, we are presumably left with the dream alone.

This work was supported in part by the National Science Foundation under Grant GS-36806. I would like to express my appreciation to Dina A. Zinnes for her criticisms of earlier drafts of this chapter.

Considerable work has been done in arms-race modeling since the pioneering efforts of Richardson, all attempting to get that dream somewhat closer to reality. This has generally pursued two different lines of attack on the problem.

The first approach is to expand the Richardson model by including more parameters, economic constraints, disaggregated measures of threat and economic burden, and so forth. Caspary, Chatterji, Wolfson, and Wright could be included here, as could Richardson himself.[4] The "submissiveness" model of Richardson is an extension of his simpler, linear model, taking in situations where one of the competing nations "gives up" the arms race and submits to being the inferior power. The problems inherent in this approach are well illustrated by Chatterji, who formulates a very elaborate model but can do very little with it analytically.

The second approach is to derive Richardson's model, or other models, from assumptions that are more "rational" than Richardson's "what people would do if they did not stop to think." Among these authors would be Brito, Simaan and Cruz, and Abelson.[5] This approach might be characterized as "rational determinism"; it argues that the arms-race process could be deterministic simply because every actor is following his own best interest by following that model, and thus there is no reason to deviate from it. The Simaan and Cruz article, utilizing dynamic game theory, is a particularly good example of this.

These approaches have continued to use deterministic models, despite the fact that none of the models have come anywhere near the accuracy one would expect if the arms race were deterministic and obeyed the proposed model. Yet to a certain extent this use of deterministic models, even in the face of what seems to be a more random process, is useful. Rapoport's observation that deterministic models are simpler to handle mathematically should not be overlooked, nor should the desire for mathematical tractability be attributed merely to laziness on the part of the modeler. In the biological sciences, for example, deterministic models are often used to study processes that are clearly dependent in part upon random events, and these models often prove to be very good approximations to those processes. In nondeterministic models, with remarkable rapidity and appallingly few useful results, one often reaches the limits of one's ability to handle the model mathematically. With few exceptions, a given amount of time invested in a deterministic model will probably yield more interesting results than that same time invested in a probabilistic model. Had we from the very beginning attempted only to use nondeterministic models to study arms races, we would probably have only a small fraction of the literature we presently have in that area, without necessarily having any results that would be more useful or interesting than those found through deterministic models.

Nevertheless, it would appear to be wise at some point to drop the deterministic assumption and pursue the implications of nondeterministic models. In fact, even if the world is indeed deterministic, we may wish to work with nondeterministic processes. Just as deterministic models can be good approximations of probabilistic processes if the random effects in those processes are either small or cancel each other out, so can a nondeterministic model be a good approximation of a deterministic process that contains a large number of deterministic variables about which little is known and whose net effect appears to be random.

The question of whether we are actually dealing with a random process or merely with a deterministic process that appears to be random may ultimately prove to be a question more suitable for philosophical debate than for empirical verification. That bastion of determinism in the nineteenth century, the physical sciences, is now probablistic in its fundamental theories. In applications, however, determinism is still of considerable use: While statistical mechanics allows that a glass of water might go up when released, one will rarely err if one predicts that it will fall to the floor.

The purpose of this chapter is to deal with a probabilistic interpretation of the arms-race process. Our interpretation will have a specific goal in mind: We will be attempting to find stochastic processes that would have the Richardson arms-race model as their expected value. To a certain extent this exercise is parallel to that of the studies that derive the Richardson model from assumptions of rational behavior on the part of the actors. We will derive the deterministic Richardson model as the expected value of a random process.

The choice of the Richardson model rather than some other arms-race model is due to three factors. The first might be called traditional: Richardson's model is certainly the model all of the other studies start from, and there is no apparent reason not to start with it. Second, the Richardson model has had a reasonably good record of providing significant empirical fits to data from arms races and has been more extensively tested than any other model.[6] It would thus appear that the Richardson model is providing at least an approximation to something going on in the real world. Third, the mathematical form of Richardson's basic model—specifically, its linearity—will make our mathematical task easier, even when dealing with stochastic processes.

In view of its rather limited objectives—the reinterpretation of an existing theory of arms races—this chapter will be primarily heuristic in nature. We are more interested in the nature and assumptions of the stochastic processes as they relate to a social process such as an arms race, rather than in the detailed mathematics involved in studying such processes. While a certain amount of mathematics is used and a knowledge of probability theory is necessary for a complete understanding of this chapter, the gist of it can be understood without recourse to equations.

THE RICHARDSON ARMS-RACE MODEL

Throughout this chapter we will be using the "discrete time" version of Richardson's model, which assumes that arms level decisions are made on a yearly basis. Richardson's original model, through its use of differential equations, implicitly assumed that decisions were made continually. While this assumption is proper when discussing accelleration or the movement of water droplets in clouds, it encounters a number of conceptual problems when applied to arms races. As best as we can observe, armaments are decided by budgetary expenditures, which occur only at discrete intervals. While the actual available military force that a nation has is continuously changing (due to recruitment, illness, equipment breakdowns, and so forth), most of this change is due to random factors that are largely independent of the intentions of the decision makers.

The discrete time model can be written as follows:

$X(t+1) = kY - aX + g$

$Y(t+1) = \ell X - bY + h$

where the parameters have the same general meanings as in Richardson's differential equation model.

In the deterministic case there are substantial differences between the analysis of a discrete-time and continuous-time model, particularly with respect to stability. Although, generally, continuous-time models are easier to work with mathematically, the discrete-time model will be easier to use when working with a Markov chain stochastic process.

STOCHASTIC PROCESSES

Any mathematical model of a dynamic system that contains random elements is a stochastic process. The term <u>stochastic</u>

means that the exact values that the variables described by the model will have in the future cannot be predicted with certainty. Instead, only the probability distributions of those variables can be predicted. This is in contrast with deterministic models, such as Richardson's, where the parameters of the model and the initial values of the variables uniquely determine the precise values of the variables for all future points in time.

The classical example of a stochastic process is the "random walk." In its more picturesque version, imagine a drunken man attempting to follow a path across an open field. Being somewhat unsteady, each step our inebriated friend takes forward also produces a step to the right or to the left. For mathematical simplicity, we can assume that each sideways step is of equal length and that the right and left direction occurs with equal probability. Figure 8.1 gives three possible routes that might be taken across the field: Each of these was produced randomly by flipping a coin at each point to determine whether the step was to the right or the left.

By analyzing this stochastic process using probability theory, we can reach a number of interesting conclusions. For example, we can prove that if it takes n forward steps to get across the field, then there are 2^n different routes that might be taken, and each of them is equally probable. We could compute the probability that the drunken man is k sideways steps from the path after r forward steps, or the probability that he will cross the path m times during his wanderings, and so forth. In short, while we cannot predict exactly which route will be taken, we can say quite a bit about the characteristics of the probability distribution of that route.

As in a deterministic model, the mathematical assumptions behind a stochastic process must be explicitly specified. One cannot become relaxed and sloppy about specifying the model "because everything is random anyway. . . ." To the contrary, in many cases the rationale for choosing particular probability distributions for the random elements of the model may be very complex. Furthermore, the mathematics involved in dealing with stochastic processes is generally more involved than that dealing with deterministic processes, since one must work with probability distribution functions rather than with single points. This can be partially avoided in many cases by working only with summary measures of the distribution, such as the expected value, rather than the distributions themselves. This approach will be used in this chapter.

In addition to wanting to know probability distributions for each point in time, one is also often concerned with the long-run behavior of the process. In deterministic systems, these questions are dealt with by studying the equilibrium and stability properties

RICHARDSON'S MODEL

FIGURE 8.1

"Random Walk" Routes, Illustrating the
Stochastic Process

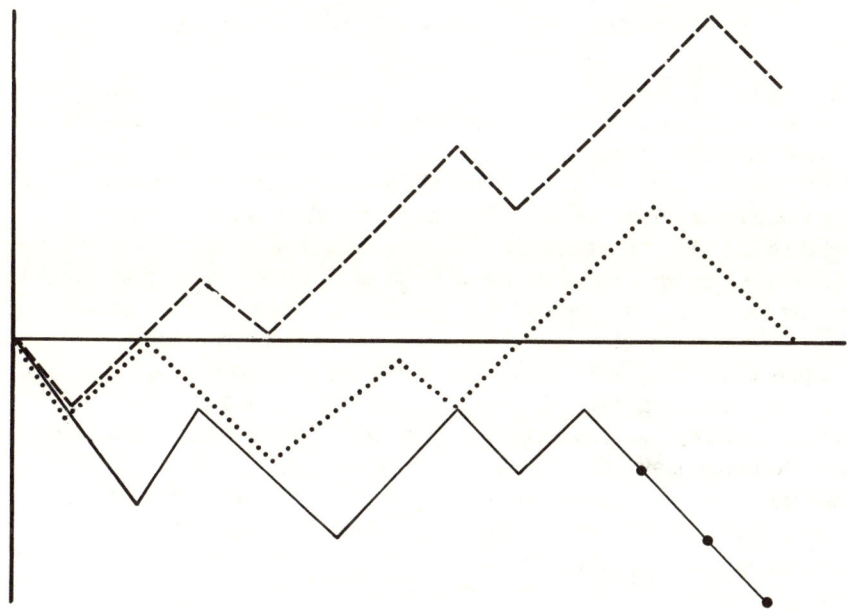

of the model. For example, many stable deterministic systems, if allowed to operate for a sufficiently long time, will "settle down" to the equilibrium point and stop changing.

Since a stochastic process is subject to random influences, we will not necessarily expect it ever to stop changing. Instead, we are interested in knowing whether the probability distribution will stop changing. A stochastic process that has this property is said to be <u>ergodic</u>. An ergodic process, instead of settling down to a single value, as a deterministic system does, settles down to a unique random variable, whose value may change but whose probability distribution does not change.

There are a number of different "standard" models of stochastic processes, many of which have been studied in great detail by mathematicians. The random walk is one such model: Its applications are much broader than merely tracking meandering drunkards across fields, seeing use in the study of Brownian motion, statistical mechanics, and nonparametric statistics. This chapter will apply some simple results from another standard model: the Markov chain. The more difficult, and potentially more productive, approach is to develop a stochastic model specific to the problem at hand, and this, of course, is how the models that are "standard" came into being.

RICHARDSON'S MODEL AS A MARKOV CHAIN

The class of stochastic processes known as Markov chains is one of the most widely studied of all stochastic processes, having been around for most of the twentieth century. Markov chains have been used in several studies in quantitative international relations.[7] Most of these applications have dealt with the changing state of the perceptions nations have of each other; in the past Markov chains have not been used specifically in the study of arms races.

A Markov chain is based upon the "transition probabilities" of the process transferring from one "state" to another. If we are modeling arms races, the "state" of the system is a level of armaments. Unlike the Richardson model, the Markov chain cannot be used to predict exactly what arms level a nation will have at the next point in time, given that the current arms levels are known. Instead, the Markov chain model only gives the exact probability distribution over a range of possible arms levels in the next time period.

For example, suppose nation X has 100 "units" of armaments and nation Y has 75 units. We can assume, rather realistically, that there are a number of different possible arms levels that each nation might have in the next year. X might increase its level to 105, decrease to 90, stay at 100, and so forth. The probabilities that X will take each of these alternatives form the transition probabilities for the Markov process. In a very simple model, involving only three alternatives, we might have the following transition probabilities:

$$X_{t+1} = \begin{cases} 95 \text{ with probability } 0.40 \\ 100 \text{ with probability } 0.20 \\ 105 \text{ with probability } 0.40 \end{cases}$$

Nation Y will have a similar function:

$$Y_{t+1} = \begin{cases} 70 \text{ with probability } 0.30 \\ 75 \text{ with probability } 0.05 \\ 80 \text{ with probability } 0.65 \end{cases}$$

If we now combine both these functions and make the further assumption that the two choices are made independently (in other words, while Y is influenced by X's armament at time t, Y does not know, or at least is not influenced by, X's armament at time t+1 when it makes its decision about its own arms level at time t+1, and similarly for X), we can deduce the following:

$$(X_{t+1}, Y_{t+1}) = \begin{array}{l} (95, 70) \text{ with probability } 0.12 \\ (95, 75) \text{ with probability } 0.02 \\ \quad \cdot \\ \quad \cdot \\ \quad \cdot \\ (105, 75) \text{ with probability } 0.02 \\ (105, 80) \text{ with probability } 0.26 \end{array}$$

The general relationship is as follows:

$(x, y) = (\text{probability } X_{t+1} = x) \cdot (\text{probability } Y_{t+1} = y)$

This is the simplist example of the type of transition that one finds in a Markov chain, a single "step" from one set of arms levels to another. In order to apply this type of stochastic process to a general arms-race model, we must elaborate it in several different ways.

First, the transition probabilities must be stated for all possible arms levels. The example we gave might be very plausible when $X_t = 100$ and $Y_t = 75$, and it could conceivably be correct for other arms values in the vicinity of those, but it wouldn't make much sense when $X_t = 1,000$ and $Y_t = 3,000$. In fact, we would probably define the model so that the transition probabilities were different for every possible armament level. This could lead to a very complicated model of course—one of the drawbacks in working with Markov chains.

Furthermore, the transition probabilities are dependent not only upon the nation's own armaments level but also upon the arms level of its opponents. Refering to our example again, we would expect the transition probabilities of X to be very different, depending on whether the arms level of Y was 75 or 150, even if X had an arms level of 100 in both cases.

In short, the transition probabilities for each nation are a function of the current levels of arms that each nation has. We will use the following notation for that function:

$T_x(p; r, s)$ = the probability that nation X has arms level $X_{t+1} = p$, given that $X_t = r$ and $Y_t = s$
$T_y(q; r, s)$ = the similar function for nation Y

As we will see below, both of these will be "probability density functions," which are the continuous-variable analogue to individual probabilities. In order to be density functions, T_x and T_y will satisfy the following:

$$\int T_x(u; r, s) \, du = 1 \quad \text{for all } (r, s)$$

$$\int T_y(v; r, s) \, dv = 1 \quad \text{for all } (r, s)$$

Another elaboration is in the number of possible arms levels the nation can have at the next time. In our example there were only three: In reality there will be a far greater number. In fact, the number of possible alternative future arms levels is so great that the mathematics is greatly simplified if one considers a continuous (that is, infinite) number of alternatives. In doing this, one uses a "probability distribution function," instead of assigning individual probabilities to each alternative. There are a number of familiar probability distribution functions available—for example, the normal distribution, which is widely used in statistics.

The use of a continuous distribution is open to some question. Some individuals have argued that an arms race is a discrete process: A government is going to decide an arms budget only down to the last dollar or so, or more likely only down to the last few million dollars. On the other hand, the amount of money spent on arms is not the sole determinant of the "arms level." Between the time the money is allocated and the time the arms are actually available for use, innumerable random factors intervene, ranging from clerical errors and bureaucratic politics to vagaries in manufacturing processes. We most likely have a continuous stochastic process by the time the arms are produced, even if the initial budget decisions were discrete and/or deterministic. While there may be some primitive arms races where a discrete model would be more appropriate (perhaps between two rival Neanderthals chipping arrowheads), in most instances the continuous model is realistic as well as tractable.

So far we have discussed only elaborations of the simple transition given earlier. What actually distinguishes a Markov chain from other stochastic processes are the restrictions on the transition functions. There are two of these.

The first, called the "stationarity property," states that the probability of transferring between two given states does not depend on time. In other words, the transition probability functions do not change as the process progresses. If the system is in the state (100, 75), the probabilities of the next state of the system will be the same whether the time is 1950 or 1970.

The second restriction, called the Markov property," says that the transition probabilities are dependent only upon the current state of the system and not upon any of the previous states. So far we have noted that the transition function can change with the different possible armaments levels of both nations involved. Mathematically, we could further elaborate so that it also depended upon the history of the arms race before the current state. However, if this were done, we would no longer have a Markov chain stochastic process.

Both the stationarity property and the Markov property are necessary in order to use the theorems associated with Markov chains. As with most restrictions, they are somewhat objectionable in terms of real-world arms races. Because of changes in governments, technology, and so forth the behavior of an arms race in 1970 will probably be quite different from the behavior in 1950. Decision makers, in deciding arms level, do take into consideration more than the current level of arms: The past behavior of the opponent nation and the past reaction of one's own nation to the arms race are certainly factors in the decision.

It is interesting to note, however, that these restrictions are precisely the same as found in the Richardson model. The usual Richardson model has no provision for changing behavior through time. The $X(t+1)$ and $Y(t+1)$ values are the same for a given (X, Y), irrespective of the time of the change. Similarly, in the Richardson model only the current level of arms is taken into consideration in determining the next level of arms. Thus, while the restrictions on the Markov chain model may be somewhat uncomfortable in real-world application, they are no more restrictive than the assumptions implicit in Richardson's model.

It should also be noted that it is possible to get around both restrictions and still work with stochastic processes where quite a lot can be done. One can include "past history" in the transition function simply by changing the definition of the "state" of the system to include not only the current value but the past values as well. This yields an "expanded" Markov process with a much more complicated state-space, but with respect to that state-space it has the Markov property. Stochastic processes where the transition probabilities vary through time can be dealt with using "stochastic differential equations." For linear equations particularly, the theory is fairly complete here.

The one other restriction we put on the process is that the two transitions be independent of each other. While this may not be strictly the situation, it is the least objectionable condition we must place on the process. Governments generally try to keep future arms levels confidential, and while speculation on an opponent's future arms level may have some effect, the final arms level itself would have little effect, since it is unknown.

Now that we have thoroughly defined the properties that the transition functions must satisfy, we can look at some of the properties of the "solution" of the model. As mentioned above, the solution of a stochastic process does not give the actual values the process will take on through time but only the probability distribution of those values. We will use the following notation for those probabilities:

$S_X(p, t)$ = probability density function for the armament level of X at time t

and similarly for $S_Y(q, t)$. By "solving" the Markov chain, we will mean arriving at values for the functions S_X and S_Y, given that we know the transition functions T_X and T_Y and that we know the initial value of the system.

For a Markov chain, the solutions are given through a relatively simple formula called the Chapman-Kolmogorov Equation. The principle behind this equation is that to find the probability that $X_t = p$, one must consider all the possible values that X_{t-1} could have had, and for each of those possible values multiply the probability that X_{t-1} actually had that value, times the probability that it took on the value p at time t, given that it had the value at t-1 (that is, the transition probability). One gets the probabilities for X_{t-1} by doing a similar exercise for X_{t-2} and so forth, working backwards until one finally reaches the initial time, where the values of the system are known. At that point, the whole business can be solved forward again to get actual values.

In practice, this is all very complicated. Since we are working with two nations, we need to consider all possible values of X_{t-1} and Y_{t-1}, and work with two separate equations. Actually solving for S_X and S_Y would be very involved, though it could be done without too much difficulty on a computer. Nevertheless, the Chapman-Kolmogorov equations themselves are easily written:

$$S_X(p, t) = \iint T_X(p; u, v) S_X(u, t-1) S_Y(v, t-1) \, du\, dv$$

$$S_Y(q, t) = \iint T_Y(q; u, v) S_X(u, t-1) S_Y(v, t-1) \, du\, dv$$

While the formal mathematics of deriving these relations is not simple, it can be seen just by looking at the equations that they are based on the idea of summing (integrating) all the possible arms levels the system could have come from times the probability that it was there. For a thorough discussion on the derivation of these equations (or most any other aspects of probability theory), see Feller.[8]

By use of these equations, we are now able to prove the result that a deterministic Richardson model could be the "expected value" of an arms race that is actually governed by a Markov process, provided that the transition function satisfies one additional requirement that we will give below. But first, we will give for purposes of reference the definition of the <u>expected value</u> of the process:

$$E_X(t) = \int S_X(u, t) \, u \, du$$

$$E_Y(t) = \int S_Y(v, t) \, v \, dv$$

This expectation is a function of time since the solution of the stochastic process is also a function of time. "Expected value" is analogous to the concept of an "average": It is the sum (integral) of all possible values the random variable might take on, times the probability that they will have that value.

Using these definitions, we have the following theorem:

<u>Theorem</u>. The expected values $E_X(t)$ and $E_Y(t)$ of a Markov chain with transition probability functions T_X and T_Y will be identical to the solutions $X(t)$ and $Y(t)$ of the Richardson model

$$X(t+1) = kY(t) - aX(t) + g$$

$$Y(t+1) = \ell X(t) - bY(t) + h$$

provided that

$$\int u T_X(u; r, s) \, du = k s - a r + g$$

$$\int v T_Y(v; r, s) \, dv = \ell r - b s + h$$

and assuming both systems start at the same initial values (X_0, Y_0).

<u>Proof</u>. We will use proof by induction. Consider $E_X(t)$ under the assumption that $E_X(t-1)$ and $E_Y(t-1)$ agreed with the solution of the Richardson model. By definition:

$$E_X(t) = \int u \, S_X(u, t) \, du$$

$$= \iiint u T_X(u; v, w) \, S_X(v, t-1) \, S_Y(w, t-1) \, dv \, dw \, du$$

$$= \iint (kw - av + g) \, S_X(v, t-1) \, S_Y(w, t-1) \, dv \, dw$$

$$= k \iint w \, S_X(v, t-1) \, S_Y(w, t-1) \, dw \, dv -$$

$$a \iint v \, S_X(v, t-1) \, S_Y(w, t-1) \, dv \, dw +$$

$$g \iint S_X(v, t-1) \, S_Y(w, t-1) \, dv \, dw$$

$$= k \, E_Y(t-1) \int S_X(v, t-1) \, dv - a \, E_X(t-1) \int S_Y(w, t-1) dw +$$

$$g \iint S_X(v, t-1) \, S_Y(w, t-1) \, dv \, dw$$

$$= k \, E_Y(t-1) = a \, E_X(t-1) + g$$

A similar argument can be made to show that

$$E_Y(t) = \ell \, E_X(t-1) - b \, E_Y(t-1) + h$$

This means that the expectation of the stochastic process can be expressed in a system of difference equations identical to the Richardson model. We further know that since the system starts at a specific point (X_0, Y_0),

$$E_X(t_0) = X_0 \text{ and } E_Y(t_0) = Y_0$$

the initial conditions on the expectation will be identical to that of the deterministic model. Therefore, $E_X(t)$ and $E_Y(t)$ will be identical to the solutions of the difference model, as was to be proven.

A few step-by-step remarks might be in order on that chain of equations. The first step is simply the definition of $E_X(t)$. In the second step, we substitute the Chapman-Kolmogorov expressions for $S_X(u, t)$. In the third step we have integrated $\int u T_X(u; v, w)$ and substituted in the value it has according to the conditions of the theorem. Step 4 multiplies this out. In step 5 we have used the fact that some of the integrals are expressions for $E_X(t-1)$ and $E_Y(t-1)$. Step 6 cleans out the remaining integrals by using the fact that the integral of a probability density function equals 1.0.

The conditions on the transition functions simply say that the expected value of the transition, given a particular state (r, s), is the same as the deterministic transition of the Richardson model. From this we can conclude that the expected value of the entire process will satisfy the Richardson model. Lest this appear to be something that should "obviously" be true, let us point that in general one does <u>not</u> get this nice relationship between the expected value of the transition and the expected value of the process satisfying a deterministic system. It is only true for linear systems, but fortunately Richardson's model is such a system. While this relationship between linear difference equations and Markov chain has undoubtedly been noticed before, I have yet to find it mentioned in any literature.

The conditions on the transition functions are relatively unrestraining and will allow us considerable diversity in those functions. For example, we might expect the transition functions to have low variance when there are few armaments in the system and higher variance when the total amount of arms is greater and the number of viable policy options increases for each nation. The shape of the density function for a given state could take a variety of forms (for example, normal, rectangular, bimodal, nonsymetrical), just as long as the expectation of that density satisfies the Richardson model.

This generalness of the transition function suggests that there is a large class of stochastic processes for which the Richardson model describes the expected value. If any of those processes actually describe what is going on in the real world, it is not surprising that Richardson's model has done rather well statistically in modeling those arms races.

LONG-TERM PROPERTIES OF A
MARKOV CHAIN

As noted earlier, some stochastic processes possess the property of being ergodic; that is, the probability distribution of the random variable eventually stops changing, even though the value of that variable may continue to fluctuate randomly. This property would enable one to study the process statistically in the long run, since a random variable whose distribution is not changing can be studied through repeated observations over time in order to estimate that probability distribution empirically. This is not possible when the distribution is continually changing through time, since each new observation is, in effect, an observation of a different random variable. Without additional a priori information on the stochastic process, it is generally impossible to obtain much information about that process statistically when the distribution is changing.

The sufficient conditions for a Markov chain to be ergodic are weak enough that they will probably be satisfied by an arms race that is following a Markov model. The formal statement of the conditions given in Feller is that "every strictly positive regular kernal K on a bounded closed interval is ergodic," where K corresponds to the transition function.[9] Translating this into somewhat less formal terminology, the theorem says that a Markov chain will be ergodic if three conditions are met.

First, the transition function is continuous with respect both to current states and to the state transferred to. In other words, there is no sudden discontinuous difference in the probability of going to a certain next arms level and the probability of going to an arms level infinitesimally above or below that level. Similarly, probabilities do not discontinuously change between a particular current state and alternative current states infinitesimally close to that state.

In general, this is merely a requirement that there be no special quantitative thresholds on the part of the decision makers, where behavior below the threshold is very different from that above it. When quantitative measures are dealt with, it is doubtful that such thresholds would exist, or even if they did whether they would still be discernible after the decisions had actually filtered down through the bureaucracy and implementation stages. Such thresholds may exist in qualitative arms races (the decision to "go nuclear" being the obvious example), but the model we have been discussing is based on continuous arms levels rather than distinct, qualitative arms levels.

It should also be noted that the condition of continuity in all arguments is a stronger condition than "regularity," but it is considerably easier to interpret empirically. See Feller for the rigorous details.[10]

Second, there is only a limited range of possible arms levels for each nation. This is the case in the real world: In most conceptual frameworks arms levels cannot drop below zero, nor can a nation expect to have an arms level higher than what it could obtain by devoting its full resources to armaments. A "closed and bounded" domain for the possible arms levels makes an ergodic Markov chain model more realistic than Richardson's deterministic model, which had as possible behaviors infinitely positive or infinitely negative arms levels when the model was unstable.

Third, the transition function must include the possibility of going from any current state to any other arms level in a single

RICHARDSON'S MODEL

step. At the extreme, this would include the possibility of going from zero arms to devoting full resources to arms in a single step.

While this condition is uncomfortable, it is not as ridiculous as it might seem at first. While there must be a <u>possibility</u> of making such transitions, the probability of such a transition can be infinitesimally small, just so long as it is not actually zero. In a similar vein, a researcher assuming that some data are normally distributed with mean zero and variance one faces the possibility that a sample point will lie between 100 and 101, with a probability of about 10^{-2170}.

In addition to the likelihood that the probabilities of drastic changes in arms levels are exceedingly small, there is the fact that nations are capable of actually making tremendous changes in armaments levels in relatively short periods of time. The United States came close to performing the "zero to full resources" transition following Pearl Harbor. Actual historical examples of such a major transition are impossible to find, not because of the absence of examples of huge increases in armaments but because of the absence of examples of nations with zero armaments.

Since these three conditions are sufficient to make a Markov chain ergodic, and all three conditions are likely to be satisfied in the real world, we can conclude that if the arms race is actually a Markov chain stochastic process, then it will probably be ergodic. If this is the case, then we can make a long-term behavior connection between a Markov chain whose expected transition is the value of a Richardson model and the deterministic Richardson model itself. We can state this as a simple theorem:

<u>Theorem</u>. If the equilibrium point of a Richardson deterministic model lies within possible arms levels of a Markov chain whose transition functions have that model as their expectation, then the expected value of the ergodic distribution of the Markov chain is identical to the equilibrium point.

<u>Proof</u>. The proof of this is quite simple. As we mentioned earlier, without proof, the ergodic distribution for a particular process is unique and does not depend upon the initial value of the process. From our earlier theorem, we know that the expectation of the Markov chain has the same values as the solution of the deterministic model. By definition of <u>equilibrium</u>, if the deterministic model started at the equilibrium point, it would stay there. Likewise, the expectation of a Markov process starting at the equilibrium point is that it will stay there. If the Markov chain is ergodic, the distribution will eventually be the ergodic distribution, and hence the expectation

of the ergodic distribution is the equilibrium point. Furthermore, since the ergodic distribution is the same for any initial values, its expectation is the same, and so the expectation of the ergodic distribution is always the equilibrium point, as we wish to prove.

This result means, among other things, that in the long run the "average" of the observed arms levels will converge to the equilibrium point of the associated Richardson model. It should be noted that this expectation will be the equilibrium point regardless of whether the deterministic system is stable or unstable. On the other hand, if the equilibrium point lies outside the permissible domain of arms levels, then without further information we can say nothing about the expectation of the ergodic distribution.

In general, we could expect that the long-run behavior of an arms race following a Markov chain would lend itself to empirical study. In all likelihood the transition functions would meet the conditions for the process to be ergodic, and the fluctuations of armament levels would settle down to two random variables whose distributions did not change. In fact, this would occur even if the Markov process did not follow a Richardson model, though in that case there would obviously be no connection between the expectation of the ergodic distribution and equilibrium points.

The problem, however, is that the "long run" that is required for the process to quiet down to the ergodic distribution may be longer than the timespan that the system remains in operation. Keynes' famous dictum, "In the long run we are all dead," may be particularly applicable to arms races. If the system can avoid major changes, then we will get the ergodic distribution, but in most cases it may be much more likely that the system itself changes (for example, the values of the Richardson coefficients change) long before the ergodic distribution is even approximated. The time it takes for the ergodic distribution to be approached depends on the detailed structure of the transition functions and on the initial conditions, so two systems corresponding to the same Richardson model may behave very differently in this respect. In short, while an arms race behaving as a Markov stochastic process opens the possibility that the probability distribution of arms levels may be empirically estimated, it does not guarantee that this will be the case.

CONCLUSION

While the extraordinary number of factors entering into political decision making may preclude the possibility of our ever arriving at a theory that will precisely predict future behavior, such as an arms race, this does not preclude the use of formal mathematical modeling in studying such behavior. In this chapter I have tried to give two examples of how a formal model that incorporates broad assumptions about the stochastic nature of the arms-race process can be used to study some of the aspects of that process.

The two theorems show that the study of a deterministic process, and in particular Richardson's linear model, could convey information about an underlying process that is actually stochastic. Since deterministic models are usually simpler to work with, this approach can often be more productive as the first attempt to study a system, even if stochastic elements are known to be present.

We have also seen that upon closer examination the random process may not be quite so hopelessly random as we first thought. In our example, if the arms race actually follows a Markov model, then it will probably also be ergodic and hence could be empirically studied to estimate a distribution function, if allowed to operate sufficiently long.

On the other hand, stochastic models are just as susceptible to problems of specification as deterministic models. Furthermore, the assumptions necessary to produce a model that can be analyzed may be rather restrictive. The theorems in this chapter were easy to prove because we were working with a stochastic process that had been thoroughly studied: The stationarity and Markov properties required by a process in order for it to be a Markov chain are not properties one would naturally choose when studying arms races. Unfortunately, more "reasonable" assumptions might quickly lead one to a very plausible model from which one could draw absolutely no conclusions.

The balance point between the problems of political plausibility and mathematical tractability is ultimately, at least in part, a matter of taste. In the vicinity of that balance, however, there would seem to be room for models of both a deterministic and stochastic nature, as both can be useful in attempting to gain some further understanding of that grand random process we call politics.

NOTES

1. Lewis F. Richardson, Arms and Insecurity (Chicago: Quadrangle Books, 1960).
2. Anatol Rapoport, "Lewis F. Richardson's Mathematical Theory of War," Journal of Conflict Resolution 1 (1957): 249-99.

3. Richardson, Arms and Insecurity, p. 12.
4. William R. Caspary, "Richardson's Model of Arms Races: Description, Critique and an Alternate Model," International Studies Quarterly 11 (1967): 63-68; Manas Chatterji, "A Model of Resolution of Conflict Between India and Pakistan," Papers, Peace Research Society (International) 12 (1969): 87-102; Murray Wolfson, "A Mathematical Model of the Cold War," Papers, Peace Research Society (International) 9 (1968): 107-24; Quincy Wright, "The Escalation of International Conflict," Journal of Conflict Resolution 9 (1965): 434-49.
5. Dagobert L. Brito, "A Dynamic Model of an Armaments Race," International Economic Review 13 (1972): 359-75; Marwan Simaan and Jose B. Cruz, Jr., "A Multistage Game Formulation of Arms Race and Control and Its Relationship to Richardson's Model," Modeling and Simulation 4 (1973): 149-53; Robert P. Abelson, "A 'Derivation' of Richardson's Equations," Journal of Conflict Resolution 7 (1963): 13-15.
6. Among others, see the following: Richardson, Arms and Insecurity, pp. 32-34; Normal Z. Alcock and Keith Lowe, "The Vietnam War as a Richardson Process," Journal of Peace Research 6 (1969): 105-11; Kendall D. Moll, The Influence of History Upon Seapower, 1865-1914 (Menlo Park, Calif.: Stanford Research Institute, 1968); Dina A. Zinnes and John V. Gillespie, "Analysis of Arms Race Models: USA vs. USSR and NATO vs. WTO," Modeling and Simulation 4 (1973): 149-54.
7. A few examples are Gordon Hilton, "The 1914 Studies— A Re-Assessment of the Evidence and Some Further Thoughts," Papers, Peace Science Society (International) 8 (1969): 117-41; Jonathan Wilkenfeld, "Models for the Analysis of Foreign Conflict Behavior of States," in Peace, War and Numbers, ed. Bruce Russett, (Beverly Hills, Calif.: Sage, 1972), pp. 275-98; Michael R. Leavitt, "Markov Processes in International Crises: An Analytical Addendum to an Event-Based Simulation of the Taiwan Straits Crises," in Experimentation and Simulation in Political Science, eds. J. A. Laponce and Paul Smoker (Toronto: University of Toronto Press, 1972), pp. 280-92; Dina A. Zinnes and Jonathan Wilkenfeld, "An Analysis of Foreign Conflict Behavior of Nations," in Comparative Foreign Policy, Theoretical Essays, ed. W. F. Hanreider (Chicago: McKay, 1971), pp. 167-213; Dina A. Zinnes, J. L. Zinnes, and R. D. McClure, "Markovian Analysis of Hostile Communications in the 1914 Crisis," in Crisis in Foreign Policy Decision Making, ed. Charles F. Hermann (New York: Free Press, 1972), pp. 139-62.
8. William Feller, An Introduction to Probability Theory and its Applications, 1 and 2 (New York: Wiley, 1971).

9. Ibid.
10. Ibid., pp. 270-74.

PART III
RICHARDSON-TYPE PROCESS MODELS

CHAPTER

9

**INTRODUCTION TO
RICHARDSON-TYPE
PROCESS MODELS**
The Editors

The models of this section are unified along at least four dimensions. Although the approach to the topic differs markedly from chapter to chapter, the models are substantively unified by a common concern for the processes that underlie national acquisition of arms. In addition, because of the nature of the topic, and because at least three of these models, to one extent or another, owe an intellectual debt to the work of Lewis Frye Richardson, there are important similarities in the structures of the models. Three such similarities can be seen. First, owing in part to the nature of the topic examined but also due in part to the intellectual heritage of Richardson, these models are all <u>time dependent</u>. We saw one such model in the previous section, Schrodt's Markovian interpretation of the Richardson model, but the other models of the last section were primarily static. In contrast, all the models of this section describe a process through time. Second, all the models postulate an interactive process: What one nation does affects the behavior of another nation, which in turn affects the first, and so on. Or seen from a different perspective, each of these models contains a "feedback" component: The behavior of the system at one point in time affects its behavior at a subsequent point in time. Finally, the first three chapters describe deterministic models. Although the term "deterministic" has a variety of meanings, it is used here to simply denote a model that does not contain a probabilistic element. In short, these models do not contain random variables. As we shall see, the fourth model, presented by Baugh, does contain a random element.

But while noting that the models share structural similarities, it is important to recognize that these facets play different roles in each model. The dynamic aspects of each model are not identical, nor does interaction necessarily occur in the same way from model to model. A comparison of the models along the three dimensions is thus instructive of the variety of ways in which these components can enter a model. Moreover, unlike the probabilistic models of the preceding section, the models of the present section are part of an extensive literature devoted to arms races generally and Richardson-process-type models more specifically. Consequently, two questions are immediately relevant: (a) Where do these models fit relative to this literature? and (b) what contribution do these models make to that literature.

THE STRUCTURE OF THE MODELS

The focus of Chapter 10 by Zinnes, Gillespie, and Rubison is entirely on the original Richardson formulation of an arms race. Unlike the remaining three chapters, Chapter 10 makes no attempt to derive a new model. Its purpose is to suggest that Richardson's interpretation of his own model was too restricted and that, given a more general interpretation, a greater understanding of the patterns of arms races can be obtained. Thus, a consideration of the time-dependency and interactive characteristics of the model discussed in this chapter is in fact a consideration of the original Richardson model. We see then that in the standard Richardson model:

$$\dot{x} = ay - bx + g \qquad (9.1)$$

$$\dot{y} = cx - dy + h \qquad (9.2)$$

where

$\dot{x}$ and $\dot{y}$ = rates at which X and Y arm
x and y = the amount of arms possessed by each side at a point in time
a and c = "threat" parameters
b and d = "fatigue" parameters
g and h = grievance parameters

there is no probabilistic element. That is, once the process begins, it grinds inexorably onwards, with the values of each variable at one point in time completely determined by the values of the variable at previous points in time; the model is dynamic as captured by the use of differential equations, and the interactive component occurs in the coupling between the two equations: Y's behavior feeds

INTRODUCTION 181

into X's armament equation and vice versa. The nature of the argument in this paper concerns the parameters a, b, c and d. When proposing the model, Richardson postulated that these parameters should always be positive. Such an assumption has serious implications for Richardson's subsequent analysis of the stability conditions of the model—his analysis of those conditions under which the arms race will approach or oscillate around the equilibrium point, the point at which the arms race stops. By requiring that the parameters be positive, Richardson can only consider one type of stable system; that is, he can only examine one way in which the two arming nations in a stable system will approach the point of rest. By allowing the parameters to be either positive or negative, a number of additional armament patterns can be seen both for stable and for unstable cases.

Chapter II by Ferejohn resembles Chapter 10 in that both present a critique of the Richardson model. However, Ferejohn's critique is of a different variety. If the Richardson arms-race literature is divided into empirical and theoretical segments (fully recognizing that some analyses fall in both categories), then while the Zinnes, Gillespie, and Rubison chapter presents a criticism of the theoretical aspects of the Richardson model, the Ferejohn chapter presents a criticism of the empirical wing. This literature has been primarily concerned with estimating the parameters of the Richardson model, namely, a, b, c, d, g, and h, as given in equations 9.1 and 9.2 above.[1] Ferejohn's criticism, based on econometrics, is that the standard estimation procedures necessarily make some implicit assumptions that raise serious questions about the usefulness of the Richardson model. Ferejohn shows that in order for the parameter estimates to be consistent, the system must be stable. But, queries Ferejohn, do we really have an arms race when the Richardson model is stable? It is important to point out that Ferejohn is assuming that stable Richardson systems will eventually reach equilibrium and that it is at this point that the arms race ceases. Thus, Ferejohn's assertion that stable systems cannot represent arms races is primarily based on what happens in the system after it reaches equilibrium. It is possible to have an arms race in a stable system—that is, both sides monotonically increase their arms—when the initial values are less than the values of the variables at equilibrium. It is also important to note that Ferejohn is assuming, with Richardson, that the parameters are positive. As Zinnes, Gillespie, and Rubison show, when no such restrictions are placed on the parameters, there exists a nonasymptotically stable case in which the armament pattern simply circles around the equilibrium point but never in fact reaches it.

Ferejohn's critique leads him to propose a new model. The primary characteristic of the new model is that it is possible for the new system to be stable—thus permitting the estimation of consistent parameters—and yet always reflect an arms race. The motivation for the model, given through an analysis of indifference curves, is provided in the second portion of the chapter. This discussion, which is subsequently formalized in the third portion, contains two important features. First, Ferejohn changes the structure of the Richardson model by adding an optimization component. While the Richardson model as given in equations 9.1 and 9.2 simply describes how two nations react to one another, Ferejohn's new model given in equations 11.2 through 11.4.2 (pp. 229-30) contains a "decision maker" who is attempting to maximize a particular goal (11.2) subject to certain constraints (11.4.1 and 11.4.2). Second, Ferejohn adds a new variable: aid. By solving the optimization problem (11.5, p. 231) and with appropriate substitutions, he obtains in 11.12 and 11.13 (pp. 232-33) an equation that very much resembles the Richardson equation except that it now contains the new variable Y_t. Ferejohn has thus shown the conditions under which it is possible to derive equation 11.13. The significance of 11.13 is that this system can be stable, thus allowing for parameter estimates, while the arms race continues by virtue of the new exogenous variable Y (mainly, D, as seen in 11.4.2).

Although the new Ferejohn model differs from the original Richardson model, the three basic components can still be seen. The model is totally deterministic: Although it now contains a goal, the assumption of optimization nevertheless still produces a deterministic system, as can be seen by examining 11.13. The model is clearly dynamic, as is evident from the time subscripts on each variable. Finally, although somewhat hidden, the model can be seen as having an interactive component: By optimizing a function of the form given in 11.2 a comparison is made between the arms levels of the two countries, M_j and M_k. However, because the newly constructed model in effect considers only <u>one</u> optimizing nation, the potential interactive component is outside the model. That is, the interaction does not occur within the model. The arms of the opponent are fed in as an exogenous variable. To model the interaction would require a consideration of <u>two</u> optimizing nations, and this would then become a differential game. Thus, Ferejohn has converted a two-nation model into a one-nation model.

In Chapter 12 Squires also presents us with a model that has its roots in Richardson. However, although both the Ferejohn and the Squires chapter begin with the Richardson model, there is an

INTRODUCTION

important difference in the treatment given the model that subsequently leads to the statement of a new model. Ferejohn changes the Richardson model by suggesting a set of assumptions (11.2 through 11.4.2) from which such a revised model can be derived. Squires, on the other hand, does not derive the reformulated Richardson model; rather, he directly modifies the Richardson equations and suggests how, through a computer simulation, the consequences of the newly postulated models might be examined.

Squires' analysis essentially suggests four main revisions in the Richardson formulation, using Richardson's extension of the model to n-nations. The first three of these revisions can be seen as unpacking or decomposing the two main components of the Richardson model, while the last revision changes the nature of the dynamic in the model. The first term on the right-hand side of equations 9.1 and 9.2 is typically known as the "threat" component of the Richardson model and is composed of the parameter a and the amount of arms of the opponent. Squires suggests that this term should be altered in two ways. First, he feels that the parameter a is in fact a function of two factors that should be explicitly modeled in the equations: the degree of trust between two nations and the distance between them. Second, Squires contends that the arms that a nation possesses must be specified: Nuclear weapons pose a different kind of threat from that of conventional weapons. This is achieved by providing two equations for each nation, one for each type of weapon, in which the trust and distance factors have different impacts. The third change that Squires suggests concerns what is typically known as the "economic burden" term in equations 9.1 and 9.2, namely the second component on the right-hand side of equations 9.1 and 9.2. His suggestion here is that alliances be permitted and that an ally helps to decrease the rate at which a nation must arm. This decrease is accomplished by adding the ally's arms to a given nation's "economic-burden" term. Based on these three new interpretations of the components of the Richardson model, Squires generates in turn three different models.

Although the changes in the components of the model provide a different interpretation of the relevant factors of an arms race, it is Squires' use of his newly formulated equations that produces the most striking contrast between his formulation and the one originally given by Richardson. The Richardson-type equations that Squires generates by changing the components of the original Richardson model are not actually used to describe the arming behavior of the nations, as was done by Richardson. Rather, these equations (12.22 and 12.23, p. 265) are used to determine the increment desired by decision makers at a specified point in time. For a given point in time a nation calculates the increments in the amounts of the two types of arms it desires vis-à-vis every other nation and chooses the largest value as its desired goal. Having set its desired goal, the nation next determines what in fact is feasible. This is accomplished by incorporating the desired values into equation 12.24 (p. 265), a function originally introduced by Caspary to approximate more closely the impact of limited resources on arming. Equation 12.24 now determines the total increment in arms of both types that is feasible given the amount of resources available (C). This total increment is then divided into the two types of weapons as determined by equations 12.26 and 12.27 (p. 266).

We see then that although the Squires model uses the Richardson equations, these equations, as modified, are used as calculation devices rather than as descriptions of the behavior of nations. In one sense, Squires is using the Richardson equations as objectives or goals comparable to the Ferejohn optimization goal given in Ferejohn's 11.2. The dynamic of the model, then, is provided by 12.24, which tells the nation what in fact it can have. The values calculated in 12.24 and reapportioned into the two weapons types in 12.26 and 12.27 feed back into the "desire" equations of 12.22 and 12.23, providing the basis for the next set of calculations. The interactive aspect of the model still comes from the coupling of the Richardson equations, but the focus is slightly different. It is not the arms of the opponent that spur a nation to increase its weapons; rather, the opponent's arms, through the medium of distance and trust, cause a nation to want to increase or decrease weapons. Whether or not the nation can in fact increase or decrease its arms is then described by equation 12.24. But while there is an important shift in emphasis between the Squires model and the original Richardson model, it is clear that the Squires model remains completely deterministic, as an examination of the key equations (12.22, 12.23, 12.24, 12.26, and 12.27) shows.

Of the four models, the Baugh model is the furthest removed from the Richardson tradition. Although the Baugh model addresses an issue that we have already seen in both the Squires and Ferejohn chapters (what is the goal that a nation seeks to achieve with respect to the amount of arms it possesses?), the issue is confronted from a different perspective. Baugh, in effect, works backwards. Suppose, he argues, that a nation's goal is to deter its opponent and that such deterrence is based on the capabilities of the weapons possessed to inflict a specified level of unacceptable damage on the opponent. The question then is, knowing the capabilities of the weapons, what mix of weapons must one have to achieve this goal? Unlike either Ferejohn or Squires, however, Baugh does not explicitly model this objective. Rather, he fights an imaginary war

INTRODUCTION 185

in which assumptions are made about the types of weapons involved, their capacities, and the strategies employed in terms of the targets selected and the sequence of events that would take place in a nuclear exchange. By varying the parameters of the model (that is, creating different scenarios), it is possible to determine the outcome of a war under varying conditions. Those arms levels that permit the nation to survive while inflicting unacceptable damage on the opponent are thus the levels of arms necessary for a successful deterrence strategy.

Unlike any of the preceeding analyses, then, the Baugh model is a model of war, not one of arms races. Yet, like the other models, its purpose is to determine some optimal level of armaments. Rather than arbitrarily specifying the desired relationship between one's own arms and those of an opponent, the needed weapons are determined through the complex calculation of the outcome of a war. The model of the war contains a number of particular parameters, and by so manipulating these parameters it is possible to find the appropriate mix to achieve deterrence.

The Baugh model is clearly dynamic since the exchange of nuclear forces as the war progresses is a sequence of events through time. But note that the dynamic occurs *in the war*, not in the arms race. In Chapters 10 through 12 the dynamic involved increasing or decreasing the amount of weapons possessed. In the Baugh model, however, there is no dynamic here: In effect, there is a simple desired level of arms for any given war scenario that produces deterrence. The interaction also occurs primarily in the war exchange. But note that the interaction is less directly coupled than was true in either the original Richardson model or the Squires revision: Once a war begins, the attacked nation must respond; hence there is interaction, but the strategy that the responding nation must employ is not dictated by the nature of the attack. There are in effect a series of possible responses that the attacked nation can take. The third difference between the Baugh model and the other three of this section is its incorporation of a random element. This primarily occurs with respect to the effectiveness of the weapons. Some of the weapons dispatched by one side will be intercepted by the opponent, and of those that in fact pass the defense of the opponent only a fraction will in fact hit designated targets.

RELATIONSHIP TO THE ARMS RACE LITERATURE

It is interesting to conclude with some comparison of these four chapters with the more general and extensive literature that exists on arms races and Richardson-type models. Where do these pieces fit with respect to that literature, and what is the contribution made? Chapter 11 can be seen as being in the mainstream of research that has sought to clarify and extend the Richardson model. Unhappy with the model itself, this literature has sought to extend the interpretation by changing the characterization of its component parts. This can be seen in Intriligator's modification of the threat term, in Caspary's modification of the economic burden term, and in Wright's proposal of additional variables, to name but a few of those who have done work in this area.[2] The proposal by Zinnes, Gillespie, and Rubison is more modest in scope; it suggests only that the assumption concerning positive parameters be dropped. The chapter differs from most of the work in this area, however, in that, with the exception of Caspary, the purpose of the chapter is to examine the consequences of such a modification. Typically, the modifications that have been proposed are so extensive that researchers are unable to assess the impact of their proposed alteration analytically.

The Ferejohn chapter fits in a slightly different tradition—one of more recent vintage. Beginning probably with the work of Brito, but moving on to encompass the work of Brito and Intriligator and of Simaan and Cruz, the Richardson arms race model has been modified by treating it as a problem in optimization, or more particularly as a problem in optimal control theory.[3] Thus, as do these other writers, Ferejohn treats the problem of an arms race from the perspective of a nation seeking to maximize some goal given certain constraints. Ferejohn also shares with Brito and with Simaan and Cruz the approach taken to the Richardson model. Thus, like these authors, Ferejohn <u>derives</u> the Richardson model from a standard problem in optimal control theory. However, while Ferejohn derives a Richardson model, he does so only for a single nation, and thus his model is closer to the work of Brito than to that of Simaan and Cruz, who derive the Richardson model from a difference game analysis. But while Ferejohn's analysis resembles the work of these other researchers, it is important to note that his point of departure is different: His motivation for creating the new model is based on problems in empirical estimation, not, as is true in the other cases, from a dissatisfaction on theoretical grounds with the Richardson model. Thus, Ferejohn's chapter links problems in empirical testing with theoretical questions of model construction.

The Squires chapter also is probably most closely allied with the tradition of changing the factors of the Richardson model as discussed above. Thus, Squires introduces a variety of new characterizations for the basic components of the Richardson model. But,

ns as was seen earlier, Squires' contribution lies in his use of the Richardson equations not as statements of the behavior of nations but as dynamic characterizations of the goals of nations. Thus, Squires' chapter can be seen as a bridge between the literature that extends the Richardson model, in which the Zinnes, Gillespie, and Rubison chapter falls, and the literature within which the Ferejohn chapter fits: the literature that alters the Richardson model to include a goal or objective component.

The Baugh chapter is more closely tied to operations research analysis and is in fact a development of a model presented by Saaty.[4] This literature is not only concerned with questions such as, "Which strategies accomplish deterrence?" but is also very specific to the capacities of particular types of weapon systems. Much of the interest lies in ascertaining effective mixes of weapons. However, the Baugh chapter can also be seen more generally as part of the optimization literature, and it is in fact similar to the more recent work of Brito and Intriligator.[5] Thus like Brito and Intriligator, Baugh's concern is with determining objectives on the basis of the outcomes of imaginary wars. Unlike Brito and Intriligator, however, Baugh's model does not contain an explicit objective—unless the general survivability function is so interpreted.

Each of these papers then falls within a recognizable tradition yet each provides a new perspective and thus a contribution to that tradition. We turn then to the details of these models.

NOTES

1. See, for example, Paul Smoker, "A Mathematical Study of the Present Arms Race," General Systems Yearbook 8 (1963): 51-60; Paul Smoker, "A Pilot Study of the Present Arms Race," General Systems Yearbook 8 (1963): 61-76; Paul Smoker, "Fear in the Arms Race: A Mathematical Study," Journal of Peace Research 1 (1964): 55-64; Norman Z. Alcock and Keith W. Lowe, "The Vietnam War as a Richardson Process," Journal of Peace Research 6 (1969): 105-13; and Dina A. Zinnes and John V. Gillespie, "Analysis of Arms Race Models: USA vs. USSR and NATO vs. WTO," Modeling and Simulation 4 (1973): 149-54.

2. Michael D. Intriligator, "Some Simple Models of Arms Races," General Systems Yearbook 9 (1964): 143-47; William R. Caspary, "Richardson's Model of Arms Races: Description, Critique and an Alternative Model," International Studies Quarterly 11 (1967): 63-88; Quincy Wright, A Study of War, 2d ed. (Chicago: University of Chicago Press, 1965).

3. Dagobert L. Brito, "A Dynamic Model of an Armaments Race," International Economic Review 13 (1972): 359-75; Dagobert L. Brito and Michael Intriligator, "Some Applications of the Maximum Principle to Problems of Arms Races," Modeling and Simulation 4 (1973): 140-44; Marwan Simaan and Jose B. Cruz, Jr., "A Multistage Game Formulation of Arms Race and Control and Its Relationship to Richardson's Model," Modeling and Simulation 4 (1973): 149-53.

4. Thomas L. Saaty, Mathematical Models of Arms Control and Disarmament (New York: Wiley, 1968).

5. Dagobert L. Brito and Michael D. Intriligator, "A General Equilibrium Model of an Armaments Race," mimeographed, n.d.; Dagobert L. Brito and Michael D. Intriligator, "An N-Country Model of an Armaments Race," mimeographed, 1974.

CHAPTER 10

A REINTERPRETATION OF THE RICHARDSON ARMS-RACE MODEL

Dina A. Zinnes
John V. Gillespie
R. Michael Rubison

An interesting anomaly has consistently appeared in the literature dealing with Richardson's original model of an arms race. When constructing his now-famous model:

$$\dot{x} = ky - ax + g \tag{10.1}$$

$$\dot{y} = \ell x - by + h \tag{10.2}$$

where $\dot{x}$ is dx/dt and $\dot{y}$ is dy/dt, Richardson asserts, almost casually, that the constants, k, ℓ, a, b, g, and h are all positive.[1] While, as we shall see, this assumption assures that the system will have certain mathematical properties, it is strange that Richardson never returns to reconsider the impact the assumption has on his model. It is strange, first, because Richardson in most of his model-building projects is forever modifying original assumptions to explore their consequences,[2] and, second, because even in Richardson's own empirical work the parameter estimates he obtains for his model are not all positive. Subsequent empirical research has further emphasized this fact: It is almost never the case that all the parameters are consistently positive.[3] Since the values of the parameters determine the location of the equilibrium point (that is, in which quadrant it will fall), whether or not the system is stable, and further, the arming-disarming pattern of two nations approaching

---

The authors wish to thank Maynard Thompson and Irwin Sandberg for their helpful suggestions on an earlier draft. Support for this research was supplied by the National Science Foundation Research Grants GS 36806 and SOC 75-04212.

equilibrium in a stable system, it is clear that the parameter value issue is not trivial. The purpose of this chapter, then, is to generalize Richardson's analysis of the equilibrium and stability characteristics of his original model by allowing the parameters to be either positive or negative. Our results, however, are based on standard and well-known results in the literature of ordinary differential equations. Thus, the purpose here is not to repeat these standard analyses but rather to consider their implications within the special context of a Richardson model.

THE MEANING OF NEGATIVE CONSTANTS

Before we turn to an analysis of the general model, however, it might be important to note the reasonableness of the proposed modification. Richardson's requirement that the parameters be positive was a natural outgrowth of his interpretation of an arms race. It must therefore be shown that negative parameter values also have a reasonable interpretation. We note first that if 10.1 and 10.2 are specifically used to describe an arms race, then it is only meaningful to assume that x and y are always nonnegative. While the interpretation of the model can be extended to more general interactive situations in which x and y assume negative values, we will restrict ourselves to arms races. The assumption that x and y are nonnegative then allows us to determine the impact of the parameters.

Richardson called the parameters k and ℓ "threat coefficients" and some have suggested that these weighting factors reflect a nation's perception of the danger posed by a potential opponent. By assuming that these parameters are positive, Richardson indicated that these weights impel a nation to increase its weapons and thus are a factor in keeping the arms race going. Obviously, then, negative values of k and ℓ, ignoring the rest of equations 10.1 and 10.2, will produce negative rates of armament—that is, disarmament. Since we are modeling arms races, one might argue that this is an irrelevant situation to the issue at hand. But this would be a rather narrow view of the potentiality of the model. If two originally belligerent nations should sign an arms limitation agreement, this could easily be reflected by negative parameters. Or if two nonbelligerent nations (k = ℓ = 0) join an alliance,[4] a negative parameter could indicate that one of the nations provides the defense for the other, allowing the latter to reallocate its governmental expenditures away from arms.[5] We can conclude then that meaningful interpretations can be given to negative values of k and ℓ, even within the context of an arms race.

In a similar vein negative values for a and b in 10.1 and 10.2 can also be shown to be reasonable. These coefficients were labeled "fatigue and expense" by Richardson and were used in his model to denote the fact that existing arms cause an economic burden for a nation. Consequently, assumed to be positive and subtracted them from the equations, these parameters push the nation toward disarmament; that is, they work against the "threat coefficients" and slow down the arms race. Clearly, however, a meaningful interpretation for negative parameters can be given. Negative parameters would multiply the negative sign, making this component positive. Consequently, negative parameters would spur the arms race on and could occur when a country's economy is heavily geared to producing weapons. In this instance weapons are not a "fatigue and expense" factor but a benefit to the country.

Finally, negative values for g and h are easily interpretable. Whereas positive values indicate that a nation has a grievance or feels hatred towards another country, negative values would suggest a feeling of friendship and cooperation.

However, although we have demonstrated the reasonableness of allowing each of the parameters to assume both positive and negative values, one might question the reasonableness of certain combinations of parameter values. The issue is really one of whether or not the parameters can be interpreted independently of one another. It is not too difficult to argue this with respect to "fatigue and expense." Since this factor reflects internal considerations, it can be argued that this parameter can be either positive or negative, regardless of the signs of the other two parameters. However, the relationship between the threat and grievance parameters is somewhat more complicated. Is it reasonable, for example, to argue that a nation can have a negative threat parameter but a positive grievance parameter (that is, that the nation fears the opponent but has no long-standing grievance against its adversary, or contrariwise has no fear but a considerable grievance)? We believe that both cases are plausible. A nation may fear a sudden newly emerging opponent that appears quite strong, yet have no history of conflict with it and therefore no grievance against the new opponent. Similarly, a nation may not really fear another yet may hold a grudge against it. Even relations between major powers might be reflected by negative or zero threat coefficients and positive grievances as, for example, France's reaction towards Germany between the world wars. Thus, we conclude that all possible combinations between positive and negative values of the parameters have reasonable interpretations.

THE CONCEPTS OF EQUILIBRIUM AND STABILITY

Because the concepts of equilibrium and stability have been widely used in the field of political science and therefore have a multitude of possible interpretations, it is important that we define precisely what is meant by these concepts when they are applied to the analysis of dynamic systems. Equilibrium in a dynamic system is that point such that change no longer occurs. In equations 10.1 and 10.2 the equilibrium point (x_0, y_0) is found by letting the rates, $\dot{x}$ and $\dot{y}$, equal zero ($\dot{x} = 0$, $\dot{y} = 0$). We can thus rewrite 10.1 and 10.2 as follows:

$$0 = ky - ax + g \tag{10.3}$$

$$0 = \ell x - by + h \tag{10.4}$$

Solving 10.3 and 10.4 simultaneously, we obtain 10.5 and 10.6:

$$x_0 = (kh + bg)/(ab - k\ell) \tag{10.5}$$

$$y_0 = (\ell g + ah)/(ab - k\ell) \tag{10.6}$$

Equations 10.5 and 10.6 describe the equilibrium point.

Given numerical values of the parameters a, b, k, ℓ, g, and h, it is possible to evaluate numerically the equilibrium point, that is, the total amount of arms nation X (x_0) and nation Y (y_0) must have if the arms race is to stop.

Stability is often most easily understood in reference to equilibrium. This type of stability is known as asymptotic stability. We will develop the concept of asymptotic stability on an intuitive basis and then proceed to a formal definition. Once asymptotic stability is understood, the more general concept of stability is easily grasped. Suppose two states X and Y have some amount of arms (x_0, y_0) different from the equilibrium values. An interesting question that can be asked is whether the dynamics of the process are propelling X and Y toward or away from the equilibrium point. If the forces are moving X and Y toward equilibrium, we say the system is asymptotically stable; if away from equilibrium, we say the system is unstable.

We will examine these two cases through the diagrams presented in Figures 10.1 and 10.2.[6]

Figure 10.1 provides an example of equations 10.3 and 10.4 where the system is as follows:

FIGURE 10.1

An Illustration of the Dynamics of the Richardson Arms Race Model: The Stable Case

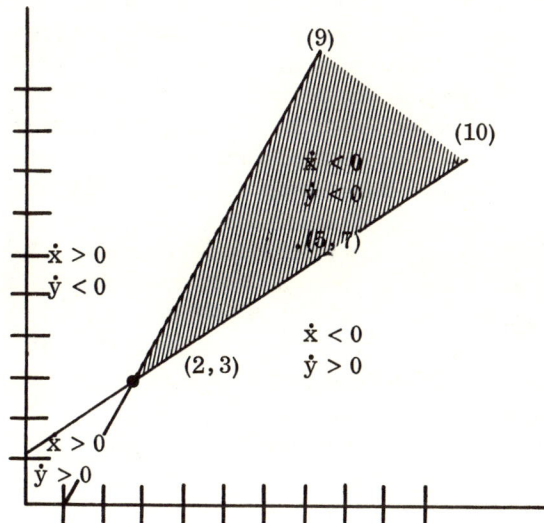

$$\dot{x} = y - 2x + 1 \tag{10.7}$$

$$\dot{y} = x - y + 1 \tag{10.8}$$

From equation 10.7 the points on the line 9:

$$y = 2x - 1 \tag{10.9}$$

satisfy $\dot{x} = 0$. Similarly, from 10.8 the points on the line 10:

$$y = x + 1 \tag{10.10}$$

satisfy $\dot{y} = 0$.

Solving 10.9 and 10.10 simultaneously, the equilibrium point occurs at point 2,3. Let us examine the values of $\dot{x}$ and $\dot{y}$ for points not on the lines 9 and 10.

Consider the point 5,7. Substituting these values into equation 10.7, $\dot{x} < 0$. Since the point 5,7 occurs below the line 9, by continuity it follows $\dot{x} < 0$ for all points below line 9. Similarly, substituting the values $(5, 7)$ into 10.8, $\dot{y} < 0$. This point occurs above the line 10. By continuity it follows $\dot{y} < 0$ for all points above line 10.

We see then that for the particular example given by 10.7 and 10.8 the region between the two lines above the equilibrium point (shaded in Figure 10.1) is an area in which both derivatives are negative. A negative derivative means the process is decelerating; a positive derivative implies that the process is accelerating. If both $\dot{x} < 0$ and $\dot{y} < 0$, the total amount of arms is decreasing, and at the next instantaneous point in time both sides will have less arms.

Let us now intuitively consider the asymptotic stability of the point $(2, 3)$. If $(2, 3)$ is asympototically stable and if the values of x and y are slightly displaced, the dynamics of the model 10.7 and 10.8 will move x and y back to the equilibrium. If point $(2, 3)$ is not asymptotically stable, when displaced, the values of x and y will not approach $(2, 3)$. Later we will show that the system 10.7 and 10.8 satisfies the conditions for asymptotic stability.

Figure 10.2 presents an asymptotically unstable example. For Figure 10.2 the system is as follows:

$$\dot{x} = y - x - 1 \tag{10.11}$$

$$\dot{y} = -2x + y + 1 \tag{10.12}$$

In Figure 10.2 the signs of $\dot{x}$ and $\dot{y}$ are displayed in the various regions. Later we will show that system 10.11 and 10.12 satisfies the conditions for stability but is not asymptotically stable.

Our discussion of stability will be simplified if we make a translation of axes to place the equilibrium point at the origin, thus eliminating the intercepts g and h in equations 10.3 and 10.4. We therefore define $\bar{x} = x - x_0$ and $\bar{y} = y - y_0$ and consequently obtain the following:

$$\dot{\bar{x}} = k\bar{y} - a\bar{x} \tag{10.13}$$

$$\dot{\bar{y}} = \ell\bar{x} - b\bar{y} \tag{10.14}$$

Let us rewrite the system 10.13 and 10.14 in matrix notation as

$$\dot{X} = AX,$$

where

RICHARDSON'S MODEL REINTERPRETED

FIGURE 10.2

An Illustration of the Dynamics of the Richardson Arms-Race Model: The Unstable Case

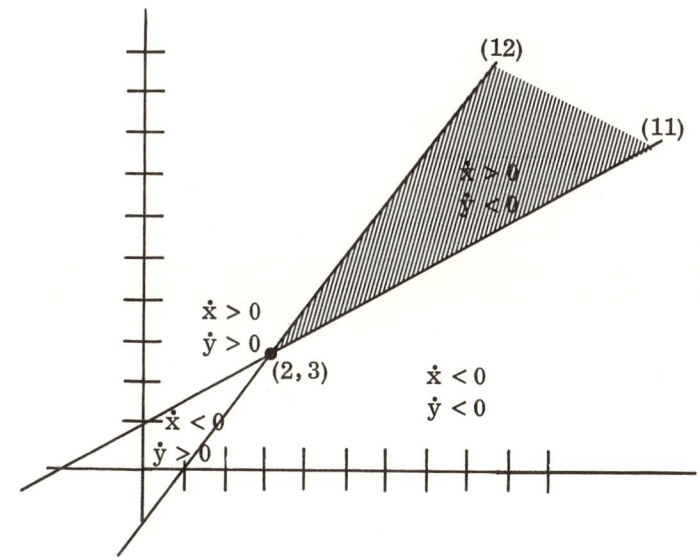

$$X = \begin{bmatrix} \bar{x}(t) \\ \bar{y}(t) \end{bmatrix}, \quad A = \begin{bmatrix} -a & k \\ \ell & -b \end{bmatrix}$$

Thus,

$$\begin{bmatrix} \dot{\bar{x}}(t) \\ \dot{\bar{y}}(t) \end{bmatrix} = \begin{bmatrix} -a & k \\ \ell & b \end{bmatrix} \begin{bmatrix} \bar{x}(t) \\ \bar{y}(t) \end{bmatrix} \tag{10.15}$$

The characteristic equation is defined as $p(\lambda) = 0$, where $p(\lambda)$ is the determinant of the matrix $(\lambda I - A)$.

Hence, for A:

$$p(\lambda) = \begin{bmatrix} \lambda + a & -k \\ -\ell & \lambda + b \end{bmatrix}$$

which yields equation 10.16:

$$p(\lambda) = \lambda^2 + (a + b)\lambda + (ab - \ell k) \qquad (10.16)$$

The characteristic values of eigenvalues are defined as the zeros of the characteristic equation. Thus, the eigenvalues of the Richardson system, 10.13 and 10.14, are given by using the quadratic formula:

$$\lambda_1 = \left[-(a+b) + \sqrt{(a+b)^2 - 4(ab - \ell k)}\right]/2 \qquad (10.17)$$

$$\lambda_2 = \left[-(a+b) - \sqrt{(a+b)^2 - 4(ab - \ell k)}\right]/2 \qquad (10.18)$$

The importance of the eigenvalues for the stability of the Richardson system is easily seen from the result in ordinary differential equations that the solution of equation 10.13, 10.14 is of the following form:

$$x(t) = f(t) e^{\lambda_i t} \qquad (10.19)$$

$$y(t) = g(t) e^{\lambda_i t} \qquad (10.20)$$

where $f(t)$ and $g(t)$ are polynomials of degree ≤ 1. With this in mind, we make the following formal definition of stability.

If $(ab - \ell k) \neq 0$ then $(0,0)$ is the only equilibrium point for the equation 10.13, 10.14.

The point $(0,0)$ is said to be __stable__ if given any $\varepsilon > 0$ there exists a $\delta > 0$ such that (i) every solution $(x[t], y[t])$ of 10.13, 10.14 in the δ neighborhood of point $(0,0)$ is defined for all time t, $t_1 < t < \infty$, and (ii) if a solution satisfies condition i it remains in the ε neighborhood of point $(0,0)$ for $t > t_1$. In addition, to have asymptotic stability of the point $(0,0)$, (iii) every solution satisfying conditions i and ii also satisfies the following:

$$\lim_{t \to \infty} x(t) = 0$$

$$\lim_{t \to \infty} y(t) = 0$$

Conditions i and ii require that for some t_1, the solution $(x[t], y[t])$ must be defined in a small neighborhood of the equilibrium point and must remain within an arbitrarily small distance from the equilibrium point. Condition iii states that $(x[t], y[t])$ will approach the equilibrium point as $t \to \infty$.

It is a well-known result in the theory of ordinary differential equations that the necessary and sufficient conditions for the asymptotic stability of a linear system, of which Richardson's equations are an example, is that the real parts of λ_1 and λ_2 (denoted by $\text{Re}[\lambda_1]$ and $\text{Re}[\lambda_2]$ be negative.[7] Furthermore, a linear system is stable but not asymptotically stable, if and only if λ_1 and λ_2 are pure complex numbers; that is, $\text{Re}(\lambda_1) = R(\lambda_2) = 0$.

Since asymptotic stability is concerned with the behavior of equations 10.19 and 10.20 as $t \to \infty$, it is necessary to examine the nature of the eigenvalues λ_1 and λ_2. From elementary algebra it is known that the properties of λ_1 and λ_2 are determined by the sign of the discriminant (D). From equations 10.17 and 10.18 the following are derived:

$$D = (a + b)^2 - 4(ab - \ell k) \tag{10.21}$$

$$D = (a - b)^2 + 4k\ell \tag{10.22}$$

Three cases can be distinguished:

Case 1. If $D > 0$, the eigenvalues (λ_1, λ_2) are distinct real numbers ($\lambda_1 \neq \lambda_2$).

Case 2. If $D < 0$, the eigenvalues (λ_1, λ_2) are distinct complex numbers. Furthermore, they are complex conjugates. Thus, $\lambda_1 = u + iv$, $\lambda_2 = u - iv$, where u and v are real numbers and $i = \sqrt{-1}$.

Case 3. If $D = 0$, the eigenvalues (λ_1, λ_2) are equal real numbers: ($\lambda_1 = \lambda_2 = -[a + b]/2$).

If $(ab - \ell k)$ in equation 10.21 is negative, the $D > 0$ (case 1). Since $D > (a + b)^2$, at least one of the real eigenvalues λ_1 or λ_2 is positive. Therefore, since $\text{Re}(\lambda_1)$ and $\text{Re}(\lambda_2)$ must be nonpositive for stability, we see that

$$(ab - \ell k) > 0 \tag{10.23}$$

is a necessary condition for stability. Furthermore, since $\text{Re}(\lambda_1) = \text{Re}(\lambda_2) = -(a+b)/2$ in both cases 2 and 3

$$(a + b) > 0 \tag{10.24}$$

is a necessary condition for asymptotic stability.

In the following section we will observe that the following two conditions,

$(ab - \ell k) > 0$

$(a + b) > 0$
(10.25)

are necessary and sufficient conditions for asympotic stability. We will also observe that the two conditions,

$(ab - \ell k) > 0$

$(a + b) = 0$
(10.26)

are necessary and sufficient for the solution to be stable but not asymptotically stable.

Consider now the implications of Richardson's assumption that all the constants must be positive. Clearly, this assumption makes equation 10.24 unnecessary, and the asymptotic stability requirements reduce to equation 10.23, as Richardson in fact discovers in his analysis. But 10.25 is less restrictive than the assumption of positive constants. Recalling that a and b are the "fatigue and expense" coefficients, 10.24 indicates that it is not possible for both of these constants to be simultaneously negative if the system is to be stable; that is, an arms race between two nations cannot be economically beneficial to both nations without the system becoming unstable. However, equation 10.24 does allow one state to have a negative "fatigue and expense" coefficient so long as the opponent's "fatigue and expense" parameter is positive and large enough to counterbalance the opponent's negative coefficient. Thus, by requiring 10.24 in place of Richardson's assumption that all constants be positive, an arms race can be stable when one side finds the race beneficial but the other finds it to be a considerable burden. There is, however, a more significant consequence of the assumption that all the constants are positive. If all the constants are assumed to be positive, then from 10.22 we see that only $(a - b)^2 + 4k\ell > 0$ is possible, and therefore $D > 0$. Consequently, this assumption only permits us to consider stability case 1. The other types of stable systems are automatically eliminated from consideration.

But of what value is it to consider each of the three stability cases? In other words, what has Richardson missed by virtue of his extra assumption on the constants? Perhaps the most significant consequence of restricting the analysis to only one of the three stability cases is that the differences in how the two nations approach equilibrium will be missed. In each of the three cases the two nations will be changing their amounts of arms through time in very different patterns. Even though all three cases are situations of stability such that, with one exception (stable but not asymptotically stable), the two nations are approaching equilibrium, the path of the approach to the equilibrium value is quite different. A second, but somewhat subsidiary consequence of not considering all three stability cases is that Richardson ignores the very interesting subcase of a stable system that is not asymptotically stable—that is, a system in which the two nations arm and disarm in an oscillating pattern within a limited range of values, thus "orbiting" the equilibrium point. We turn then to a consideration of the consequences of the three stability cases.

PATTERNS OF STABILITY

Before examining each of the three stability cases, it is useful to sketch the outlines of the argument that will be followed. Since we have translated the equilibrium point to the origin we know that in the asymptotically stable cases $\bar{x}(t)$ and $\bar{y}(t)$ move to the origin. We wish to examine the movement of the trajectory $(\bar{x}[t], \bar{y}[t])$ for $t \varepsilon (0, \infty)$ in the (x,y) plane. For each value of t we obtain a value for $\bar{x}$ and $\bar{y}$, which we can plot as shown, for example, in Figures 10.3A or 10.3B. What we are interested in is how the trajectory $(\bar{x}[t], \bar{y}[t])$ behaves in the three stability cases. By comparing Figures 10.3A and 10.3B it is easily seen that differences in the <u>way</u> in which x and y approach equilibrium in asymptotically stable cases has important implications for understanding an arms race. One important difference between Figures 10.3A and 10.3B is that in 10.3A both nations are disarming, (that is, the amount of arms that each side has decreases as time increases), while in Figure 10.3B the two nations' armaments both increase and decrease as they approach equilibrium. If the reader finds 10.3B somewhat disconcerting, since it implies, for example, that at t, nation X has a negative amount of arms, he should recall that we have translated the equilibrium point to the origin. We will show that the <u>path</u> of the trajectory $(\bar{x}[t], \bar{y}[t])$ is important for understanding an arms race. We turn now to a consideration of the factors that govern the paths.

From our previous discussion we know that the behavior of the trajectory $(\bar{x}[t], \bar{y}[t])$ is determined by λ_1 and λ_2 as given in equations 10.17 and 10.18. We will perform a simple transformation on $\bar{x}$ and $\bar{y}$ so that only one λ will appear in each solution of 10.13 and 10.14. For example,

FIGURE 10.3

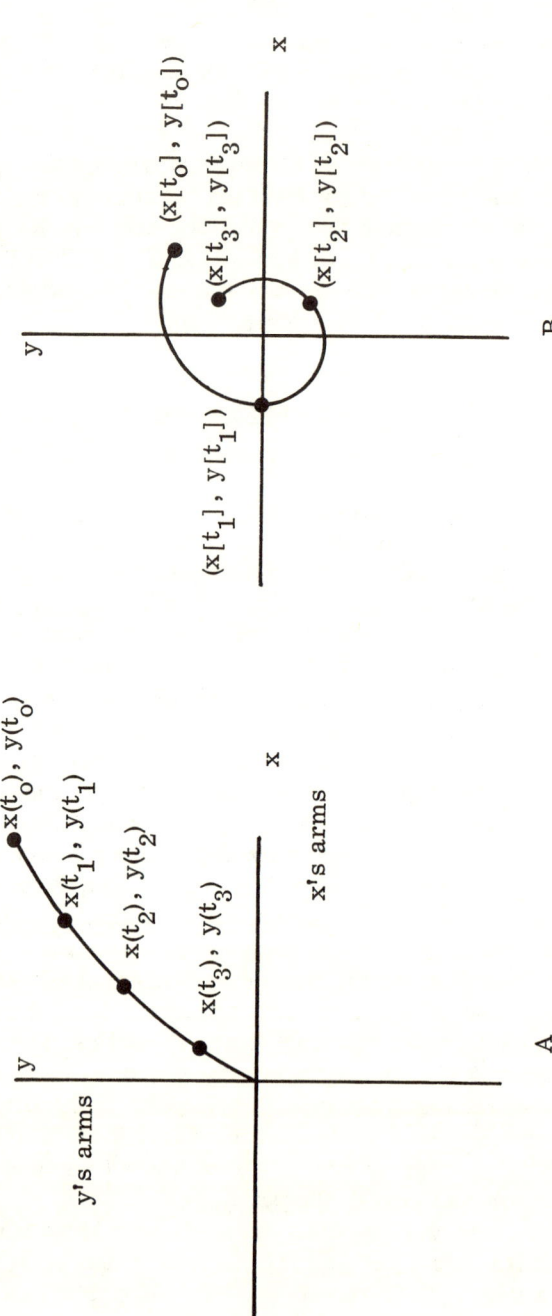

Trajectory of Arms Race in Asymptotically Stable Case: Mutual Disarmament

Trajectory of Arms Race in Asymptotically Stable Case: Increases and Decreases in Arms

$$\tilde{x}(t) = C_1 e^{\lambda_1 t} \qquad (10.27)$$

$$\tilde{y}(t) = C_2 e^{\lambda_2 t} \qquad (10.28)$$

where $\tilde{x}(t)$ and $\tilde{y}(t)$ are solutions of equations 10.13 and 10.14. An examination of what happens in 10.27 and 10.28 as t increases within each of the three stability cases is relatively straightforward. We now turn to a consideration of each case.

Case 1: $D > 0$*

We define the transformations as follows:

$$\xi \equiv \ell\bar{x} + (\lambda_1 + a)\bar{y} \qquad (10.29)$$

$$\eta \equiv \ell\bar{x} + (\lambda_2 + a)\bar{y} \qquad (10.30)$$

and note from 10.17 and 10.18 that

$$\lambda_1 + \lambda_2 = -(a + b) \qquad (10.31)$$

$$\lambda_1 \lambda_2 = ab - \ell k \qquad (10.32)$$

differentiating 10.29 and 10.30, we obtain the following:

$$\dot{\xi} = \ell\dot{\bar{x}} + (\lambda_1 + a)\dot{\bar{y}} \qquad (10.33)$$

$$\dot{\eta} = \ell\dot{\bar{x}} + (\lambda_2 + a)\dot{\bar{y}} \qquad (10.34)$$

Substituting 10.13 and 10.14 into 10.33 and 10.34 and simplifying using 10.31 and 10.32, we obtain the solutions:

$$\xi(t) = \xi(0)e^{\lambda_1 t} \qquad (10.35)$$

$$\eta(t) = \eta(0)e^{\lambda_2 t} \qquad (10.36)$$

where $\xi(0)$ and $\eta(0)$ are the initial conditions. For asymptotic stability, it follows from 10.35 and 10.36 that $\lambda_1 < 0$ and $\lambda_2 < 0$.

Examining 10.35 and 10.3 we note immediately that $e^{\lambda_1 t}$ and $e^{\lambda_2 t}$ are positive. Consequently, if the initial conditions are positive,

---

*Eigenvalues real and distinct, $\lambda_1 \neq \lambda_2$.

$\xi(0) > 0$ and $\eta(0) > 0$, 10.35 and 10.36 will be positive for all finite t. Similarly, if $\xi(0) < 0$ and $\eta(0) > 0$, equation 10.35 will be negative and 10.36 positive. In general $\xi(t)$ and $\eta(t)$ begin and remain in the same quadrant. In short, the ξ axis and the η axis are barriers. These results are shown graphically in Figure 10.4.

The significance of this result can perhaps be more easily shown graphically. First, we will perform the inverse transformation to obtain the images of the ξ and η axes in the $(\bar{x}, \bar{y})$ plane. From equations 10.29 and 10.30 these images are given by the following:

$$\bar{y} = (-\ell/[\lambda_1 + a])\bar{x} \qquad (10.37)$$

$$\bar{y} = (-\ell/[\lambda_2 + a])\bar{x} \qquad (10.38)$$

where λ_1 and λ_2 are defined by 10.17 and 10.18. Figure 10.5 is a representation of equations 10.37 and 10.38 in (x, y) plane. In Figure 5 lines (10.37) and (10.38) are barriers as identified by Richardson.[8]

Thus we observe that there are two consequences implicit in being in case 1. First, the approach to equilibrium involves a

FIGURE 10.4

Trajectory and Barriers in Case I:
(ξ, η) Plane

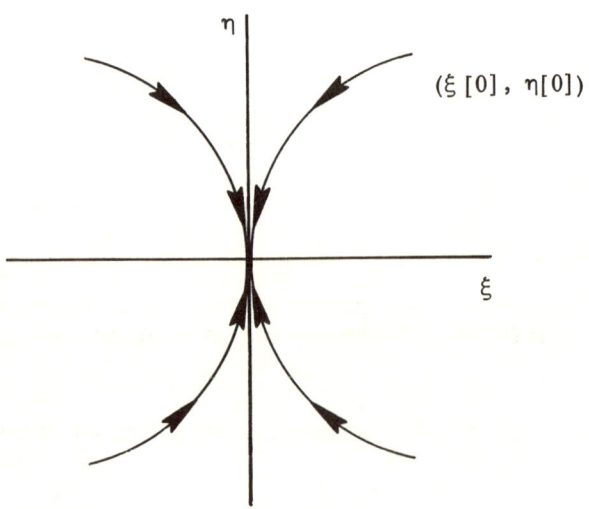

FIGURE 10.5

Trajectory and Barriers in Case 1:
(x, y) Plane

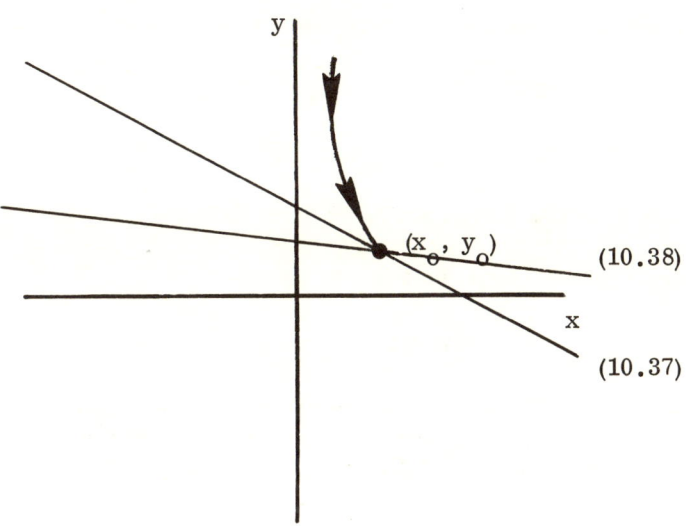

monotonic decrease in arms in the transformed plane. Second, there are two barriers neither of which can be crossed.

Case 2. $D < 0$*

We define the transformations as follows:

$$\psi \equiv \ell \bar{x} + (u + a) \bar{y} \tag{10.39}$$

$$\phi \equiv v \bar{y} \tag{10.40}$$

where u and v are real numbers and

$$\lambda_1 = u + iv \tag{10.41}$$

$$\lambda_2 = u - iv \tag{10.42}$$

---

*Eigenvalues are complex conjugates.

or referring back to equations 10.17 and 10.18:

$$u = -(a + b)/2 \tag{10.43}$$

$$v = \sqrt{D}/2 \tag{10.44}$$

Differentiating equations 10.39 and 10.40, we obtain the following:

$$\dot{\psi} = u\psi - v\phi \tag{10.45}$$

$$\dot{\phi} = v\psi + u\phi \tag{10.46}$$

whose solutions can be shown to be as follows:

$$\psi(t) = c_1 e^{ut} \cos(vt + \theta) \tag{10.47}$$

$$\phi(t) = c_1 e^{ut} \sin(vt + \theta) \tag{10.48}$$

Consider two subcases of equations 10.47 and 10.48: (2A) $u = (a+b)/2 = 0$, (2B) $u = (a+b)/2 < 0$. The subcase of $u > 0$ is not considered because it implies that the system is not stable and hence not relevant to the present discussion.

Subcase 2A. $u = 0$

If $u = 0$, equations 10.47 and 10.48 become 10.49 and 10.50:

$$\psi(t) = c_1 \cos(vt + \theta) \tag{10.49}$$

$$\phi(t) = c_1 \sin(vt + \theta) \tag{10.50}$$

Furthermore, we know that since $-1 < \cos(\theta) < 1$ and $-1 < \sin(\theta) < 1$, it must be the case that as $t \to \infty$, the trajectory ($\psi[t]$, $\phi[t]$) is a circle whose radius depends on c_1. Since c_1 is in turn dependent on the initial condition, in this first subcase the initial condition determines the radius of the circle in Figure 10.6. The system orbits around the equilibrium point in the (ψ, ϕ) plane. Three conclusions can be drawn in this case. First, the system will never reach the equilibrium point. The system is stable but not asymptotically stable, meeting conditions i and ii of the definition, but not condition iii. Second, the pattern of behavior of the two nations will involve oscillations between increasing and decreasing the amount of arms of the part of both sides. But these oscillations will be confined to a given set of values determined by the initial

FIGURE 10.6

Trajectory and Barriers in Case 2,
subcase a: (φ, ψ) Plane

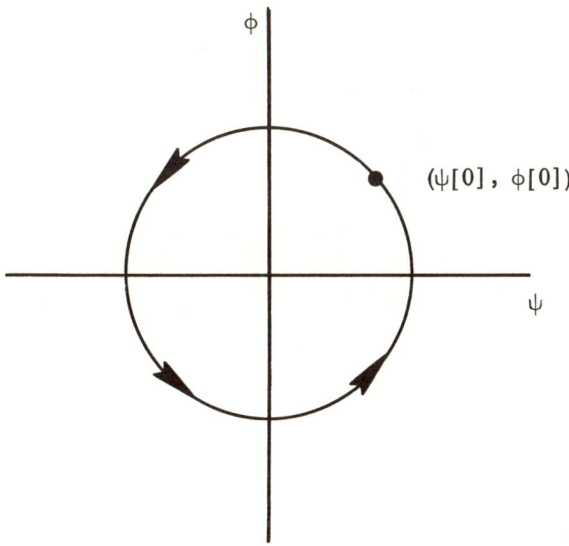

condition that in turn specifies the radius of the circle on which the arming behavior will orbit equilibrium. Third, there are not any barriers. The two arming nations are not restricted to any quadrant in the (ψ, φ) plane. Figure 10.7, which uses the inverse transformation to obtain the image of the ψ and φ axes in the (x, y) plane, shows that there are no barriers.

Subcase 2B. u < 0

The principle difference between subcases 2A and 2B is that in the later e^{ut} becomes operative. Since u < 0, then as t increases the value multiplying either cos or sin is decreasing. As a result, the trajectory (ψ, φ) spirals into the origin as shown in Figure 10.8. The conclusion we can draw from this case is that while X and Y will both arm and disarm in the oscillating pattern similar to subcase 2A, the total amount of arms of both sides is continually shrinking, and the system approaches the equilibrium point. Furthermore, as was true in subcase 2A, Figures 10.8 and 10.9 show that there are no barriers.

FIGURE 10.7

Trajectory and Barriers in Case 2,
subcase a: (x,y) Plane

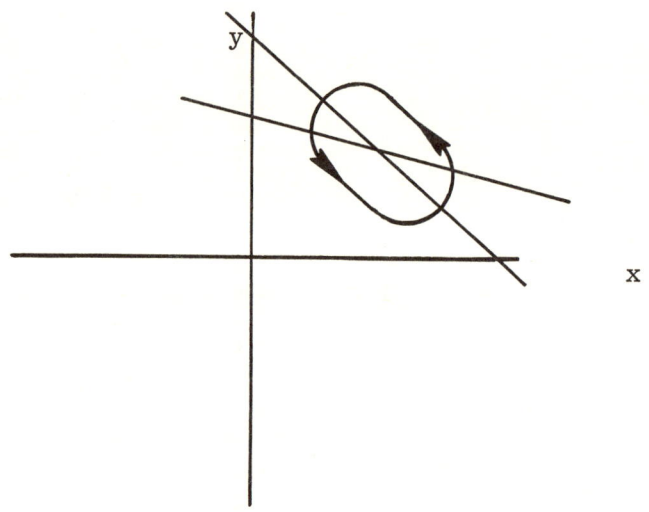

FIGURE 10.8

Trajectory and Barriers in Case 2,
subcase b: (ϕ, ψ) Plane

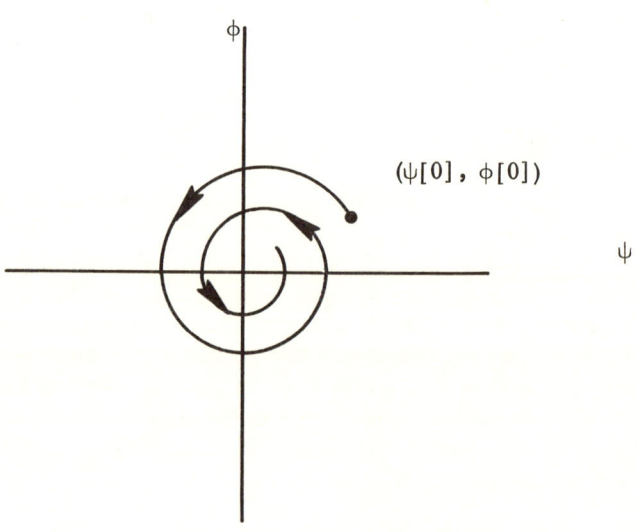

FIGURE 10.9

Trajectory and Barriers in Case 2,
subcase b: (x,y) Plane

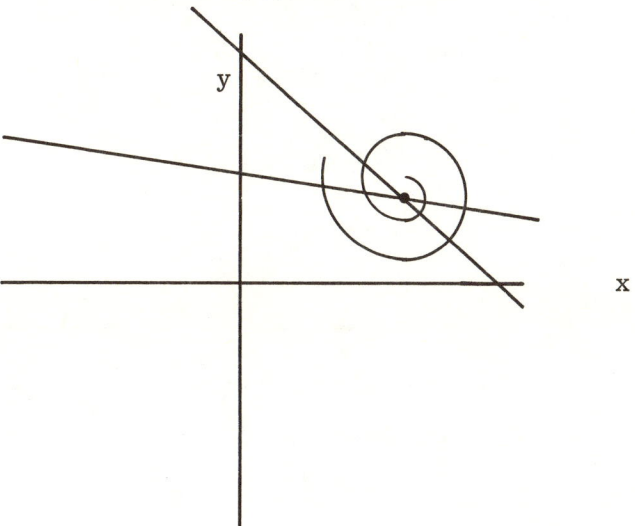

Case 3. $D = 0$*

Since $D = 0$ in equation 10.22, we observe that $(a - b)^2$ must be zero or positive. If $(a - b)^2 > 0$, then either ℓ or k, but not both, must be negative. If $(a - b)^2 = 0$, then either ℓ or k must be zero. This yields three subcases, each of which must be considered: (3A) $\ell = k = 0$; (3B) $k \neq 0$; and (3C) $\ell \neq 0$.

Subcase 3A. $\ell = k = 0$

Under this condition, the original system 10.13 and 10.14 becomes the following:

$$\dot{\bar{x}} = -a\bar{x} \qquad (10.51)$$

$$\dot{\bar{y}} = -b\bar{y} \qquad (10.52)$$

From equations 10.51 and 10.52 it can be seen that the condition for asymptotic stability is $a = b > 0$. Hence, as t increases, x(t)

---

*Eigenvalues are real but equal, $\lambda_1 = \lambda_2 = -(a + b)/2$.

FIGURE 10.10

Trajectory and Barriers in Case 3,
subcase a: (x,y) Plane

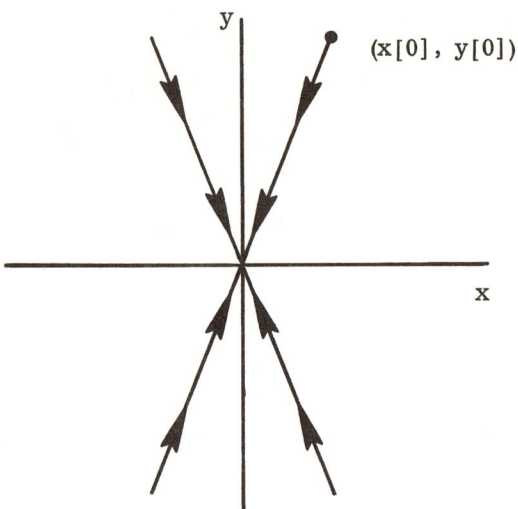

and y(t) approach the origin along a straight line whose slope is determined by the initial condition, as shown in Figure 10.10. Note that no transformation was required in this subcase, so we are in the original (x, y) plane. In the sense that there is a monotonic decrease in arms by both sides in this case, there is a similarity here with case 1.

Subcase 3B. $k \neq 0$

Define the following transformation:

$$\rho \equiv ([a - b] / [2k])\bar{x} + \bar{y} \qquad (10.53)$$

$$\omega \equiv (1/k)\bar{x} \qquad (10.54)$$

When differentiated, 10.53 and 10.54 used with 10.13 and 10.14, yield the following:

$$\dot{\rho} = (-[a + b]/2)\rho \qquad (10.55)$$

$$\dot{\omega} = \rho - ([a + b]/2)\omega \qquad (10.56$$

RICHARDSON'S MODEL REINTERPRETED

The solution to 10.55 and 10.56 is as follows:

$$\rho(t) = \rho(0)e^{(-t[a+b])/2} \qquad (10.57)$$

$$\omega(t) = (\omega(0) + \rho(0)t)e^{(-t[a+b])/2} \qquad (10.58)$$

Obviously when $a + b > 0$, equations 10.57 and 10.58 are asymptotically stable, and the arms race will approach the equilibrium point. Figure 10.11 demonstrates the case where $\rho(0)$ and $\omega(0)$ have the same sign and the trajectory (ρ, ω) never crosses either axis. Figure 10.12 shows the case where $\rho(0)$ and $\omega(0)$ are of different sign and trajectory (ρ, ω) crosses only the ρ axis.

The implications of these results for an arms race are best shown by finding the image ω axis in the (x, y) plane. It is given by equation 10.59:

$$\bar{y} = ([b - a]/zk)\bar{x} \qquad (10.59)$$

A typical inverse transformation is shown in Figure 10.13, where once again we are not translating the equilibrium point to the origin. The equilibrium point is on the barrier z. Thus, if the system begins in the shaded region, it is confined to that region; that is,

FIGURE 10.11

Trajectory and Barriers in Case 3, subcase b:
$\rho(0)$ and $\omega(0)$ Have Same Sign

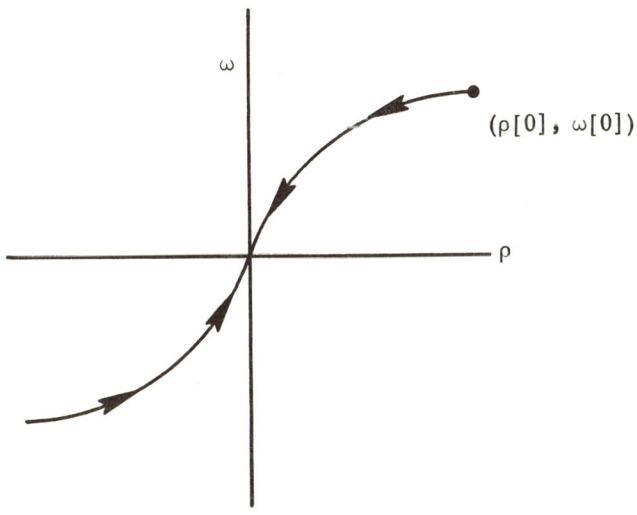

FIGURE 10.12

Trajectory and Barriers in Case 3, subcase b:
ρ(0) and ω(0) of Different Sign

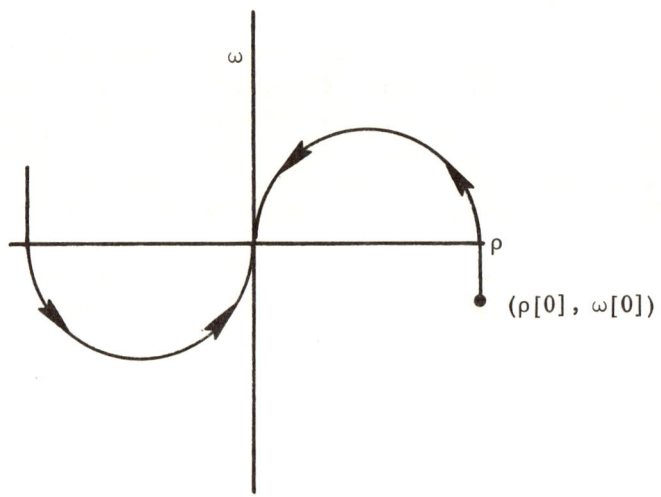

FIGURE 10.13

Trajectory and Barriers in Case 3, subcase b:
(x,y) Plane, Negative Slope

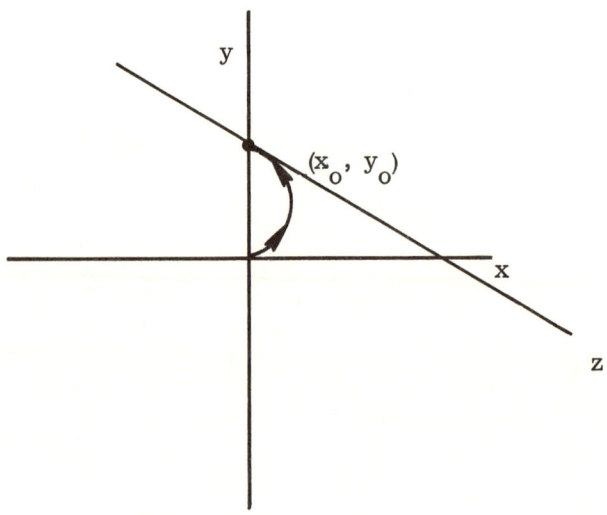

the z line indicates the limit that is placed on the combined amount of arms of the two nations.

There is yet another interesting consequence of this subcase. Figure 10.13 depicts equation 10.59 as having a negative slope. But the stability conditions do not necessarily imply that this will always be the case; the line z could have a positive slope, as shown in Figure 10.14. The surprising result that occurs when we compare Figures 10.13 and 10.14 is that the negative slope of Figure 10.13 places considerably greater restrictions on the values of the initial conditions for stability to occur. In Figure 10.14 we see that the initial amount of arms possessed by X can be of any value and the (x[t], y[t]) trajectory will lie in the shaded region bounded by the z barrier.

Subcase 3C. $\ell \neq 0$

It should not be difficult to see that the argument in this case is identical to that presented for subcase 3B. In the transformation given in equations 10.53 and 10.54 we substitute ℓ for k, and the solutions are the same. The difference occurs when we translate

FIGURE 10.14

Trajectory and Barriers in Case 3, subcase b: (x,y) Plane, Positive Slope

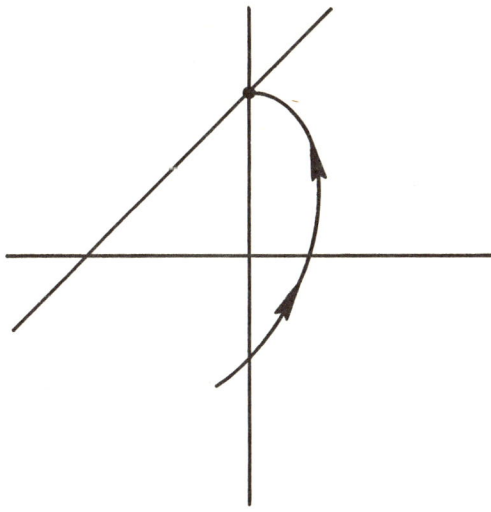

the ρ and ω axes into the (x, y) plane. Here we find that the barrier is given by

$$\bar{y} = ([2\ell]/[b-a])\bar{x} \qquad (10.60)$$

We have discussed all three of the stability cases. For each case we have noted the barriers when such exist. We now have detailed the necessary and sufficient conditions for stability (10.26) and asymptotic stability (10.25) without the sign constraints imposed by Richardson. In addition, for each stability case we have shown the trajectories of the two nations in their approach toward the equilibrium point. Different stability cases yield different trajectories and barriers that cannot be transversed.

PATTERNS OF INSTABILITY

It should be obvious that for each of the above three cases, though not for all subcases, there will be corrollary patterns of instability. Corresponding to case 1, depicted in Figure 10.4, the trajectory would move out and away from the initial condition, as shown in Figure 10.15. In case 2, as shown in Figure 10.8 we obtain a spiral that spins out and away from the initial condition. There would be of course no corresponding condition for subcase 2A; this is seen in Figure 10.16. In case 3 the direction of the trajectories of x(t) and y(t) move in the opposite direction from that shown in Figures 10.10 and 10.11, as depicted in Figures 10.17 and 10.18. In addition to these three cases there will be one further unstable case as shown in Figure 10.19. This occurs when D is positive and $ab - \ell k < 0$.

STABILITY IN THE RIVALRY MODEL

Having constructed and analyzed his original model (equation 10.1 and 10.2), Richardson considered a slight modification and introduced his Rivalry model[9]:

$$\dot{x} = k'(y - x) - a'x + g' \qquad (10.61)$$

$$\dot{y} = \ell'(x - y) - b'y + h' \qquad (10.62)$$

FIGURE 10.15

Instability in Case 1

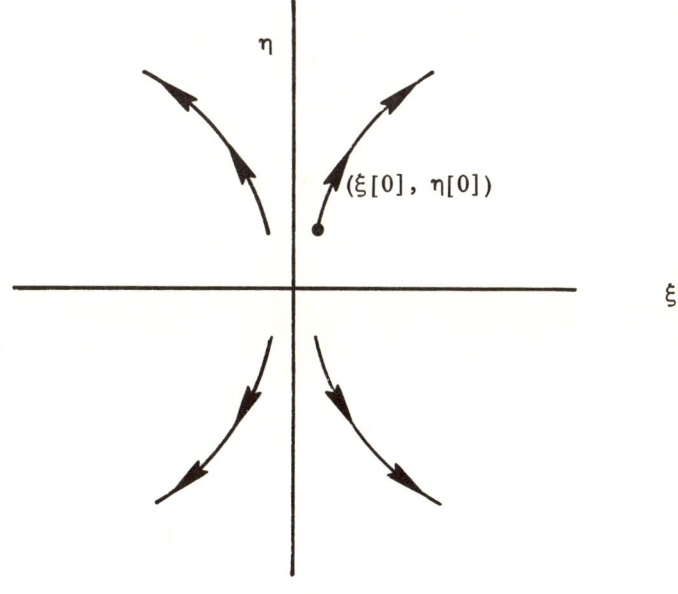

FIGURE 10.16

Instability in Case 2, subcase b

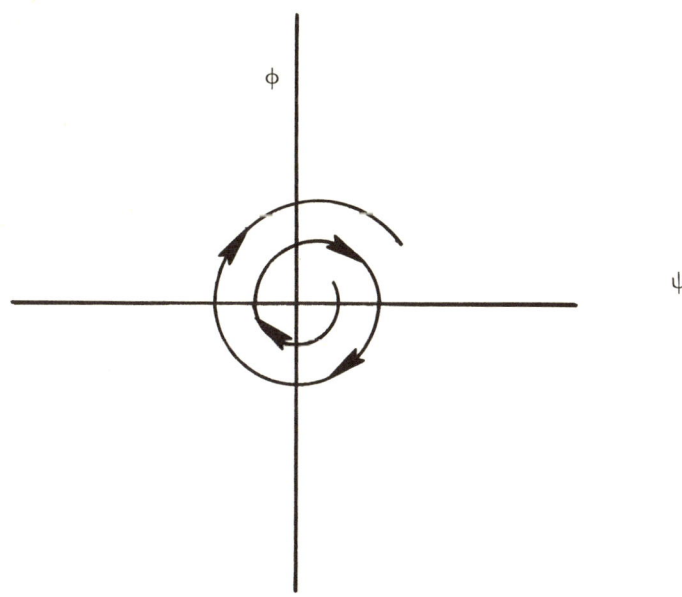

FIGURE 10.17

Instability in Case 3, subcase a

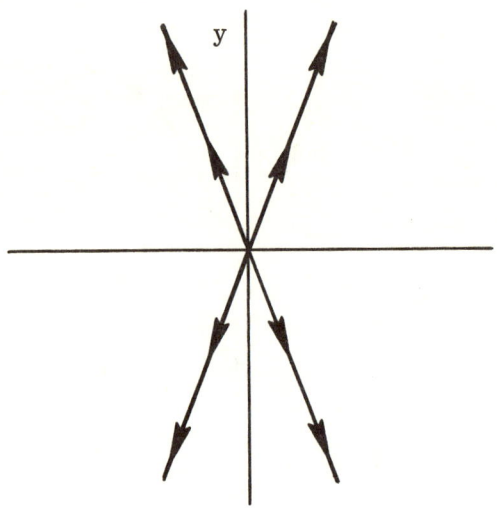

FIGURE 10.18

Instability in Case 3, subcase b

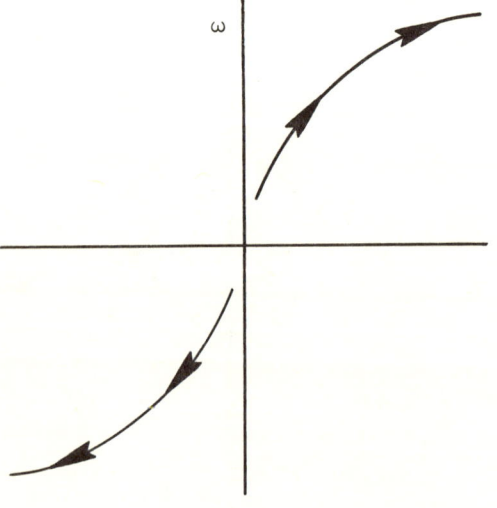

FIGURE 10.19

Instability When D > 0 and (ab − ℓk) < 0

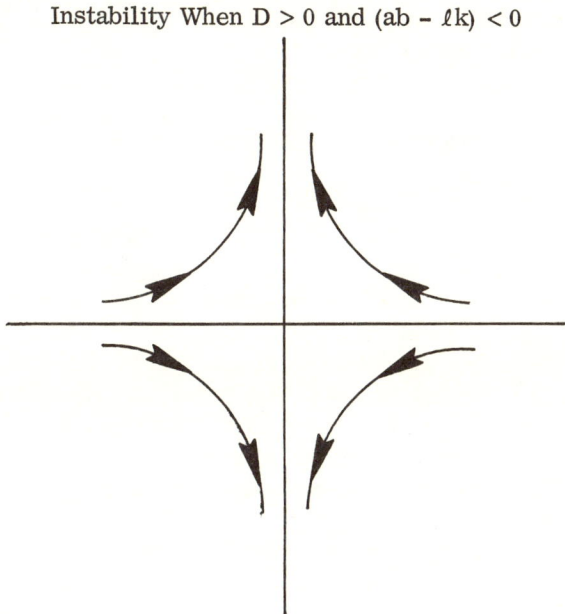

Under his assumptions concerning the signs of the parameters, Richardson discovered that the rivalry model was always asymptotically stable. Consequently, he discarded the model as uninteresting because historically not all arms races have been stable. From our earlier discussion, it can be shown that the inherent asymptotic stability of this model is a product of Richardson's assumption that all parameters are positive.

We note first the equivalence between the original model of equations 10.1 and 10.2 and the Rivalry model of equations 10.61 and 10.62 by writing the original model as follows:

$$\dot{x} = ky - ax + g = k(y - x) - (a - k)x + g \qquad (10.63)$$

$$\dot{y} = \ell x - by + h = \ell(x - y) - (b - \ell)y + h \qquad (10.64)$$

Setting $k' = k$, $\ell' = \ell$, $a' = (a - k)$, and $b' = (b - \ell)$, we see that equations 10.63 and 10.64 reduce to equations 10.61 and 10.62. In the original model the assumption of positive constants only eliminated the need for condition 10.24; it was still necessary to specify condition 10.23, since there was no reason to believe that $ab - k\ell > 0$. However, by assuming the constants k', a', ℓ', and b' to be positive in equations 10.61 and 10.62 we see that Richardson has in effect specified that (a - k) and (b - ℓ) are both positive. Therefore, a > k > 0 and b > ℓ > 0. Consequently, ab - kℓ > 0. We see that by assuming positive constants, the stability conditions are always met in the rivalry model.

SUMMARY AND CONCLUSION

The purpose of this chapter has been to extend Richardson's analysis of his original arms-race model by discarding the somewhat artificial restriction that all the constants of the model be positive. We have shown that the assumption of positive constants led Richardson to consider only one very special case of stability and did not allow him to see that there could be a variety of different ways two nations could reach equilibrium.[10] We saw further that the barriers that he found do not necessarily exist in all the stability cases and that they differ from case to case in those instances in which they do exist. Dropping the assumption of positive constants also made it possible to observe a very special case of stability in which an equilibrium point would never be reached: where two nations armed and disarmed in a pattern traced by a circle. The most important general conclusion from these analyses is that there is a variety of different patterns of stable arms races. Similarly, there is a corresponding variety of different unstable arms races. Finally, we showed that the positive constant assumption, when applied to the Rivalry model, made that model inherently stable. Richardson's conclusion that this model is always stable is not an artifact of the model but of the additional assumption that the constants must be positive.

NOTES

1. Lewis F. Richardson, Arms and Insecurity (Chicago: Quadrangle Books, 1960).
2. For examples, see Lewis F. Richardson, Statistics of Deadly Quarrels (Chicago: Quadrangle Books, 1960).
3. See, for example, Paul Smoker, "A Mathematical Study of the Present Arms Race," General Systems 8 (1963): 51-60; Paul Smoker, "A Pilot Study of the Present Arms Race," General Systems 8 (1963): 61-76; Dina A. Zinnes and John V. Gillespie, "Analysis of Arms Race Models: US vs. USSR and NATO vs. WTO," Modeling and Simulation 4 (1973): 145-48.

4. See for example Philip A. Schrodt, "Richardson's N-Nation Model and the Balance of Power," paper presented at International Studies Association, 1975.

5. Mancur Olson, Jr., and Richard Zeckhauser, "An Economic Theory of Alliances," Review of Economics and Statistics 48 (1966): 266-79.

6. For a more complete discussion of this intuitive argument, see Anatol Rapoport, Fights, Games and Debates (Ann Arbor: University of Michigan Press, 1961); Dina A. Zinnes, Contemporary Research in International Relations (New York: Free Press, 1976), Ch. 14.

7. For a complete discussion of the solution to differential equations, see L. S. Pontryagin, Ordinary Differential Equations (Reading, Mass.: Addison Wesley, 1962); D. A. Sanchez, Ordinary Differential Equations and Stability Theory: An Introduction (San Francisco: Freeman, 1968).

8. Lewis F. Richardson, Arms and Insecurity, pp. 28-29.

9. Ibid., pp. 35-36.

10. Dragoslav D. Siljak, "On Stability of the Arms Race," in Mathematical Systems in International Relations Research, ed. John V. Gillespie and Dina A. Zinnes (New York: Praeger), 1976.

CHAPTER 11

ON THE EFFECTS OF AID TO NATIONS IN ARMS RACES
John A. Ferejohn

THE RICHARDSON MODEL

The arms race literature in political science has dwelt heavily (indeed almost doted) upon the pioneering work of Lewis Richardson.[1] Richardson's principal contribution was twofold: (a) to characterize an arms race as a set of linear differential equations and (b) to produce behaviorally plausible interpretations of the parameters in the model. To keep outside reference at a minimum, we will summarize the relevant parts of his work. Consider two nations, and let x be the arms expenditure of one and y the arms expenditure of the other. Then Richardson's model for an arms race is as follows:

$$dx/dt = ax + by + c$$
$$dy/dt = dx + ey + f$$

(11.1)

He reasons that a and e should be negative, and he called them "fatigue" coefficients, arguing that in the absence of external threat nations will prefer to decrease military expenditure. He called c and f "grievance" coefficients: If positive, they maintain military expenditures away from zero in the absence of external

---

Research for this paper was conducted under the auspices of the Brookings Institution. An earlier version was presented at the Annual Meetings of the American Statistical Association, December 28-30, 1970. The author wishes to thank Talbot Page, David Seidman, and David Grether for their critical remarks.

pressure; if there is external pressure, they accelerate the rate of growth of arms expenditure. He called b and d the "reaction" coefficients; they characterize the response of each nation to the other's level of arms expenditure.

Richardson's analysis is to categorize stationary points of the system: points where neither nation is increasing or decreasing arms expenditures. These are the points where $dx/dt = dy/dt = 0$. He shows that there are two interesting kinds of stationary points depending on the coefficients:

1. Stable points. If (x_0, y_0) is a stable point, then given any vector (x,y) near (x_0, y_0), the system will converge to (x_0, y_0).
2. Unstable points. If (x_0, y_0) is unstable and stationary, then if (x,y) is different from (x_0, y_0), the system will diverge from (x_0, y_0), and one or both x and y will tend to infinity (either oscillating or in one direction).

The sufficient condition on the coefficients for determining which of these two cases holds, can be written variously:

1. $ae < bd \rightarrow$ instability
2. max root of $\begin{pmatrix} a & b \\ d & e \end{pmatrix} > 0 \rightarrow$ instability

Richardson carries his analysis over to the case of more than two nations. Criterion 2 is, of course, still applicable. Though we will not go into it, there are several obvious ways this line of thought can be extended. Milstein and Mitchell characterize the two-nation arms race as a pair of second-order differential equations.[2] The coefficients in that case also seem to have clear interpretation, and similar stability conditions may be derived. Peter Busch provides an adequate survey of the field for those who want to pursue this line of thought.[3]

What interests us more is the following question: Can one ever empirically identify an arms race? That is, is it possible to estimate the coefficients in the Richardson model? Our efforts here will show that (a) the estimation problems in the Richardson model are practically insuperable; (b) the estimation of the competitive military situation between nations is important for evaluating U.S. aid policies; (c) useful arms race models can be introduced that are empirically more plausible than the Richardson model and its variants and that permit empirical estimation. The outline of the chapter will be as follows: The first part will demonstrate the empirical quandary of Richardson-type models. The second part will introduce graphical analysis of U.S. military and domestic aid policies to reactions in arms competition. The third part will introduce a model that captures the essential aspects of the graphical analysis and that permits econometric estimation. The fourth part will evaluate United States aid policies and indicate alternative approaches.

EMPIRICAL QUANDARY OF RICHARDSON-TYPE MODELS

The Richardson model would not be such a bad one if it were not taken so seriously. It has certain very plausible features, especially when written down in difference equation form rather than in differential equations as above. It can be written as follows:

$$\Delta x_t = x_t - x_{t-1} = ax_{t-1} + by_{t-1} + c$$

or

$$x_t = (1 + a)x_{t-1} + by_{t-1} + c$$

The decision maker looks at what the other nation did last time, considers the cost to himself of maintaining a large military budget, adds a constant amount (perhaps for controlling domestic disorder, perhaps for peace of mind), and then computes his next period budget. The other nation does the same thing. This has a comforting ring to it in that no great intellectual task is required of decision makers.

Several scholars, Richardson included, have made attempts to estimate the coefficients of this model directly. The usual procedure, whether written down explicitly or not, is to tack an error term onto each question, obtaining the following:

$$x_t = (1 + a)x_{t-1} + by_{t-1} + c + \varepsilon_t$$
$$y_t = dx_{t-1} + (1 + e)y_{t-1} + f + \eta_t$$
(11.1.1)

I shall write this in vector form as follows:

$$x(t) = Cx(t-1) + \varepsilon_t \qquad (11.1.2)$$

where

EFFECTS OF AID ON ARMS RACES

$$x(t) = \begin{pmatrix} x_t - \bar{x} \\ y_t - \bar{y} \end{pmatrix} \quad \text{where } \bar{x} \text{ and } \bar{y} \text{ are equilibrium values of } x(t) \text{ and } y(t)$$

$$C = \begin{pmatrix} 1+a & b \\ d & 1+e \end{pmatrix} \quad \varepsilon_t = \begin{pmatrix} \varepsilon_t \\ \eta_t \end{pmatrix}$$

For purpose of simplicity take x(0) to be a constant. The assumptions are the usual ones for application of least squares:

1. $E(\varepsilon_t) = 0$
2. $\text{Var}(\varepsilon_t) = E(\varepsilon_t \varepsilon_t') = \Omega$ a positive definite matrix
3. $\text{Cov}(\varepsilon_t \varepsilon_\tau') = E(\varepsilon_t \varepsilon_\tau') = 0$ for $t \neq \tau$

The difference equation solution of 11.1.2 can be written:

$$x(t) = C^t x(0) + \sum_{k=0}^{t-1} C^k \varepsilon_{t-k} \tag{11.1.3}$$

The following results are easy to obtain:

$$Ex(t) = C^t x(0) + E\left(\sum_{k=0}^{t-1} C^k \varepsilon_{t-k}\right)' = C^t x(0) \tag{11.1.4}$$

$$\text{Var}(x[t]) = E\left(\sum_{k=0}^{t-1} C^k \varepsilon_{t-k}\right)\left(\sum_{k=0}^{t-1} C^k \varepsilon_{t-k}\right)' = \sum_{k=0}^{t-1} C^k \Omega C^{k'} \tag{11.1.5}$$

It is apparent that the behavior of x(t) depends on the matrix C. If C^t gets small as t gets large, the variance of x(t) will converge to a constant. The stability conditions on C are slightly different from the ones employed in the introduction, since a 1 was added to each diagonal element. We have

$$\lim_{t \to \infty} C^t = 0$$

if and only if the roots of C are less than one in absolute value.

Some results from least-squares theory are now in order. It is well known that in models of the form 11.1.2, least squares yield biased estimates even when the matrix C is stable.[4] Some authors have, on the other hand, found asymptotic expressions for the bias which will allow for cheap corrections.[5] For C stable, least-squares estimates are consistent.

The repeated stipulation that C be stable ought to give pause to students of arms competition. If C is stable, then one must wonder if there really is a true "arms race" between nations. Such cases may not be of great interest compared to the case where C is unstable. The rather fragile properties of the least-squares estimator of C are obtained only in the case where there seems to be no arms race to speak of. What if there is?

Suppose there are roots of C that are greater than one in absolute value. Anderson has studied the case where all the roots of C are greater than 1.0.[6] He shows that if and only if the ε_t are normally distributed, the limiting distribution of the least-squares estimator Ĉ about C is Cauchy. (Note that the variance of a Cauchy distribution is infinite and that the mean of such distribution exists only in a special sense.) If the ε_t are not assumed to be normal, no limiting distribution at all may exist. Where only some of the roots of C are greater than one, research has not been done (to the author's knowledge). We think this situation is nearly hopeless: In the case of greatest interest, estimation of the arms-race structure with any reliability is just about impossible.

A GRAPHICAL ANALYSIS OF MILITARY AID

Throughout this section the decision makers are assumed to be dictators or at least homogeneous ruling groups. This assumption is made for two reasons. First, we want to be able to use indifference maps, so we shall need well-behaved social preferences at least. Second, we do not want to have to worry about the control over the relevant resources within the nation. In other words, the decision makers are assumed to be able to make allocational decisions and to enforce them.

The decision maker of a nation is faced with an allocation problem each year. He is given a total budget Y_t, and he can spend it to buy two kinds of goods: domestic goods (D_t) and military goods (M_t). It seems reasonable to postulate that domestic goods are valuable to each decision maker (which simply means that there is no satiation point for domestic goods). Second, we postulate a condition of arms competition: If the opposing nation raises its budget, then the marginal value of a military good to the first nation is increased.

In view of the manner in which budgeting decisions are actually reached in most nations, we shall be able to remove most of the strategic elements of the situation. That is, each nation essentially reacts to what the other did last time, or, what is substantially the same (and mathematically identical), each nation reacts to its forecast of what the other will do this time. Thus, the model assumes there is no negotiation over the levels of the military budget. This seems to be entirely plausible and to capture the essence of the situation. (The reader might observe that this assumption makes the postulated situation share many of the features of the Prisoner's Dilemma game.[7])

The situation for a single nation is shown in Figure 11.1. The assumptions above allow me to use indifference curves. The indifference curves are drawn under the assumption that the competing nations' arms expenditures in the previous period are fixed at some definite level. The optimal point is where the budgetary constraint is tangent to I, and here M dollars are allocated to the military, and Y - M = D dollars are given over to domestic expenditures.

Suppose now that the nation is given some unrestricted aid and that it receives this aid before formulating its budget. Such aid

FIGURE 11.1

The Decision Maker's Allocation Problem

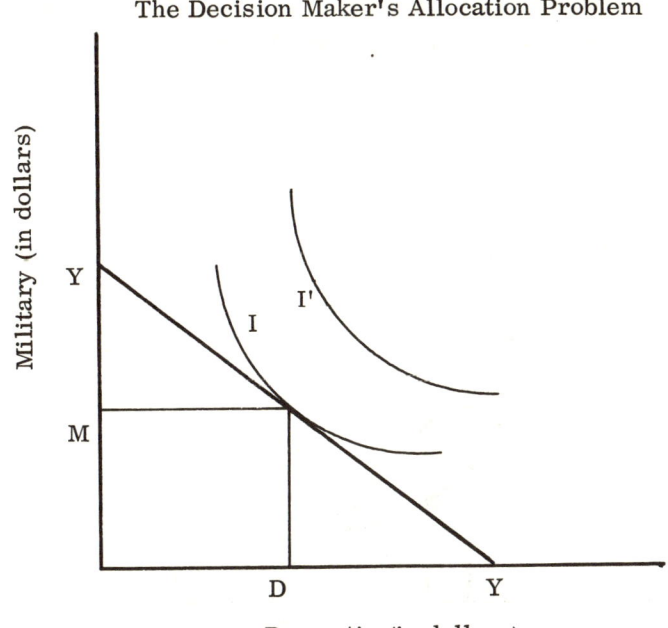

can be seen as a simple shift of the budget line: the nation now has a budget of size $Y_t + A_t$. Figure 11.2 shows that effect on the size of the military and domestic budgets. $\Delta M + \Delta D = A_t$.

Now consider the case when purely military aid is given. I assume that if aid is given in the form of military goods, it cannot be sold and the money transferred into domestic expenditure. Two cases are of interest: (a) the military aid is received prior to the formulation of the budget; (b) it is received after the budget is formulated. Figure 11.3 illustrates the first case. The effect of restricted aid to the military in this case is to change the shape of the budgetary constraint. The new constraint is now ABC'. In the figure there is no difference between the allocation under a purely military aid restriction and the allocation that would have been achieved if the aid were not restricted.

Figure 11.4 illustrates a case where different allocations are achieved. If aid is unrestricted, the new budget constraint is AA', and the optimal amount of military goods is $M + M_{pa}$ (where pa stands for pure aid). If aid is military, the budget constraint is ABC', and the military goods allocation if $M + M_{ma}$. The peculiar features of this example are noteworthy. Notice that in order to get a discrepancy between the amount of military goods in the two

FIGURE 11.2

The Effect of Unrestricted Aid on the
Allocation of the Budget

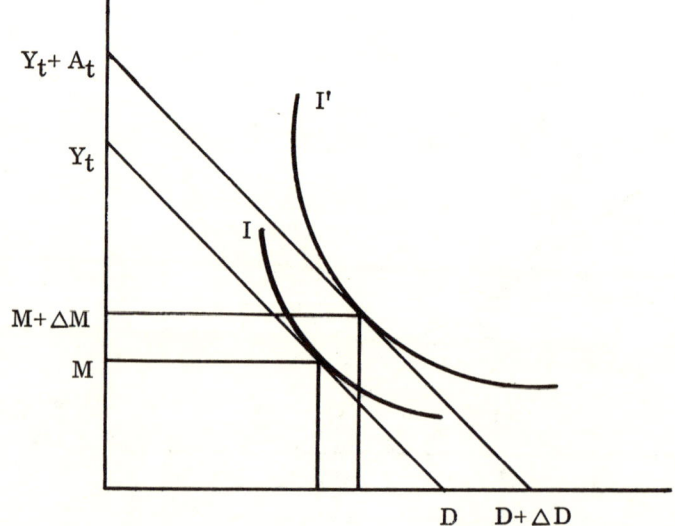

FIGURE 11.3

The Effect of Military Aid on the Budget When the Aid Is Received Prior to Budget Formation

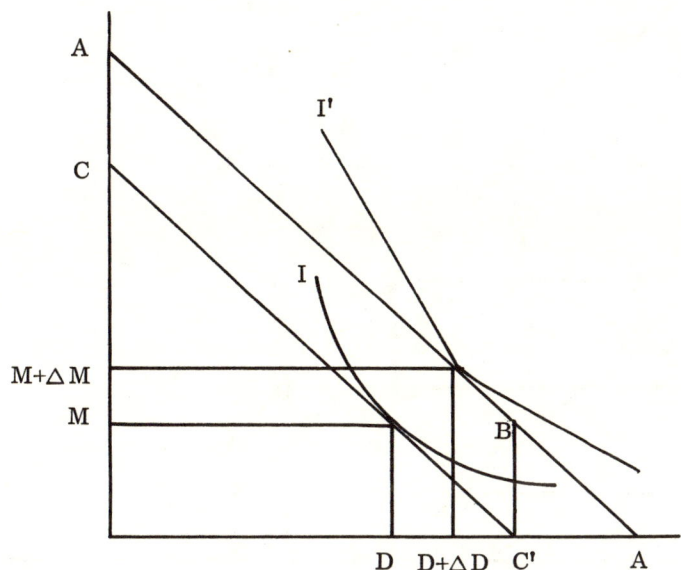

situations (a) there has to be a large amount of aid given relative to the size of the original budget (CC'), and (b) the taste of the dictator must be strongly in the direction of domestic goods (in other words, budget distortion will most likely occur in peace-loving nations).

Now consider the case where military aid is given after budget formulation. This case is a little less straightforward than previous ones. On the face of it, the nation simply decides on its optimal level of military expenditure and then the military aid is simply added on, as in Figure 11.5, to produce the total $M + \Delta M$. It is tempting to observe that the amount of military aid given implies a new budget constraint and a new military goods allocation $M + \Delta M'$ that is always less than $M + \Delta M$. The problem is that this diagram is an accurate reflection of the situation only where the military aid is a pure windfall. That is, the decision maker expected to receive nothing. This clearly is a situation of limited applicability.

In the case where military aid is not a windfall, a similar conclusion can be shown to follow. To produce this result we shall

FIGURE 11.4

The Effect of Military Aid on the Budget

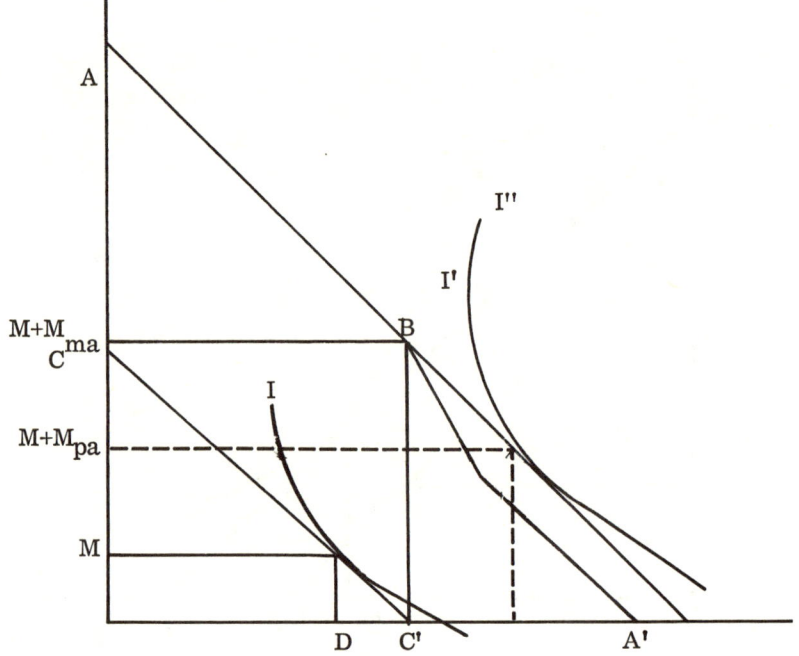

need a couple of additional concepts. Suppose military aid A is seen by the decision maker as a random variable with a known expected value $a = E(A)$. This expected value is to be interpreted as the decision maker's "forecast" of the aid he expects to receive. Assume, second, that the probability distribution is symmetric about the expected value. Now then, we argue that the costs of a wrong guess as to the size of aid forthcoming are generally asymmetric. That is, if he gets more aid than expected, the loss he suffers is in the form of an opportunity cost. If he gets less aid than expected, then the penalty he pays is in terms of a loss of security. We would suspect that the second of these costs is generally (in arms-race situations) the more severe. If this is true, then the result is again that there will be a tendency to allocate too much for military goods.*

---

*It is instructive to consider the case where the opportunity loss per dollar is greater than the security loss. This should occur where there is substantial threat of domestic insecurity.

EFFECTS OF AID ON ARMS RACES

The analysis above has been carried out under the supposition that the other nation's military budget for the previous period was fixed. We still do not consider it reasonable to drop that assumption. However, it is useful to draw a figure that shows a couple of different conditional indifference curves. The two indifference curves show that shifts in the military allocations of the other nation (nation 2) shift the tastes of the dictator of nation 1. This example opens the way to a systemic analysis of foreign aid.

So far we have looked at the effects on a single nation of given military and/or domestic aid. Traditional graphical tools have shown some of the effects of foreign aid. The peculiar aspects of the situation, as shown in Figure 11.6, have not been exploited. That is, since the two nations are in an arms race, aid to one nation will affect the future allocations of the other. An aid policy

FIGURE 11.5

The Effect of Military Aid Given After
Budget Formation

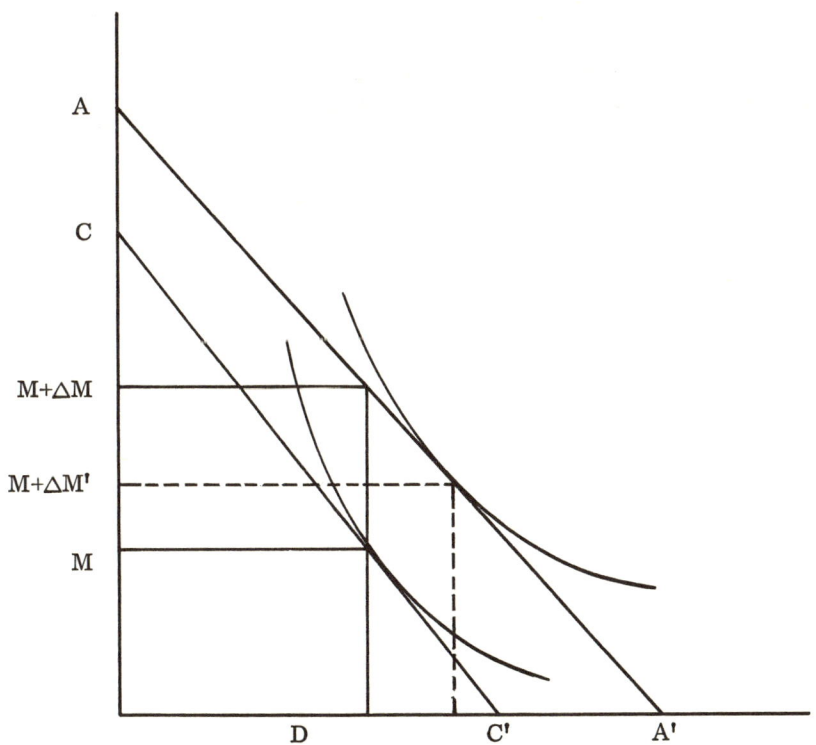

FIGURE 11.6

The Effect of Increased Military Expenditure
to the Other Nations

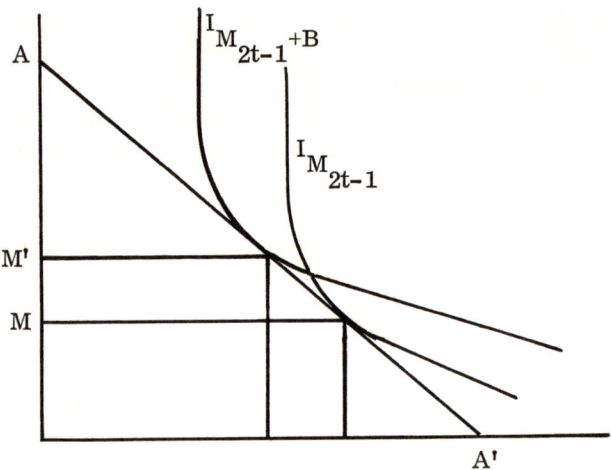

is conceived as a stream of aid to each nation. This policy will
cause each nation to generate a different military expenditure stream
than it would have, had there been no aid; likewise, with the streams
of domestic expenditures. The difference between the domestic
expenditure streams, given different aid policies, is a measure
of the cost or the benefit of the aid policy to the passive consuming
populaces of the two nations. In order to pursue this idea, we shall
jetison the diagrammatic implements employed so far and formulate
a mathematical model that will permit the assessment of alternative
policies.

Summarizing, we argue that in the simple two-nation world
several sources of explanation will exist for changes in military
expenditures by nation 1:

1. Changes in income Y_t (or general grants)
2. Changes in aid
3. Changes in military expenditures by nation 2
4. Exogenous shifts in the utility function (change in valuation of military expenditures)

The Richardson model only attempts to ascertain type 3 shifts.
In a world where all four sources of change are operating, it is

clearly an inadequate starting point for an empirical model. We shall restrict ourselves to types 1 through 3 only, since data are available only in short time series.

A MODEL

The behavioral model we have produced has several specific underlying assumptions:

1. Nations are rational: They maximize a utility function in determining their actual budget each year.
2. The information that one nation has about the other comes only through arms budgets.
3. There is no bureaucratic inertia in budget implementation. Military budgets in successive years could conceivably be of drastically different sizes, and there would still be no problem of mobilization or demobilization to achieve them.
4. There is no learning. Each nation's policies toward its competitors are fixed and immutable. They cannot escape the arms-race condition.
5. There is no investment in the model. Each nation receives its income exogenously and spends it on military and nonmilitary goods. The next period's income has nothing to do with past allocations.

These assumptions are essential to the particular model below, but some can be dropped easily, while others are more difficult to get rid of. At the end of the chapter we will point out some directions in which research might profitably go.

The postulated model* is written as follows for nation j:

$$U_{jt} = AD_{jt}^{\alpha j}(M_{jt} - \gamma_j M_{kt}^* - K_j)^{\beta j} \quad j = 1, 2; k \neq j \quad (11.2)$$

where

$$M_{kt}^* = \lambda_j M_{kt-1}^* + (1 - \lambda_j)M_{kt-1} \quad (11.3)$$

and the decision maker maximizes equation 11.2 subject to the following constraints:

---

*The reader should be aware that an indifference curve is merely a curve of constant utility obtained by setting the utility function equal to a constant and tracing out the path of one argument as an implicit

$$M_{jt} \geq \gamma_j M_{kt}^* + K_j \tag{11.4.1}$$

$$M_{jt} + D_{jt} = Y_{jt} \tag{11.4.2}$$

The variables are defined below:

U_{jt} = Utility level of nation j at time t
D_{jt} = Domestic spending of nation j at time t
M_{jt} = Military spending of nation j at time t
M_{kt}^* = Nation j's forecast of what nation k will spend on military goods at time t
α_j = Elasticity of utility with respect to domestic spending
β_j = Elasticity of utility with respect to military spending in excess of the lower arms-race path
γ_j = Arms expenditure standard
λ_j = Forecast parameter. Coefficient of faith in last periodic forecast
K_j = Lower limit of arms spending ignoring outside competition.

Some features should be noted before proceeding. Equation 11.3 is known as the forecasting equation. It allows each decision maker to predict what the other will do, based on his behavior in the previous period. Note that if $\lambda_j = 1$, $M_{kt}^* = M_{kt-1}^*$, which means that the decision maker expects the other nation to allocate the same amount to military spending each time. If $\lambda_j = 0$, then $M_{kt}^* = M_{kt-1}$. In this case the decision maker expects the other nation to maintain his last period spending level; no credibility at all is given his earlier guess. Where λ_j is between zero and one, the decision maker modifies his forecast by using the available data from period t-1.

The first constraint, equation 11.4.1, indicates that the nation has a minimum standard for defense expenditures each period. K_j might be seen as the amount needed to maintain domestic tranquility. The parameter γ_j has analogues with the reaction parameter in Richardson's model. Numerous scholars have done research which indicates that γ_j has a behavioral meaning; that is, in many cases nations actually have an arms standard that can be

---

function of the other. We make this remark so that the reader unfamiliar with these methods can see that no leap has been attempted when going from the indifference curve analysis of the section, "A Graphical Analysis of Military Aid," to the utility-maximizing model of this section. These are simply two ways of looking at the same thing.

written in this form.[8] It ought also to be remarked that K_j, α_j, β_j, γ_j, and A are assumed to be positive.

We shall omit the technical steps and assert that the first order condition obtained from maximizing equation 11.2 subject to the budget constraint is as follows:

$$\alpha_j/D_{jt} = \beta_j/(M_{jt} - \gamma_j M_{kt}^* - K_j) \tag{11.5}$$

This condition is equivalent to the statement that the gain from shifting an additional dollar to military goods is zero at the point characterized by equation 11.5. Noting that $Y_{jt} = D_{jt} + M_{jt}$ and solving equation 11.5 for military expenditure in terms of national income, the following equality is derived:

$$M_{jt} = [\beta_j/(\alpha_j + \beta_j)] Y_{jt} + [(\alpha_j \gamma_j)/(\alpha_j + \beta_j)] M_{kt}^* + (\alpha_j K_j)/(\alpha_j + \beta_j) \tag{11.6}$$

Let $b_j = \beta_j/(\alpha_j + \beta_j)$, $a_j = \alpha_j/(\alpha_j + \beta_j)$. Thus $a_j + b_j = 1$. Therefore,

$$M_{jt} = b_j Y_{jt} + a_j \gamma_j M_{kt}^* + a_j K_j \tag{11.7}$$

Now we turn to the forecasting equation and solve for M_{kt}^* in terms of the past actual expenditures of nation k.

$$\begin{aligned} M_{kt}^* &= \lambda_j M_{kt-1}^* + (1 - \lambda_j) M_{kt-1} \\ &= \lambda_j [\lambda_j M_{kt-2}^* + (1 - \lambda_j) M_{kt-2}] + (1-\lambda_j) M_{kt-1} \\ &\vdots \\ &= \lambda_j^{t'} M_{kt-t'}^* + (1 - \lambda_j) \sum_{i=1}^{t'-1} \lambda_j^{i-1} M_{kt-i} \end{aligned} \tag{11.8}$$

If $0 < \lambda_j < 1$, we can write the following:

$$M_{kt}^* = (1 - \lambda_j) \sum_{1}^{\infty} \lambda_j^{i-1} M_{kt-i} \tag{11.9}$$

This equation displays the dependence of the forecasts M_{kt}^* on all the past data. In the economic literature this form of relationship is known as a Koyck distributed lag. We shall substitute equation 11.9 into equation 11.7 obtaining the following:

$$M_{jt} = b_j Y_{jt} + (1 - b_j)\gamma_j(1 - \lambda_j) \sum_{i=1}^{\infty} \lambda_j^{i-1} M_{kt-i} + (1 - b_j)K_j$$

(11.10)

Let $c_j = (1 - b)\gamma_j(1 - \lambda_j)$ and note that each of the terms in the infinite sum from $i = 2$ on appear in the formula for M_{jt-1}. Then,

$$M_{jt} = b_j Y_{jt} + c_j M_{kt-1} + \lambda_j M_{jt-1} + \lambda_j b_j Y_{jt-1} - (1 - b_j)K_j \lambda_j + (1 - b_j)K_j$$

(11.11)

$$M_{jt} = b_j Y_{jt} - \lambda_j b_j Y_{jt-1} + c_j M_{kt-1} + \lambda_j M_{jt-1} + (1 - b_j)(1 - \lambda_j)K_j$$

(11.12)

The reader should observe some similarities between the Richardson model and equation 11.12. It is essentially the same model with the exception that there are two additional variables: Y_{jt} and Y_{jt-1}. Carrying through the same analysis for nation k and switching to vector notation will facilitate the comparison.

$$M_t = \begin{pmatrix} M_{1t} \\ M_{2t} \end{pmatrix}$$

$$Y_t = \begin{pmatrix} Y_{1t} \\ Y_{1t-1} \\ Y_{2t} \\ Y_{2t-1} \end{pmatrix}$$

$$A = \begin{pmatrix} \lambda_1 & c_1 \\ c_2 & \lambda_2 \end{pmatrix}$$

$$\varepsilon_t = \begin{pmatrix} \varepsilon_{1t} \\ \varepsilon_{2t} \end{pmatrix}$$

Notation:

$$B = \begin{pmatrix} b_1 & -\lambda_1 b_1 & 0 & 0 \\ 0 & 0 & b_2 & -\lambda_2 b_2 \end{pmatrix}$$

$$K = \begin{pmatrix} (1-b_1)K_1(1-\lambda_1) \\ (1-b_2)K_2(1-\lambda_2) \end{pmatrix}$$

We shall make the same assumptions about ε_t as were made in the first part of this article in discussing the Richardson model.* The model is now written as follows:

$$M_t = AM_{t-1} + BY_t + K + \varepsilon_t \qquad (11.13)$$

The solution to this first order difference equation 11.13 can be found by backward iteration to be :

$$M_t = A^t M_0 + \sum_{i=0}^{t-1} A^i BY_{t-i} + \sum_{i=0}^{t-1} A^i \varepsilon_{t-i} + \sum_{i=0}^{t-1} A^i K \qquad (11.14)$$

It is again clear that the matrix of coefficients A determines the behavior of the system. The reader can refer back to the first part of this chapter and carry through the same analysis for this case. The conclusion of that analysis, it will be recalled, was that if A is "stable" then estimation of the system is reasonably straightforward. The stability condition for A which was introduced was that the characteristic roots of A be less than one in absolute value. Using that section for reference, we produce the stability condition for the matrix A.

$$\left| (\lambda_1 + \lambda_2 \pm \sqrt{(\lambda_1 - \lambda_2)^2 + 4c_1 c_2})/2 \right| \leq 1 \qquad (11.15)$$

The next task is to show that there can indeed be an arms race while the matrix A remains mathematically stable. We ask the reader to take note of the confusion that can easily arise hereafter in the discussion if he does not religiously adhere to the word usage we have adopted. The word "stable" is used only in the technical sense.

Assume now that A is stable. This implies that $\lim_{t \to \infty} A^t = 0$ and equation 11.14 can be rewritten as follows:

---

*For the moment, the behavior implications of the various possible assumptions about the ε_t will be ignored. These considerations will be discussed in the following section.

$$M_t = \sum_{i=0}^{\infty} A^i BY_{t-i} + \sum_{i=0}^{\infty} A^i \varepsilon_{t-i} + (I - A)^{-1} K \tag{11.16}$$

Equation 11.16 is generally known as the "final form" of an econometric system. It conveys the idea that practically all the military expenditure that is generated in the system comes from the national incomes of the two nations. If an arms race is described as a continued upward trend in military expenditures, then this form of the system shows that the incomes of the nation must be growing at a proportionate rate. This triviality, to the wise observer, allows us naive empiricists to observe that there is a class of cases for this model both where there are arms races and where it is possible to estimate their structure* (that is, the matrices A and B). The Richardson model had no such class. This class, call it α for convenience, is described mathematically as the set of permissible structures (A, B) where the stability constraints (equation 11.15) hold with strong inequality. A permissible structure is one where the appropriate inequalities hold for the parameters (that is, $0 < \lambda_j < 1$, $\gamma_j > 0$, and so on).

A numerical illustration will bring some of the features of the model out into the open. Here is a set of plausible parameter values:

$\lambda_1 = \lambda_2 = 0.5$
$\gamma_1 = \gamma_2 = 0.222$
$b_1 = b_2 = 0.1$
$k_1 = k_2 = 0$

Now assume that the economies of nations 1 and 2 exhibit no growth at all and, for the moment, that there are no errors in the equations. We can then write the following from equation 11.16:

$$M_t = (I - A)^{-1} BY \tag{11.17}$$

In this case each nation spends the same amount on military goods each year.

$$\begin{aligned} M_1 &= 0.088Y_1 + 0.049Y_2 \\ M_2 &= 0.049Y_1 + 0.088Y_2 \end{aligned} \tag{11.18}$$

---

*This idea implicitly introduces for any model a class of structures that is practically inestimable. The "size" of this class depends on the model adopted.

And, for both nations considered together:

$$M_1 + M_2 = 0.137(Y_1 + Y_2) \qquad (11.19)$$

That is, 13.7 percent of the total expenditures by both nations are spent on the military. Now consider what happens when aid is given to one of the nations at some time. We shall call this the "one-shot" aid case. Figure 11.7 depicts the effects compared to the no-aid case. Suppose, for ease of comparison, that the one-shot aid is equal to one dollar. Then, in the first period, nation 1 (the recipient nation) would spend an extra $0.10 on military goods. The following period, nation 2 would spend $0.05 on military goods; whereas the first nation would spend a penny less than in the no-aid case. The pattern is clear enough. The dollar's worth of aid to one nation has continuing effects on both nations' arms expenditures. In the simple model presented here, nation 2's increased military expenditure is removed entirely from its domestic spending. The proportion of total expenditures spent on the military can easily be computed for each time period. In this case the numbers depend on what Y_1 and Y_2 are, so I will just give the results algebraically (Table 11.1).

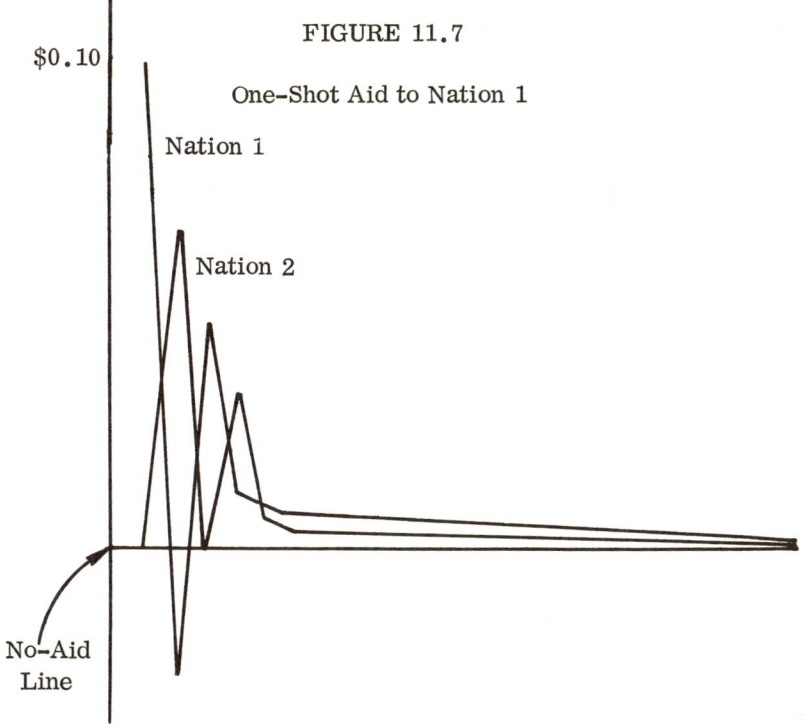

FIGURE 11.7

One-Shot Aid to Nation 1

TABLE 11.1

Proportion of Total Expenditures Used for
Military Spending

Time Period	Proportion
1	$-0.037/(Y_1 + Y_2) + 1$
2	$0.04/(Y_1 + Y_2)$
3	$0.024/(Y_1 + Y_2)$
4	$0.014/(Y_1 + Y_2)$
5	$0.009/(Y_1 + Y_2)$
6	$0.005/(Y_1 + Y_2)$
.	.
.	.
.	.

The same methods permit an analysis of a policy of a continuing aid to one of the two nations. Figure 11.8 shows the effects in dollars of one dollar's worth of aid to nation 1 at each time period. The result is that, after a few years, about 20 additional cents per year are spent by both nations on arms.

Two further areas need to be explored. The first is the distinction between military and nonmilitary aid. The second is the question of whether aid is received before or after budget formulation. The graphical analysis of military aid indicated that when aid is given in advance of budget formulation, it is unimportant whether or not it is specifically military aid except in the case where the military aid grant is larger than the total arms budget would have been without it. On the other hand, when aid is given after budget formulation, then the distinction between military and unrestricted aid is important. A very simple model of this case is presented below. We shall refer to it henceforward as the "late-aid" model. The modifications of the previous model are that the utility function is now written as follows:

$$U_{jt} = AD_{jt}^{\alpha j}(M_{jt} + A_{jt}^* - \gamma_j M_{kt}^* - K_j)^{\beta j} \tag{11.20}$$

$$j = 1, 2; \ k \neq j$$

$$A_{jt}^* = \delta_j A_{jt-1}^* + (1 - \delta_j)A_{jt-1} \tag{11.21}$$

EFFECTS OF AID ON ARMS RACES

A_{jt} and A_{jt}^* are military aid to nation j at time t and expected (or forecasted) military aid to nation j at time t. The only data the nation uses to forecast military aid at time t+1 are the data on aid that it has received earlier. Exactly the same steps as above are used to derive a form similar to equation 11.12:

$$M_{jt} = \alpha_{1j} Y_{jt} + \alpha_{2j} Y_{t-1} + \alpha_{3j} Y_{t-2} + \alpha_{4j} M_{kt-1} + \alpha_{5j} M_{kt-2}$$
$$+ \alpha_{6j} M_{jt-1} + \alpha_{7j} M_{jt-2} + \alpha_{8j} A_{jt-1} + \alpha_{9j} A_{jt-2} + \alpha_{10j} \qquad (11.22)$$

where

$\alpha_{1j} = b_j$
$\alpha_{2j} = -(\lambda_j + \delta_j) b_j$
$\alpha_{3j} = \delta_j \lambda_j b_j$
$\alpha_{4j} = c_j$
$\alpha_{5j} = -\delta_j c_j$
$\alpha_{6j} = -(\lambda_j + \delta_j)$
$\alpha_{7j} = -\delta_j \lambda_j$
$\alpha_{8j} = -(1 - b_j)(1 - \delta_j)$
$\alpha_{9j} = (1 - b_j)(1 - \delta_j) \lambda_j$
$\alpha_{10j} = K_j (1 - b_j)(1 - \lambda_j)(1 - \delta_j)$

FIGURE 11.8

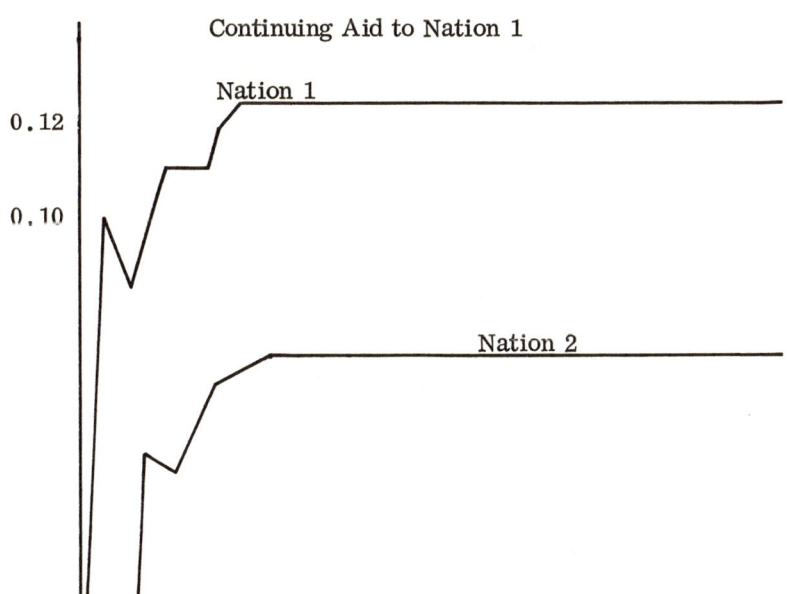

Continuing Aid to Nation 1

Some conclusions can be derived from the late-aid model. If a nation receives military aid one year as a pure windfall and it expects to receive such aid thereafter, the effect of the one-shot policy is to depress the military expenditures of both nations. They gradually reapproach their no-aid equilibrium lines. Under the assertion that $\delta_1 = \delta_2 = 0.2$, continuing military aid to one nation appears to impose a tax on the other nation that stabilizes at about 33 cents for each dollar of military aid. This is a more severe effect than was obtained with the earlier model.

ESTIMATION AND ANALYSIS

The earlier parts of this chapter were constructed in the uncomplicated world of theory. We direct ourselves now to the question of whether this endeavor has any connection with reality. We chose India and Pakistan as an example of two nations in an arms race even though some of the assumptions of the model seem to be violated. First, neither nation is a dictatorship. All that is required here is that the ruling group is sufficiently cohesive to hold a consistent schedule of preferences and be able to enforce it. Whether this weaker assumption is "true enough" will await an evaluation of the results. Second, there are other nations nearby that complicate the situation—particularly, China. We estimate two alternative specifications to deal with this case: one in which China is altogether ignored; the other in which India reacts to Pakistan and China together, whereas Pakistan reacts only to India.

Another feature of the model is that everything is done in money terms. The arms that are represented by the budgetary choices are ignored. Therefore, phenomena such as "qualitative" arms races must be ignored. The importance of this omission is clearer when consideration is directed toward Multiple Independently Targeted Reentry Vehicles (MIRV)—a cheap but escalatory step in the U.S.-Soviet arms race.

Our guess is that technological advances in weapons' effectiveness will not be as dramatic in developing countries, and so the fact that the arms race is represented in dollar terms will not distort things overmuch. If there is such a thing as a rate of technological progress in weapons' effectiveness, then nations could in fact escalate their positions in the race while maintaining constant budgets and simply replacing older weapons as they become obsolete with more effective ones. If this is the case, then the coefficients γ_j will be underestimated in the procedure given below. In any case we believe this idea can be incorporated into the model if independent

EFFECTS OF AID ON ARMS RACES

estimates of the rate of technological progress in weapons' effectiveness are available for the technologies employed by the nations being studied. This topic will not be explored here.

In the fourth part of this chapter "A Model," the decision maker was assumed to forecast the other nation's military expenditure for the current year and then determine his own expenditure by maximizing his utility function. Equation 11.7 represented this decision rule behaviorally. It is reproduced here:

$$M_{jt} = b_j Y_{jt} + a_j \gamma_j M_{kt}^* + a_j K_j$$

$$M_{kt}^* = \lambda_j M_{kt-1}^* + (1 - \lambda_j) M_{kt-1}$$

This will be called the "behavioral form" of the model. Another equivalent form was given in equation 11.12 by eliminating M_{kt}^* as follows:

$$M_{jt} = b_j Y_{jt} - \lambda_j b_j Y_{jt-1} + c_j M_{kt-1} + \lambda_j M_{jt-1} + (1 - b_j)(1 - \lambda_j) K_j$$

This is called the "autoregressive form" of the model. There are several possible sources for the error in the model. The following four types should constitute the bulk of it:

1. Arms expenditures of other nations not represented in the model (such as the USSR)
2. Military or domestic aid from various sources
3. Varying domestic pressures for more or less expenditures summarized in the K_j term
4. Lumpiness of expenditures (for example, the difference between buying ten jets or eleven is a large monetary quantity; precise marginal adjustments are ruled out under these conditions)

Sources 1 and 2 should be the principal systematic components in the error term—and these components should be highly autocorrelated. Source 4 ought not to show any systematic evolution in short time periods. We cannot feel any great confidence in thinking about the process of source-3-type errors, but in any case negative autocorrelation for this component seems unlikely. This reasoning indicates that one ought to allow for the possibility of autocorrelation in the specification of the errors. We shall assume that the errors are governed by the simplest imaginable process: a first-order stochastic difference equation. Thus we have the following:

$$M_{jt} = b_j Y_{jt} - b_j \lambda_j Y_{jt-1} + c_j M_{kt-1} + \lambda_j M_{jt-1} + (1 - b_j)(1 - \lambda_j) K_j + \varepsilon_j \tag{11.23}$$

where $\varepsilon_{jt} = \rho_j \varepsilon_{jt-1} + \eta_{jt}$

Equation 11.23 can be rewritten as follows:

$$M_{jt} = b_j Y_{jt} - (\lambda_j + \rho_j) M_{jt-1} - \rho_j \lambda_j b_j Y_{jt-2} + c_j M_{kt-1} - \rho_j c_j M_{kt-2}$$
$$+ (\lambda_j + \rho_j) M_{jt-1} - \rho_j \lambda_j M_{jt-2} + (1 - b_j)(1 - \lambda_j)(1 - \rho_j) K_j + \eta_{jt}$$
$$(11.24)$$

We shall try to obtain estimates for the parameters in equation 11.24.*

Estimation of equation 11.24 cannot proceed directly by use of ordinary least squares since the parameters contained in it are subject to some constraints. Let

$\beta_1 = b_j$
$\beta_2 = -(\lambda_j + \rho_j) b_j$
$\beta_3 = \rho_j \lambda_j b_j$
$\beta_4 = c_j$
$\beta_5 = \rho_j c_j$
$\beta_6 = (\lambda_j + c_j)$
$\beta_7 = -\rho_j \lambda_j$
$\beta_8 = (1 - b_j)(1 - \lambda_j)(1 - \rho_j) K_j$

Then the following is required:

$$-\beta_2/\beta_6 = \beta_1 = -\beta_3/\beta_7, \quad (\beta_4 \beta_7)/\beta_5 + \beta_5/\beta_4 = \beta_6 \qquad (11.25)$$

A few procedures are possible:

1. Minimize the sum of squares of equation 11.24 subject to the constraints 11.25. Then solve for the parameters of interest.

---

*The data were collected from the Stockholm International Peace Research Institute, <u>Yearbook of World Armaments and Disarmament 1969/1970</u> (Stockholm: Almquist and Wiksell, 1970), and the Agency for International Development (AID). The military expenditures series for India and Pakistan from 1950 to 1969 in constant U.S. dollars (the CPI for each country was used as a deflator) were obtained from the Stockholm International Peace Research Institute's publication. GNP information was gathered from AID. They also provided whatever data we present here on U.S. aid to the two nations. It ought to be remembered that military aid from the United States to Pakistan and, to a lesser extent, to India is largely classified.

EFFECTS OF AID ON ARMS RACES   241

2. Employ Durbin's method, which is summarized here; it must be
   applied to equation 11.23:
   a. Estimate equation 11.23. This gives a consistent estimator
      of λ_j.
   b. Substitute this estimator into equation 11.23 and note that
      the resulting equation is linear in its parameters and will
      give estimates of b_j, c_j, K_j.
   c. Now let λ_j be estimated after substituting back in equation
      11.23 for these parameters. Continue this procedure until
      there is convergence.

In order, the first alternative was rejected since complicated
nonlinear equations had to be solved. The second alternative was
chosen after the following modifications: First, we used a grid of
values for λ_j in order to get a starting value; second, an autoregressive correction was employed at each step that also employed a grid
on ρ_j. This method converged fairly rapidly: Four or five iterations
were all that were necessary.

There is some question as to how much faith to have in the
estimates presented here. Variances are not presented since the
distribution of the parameters is not necessarily even asymptotically
normal and since the computation of the variances is very tedious.[9]
We shall therefore only indicate by an asterisk (*) any parameters
that were observed to be unstable during the estimation algorithm.

The first model presented is with India reacting to Pakistan
(model 1):

	b_j	c_j	λ_j	ρ_j	R^2	Dw	K
Pakistan	0.0072*	0.0892	0.599	-0.139	0.848	2.040	12.75
India	0.0169	0.2614*	0.843	0.292	0.875	1.946	0

From the table and the derivations in the fourth part of this chapter,
"A Model," the following estimates of γ_j were obtained: $\gamma_I = 1.66$
$\gamma_p = 0.224$. This indicates a higher arms standard for India relative
to Pakistan than the reverse. Residual plots from the two equations
are printed as Figures 11.9 and 11.10.

The residuals in Figure 11.9 indicate outliers in 1952, 1957,
1964, 1965, 1966, and 1967 in Pakistan. Extreme years for India
were 1962, 1963, and 1964. Examination of the original data
(Figure 11.11) shows that India's military expenditures increased
gradually from 1951 to 1961, at which point they grew rapidly for
two years. Since 1964 Indian military expenditures have been slowly
declining. Comparison of Pakistan's military expenditures (Figure
11.12) with India's indicates that Pakistan reacted to India's military
expansion with about a two- to three-year lag. The data seem to

FIGURE 11.9

Residual Plot for Pakistan for Model 1
($U.S. millions)

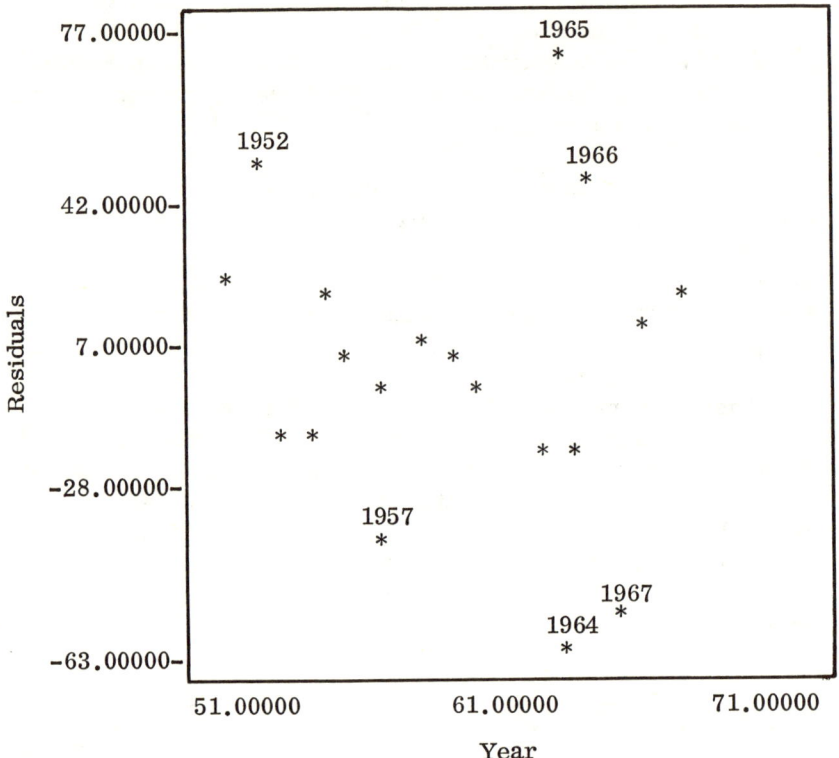

indicate that both have found new expenditure plateaus that are much higher than their plateaus prior to 1962. The model we have presented incorporates this lag phenomenon in a sort of "credibility" parameter (λ). It would indicate that Pakistan did not immediately react to India since Pakistan might have thought that the additional Indian arms were focused elsewhere (namely, China). Another interpretation, perhaps a more plausible one, is that it took a couple of years for Pakistan to gear up its armed forces. The lag might be purely technological.

These considerations indicate that the two main phenomena in the model, India's arms takeoff in 1962 and 1963 and the subsequent leveling off of her arms expenditures, were caused by forces exogenous to the model. The cause of the takeoff was most likely the breakout of Indian-Chinese hostilities in 1962 and 1963. The downturn of Indian expenditures did not abate even after the incidents with Pakistan. Pakistan's expenditures peaked at the beginning of the India-Pakistan conflict. The main inadequacy of the model would seem to be that a major exogenous shock occurred during the period; that shock (Chinese-Indian war) appears to have lifted the arms budget plateaus of both nations.

An examination of the residuals of the India equation of model 1 indicates the presence of extreme outliers in 1962 and 1963. These residuals suggest that the influence of the exogenous shock on the model in 1962-63 may have exerted some great effect on the parameter estimates.

FIGURE 11.10

Residual Plot for India for Model 1
($U.S. millions)

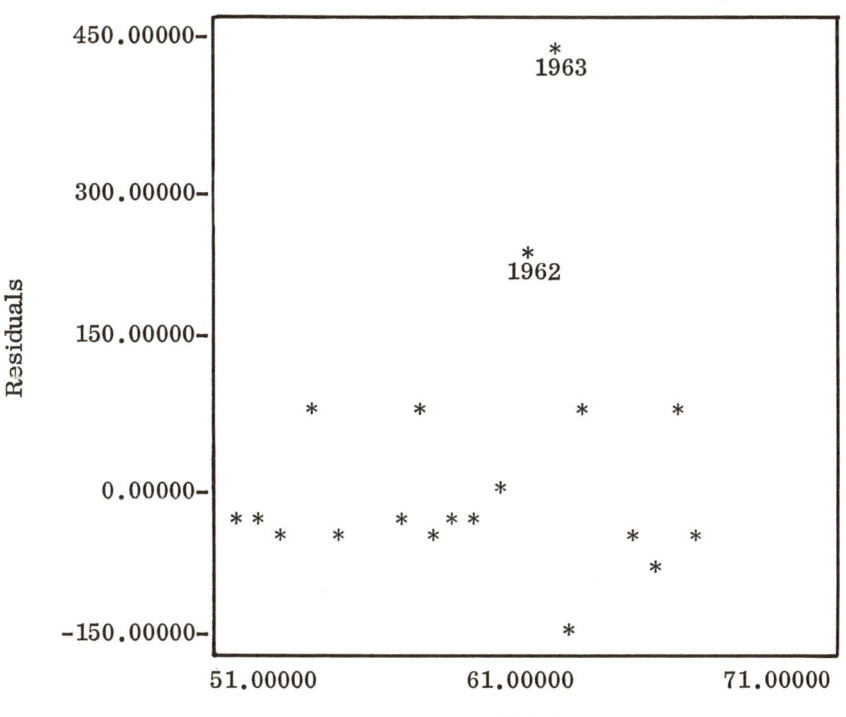

FIGURE 11.11

India's Military Expenditures
($U.S. millions)

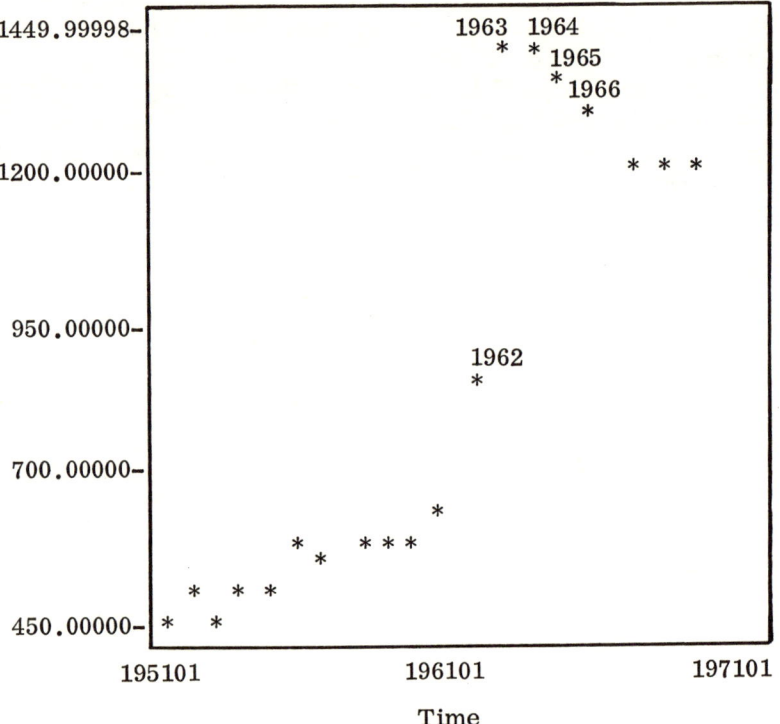

The Indian equation was reestimated with a dummy variable (an intercept dummy) for the years 1962-63 and the new estimates are given as follows:

b_I	c_I	λ_I	ρ_I	R^2_I	Dw_I	Dum_I
0.0152	0.09464	0.913	-0.519	0.93	2.158	375.1

The fit of the equation has increased perceptably. The residuals are presented in Figure 11.13. The implied estimate of γ_I, the arms standard toward Pakistan, is 1.11.

Using the revised version of model 1 it is a simple step to evaluate the hypothetical aid policies presented in the fourth section of this chapter. The nations, India and Pakistan, are not symmetric

EFFECTS OF AID ON ARMS RACES

as were those of the numerical example, so I shall present four streams of effects over time rather than two. The effects are generally of a smaller order than those presented in the example, but considered in terms of the aid that the United States actually presents to these nations, the effects are respectable. Figures 11.14 and 11.15 show the results of the two alternative policies examined in the third section.

For the reader to appreciate the size of the effects shown in the figures, we must cite actual aid given to Pakistan and India. In 1962 U.S. economic aid to Pakistan was $422.2 million, and to India it was $763.1 million. Now consider the case where the United States only gives aid to India. The result of this is that India

FIGURE 11.12

Pakistan's Military Expenditures
($U.S. millions)

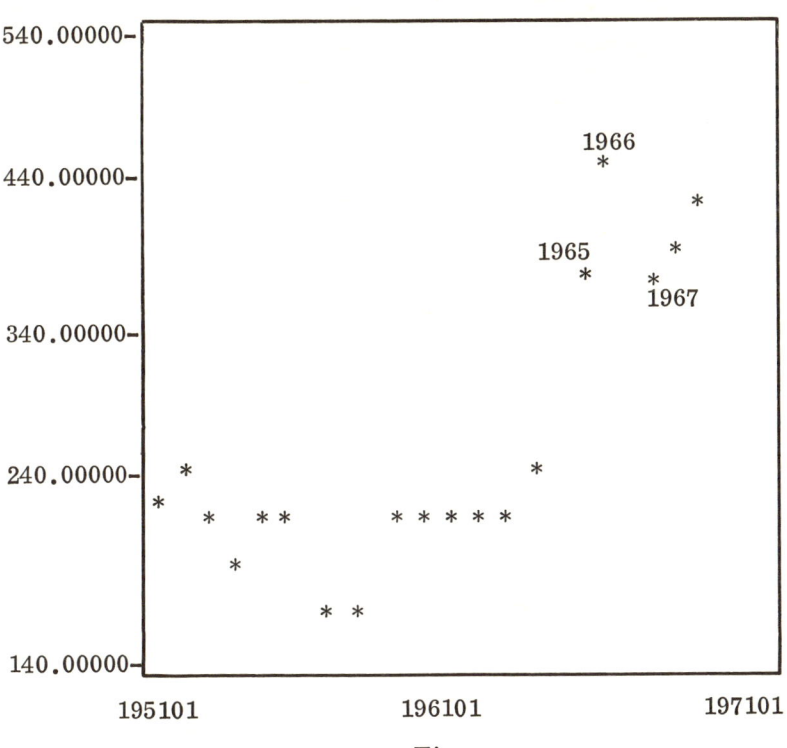

FIGURE 11.13

Residuals for the Revised India Equation
($U.S. millions)

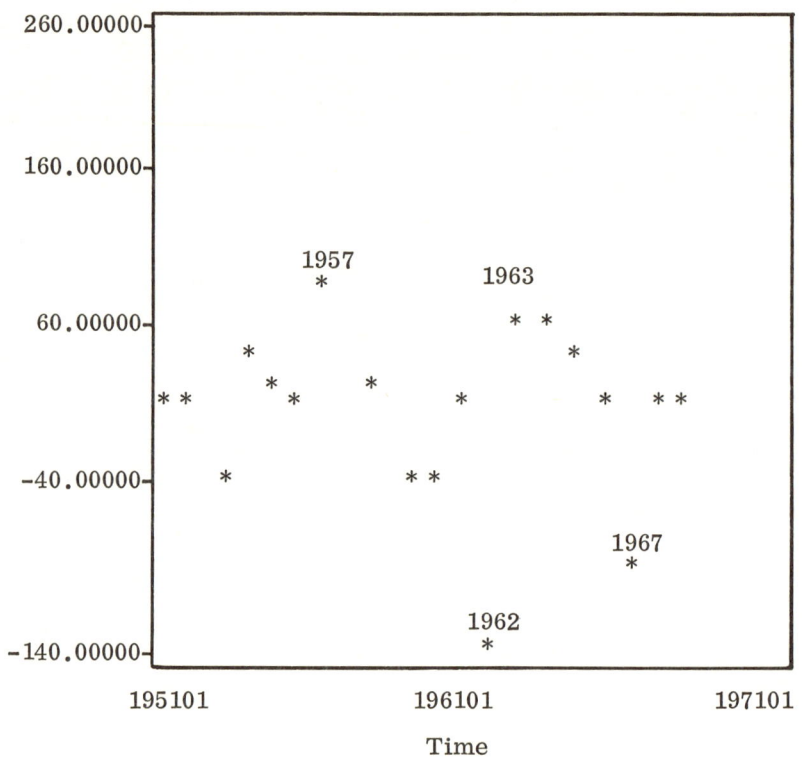

will spend an additional $11.6 million on arms in the first year.
Following this Pakistan will spend $2 million, then $1.1 million.
The total effect on Pakistani military budgets over a 25-year period
is about $5.5 million, the bulk of this ($4.1 million) occurring
within five years of the aid grant to India. Twenty-five years after
the grant, India is still spending $116,000 more on the military
than she would have without the one-shot grant; Pakistan is still
spending $44,000 more. This analysis indicates that the burdens
on Pakistan from one-shot aid to India can be fairly sizable and
that they will continue for years after the discontinuence of the
policy. Figure 11.16 shows the effects of the actual aid policy to
India from 1958 to 1969 under the assumption that no aid goes to

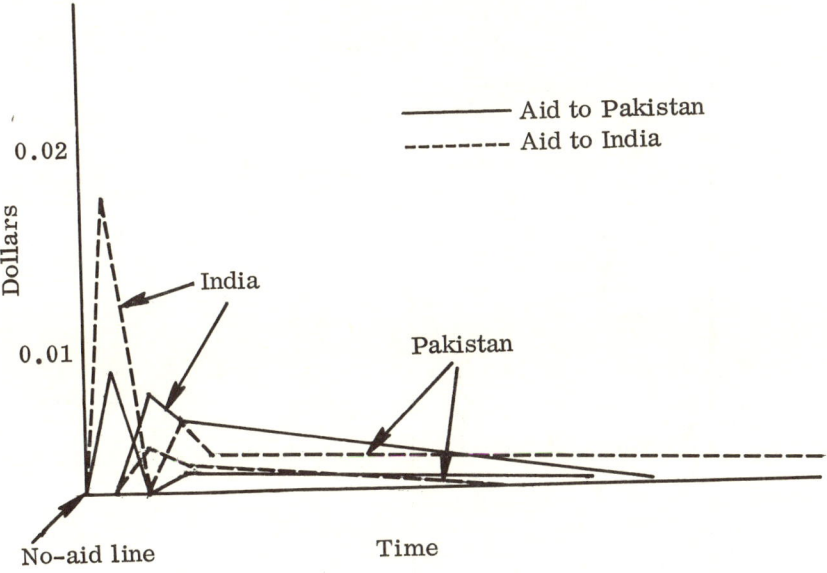

FIGURE 11.14

One-Shot Aid Policies

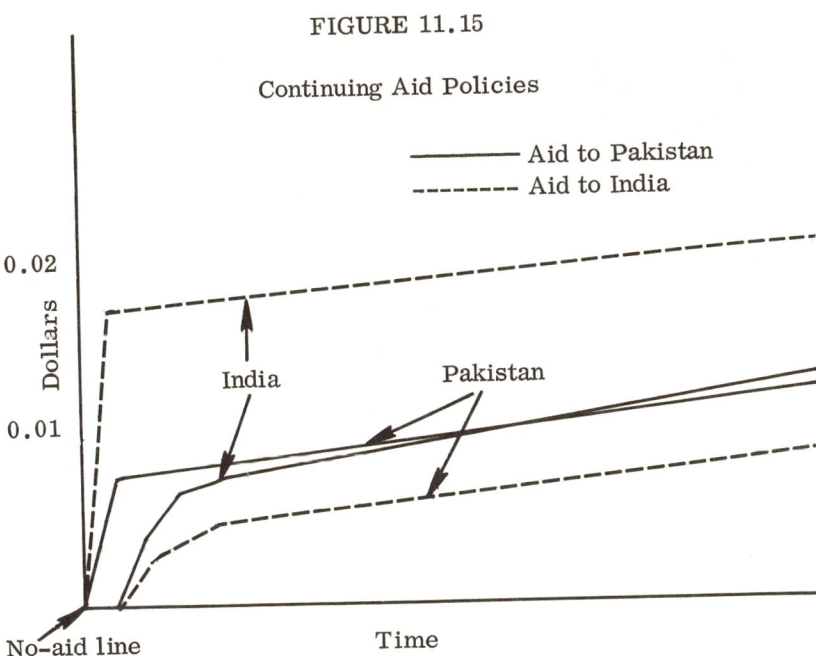

FIGURE 11.15

Continuing Aid Policies

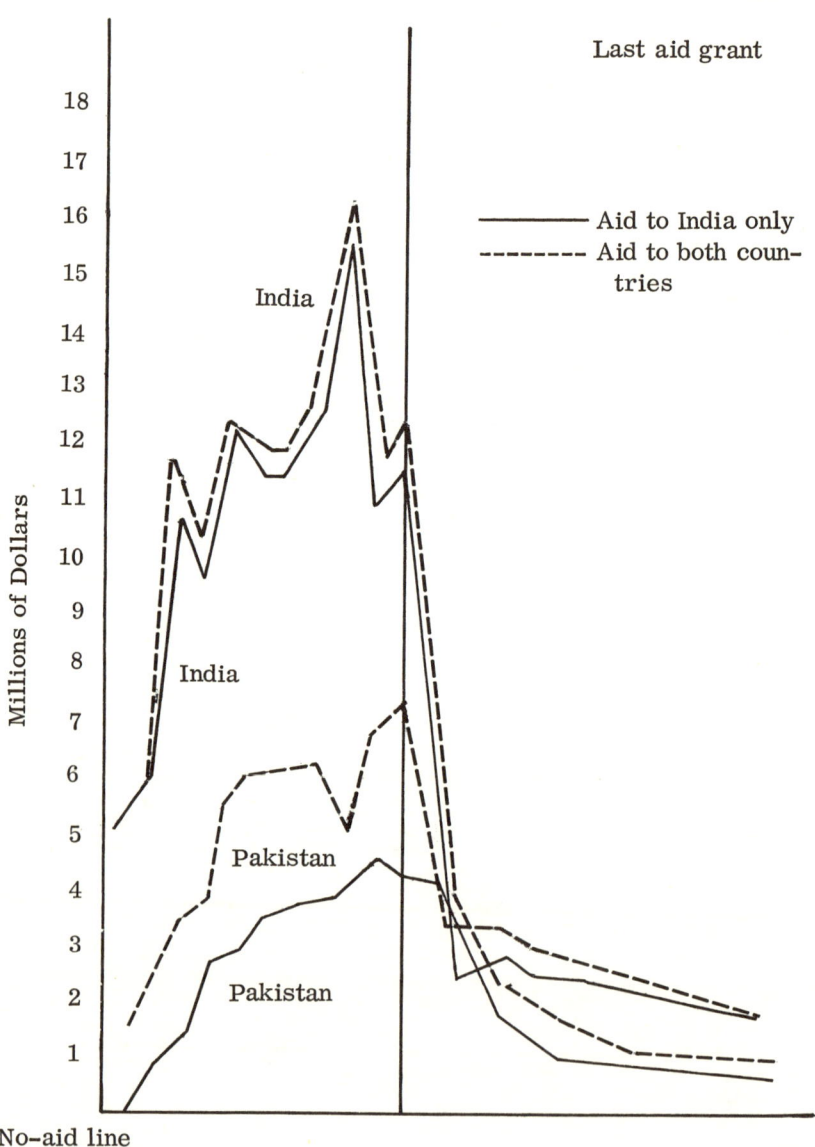

FIGURE 11.16

Estimated Effects of Actual Aid Given to the Two Nations ($U.S. millions)

EFFECTS OF AID ON ARMS RACES

Pakistan. The same graph displays the effects of the actual domestic aid policies to both nations over the same period.

An alternative specification for the Indian specification was also tried out. In it (model 2) India reacts to Chinese plus Pakistani military expenditures rather than to Pakistan's military expenditures alone. We leave it to the reader to decide whether model 1 or model 2 is more realistic. The estimates are presented below.

b_I	c_I	λ_I	ρ_I	R^2_I	Dw_I
0.0129	0.0578	0.4949	0.601	0.8858	1.8

Using a dummy variable for 1962-63 as is suggested by the residuals, the revised estimates are as follows:

b_I	c_I	λ_I	ρ_I	R^2_I	Dw_I	Dum_I
0.012	0.051	0.566	0.378	0.94	2.02	321.1

The analysis of the impact of foreign aid is not carried through in this case. The sizes of the coefficients can be compared with those for the revised version of model 1 and the following conclusions are apparent. The income (b) and reaction (c) effects are generally less pronounced in this model so that U.S. aid to Pakistan or India will cause less increase in Indian military spending. The Indian military spending curve will be smoother since there is heavier reliance on past budgets. Note also that the fit is not so good as that of revised model 1.

Since military aid to each of these countries is largely classified, there can be no analysis of the late-aid model introduced in the third part of this chapter. Consequently, it seems useless at this stage to distinguish between military and domestic aid. The results of this chapter, therefore, actually constitute an evaluation of one set of effects of aid programs to these two nations. The analysis in the fourth part, "A Model," demonstrated that were it possible to estimate the late-aid model, one would expect more pronounced effects than those described herein.

CONCLUSIONS

What conclusions can be drawn from this analysis? First, aid to nations in arms races, whether domestic, military, or unrestricted, has the effect of imposing a burden on the domestic economies of the nations not receiving aid. Second, the effects continue long after the aid policy is discontinued. Third, the effect of introducing uncertainty into a military aid policy with respect to nations in arms races is to cause budgetary distortion in the direction of increased military spending.

These conclusions suggest that these effects of an aid policy be taken into account in policy formulation. It might be possible to devise a policy of compensation to correct the burdens imposed on nonrecipients. Of course, given the loose structure of the India-Pakistan arms race and our lack of knowledge about how to evaluate the welfare consequences of these policies, it is possible that a compensation policy might not be required.

We have introduced models that examine only one set of effects of a U.S. policy. There are at least two other factors that need to be considered. First, if the effects of domestic aid on the growth of the nations' incomes were known, it might be possible to have a policy that compensated for the loss in domestic spending observed here. However, it should be clear that the amount spent on the military would be even greater in the presence of expanded national incomes. Second, if the United States gives aid to one nation and not to the other, the second nation suffers a loss in domestic spending. This may lead to reduced domestic stability in that nation and a demand for higher military expenditures (for domestic reasons)— a shift in b. This shift in the tastes of the government was not estimated here because there were so few data points available. An analysis of this effect may show that U.S. policy is counterproductive in terms of maintaining stability in the Third World.

Too much should not be made, therefore, of the policy implications of the models.

There are several possible directions for possible extension of the theory. One is to incorporate investment so that income is no longer purely exogenous. A second is to allow for some shifts in the parameters. It might also be possible to extend the theory to cases of more than two nations and thence to alliances of nations. The problem encountered in the third suggestion is that of the "free rider." We have tried various methods of dealing with this but none has yet proved satisfactory—essentially, a satisfactory solution must rest on a theory of burden sharing in alliances. It is also possible to build some inertia into the model so that the hypothesis of "mobilization lag," as opposed to a "credibility lag" discussed earlier, can be separated. Lastly, the prediction equation for what the other nation will spend is taken as fixed. It might be possible to build a theory for this element that is more refined than simply allowing for a shift in λ for a whole period. Each of these avenues warrants some investigation so that a useful policy model may be constructed that has some hope of evaluating the full effects of alternative aid policies.

NOTES

1. For an example of his work, see Lewis F. Richardson, Arms and Insecurity (Chicago: Quadrangle Books), 1960.
2. Jeffrey S. Milstein and William S. Mitchell, "Computer Simulation of International Processes," Yale Papers in Political Science, no. 38 (New Haven, Conn.: Yale University Press, 1968).
3. Peter Busch, "Mathematical Models of Arms Races," in What Price Vigilance? ed. Bruce M. Russett (New Haven, Conn.: Yale University Press, 1970), pp. 193-233.
4. J. Johnston, Econometric Methods (New York: McGraw-Hill, 1963).
5. F.G.C. Marriott and J. A. Pope, "Bias in the Estimation of Auto-correlations," Biometrika 41 (1954): 390-396; John S. White, "Asymptotic Expansions for the Mean and Variance of the Serial Correlation Coefficient," Biometrika 48 (1961): 85-94; E. Malinvaud, Statistical Methods of Econometrics (Chicago: Rand McNally, 1966).
6. T. W. Anderson, "On Asymptotic Distributions of Estimates of Parameters of Stochastic Deference Equations," Annals of Mathematical Statistics 30 (1959): 676-87.
7. See Anatol Rapoport and A. M. Chammah, Prisoner's Dilemma (Ann Arbor: University of Michigan Press, 1965).
8. See for example Kendall D. Moll, The Influence of History upon Seapower, 1865-1914 (Menlo Park: Stanford Research Institute, 1968).
9. Malinvaud, Statistical Methods, p. 305.

CHAPTER 12

THREE MODELS OF ARMS RACES
Michael L. Squires

Mathematical models of arms races have been a topic of interest to students of international relations for about 15 years. The field, which originated with the work of Lewis F. Richardson, has concentrated on mathematical models of two-nation systems or, in a few cases, n-nation systems with no alliance ties.[1] The basic Richardson model, in addition, uses only an approximation for economic constraints. Finally, the developments in military technology have created a distinct conceptual difference between fission or fusion weapons and those using conventional explosives. The Richardson model blurs this important difference.

This chapter presents three n-nation models of the arms race that progressively introduce modifications to the basic Richardson model. Model 1 uses an elaboration of the action-reaction concept based on Boulding's notion of unconditional viability; a division of weapons systems into two classes, called "strategic weapons" and "conventional weapons"; a perceptual variable called "trust"; and an economic constraint function taken from Caspary.[2] Model 2 introduces defensive alliances in a static manner; model 3 adds a mechanism for the incremental change of alliances, which makes the alliance structure of the n-nation system a dynamic part of the arms-race model.

A stability analysis is made of model 1 only; models 2 and 3, which cannot be simply reduced to two-nation systems, are not given a similar treatment. A full analysis of the properties of model 3, using the method of sensitivity testing of a computer simulation, is planned for a later date.

Written while the author was in residence at Indiana University.

THREE MODELS OF ARMS RACES

DISCUSSION

The basic Richardson model is a two-equation simultaneous differential equation model based on the following equations:

$$dY/dt = kX - aY + g \qquad (12.1)$$

where Y is the arms expenditure of nation y

$$dX/dt = k'Y + a'X + h \qquad (12.2)$$

where X is the arms expenditure of nation x

The coefficients k and k' are reaction constants, which modify the effect of nation x's expenditure on y, and vice versa. The coefficients a and a' are "cost and fatigue" coefficients, which tend to reduce the rate of expenditure from the level indicated by a nation's considering only arms expenditures of the other nation. The two remaining coefficients, g and h, are grievance coefficients, which indicate the rate of arms expenditure that would exist in the absence of any expenditure by the other nation.

The two variables X and Y used in the original Richardson model were defined in terms of arms expenditures. Sometimes X and Y have also been defined as arms stocks; this substitution, however, raises questions about the attrition of weapons through wear and tear and, more importantly, the question of the comparability of measures of different nations' arms stocks. The units of measurement for arms stocks have usually been in terms of numbers of weapons; in some cases the units have been in terms of the military power of the arms stocks. The original Richardson formulation has the advantage of easily being made operable, which is not the case with other definitions of X and Y. This chapter will not address this question directly; I will, however, indicate the quantity being measured by the variables X and Y.

The Richardson model can be reinterpreted, following Caspary, if we manipulate the two equations by (a) dividing through each equation by its cost and fatigue coefficient, (b) collecting terms, and (c) multiplying each equation through by its cost and fatigue coefficient.[3] Thus, equation 12.1 becomes the following:

$$dY/dt = a[(k/a)X - Y + (g/a)] \qquad (12.3)$$

Similarly, for the second equation in the Richardson system we find the following:

$$dX/dt = a'[(k'/a')Y - X + (h/a')] \qquad (12.4)$$

In this form the coefficients take on new interpretations. If Y is less than (k/a)X, then nation y's expenditure would tend to increase. Similarly, if Y is larger than (k/a)X, then nation y's expenditure would tend to decrease. The coefficient k/a is a measure of the proportion of nation x's expenditure that nation y wishes to match; a similar interpretation is possible for the coefficient $(k'/a')^2$.

We turn now to a different task: elaborating the Richardson model. The Richardson model, in the form of equations 12.3 and 12.4, will be modified so that a more realistic form of economic constraint is applied, the k/a parameter "unpacked" into two different parameters, the single aggregate measure of arms stocks disaggregated into a variable representing strategic weapons and a variable representing conventional weapons, and an N-nation formulation of the model created with alliances as a dynamic part of the model.

ECONOMIC CONSTRAINTS

The economic constraint term used by Richardson was modified by Caspary in a paper that also adopted the comparison of levels notion developed above. Caspary noted that the Richardson model was only a good approximation if the level of defense expenditure was on the order of 10 percent of the total GNP. Furthermore, the Richardson model allows infinitely large rates of increase in arms expenditure, an obvious impossibility in any real economic system. Caspary solves these problems by converting the model into a two-stage process. The Richardson model is used as a first stage that produces not the actual rate of change but a desired change in arms stocks. The desired change is then converted into a desired expenditure, and the desired expenditure then moderated by an economic constraint function that takes into consideration the costs of maintaining existing arms stocks.

The first stage of the model is identical in form to the Richardson model, with the exception that dY/dt has been replaced by D, the desired change; for nation y, dX/dt has been replaced by D', the desired change for nation x.

$$D = (k/a)Y - X + g/a \qquad (12.5)$$

$$D' = (k'/a')X - Y + h/a' \qquad (12.6)$$

THREE MODELS OF ARMS RACES

In the second stage the desired increment in arms is moderated by an exponential economic constraint function. This function relates C, the maximum production possible, and the desired increment in arms stocks D to the actual arms stock increment f(D, C) in the following way:

$$f(D, C) = C(1 - e^{-D/C}) \qquad (12.7)$$

If $D < C$, then f(D, C) is nearly as large as D; as D increases to C, f(D, C) increases at a slower rate, approaching C as a limit as D increases without limit.

We can now give the exact form of the second stage of Caspary's model. If we let N be the unit cost of new arms stocks, M be the maintenance costs of existing stocks, and a and p be constants, then the rate of change of y's expenditures dY/dt is related to the desired increment D' in the following way:

$$dY/dt = a/p(C - MY)[1 - e^{-(ND)/C}] \qquad (12.8)$$

Similarly, for nation x we have the following:

$$dX/dt = a'/p'(C' - M'X)[1 - e^{-(N'D')/C'}] \qquad (12.9)$$

To summarize, the Caspary modification of the Richardson model has been adapted for the three models presented in this chapter. The fundamental structure of the models is Caspary's concept of a desired arms stock and an actual rate of increase moderated by an economic constraint function.

DESIRED ARMS STOCKS, UNCONDITIONAL VIABILITY, AND TRUST

Richardson's model, interpreted as a desired ratio model, fails to explain how a nation y decides what proportion of nation x's arms stock is needs to possess. Returning to the model given in equations 12.3 and 12.4, we will interpret X and Y as total arms stocks and not as expenditures.

If we assume that both g and h are zero, we find that dX/dt and dY/dt are zero if the following conditions hold:

$$\text{If } (k/a)X = Y, \text{ then } dY/dt = 0 \qquad (12.10)$$

$$\text{If } (k'/a')Y = X, \text{ then } dX/dt = 0 \qquad (12.11)$$

Equations 12.10 and 12.11 may be interpreted to mean that there is some desired proportion k/a of x's arms stocks that y desires; similarly, for x there is some proportion k'/a' of y's arms stock. If the arms stock is below the desired amount, there is an impetus to arm; if the arms stock is above the desired amount, there is an impetus to reduce arms stocks.

The alternate formulation of the Richardson model does not attempt to supply an interpretation of the coefficients k/a and k'/a'. We introduce here two factors that, taken together, are assumed to produce the coefficients k/a and k'/a'. These factors are the arms stocks necessary for unconditional viability and the probability perceived by one nation that hostilities will occur between it and another nation.

Boulding introduced "unconditional viability" as a relative measure of the military power of two nations. He assumed that the military power of a nation could be expressed as a single number; this power was then reduced by a linear function as the distance from the nation increased. A second state was considered unconditionally viable if its own military power, measured at its borders, was greater than or equal to the military power of the first state reduced by the distance between the two nations.

Unconditional viability can be introduced to the Richardson model by changing the basis for comparing arms stocks. If we define the variables X and Y as representing arms stocks measured in units of military power the coefficients k/a and k'/a' become measures of the desired ratio of military power for y and x. If military power is reduced by distance, then the military power of nation x will be reduced by a factor d_{yx} that is less than one and is a function of the distance between nation x and nation y. Nation y will now be comparing its own military power at home to the military power nation x can project at nation y's borders. If we insert this comparison into equation 12.3, we get the following:

$$dY/dt = a[bd_{yx}X - Y + (g/a)] \qquad (12.12)$$

where $k/a = bd_{xy}$. A similar substitution into equation 12.4 yields the following:

$$dX/dt = a'[b'd_{xy}Y - X + (h/a')] \qquad (12.13)$$

where $k'/a' = b'd_{xy}$.

The coefficients k/a and k'/a' have been replaced by three new coefficients b, b', and d; d is dependent on distance (therefore, $d_{xy} = d_{yx}$), and both b and b' are as yet undefined coefficients that are assumed to be dependent on national policy.

THREE MODELS OF ARMS RACES

Equations 12.12 and 12.13 are identical in form to equations 12.3 and 12.4; we have simply substituted a new set of coefficients for k/a and k'/a'. The new coefficients now provide a partial interpretation of the "desired ratio of forces" in terms of the military power necessary for unconditional viability.

Unconditional viability assumes that the outcome of military conflicts is a simple function of two variables: the military power of nation x and the military power of nation y, both measured at a certain point. If the military power of nation y is greater or equal to the military power of nation x and the point of measurement is on the border of nation y, then nation y is unconditionally viable. If the military power of nation x as measured at the border of nation y is greater than the military power of nation y, then nation y is not unconditionally viable. This deterministic arrangement is not true for real warfare. The amount of force necessary to deter attack is frequently much smaller than the amount needed to defeat the attacker decisively; all that is necessary is to make the cost of attacking too high for the payoff in political or territorial gains. Similarly, certain victory for the attacker usually means a ratio of offensive forces of at least 2:1, and more often 3:1. This factor must be taken into account in the comparison of military power.

The coefficients b and b' will now be replaced by an expression $(1-\tau)$, where τ is a measure of trust. We will define trust in terms of a perceptual variable p: p_{yx} is the probability of hostilities breaking out between x and y as perceived by y; p_{xy} is the same probability as perceived by x. It is clear that p_{xy} is not necessarily equal to p_{yx}. If nation y perceives the possibility of hostilities breaking out between itself and nation x as being small, then nation y will not require arms stocks so large as those necessary for unconditional viability. If nation y perceives that the probability of hostilities breaking out with nation x is high, then nation y will desire more arms stocks than if the perceived probability were low. If nation y intends to attack nation x preemptively, then the perceived probability of hostilities would be very high, and nation y would desire more arms stocks than would be necessary for unconditional viability.

This can be expressed in terms of "trust." If p_{yx} is small, then we say that y trusts x; if p_{yx} is large, then y does not trust x. In terms of "trust" we see that if nation y trusts nation x, then nation y will be satisfied with less than the arms stock necessary for unconditional viability; if nation y does not trust nation x, then nation y will desire arms stocks larger than those necessary for unconditional viability.

There is a simple expression that relates the perceived probability of hostilities to trust in the manner required. If p_{xy} represents the perceived probability of hostilities, and τ_{xy} represents the level of trust nation y has for nation x, then we can form the following expression relating p_{xy} and τ_{xy}:

$$\tau_{xy} = (1 - 2p_{xy})/(1 - p_{xy}) \qquad (12.14)$$

This function has the following properties. If p is zero, then τ is one; if p is between one and one-half, then τ is between one and zero; if p equals one-half, then τ equals zero; finally, if p is less than one-half, then τ is negative, tending to minus infinity as p approaches zero.

The concept of trust can be introduced into the Richardson model if an additional assumption is made. This assumption is that nation y desires as its own arms stock, measured in units of power, the quantity $(1 - \tau_{yx})$ times the arms stock necessary for unconditional viability. Substantively, this expression indicates that nation y will desire less than the arms stock necessary for unconditional viability if the perceived probability of hostilities is less than one-half; if the perceived probability of hostilities exceeds one-half, then nation y will desire more than the arms stock necessary for unconditional viability, tending to plus infinity as p goes to one.

The expression relating trust to desired ratios of arms stocks can be introduced into equations 12.12 and 12.13, yielding the following:

$$dY/dt = a[(1-\tau_{yx})d_{yx}X - Y + (g/a)] \qquad (12.15)$$

$$dX/dt = a'[(1-\tau_{xy})d_{xy}Y - X + (h/a')] \qquad (12.16)$$

The equations are still identical in form to 12.3 and 12.4; the only change is that the coefficients k/a and k'/a' are now replaced by expressions containing τ and d, which have been given meaning in terms of national perceptions and dyadic distances.

ALLIANCES

The discussions to this point have been based on a two-nation model. We now turn to models with more than two nations; these are termed N-nation models. A number of new possibilities emerge in a N-nation model that did not exist in a two-nation model; in particular, one possibility is that of defensive alliances. A defensive alliance is an agreement between two nations that the armed forces of one will aid the other if either of the two nations is attacked by

THREE MODELS OF ARMS RACES 259

a third nation. The immediate effect of such an alliance is that of reducing the size of the military forces both must keep in order to remain unconditionally viable. A defensive alliance assumes that the two nations entering into it are relatively friendly to each other. In terms of the model as it has been developed, the perceived probability of hostilities breaking out between the two alliance members is below a certain level for both members. Both nations "trust" each other. Defensive alliances can therefore be added to the basic model by tying them to the variables p and τ.

A new variable, e, is necessary to add defensive alliances to the model. This variable e has only two values, one or zero. In addition, $e_{xy} = e_{yx}$ (if nation y is allied to nation x, nation x is allied to nation y). This model is meant to apply only to international systems in which each nation highly desires alliance with any "trustworthy" nation. Thus, if the perceived probability of hostilities is low as perceived by both nations (which is equivalent to saying that the two nations x and y trust each other at a certain level), then we will say that nation x and nation y are in a defensive alliance and that the coefficient e_{xy} has the value of one. If p_{yx} or P_{xy} do not satisfy the condition that they be both low, then we say that nation x and nation y are not in a defensive alliance, and the coefficient e_{xy} is zero.

The contribution of defensive alliances to a nation's military power can be interpreted in two ways: (a) by the amount of power that the ally can exert at its partner's border or (b) by the amount of power that the ally can exert at the possible enemy's border. We shall use the former as the definition of the contribution of an ally to a defensive alliance, as it will always lead to unique values for the contribution of allies to defense. Interpretation a is also clearly defensive; this is not necessarily true for interpretation b.

Let us define a simple three-nation system in which to model the effect of defensive alliances. There are three nations: nation x, with arms stock (measured in units of military power) X; nation y, with arms stock Y; and nation w, with arms stock W. Nation x and nation w are allied (that is, $e_{xw} = e_{wx} = 1$); no other alliance exists. The effect of defensive alliances can be studied by examining the contribution of nation w's arms stocks to nation x's arms stocks when determining the rate of change of nation x's arms stocks with respect to nation y.

Nation x needs a level of military power equivalent to $d_{xy}Y$ to be unconditionally viable, since it has available its own military power, X, and that of its ally as measured at nation x's border, $d_{xw}W$. The total military power available to nation x from both its own military forces and those of its ally w is therefore $X + d_{xw}W$. If this expression is substituted into equation 12.16, we obtain the following:

$$dX/dt = a'[(1-\tau_{xy})d_{xy}Y - (X + d_{xw}W) + g/a'] \quad (12.17)$$

We can expand this equation to include all nations in the system by introducing the coefficient e and summing the contributions by allies over all nations in the system, arriving at the following:

$$dX/dt = a'[(1-\tau_{xy})d_{xy}Y - (X + \sum_{i=1}^{N} e_{xi}d_{xi}I_i) + g/a'] \quad (12.18)$$

where e_{xi} is one, if nation x and nation i are allied, zero otherwise; I_i is the arms stock of nation i; and d_{xi} is the coefficient depending on distance that reduces the military power of the arms stock.

Equation 12.18 raises some questions about the methods to be used for solving the system of equations. The equation is no longer an equation in two unknowns; it is an equation in at least two but possibly more unknowns. In addition, the rate of increase determined from equation 12.18 is only based on a reaction to one nation; some method of summing over all nations in the system must also be found. These problems will be dealt with during the formal presentation of model 1.

CONVENTIONAL WEAPONS AND STRATEGIC WEAPONS

Weapons systems can be used in two distinct ways. The most common use is that of waging limited war against adversaries over limited goals. These goals do not include the elimination of major members of the international system from that system; the types of actions may range from "police actions," such as the recent U.S. actions in Cambodia, to major conventional wars between minor system members, such as Israel and Egypt. The second method for using weapons systems is that of strategic war. A strategic war is one in which the goal is the elimination of a major international-system member from the international system.

Weapons systems whose major purpose is that of waging strategic war are termed "strategic weapons systems"; weapons systems whose major purpose is that of waging limited war are termed "general purpose forces."

Prior to World War II the most important strategic weapon was the battleship. The destruction of the enemy's battle fleet was considered to be the decisive engagement of a strategic war. The battleship, however, could be used in limited wars; it was therefore a dual-purpose weapons system. The assumption that arms stocks and the expenditures for those arms stocks could be treated as an undifferentiated mass was therefore not completely unrealistic. The post-World War II era, however, has led to the development of weapons systems that have a single purpose. The land-based ICBMs of the United States and the Soviet Union clearly have only a minor role in a limited war. Similarly, the intervention forces possessed by former colonial powers do not have a major strategic role. These developments make it necessary to drop the assumption that weapons systems or the expenditures for those weapons systems can be treated as an undifferentiated mass.

In this chapter it is assumed that all weapons systems can be placed into one of two categories: strategic weapons and conventional weapons. This classification system has some obvious problems; for example, the B-52 bomber has a major strategic role as a nuclear bomber, but it also has a major tactical-conventional role as a high-altitude conventional bomber. On balance it seems more reasonable to use two separate categories for weapons systems than to use a single category that equates SS-18s with field howitzers.

The division of weapon systems into two different categories requires that the rate of change of arms stocks be derived from two terms: a rate of change for strategic arms and a rate of change for conventional arms. These two rates must also be constrained so that the combined rate of change is economically feasible.

DIFFERENTIAL EQUATIONS AND DIFFERENCE EQUATIONS

There are essentially two different methods for formulating and analyzing mathematical models. The first method, which was used by Richardson, is that of differential equations; the second method is that of difference equations. Differential equations are defined in terms of continuous time; difference equations are defined in terms of discrete time. The solution of differential equations has been extensively studied, but unfortunately the system of differential equations that is generated from model 1 is not susceptible to such solutions. The model is also too complex for analytical solution using difference-equation methods; however, the method of difference equations does provide a means of studying the model. We can define the model in terms of difference equations, convert those equations into a computer program, and then examine the characteristics of the model through the behavior of the computer program or simulation. The translation of the model into a computer program allows the researcher with relative ease to examine the behavior of the model under many different conditions. Although a general solution cannot be found, the behavior of the model is investigated through sensitivity testing. The use of a computer simulation allows us to examine a model whose N is limited only by computer hardware.

A computer simulation gives away a great deal of predictive power for this advantage. Prediction, in the nomological-deductive sense, is based on a deduction from a covering law. We have in a computer simulation such a covering law, but our knowledge is not based strictly on deduction. The researcher may discover some of the interrelationships in the model but does not have the means of finding all of the relationships and cannot make statements of a law-like nature. In the case where the number of interacting elements is large, as in multinational arms races, a computer simulation is still the best first step towards an analytical solution of the model.

This model, therefore, will be based on difference equations and upon an assumption of discrete time. It is assumed that nation-states can only change allocations of economic resources once a year; between those times the allocation is fixed.

MODEL 1: A DIFFERENCE EQUATION MODEL CONVERTIBLE INTO A COMPUTER SIMULATION

We have now seen in the discussion above all the elements of model 1. These elements are Caspary's modification of the Richardson model, including the economic constraint function; an elaboration of the desired ratio of forces in terms of unconditional viability and a perceived probability of hostilities; and a division of weapons into strategic and conventional types. Model 1 will not contain defensive alliances. The general form of the model has also been defined; model 1 will be a difference-equation model convertible into a computer simulation.

Caspary's model was based on two equations. The first equation related the arms stocks of nation x and nation y to the desired increment of arms stocks; the second equation converted the desired increment in arms stocks to a desired expenditure, moderating this expenditure by an economic constraint function that took into account maintenance costs. Model 1 will use the basic structure of Caspary's model; however, it will consider arms stocks that are divided into two types that cannot be substituted for each other and that are measured in units of military power. There will be one equation that relates the conventional arms stock of nation y to the conventional arms stock of nation x, which determines a desired increment in conventional arms; a similar equation will relate nation y's and nation x's strategic arms to produce a desired increment in strategic arms. The two desired increments will be summed to create a total desired increase; this total desired increase will be moderated by an economic constraint function similar to Caspary's, but one that does not take into account maintenance costs. The actual increment in arms will then be allocated to conventional and strategic arms.

The principal differences between Caspary's formulation and model 1 lie in the elaboration of the coefficients of the model in terms of national attributes and policies. The characteristics used in the model are economic resources, arms stocks, distances between nations, and an index of trust. The characteristics will now be defined so that they may be added to the structure discussed above.

The first characteristic, economic resources, is easily defined. The economic resources of a nation-state are the total amount of goods and services that may be produced during an arbitrary time period. The amount of goods and services available to the ith country during time period t is defined as C_{it}.

The second characteristic, arms stocks, is measured in units of military power at some time t. The arms stocks of nation i consist of two types: strategic arms, denoted by Z_{it}, and conventional arms, denoted by Y_{it}. The total of Z_{it} and Y_{it} is T_{it}. The existence of a total does not imply that strategic weapons and conventional weapons can substitute for each other. T_{ij} is a measure of military power defined only for intermediate computational purposes.

The two types of arms stocks are distinct not only in their destructive capabilities, but also in the way they are affected by a third important factor, distance between nations. The effect of strategic arms is assumed to be independent of distance. However, the effect of conventional arms is proportional to $(r_{ij})^{-2}$, where r is the shortest distance between the borders of nation i and nation j.* This reduction of military power can be represented by a coefficient d, such that the military power of nation i's

---

*Arms stocks are assumed to be kept within the borders of the nation producing them. This assumption does not rule out fixed foreign bases, as national boundaries may be redrawn to include such bases. However, the assumption clearly excludes "moving bases" or naval task forces.

conventional arms stock, Y_{it}, at a distance r_{ij} from nation i, is equal to $d_{ij}Y_{it}$. The relationship between this coefficient and distance (r_{ij}) is such that if distance is zero, the coefficient d is one. As distance increases, d will decrease as a square of the distance. Since our model employs only one type of conventional weapon, we will use the characteristics of the jet fighter bomber that with its range of 1,000 miles is the longest-range conventional weapon in general use. At 500 miles we will assume that half the available military power remains. Thus, the reduction of military power by distance is expressed by the following equation:

$$d_{ij} = (1)/[(r_{ij})/(1,200) + 1]^2 \qquad (12.19)$$

Hence, if r_{ij} is zero, d_{ij} is one; if r_{ij} is 500 miles, d_{ij} is 0.5; if r_{ij} is 5,000 miles, d_{ij} is 0.04.

The fourth important characteristic incorporated in the models is trust. The trust coefficient τ_{ij} is a constant in model 1. This assumption is a reasonable one if the period of time modelled is short—less than ten years.

We can now insert the variables and coefficients into the first stage of the model. In this stage, nation-states estimate the desired increment to their arms stocks for each possible adversary. We will define all of the equations in terms of nation i comparing its arms with nation j. Let the desired change in j's conventional arms due to i's conventional arms stock be ΔYD_{ijt}; the desired change in j's strategic weapons is ΔZD_{ijt}. We now have one equation relating i's conventional weapons to j's, and another equation linking i's strategic weapons to j's:

$$\Delta YD_{ijt} = a[(k/a)Y_{jt} - Y_{it} + (g/a)] \qquad (12.20)$$

$$\Delta ZD_{ijt} = a[(k/a)Z_{jt} - Z_{it} + (g/a)] \qquad (12.21)$$

Nations may react differently to changes in strategic arms than to changes in conventional arms; we therefore replace "a" in equation 12.20 by R_i and "a" in equation 12.21 by S_i. These constants are reaction constants that are unique for each nation-state i and indicate the rate at which that nation-state wishes to react to perceived differences between the desired and the actual arms stocks. In equation 12.20 k/a is replaced by $(1-\tau_{ij})d_{ij}$; in equation 12.21 k/a is replaced by $(1-\tau_{ij})$. We shall assume that both g and h are zero in order to simplify the model. Thus, the desired increment at time t in the conventional arms stock of nation i with respect to nation j's conventional arms is ΔYD_{ijt}, which is given by the following:

$$\Delta YD_{ijt} = R_i \left[\left| (1-\tau_{ijt})(d_{ij}Y_{jt}) \right| - Y_{it} \right] \tag{12.22}$$

If ΔYD_{ijt} is zero or negative, nation i is satisfied; otherwise, it is unsatisfied. The desired increment at time t in the strategic arms stock of nation i with respect to nation j's strategic arms stock is ΔZD_{ijt}, which is given by the following:

$$\Delta ZD_{ijt} = S_i \left| (1-\tau_{ij})Z_{jt} - Z_{it} \right| \tag{12.23}$$

We have now described the process by which nation-states estimate the desired increment to their conventional and strategic arms stocks for each of the possible N-1 adversaries. We must now define a function that aggregates the N-1 individual threats into a single value for the desired increment in arms. We shall assume that nation i will never be attacked by more than one nation at a time. Offensive alliances are ruled out. Thus, we need to consider only the N-1 dyads containing i. For each dyad (i,j) there is a desired increment in conventional arms ΔYD_{ijt} and a desired increment in strategic arms ΔZD_{ijt}. These desired increments may be positive, negative, or zero. Among the N-1 desired increments in conventional arms there must be one that is greater or equal to any of the other N-2 desired increments ΔYD_{ijt}. Let the nation evoking this increment be called m. Similarly, among the N-1 desired increments in strategic arms there must be one that is greater than or equal to any other of the N-2 desired increments ΔZD_{ijt}. Let the nation causing this increment be called n. The increment in conventional arms desired by nation i with respect to nation m, or ΔYD_{imt}, is the desired increment in conventional arms for nation i at time t. We will call this desired increment ΔYD_{it}. The similar maximum value for strategic arms, ΔZD_{int}, will be the desired increment in strategic arms ΔZD_{it}.

We have now defined a functional relationship between the arms stock of each nation and the desired changes in conventional and strategic arms for each nation. These desired changes must be moderated by the second stage of the model, which poses economic constraints. The maximum increment is C_{it}. The actual change in total arms stocks is ΔAT_{it} and is related to the desired changes in arms stocks in the following way:

$$\left| \Delta AT_{it} \right| = C_{it}[1-e^{-f}] \tag{12.24}$$

where f is the expression

$$f = [\left| \Delta ZD_{it} \right| + \left| \Delta YD_{it} \right|]/C_{it} \tag{12.25}$$

This expression has the property that $|\Delta AT_{it}|$ approaches $|\Delta ZD_{it}| + |\Delta YD_{it}|$, if $|\Delta ZD_{it}| + |\Delta YD_{it}| \ll C_{it}$. Similarly, as $|\Delta ZD_{it}| + |\Delta YD_{it}|$ approaches and passes C_{it}, $|\Delta AT_{it}|$ approaches C_{it} as a limit.*

This actual change in total arms stocks ΔAT_{it} is composed of an actual change in conventional arms ΔAY_{it} and an actual change in strategic arms ΔAZ_{it}. The actual changes ΔAY_{it} and ΔAZ_{it} are in proportion to the contribution of each type of arms stock to the total desired change. The desired and actual increments are related by the following equations, where the actual change in conventional arms stocks is identical in sign to ΔYD_{it}, and the actual change in strategic arms stocks is identical in sign to ΔZD_{it}:

$$|\Delta AY_{it}| = |\Delta AT_{it}| \{(|\Delta YD_{it}|)/(|\Delta YD_{it}| + |\Delta ZD_{it}|)\} \quad (12.26)$$

$$|\Delta AZ_{it}| = |\Delta AT_{it}| \{(|\Delta ZD_{it}|)/(|\Delta YD_{it}| + |\Delta ZD_{it}|)\} \quad (12.27)$$

The absolute values are used to eliminate problems that arise when one desired increment is much larger in absolute value than the other desired increment and is of opposite sign.

Having computed actual changes, we can now complete the loop by computing the arms stocks for the next time period, t+1. The total conventional arms stock at time t+1 is $Y_{i,t+1}$, which is equal to $Y_{it} + \Delta AY_{it}$; the total strategic arms stock at time t+1 is $Z_{i,t+1}$, which is equal to $Z_{it} + \Delta AZ_{it}$.

We have now completed the presentation of model 1. This model is based on a simplified version of a model by Caspary, with some of the coefficients elaborated in terms of Boulding's notion of unconditional viability and a perceived probability of hostilities. Each nation's decision makers compare their arms stocks, both strategic and conventional, with all other nations in the system. There are N-1 desired increments for each weapon system type; the decision makers of each nation choose the largest desired increment for each weapons-system type; the desired increments for each weapons-system type are combined into a total desired increment, which is moderated by an economic constraint. The result of the economic constraint function is the total actual increment, which is apportioned into an actual increment in conventional arms and an actual increment in strategic arms. The actual incre-

---

*We use the absolute values of ΔZD_{it} and ΔYD_{it} in order to avoid mathematical problems that arise if f goes negative. This function makes the maximum possible decrease in the total arms stock equal to minus $[|\Delta ZD_{it}| + |\Delta YD_{it}|]$.

THREE MODELS OF ARMS RACES

ments are added to the existing arms stocks, producing the existing arms stocks for the next time period.

MODEL 2: ADDITION OF DEFENSIVE ALLIANCES

The second model differs from the first by including defensive alliances. In this model defensive alliances are a static part of the model; the nations allied are predetermined and do not change during the operation of the model. In order to introduce defensive alliances we define a new parameter, e_{ij}. This parameter is zero for all values of τ_{ij} less than some value ε; $0 \leq \varepsilon \leq 1$ represents the minimum level of trust necessary for defensive alliances. When both τ_{ij} and τ_{ji} are greater than ε, we say that nation i may now depend on j for military support (and vice versa) or that nation i and nation j are in a defensive alliance. In this case, $e_{ij} = e_{ji} = 1$.

The definition of the desired change in arms stocks is now changed so that the military power of nation i's allies is included in the computation. The desired increment in conventional arms, ΔYD_{ijt}, is now as follows:

$$\Delta YD_{ijt} = R_i[(1-\tau_{ij})d_{ij}Y_{jt} - (Y_{it} + \sum_{k=1}^{N} e_{ik}d_{ki}Y_{kt})] \qquad (12.28)$$

The equivalent expression for the desired change in strategic arms stocks ΔZD_{ijt} is as follows:

$$\Delta ZD_{ijt} = S_i[(1-\tau_{ij})Z_{jt} - (Z_{it} + \sum_{k=1}^{N} e_{ik}Z_{kt})] \qquad (12.29)$$

From this point on model 1 and model 2 are the same. The computation of the desired increments and the actual increments, given economic constraints, are identical with those for model 1.

MODEL 3: DEFENSIVE ALLIANCES AS A DYNAMIC COMPONENT

The third model makes defensive alliances a dynamic part of the model. This model, model 3, is identical to model 2 up to the state when the actual rates of change of conventional and strategic arms are computed. It is at this point that another difference equation is added.

We have defined the relationship between ΔZD_{it}, ΔYD_{it}, and ΔAT_{it} in equations 12.24 and 12.25. If $|\Delta AT_{it}|$ is not equal to zero, then i was unable to arm or disarm at the rate actually desired but was forced by economic limitations to arm or disarm at some lower rate. We shall assume that i will act to minimize this discrepancy by changing the pattern of τ_{ij}'s (and the associated e_{ij}'s). We shall assume that i will change only one τ_{ij} (and possibly its associated e_{ij}) in one time period. In particular, we will assume that i will change the τ_{ij} that will reduce the discrepancy the most, subject to a constraint.

The former parameter τ_{ij} therefore becomes a variable, τ_{ijt}; the associated parameter e_{ij} also becomes a variable, e_{ijt}. We wish to limit the maximum possible change for any τ_{ijt} and its associated e_{ijt}; in particular, we wish to make the maximum possible change a function of the discrepancy between ΔDT_{it} and ΔAT_{it}. This maximum possible change must be subject to the constraint that τ_{ijt} is less than or equal to one and greater than or equal to zero.

The discussion above suggests the following formulation for computing $\Delta \tau_{ijt}$, the maximum possible change in τ_{ijt} in terms of the perceived discrepancy between the desired change and the actual change in arms stocks. We let the perceived discrepancy between the desired change in arms stocks and the actual change in arms stocks be δ_{it} where

$$\delta_{it} = A_i [\Delta DT_{it} - \Delta AT_{it}] \tag{12.30}$$

where $\Delta DT_{it} = \Delta YD_{it} + \Delta ZD_{it}$; $\Delta AT_{it} = \Delta AY_{it} + \Delta AZ_{it}$; A_i is a reaction constant. The maximum possible change in any τ_{ijt} is τ_{ijt} where

$$1 - \tau_{ijt} \geq \Delta \tau_{ijt} \geq -\tau_{ijt} \tag{12.31}$$

if $\delta_{it} > 0$, then

$$\Delta \tau_{ijt} = [1 - \tau_{ijt}][1 - e^{-g}] + G_{ij} \tag{12.32}$$

if $\delta_{it} < 0$, then

$$\Delta \tau_{ijt} = \tau_{ijt}[1 - e^{-h}] + G_{ij} \tag{12.33}$$

where $g = |\tau_{it}/(1-\tau_{ijt})|$ and $h = |\delta_{it}/\tau_{ijt}|$. It should be noted that G_{it} is a grievance term; there may be some nation-states with which i will not ally under any circumstances, and other nation-states with which i allies easily. G_{it} is a constant that is negative if nation i is predisposed not to trust nation-state j and positive if nation i is predisposed to trust nation j.

The perceived discrepancy between the desired rate of change and the actual change in arms stocks, given that the jth trust coefficient, as changed by $\Delta \tau_{ijt}$, is $\delta_{it(j)}$. The discrepancy is computed by substituting $\tau_{ijt} + \Delta \tau_{ijt}$ for every occurrence of τ_{ijt} in the computation of ΔYD_{it} and ΔZD_{it}. A change in a τ_{ijt} may also involve a change in the associated e_{ijt} if the τ_{ijt} becomes larger or smaller than the value of ε. If τ_{ijt} was originally greater than ε and becomes smaller than ε, then we say that i's trust in j has decreased below the threshold for alliance and that i and j are no longer tied in a defensive alliance. Similarly, if τ_{ijt} was originally less than ε and becomes larger than ε, then we say that nation i and nation j are now tied in a defensive alliance.

We have N-1 possible discrepancies $\delta_{it(j)}$, each based on a single alliance change, and one δ_{it}, based on no change at all. There must be some δ that is at least as small as any other δ; if there is more than one, we choose the δ with the smallest $\Delta \tau_{ijt}$. This δ is called δ_{ilt} and has associated with it a $\Delta \tau_{ilt}$. If we now change the trust coefficient τ_{ilt} by adding this $\Delta \tau_{ilt}$ and use this new alliance structure to compute the new desired increments to arms stocks, we will have reduced to a minimum the discrepancy between the desired increments and the actual increments, given the constraints on alliance change. The computation of actual increments and the new totals for each type of arms stock proceeds as in model 1 from this point.

We are now ready to summarize the sequence of computations in one iteration of model 3. First, the decision makers of nation i compute the desired rate of change of each type of arms stock in the absence of any change in alliance structure. The decision makers of nation i now compute the actual rate of change in arms stocks that would result from this desired increment and find the discrepancy between the actual increment, given no alliance change, and the desired increments. If this discrepancy is not zero, then the decision makers of nation i examine each dyadic relationship, computing the possible change in the trust coefficient with each nation. The N-1 possible changes in trust coefficients lead to N-1 possible changes in the desired increment for each type of arms and N-1 possible changes in the actual increment for each type of arms stock. The decision makers choose the trust coefficient change that minimizes the difference between the desired arms increments and the actual arms increments. This actual increment is then added to each type of arms stock, leading to the existing arms stock for the next iteration of the model.

Two additional assumptions might be made in order to fit reality better. First, we may make the actual possible change in strategic arms zero if nation i has less than some threshold value of C_{it}. This assumption corresponds to the cost and technological knowledge required to build strategic forces. Second, the pattern of alliances may be specified such that moving closer to one nation in terms of trust necessarily requires changes in the amount of trust for other nations. In other words, we may assume that it is impossible for a nation to trust all other nations simultaneously.

The time period during which this model is valid is limited by two factors: the rate at which nations change alliances in the real world, and the rate at which weapons systems wear out. The first factor places a lower bound on the length of time—it would be unreasonable to use this model to study a time period of one day. The lack of a function reflecting the attrition of arms stocks through wear means that the model will become increasingly unrealistic. This factor places an upper bound on the period that can be modeled.

Some inferences may be made immediately from the third model. The relationship between desired total increment and actual total increment insures that the presence of a power or set of powers that possess strategic weapons will force powers not able to build strategic weapons to ally with at least one of the powers possessing strategic weapons. The same would take place if one or more nations had much larger conventional arms stocks than any other nation in the system and the smaller powers were restricted by economic constraints from adding substantially to their conventional arms stocks.

STABILITY CONDITIONS FOR MODEL 1

We can obtain the analytical conditions for stability in model 1 by a number of simplifying assumptions. We will assume that there are only two nations in the arms race. We recall that the equation giving the desired increment in conventional arms in model 1 was as follows:

$$\Delta YD_{it} = R_i [1 - \tau_{im})(d_{im} Y_{mt}) - Y_{it}]$$

where m was the nation for which nation i desired the largest increment in conventional arms. If we assume that the arms race is a two-nation arms race, then there are only two comparisons to be made:

$$\Delta YD_{1t} = R_1[(1-\tan_{12})(d_{12}Y_{2t}) - Y_{1t}]$$

$$\Delta YD_{2t} = R_2[(1-\tan_{21})(d_{21}Y_{1t}) - Y_{2t}]$$

If the arms race is to stabilize, it must be the case that $\Delta YD_{12} = \Delta YD_{21} = 0$. A similar condition must, of course, hold for strategic weapons if the total arms stocks of both nations are to hold constant. The stability conditions for strategic weapons may be found by making the appropriate substitution in the stability conditions for conventional arms.

By multiplying through and collecting terms, we can simplify the first equation into the following form:

$$\Delta YD_{1t} = [R_1 d_{12} - \tau_{12} R_1 d_{12}] Y_{2t} - R_1 Y_{1t}$$

It is quite clear that the model is a variation on the Richardson model; the major differences are the disaggregation of arms into two types and the absence of a "grievance" term. According to Richardson the equilibrium conditions for the transformed differential equations are that $\alpha\beta$ be greater or equal to ℓk, where

$$dX/dt = kY - \alpha X$$

$$dY/dt = \ell X - \beta Y$$

The Richardson stability condition applied to model 1 indicates that the model is invariably in equilibrium. If we let $k = [R_1 d_{12} = \tau_{12} R_1 d_{12}]$; $\ell = [R_2 d_{21} - \tau_{21} R_2 d_{21}]$; $\alpha = R_1$; and $\beta = R_2$, and form the inequality, we find the following:

$$[R_1 d_{12}(1-\tau_{12})][R_2 d_{21}(1-\tau_{21})] < R_1 R_2$$

Or, dividing through by $R_1 R_2$ we find the following:

$$[d_{12}(1-\tau_{12})][d_{21}(1-\tau_{21})] < 1$$

But, since it is the case that $d_{ij} \leq 1$, and $\tau_{ij} \leq 1$, it must always be the case that this inequality holds. Since at least one run of the computer simulation has ended with arms stocks taking on values greater than 10^{99} in the first iteration, this inequality is not applicable. Therefore, the similarity in form between the Richardson differential equations and the difference equations posited in this model do not entail the validity of the Richardson stability analysis for the difference equation model.

A necessary stability condition does exist, however. Stated without proof, the condition is as follows:

$$R_1 R_2 d_{12} d_{21} [1-\tau_{12}][1-\tau_{12}] < 1$$

The condition for strategic arms races is as follows:

$$S_1 S_2 [1-\tau_{12}][1-\tau_{21}] < 1$$

The first model was tested in a simulation, and the predicted values of $R_1 R_2$ agreed with the values that generated stable "arms races." The simulation moderated the desired rate of increase with an economic constraint; in addition, the desired rate of increase was also set to zero if it was less than one in absolute value in order to eliminate "divide by zero" messages. The computer simulation is therefore more stable than the analytical model. One set of runs that used only conventional weapons in a two-nation arms race remained stable even when $R_1 R_2$ was 1.56; the maximum value for stability, according to the criterion, was 1.02. The economic constraint of the first nation was 15, and its initial stock of conventional arms was 150; the economic constraint of the second nation was 20, and its initial stock of conventional arms was 200. The arms stock nearly doubled after 95 iterations when $R_1 R_2$ was 81.

CONCLUSION

Three models of arms races have now been presented. These three models begin with a basic structure derived from Caspary's modifications to the Richardson arms race model. This basic structure is modified in model 1 by the elaboration of the "desired proportion" coefficient in terms of Boulding's unconditional-viability notion and a perceived probability of hostilities. Model 2 introduces static defensive alliances. Model 3 takes those defensive alliances and makes them a dynamic part of the model. All three models are N-nation models using an economic constraint function that prohibits unrealistically large actual increments to arms stocks. These elaborations, it is hoped, make the models a better fit to reality.

NOTES

1. See Lewis F. Richardson, <u>Arms and Insecurity</u> (Chicago: Quadrangle Books, 1960).

2. Kenneth Boulding, Conflict and Defense (New York: Harper & Row, 1962); William F. Caspary, "Richardson's Model of Arms Races: Description, Critique, and an Alternative Model," International Studies Quarterly 11 (1967): 63-88.

3. Caspary, "Richardson's Model."

CHAPTER 13

AN OPERATIONS ANALYSIS MODEL FOR THE STUDY OF NUCLEAR MISSILE SYSTEM POLICIES
William H. Baugh

Since the end of World War II strategic weapons systems have received increasingly intensive study. How they would effect subsequent wars and how they themselves are affected by policy changes determine evaluation of both existing and potential weapons programs and consideration of arms limitations. The latter, though hardly a new field of study, has become better known in the last few years since the Strategic Arms Limitation (SALT) talks between the United States and the Soviet Union set limited ceilings on certain types of nuclear weapons. The advent of the SALT talks expanded the scope of strategic studies from evaluation of moves in a game without communication to the posing of alternatives in a mixed-motive game with some communication. The result is a cycle of studies of alternative policies questioning the feasibility of arms limitations and their effects on a future to be virtually created by shifts in present policies.

This chapter is devoted to an explication of one of the tools used in such studies, an operations analysis model denoted DETER/YIELD. This model belongs to the family of "nuclear exchange models," so called because it is used to calculate sets of answers to the question, "If a nuclear war were fought in this way, with these weapons, what would be the results?" Expected results under different conditions can be compared to determine the effect of policy changes, such as shifts in the number and targeting of missiles on specific "figures of merit" such as security levels, numbers of targets destroyed, or numbers of missiles surviving attack.

Construction of DETER/YIELD begins from an assumption set that includes the strategic doctrine of "mutual assured destruction," under which any war between the United States and the Soviet Union would begin with a "counterforce" strike against missiles, followed by a retaliatory "countervalue" strike against cities. This assumption about strategic doctrine determines the structure of the nuclear exchange. The model is then expressed in mathematical form, with parameters being included to represent numbers of missiles of different types, numbers and capabilities of warheads, and so forth. We can then study the effects of policy changes by expressing policy shifts as changes in one or more of the included parameters. DETER/YIELD is a two-nation expected-value model; it includes both intercontinental ballistic missiles (ICBMs) and submarine-launched ballistic missiles (SLBMs) but is highly aggregated, allowing only two types of each on each side; it is solved numerically by computer; and it allows a limited form of simulation in which parameter changes can be linearly extrapolated over any number of time periods from initial values to final values.

Use of nuclear-exchange models for policy study has several advantages. Such models make possible the calculation of a few summary figures of merit for evaluation, reducing the complexity of a highly complicated system in which we cannot perform direct experiments. A large number of parameters may be included; DETER/YIELD includes the following: (a) types of missiles and the numbers of each; (b) number, explosive yield, and accuracy of warheads on each missile; (c) numbers and effectiveness of antiballistic missiles (ABMs) in the system; (d) deployment patterns of those ABMs to protect either missiles or cities; (e) numbers of "value" targets (generally cities) in each nation; (f) strategies and action sequences to be followed; (g) patterns of allocating warheads to targets; (h) target capabilities of resistance ("hardness"); (i) grouping factors, such as the number of missiles on an individual ballistic missile submarine and the number of such submarines on patrol at any given time; (j) bases of decision making in the system; and (k) the history of the system as it affects current parameter values. Moreover, complex interaction effects are automatically accounted for, since any one of several different parameter shifts or combinations of such shifts may produce the same effect, and each side's parameter values affect both side's figures of merit.

The most important interaction effect, however, is deterrence. In the modern deterrent system, security is not defined as maintenance of high absolute, or even high relative, levels of armament. Rather, security is measured by the potential destructive effect one side can reasonably expect to return to the other. Analysts of strategy commonly refer to this as an "assured destruction capability," so that a doctrine of balanced deterrence becomes a doctrine of "mutual assured destruction." However, since any given individual warhead has only a certain probability of destroying its intended target, no capability can be absolutely "assured." A better figure of merit is the Expected Countervalue Retaliation (ECVR), the fraction of "value" targets expected to be destroyed in retaliation even after suffering an initial attack. If the ECVR is sufficiently high, the opponent will not attack; it can then be said that the opponent is deterred by the defense's "sufficiency" in strategic weapons. DETER/YIELD calculates the ECVR for each side, along with the Expected Counterforce Survivability (ECFS), the fraction of missiles expected to survive a first strike directed at military ("force") targets, and the separate expected surviving fractions of ICBMs and SLBMs.

DETER/YIELD is far from being the most elaborate member of the family of nuclear-exchange models. For purposes of comparison, it is convenient to order such models according to the extent to which weapons types are disaggregated. At one end of an aggregation-disaggregation continuum could be placed a single-weapon-type model, such as Thomas Saaty's multiple independently targetable reentry vehicle (MIRV) model.[1] This is a very simple static model for studying the effect of MIRVing on the number of missiles required to hold the ECFS constant. The author's NUKEM and early DETER models involve many parameters and two nations but only one or two missile types per side.[2] DETER/YIELD includes four types of missiles per side, incorporates additional missile performance parameters, includes provision for interactive computer calculation, and introduces a limited form of simulation over a period in which parameters are linearly changed. The Arsenal Exchange Model (AEM) developed by Martin Marietta Corporation for the Department of Defense is a dynamic, stochastic model and requires numerical calculation. It allows manned bombers as well as missiles, and four possible war scenarios, ranging from a single-strike war to a three-strike war. And the current ultimate in disaggregation is the Strategic International Relations Nuclear Exchange Model (SIR NEM) developed by the Academy for Interscience Methodology in Chicago for the United States Arms Control and Disarmament Agency, a dynamic, stochastic model with variable war scenarios that allow for at least 50 different types of weapons and targets in both nations, plus blast, radiation, and fallout effects of those weapons. The primary goal of increasing disaggregation and complexity must be to achieve a more complete and realistic model. It is unclear at what point the process yields diminishing returns, but the derivation and use of DETER/YIELD will make clear a number of reasons why a more detailed model might be desired.

In what follows in this chapter, the nuclear-exchange model DETER/YIELD will first be developed as a set of assumptions about the essential features of the U.S.-Soviet strategic ballistic missile system. The assumptions will then be translated into mathematical form. Several sample applications will be examined, and a brief discussion of some avenues for the further development and application of the model will conclude the study. An application of the DETER/YIELD model to the study of some possible SALT II arms-reduction schemes has been published elsewhere by the author[3]; this chapter contains a considerably more detailed derivation of the model, followed by a different set of applications.

DEVELOPMENT OF THE MODEL AS AN ASSUMPTION SET

The assumption about strategic doctrine mentioned earlier is only one of the assumptions required to determine the structure of the model. In this section those assumptions are grouped into three categories: political, weapons, and strategic doctrine and usage assumptions.

Political Assumptions

These assumptions are statements about the system of nation-states involved, the actors in that system, and their methods of decision making.

A1: <u>Two Nation-States</u>. The modeled system has two nation-states, denoted the United States and the Soviet Union.

A2: <u>Economic and Technological Symmetry</u>. The two sides have gross economic and technological symmetry; a weapons development possible to one is also possible to the other after a "lag time" not exceeding a few years.

A3: <u>Value Targets</u>. Each nation-state has a number of value targets subject to retaliatory attack because of their nonmilitary worth to the nation. Significant value targets include infrastructure items such as docks and dams but are usually cities. The number of value targets is a parameter of the model. A large and important city may be counted as several targets, so it is not necessary to assume that there is more than one type or size of value target.

A4: <u>Rational and Unitary Actors</u>. The two nation-states are treated as unitary actors, without consideration of bureaucratic politics or other interactions below the nation-state level. In a general sense, the nations are considered to follow the postulates of rational action as outlined by Downs[4]; decisions are made so as to maximize expected net benefits.

A5: <u>Strategic Action Bases</u>. The bases for action decisions in strategic war are the strategic position of the nation-state vis-à-vis its opponents and other factors, such as evaluation of expected losses and benefits in strategic war.

A6: <u>ABM Deployments</u>. Each side will have 100 ABMs operational beginning in 1975. The Soviet site will protect Moscow and environs, while the U.S. site will protect a Minuteman missile field near Grand Forks, North Dakota. These deployments conform to the limits set by the ABM Treaty of 1972 as modified by the 1974 ABM Protocol.[5] Each site will have ABMs of a single type.

Weapons Assumptions

These assumptions are statements about the types and properties of weapons and targets included in the model.

A7: <u>Weapons Types</u>. Only strategic ballistic missile systems and their associated weapons are considered. The relevant terms are as follows:
- ABMs: Antiballistic missiles (see also assumption A6)
- ICBMs: Intercontinental ballistic missiles
- MARVs: Maneuverable reentry vehicles—an advanced MIRV with terminal guidance to target
- MIRVs: Multiple independently targetable reentry vehicles, or, for convenience, multiple warheads
- MRVs: Multiple reentry vehicles—several warheads launched by one missile at essentially the same target area
- SSBNs: Missile-carrying submarines, generally nuclear powered

A8: <u>Missile Varieties</u>. Each side is allowed four types of missiles: two SLBM types and two ICBM types. Accurate modeling requires that a change in the number of warheads per missile be represented as a change from one missile type (with n warheads) to another (with m warheads, m ≠ n).

A9: <u>MIRVing</u>. Subject to the limitation of assumption A8, some fraction of the missiles of each type on each side may be equipped with multiple warheads—that is MRVs, MIRVs, or MARVs. Missiles so equipped will be said to be MIRVed.

A10: <u>Warhead Properties</u>. The essential properties of missile/warhead combinations are summarized in the following two parameters:

    CEP: "Circular error probable," an accuracy measure denoting the radius of a circle centered on a ground target and large enough that half the warheads launched at the target are expected to fall within the circle

    Yield: Explosive power of a warhead

A11: <u>Target Properties</u>. The key property of a target is its ability to resist destruction. Here that resistance will be taken as "hardness," the resistance to destruction by blast effects. Hardness is the amount of atmospheric pressure increase ("overpressure") required to destroy the target; it may be 1,000 pounds or more for a missile silo and as little as five to ten pounds for a city. Hardness thus provides a sufficient parameter for distinguishing between military and value targets.

A12: <u>ABMs Uniformly Effective</u>. The ABMs of one nation-state may not be as effective as the opponent's ABMs, but they have equal probability of destroying any <u>type</u> of incoming warhead. This does not rule out the use of decoys that could help "use up" defending ABMs, although such decoys are not included in DETER/YIELD.

                Strategic Doctrine and Usage Assumptions

The United States and the Soviet Union are members of a strategic deterrent system that rests upon a combination of (a) enormous destructive power in any single strategic weapon, such as a missile warhead, and (b) a related technological superiority of offense over defense. Construction of a nuclear-exchange model requires an explicit statement of the way in which weapons would be

280   MATHEMATICAL MODELS IN INTERNATIONAL RELATIONS

used in war. In addition, relating the figures of merit used in the model to other concepts, such as deterrence and strategic sufficiency, requires statements about the circumstances in which war would be initiated.

A13: Basic Deterrent Strategy. A strategic war in the two-nation-state system would consist of only the following two steps:
1. A counterforce (CF) attack by one nation-state, using all available missiles to attack the opponent's missiles; this attack is an attempt to wipe out the opponent's military strength and thus his means of retaliation.
2. A countervalue (CV) retaliation by the other nation-state, utilizing up to the total number of surviving available missiles to retaliate against the attacker's cities, population centers, factories, and other valuable resources.[6]

The two-stage war scenario of this Basic Deterrent Strategy is extremely stringent, and it does not take account of the likelihood that at least a few missiles would be withheld from initial use in order to permit later stages of bargaining. Yet such later stages would depend at least in part on the outcome probabilities of events in the first two stages, and would thus be difficult to predict. Presumably, the few missiles involved would not introduce large changes in either the ECFS or the ECVR, so the simplification introduced by assumption A13 can be justified. The sequence of steps involved in a war under this assumption is summarized in Figure 13.1.

A14: Maximum Acceptable Loss Fraction. The decision makers of a nation-state will not initiate strategic war if their Expected Loss Fraction (ELF) exceeds a specifiable level that we will call the Maximum Acceptable Loss Fraction (MALF). The ELF of one side is equal to the ECVR of the other side.

A15: Systemic Stability. If each side's ELF is greater than its MALF, no war will be initiated in the system, and the condition of systemic stability obtains.

A16: War Possibility. If the ELF is less than the MALF for one side that side *may* initiate war.

These assumptions, together with assumption A13, depict a system in which both sides hold to the strategic doctrine of

FIGURE 13.1

Schematic Representation and Action Summary
for Assumed Missile Exchange

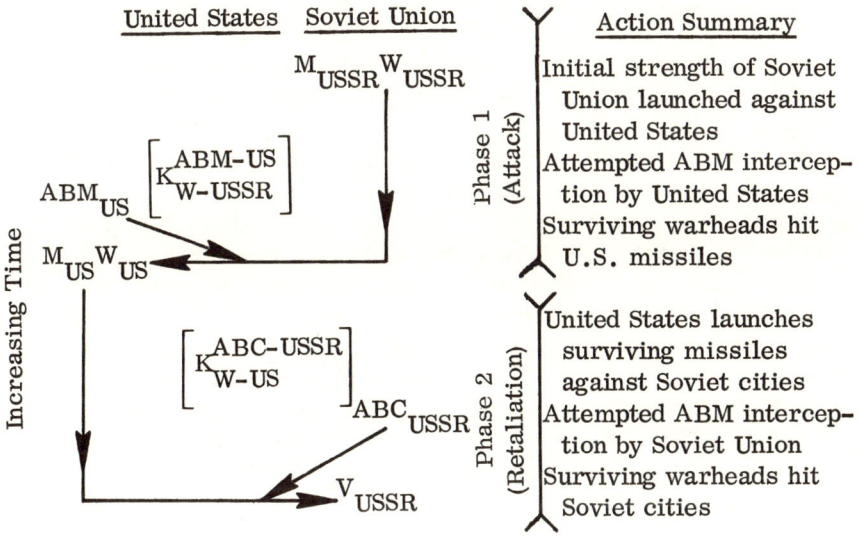

Symbol	Description
ABC	Antiballistic missiles defending value targets (cities).
ABM	Antiballistic missiles defending missiles.
K_{2-K}^{1-J}	Expected kill probability of a weapon of type 1 owned by nation J against a weapon or target of type 2 owned by nation K.
N	Quantity of strategic ballistic missiles (ICBMs or SLBMs).
V	Number of value targets (generally cities) in a nation-state.
W	Number of warheads ("reentry vehicles" or RVs) on a missile.

Subscripts denote the nation-state that "owns" a missile or target.

Note: The quantities in brackets are kill probabilities or effectiveness parameters.

"mutual assured destruction." Systemic stability results when each side's sufficiency in strategic weapons deters the other side; war is avoided because overwhelming destruction (ELF greater than MALF) is "assured." Assumption A16 does not necessarily rule out the possibility of restraint, but it is assumed that war becomes possible in the system whenever the ECVR of one side falls below the MALF of the other side—that is, whenever one side can initiate war without expecting unbearable retaliation. Policy changes regarding strategic weapons must be evaluated against such a possible loss of systemic stability. The strategic and usage assumptions may thus be seen as statements about how the decision makers of the two sides evaluate their own possible policy changes and their opponent's actions, using ECFS and the ECVR as figures of merit. This does not necessarily imply that the opponent's <u>intentions</u> are inferred from his capabilities; the logic of the deterrent system simply dictates that each side must guard against the opponent's capabilities. Since the emergence of the modern deterrent system both the United States and the Soviet Union have shown signs of reaction to the capabilities of the opponent, regardless of announced intentions such as "no first strike" or "no first use of nuclear weapons." The continuing concern over inspection and verification under the SALT agreements seems to imply that both sides fear that actions supportive of hostile intent could be falsified or hidden.[7]

DEVELOPMENT OF THE MODEL IN MATHEMATICAL FORM

Structure and Sequence of Action

The nuclear exchange model DETER/YIELD can be expressed as a small set of equations. The main equations are those that express the figures of merit ECFS and ECVR in terms of the many parameters enumerated above. There is one such equation for each nation; since the equations are equivalent except for nation subscripts, the derivation that follows is limited to the case in which the Soviet Union initiates attack against the United States. The structure of the main equations follows from the assumed sequence of the nuclear exchange, as summarized in Figure 13.1. The ECFS is first calculated and then used in the calculation of the ECVR.

The war scenario or sequence of action is fixed by assumption A13. When a set of parameter values is read in, the model calculates the "consequences" in the form of the figures of merit ECFS and ECVR. It is then possible to represent a policy change by changing one or more parameters and comparing the results. This is facilitated by a program feature that allows a limited form of simulation in which "initial" and "final" parameter values are read in and the figures of merit are calculated for each of a specified number of "time" periods using a linear extrapolation from initial to final parameter values. Some of the parameter values, such as those for present numbers of missiles, are well known from "open literature" data. Others, such as those for ABM effectiveness, must be estimated from much more limited data. If the referent world values are not well known, the model may still be used to determine how sensitive the results are to variation of selected parameters over "reasonable" ranges of values. Parameter values may also be projected for alternative futures under whatever policy alternatives one wishes to examine.

The remaining equations of the model are used to calculate the probability that targets survive attack. It is necessary both to specify the survival probability for a single target of a specific type attacked by a single warhead of a specific type, and to calculate the survival probability for a set of targets attacked by a set of warheads. The latter problem arises from the fact that the ratio of warheads to targets will generally not be integral; the calculation is performed by the General Survivability Function (GSF), as described below. The ECFS and ECVR equations require nested use of the GSF functional form.

The General Survivability Function

Under the Basic Deterrent Strategy, assumption A13, and as shown in Figure 13.1, there are four stages at which a number of attackers is set upon a number of targets. Since there are likely to be multiple types of attackers and multiple types of targets at some of the four stages, the description of each attack will require statement of a prior allocation of specific attacker types to specific target types. This problem will be taken up in the following sections, as each stage of attack is described in detail. We turn first, in this section, to the problem of determining the probability that a set of targets of one type survives attack from a set of attackers of one type, when the ratio of attackers to targets is not an integer.

The allocation of attackers to targets, when the attacker/target ratio is nonintegral, is expressed in the following assumption:

A17: <u>General Survivability Function</u>. The ratio of attackers to targets is not generally integral. A certain fraction of targets will thus be attacked by "a" attackers, where a is an integer, and the remaining fraction of targets will be attacked by a+1 attackers. No distinction is made between targets of the same type when attackers are assigned. (Recall that a target may be a portion of a city, by assumption A3 on value targets.)

To operationalize this assumption, let the following specifications be made:

    $f(a,b)$:   Probability that a target survives attack by a number of attackers

    a: Attack multiplicity $=_{df.}$ (number of attackers)/(Number of targets)

    b: Kill probability for a single attacker directed against a single target

    $a =_{df.}$: $\{a\} + r$ (13.1)

    $x = \{a\}$: means x = the greatest integer $\leq a$ (a standard mathematical usage)

    r: Fractional part of a; $r = a - \{a\}$

If the attack multiplicity, a, is integral, there are precisely a attackers per target. The probability of survival of a single target in one such attack is $(1-b)$, and for multiple attackers $f(a,b) = (1-b)^a$. But a will not in general be integral, and by assumption A17 the nonintegral portion of the attack multiplicity is uniformly distributed; that is, there is an additional, fractional probability of attack for any single target. Thus, we obtain the following general form for the GSF:

$$f(a,b) = (1 - b)^{\{a\}} (1 - r \cdot b) \qquad (13.2)$$

It is now evident that the behavior of this function is reasonable for extreme values of the parameters representing kill probability and attack multiplicity. As kill probability, b, approaches zero, $f(a,b)$ approaches unity, indicating that as kill probability approaches zero, survivability approaches unity. And as the attack multiplicity, a, becomes very large, $f(a,b)$ approaches zero, so long as $b \neq 0$, indicating that so long as the kill probability is nonzero, the survivability approaches zero as the ratio of attackers to targets becomes very large. Finally, as the attack multiplicity, a, approaches zero, the survivability, $f(a,b)$ again approaches unity, indicating that as the number of attackers approaches zero the situation approaches survival of all targets. These findings indicate that the GSF ($f[a,b]$) shows the behaviors expected for extreme values of the attack-multiplicity and kill-probability parameters.

The GSF leads to mathematical complexities but gives a more accurate calculation than the alternatives of assuming that each target is attacked by the same number of attackers, or by a fractional number of attackers, which may be nonintegral. Test calculations show that such assumptions mask certain subtle interaction effects, especially in the most important referent world case, when the attack multiplicity is low—say, in the range of one to three.

At this point, some explanatory remarks concerning the use of the GSF are in order. The GSF is a continuous function but is only piecewise linear; thus, it is not continuously differentiable. Very large changes of slope occur when the attack multiplicity is not more than five. This low range of values is most likely given present and projected weapons quantities and is thus of greatest interest. If the GSF were continuously differentiable, the behavior of figures of merit (including maxima and minima) under parameter changes could be obtained from the model by straightforward calculus, and there would be considerably less need for computer calculation.

Test calculations were run using a continuously differentiable form of the GSF; for convenience let this be called the CDGSF. The CDGSF allows a target to be attacked by a fractional number of attackers, in contrast to assumption A17. Its formula is simply $CDGSF = (1-b)^a$, using the specifications (equation 13.1). The graph of the CDGSF is a continuous smooth curve that touches the graph of the GSF only at the points at which attack multiplicity, a, is integral. Consequently, we expect that the two functions will yield results that differ least when the attack multiplicity is nearly integral. Moreover, the differences between the two functions are greatest when attack multiplicity is small. The CDGSF should tend to predict higher survivabilities than the GSF, but this does not necessarily predict that the figures of merit will all be similarly affected, since they involve "nested" attacks. For example, the CDGSF may predict that more Soviet warheads will penetrate a U.S. defense of ICBMs, but it may also predict that more of the ICBMs would survive an attack if the incoming number of warheads were unchanged, so the effect of using the CDGSF in calculating the figure of merit ICBMSF1 (relative to using the GSF) is not obvious.

As expected, test calculations indicated that use of the CDGSF increased some calculated figures of merit and lowered others, and the changes were least when attack multiplicities were large and kill probabilities low. Thus, for most of the cases reported in the applications section of this chapter, there was almost no effect on expected SLBM survivabilities, SLBMSF. In contrast, when attack multiplicities were low, as for example in the 1975 ABM projections reported below, the figures of merit were strongly affected. For the cases reported here, the maximum shifts in figures of merit were about 16 percent. Other test cases have shown shifts of some 45 percent when there were many warheads per missile and the probability of a warhead destroying its target was large. On the basis of such test calculations we conclude that the greater accuracy resulting from use of the GSF justifies the increased difficulty. There are indications that comparable approaches are used in the classified literature.[8]

The Counterforce (First) Strike*

The problem of the allocation of attacker types to target types at each attack stage may be approached by building up from highly disaggregated levels, starting with a single missile type and moving on to derivation of the aggregation procedures necessary to obtain the figure of merit ECFS. (ECVR is calculated for the second, or CV, strike.) In this section the equation for $ECFS_{US}$ will be developed, on the assumption that war is initiated by the Soviet Union. Analogous procedures starting from the assumption of a U.S. first strike would yield the corresponding equation for $ECFS_{USSR}$. Referring to Figure 13.1, the assumed war begins with the launching of Soviet missiles, M_{USSR}, at U.S. missiles, M_{US}. Individual warheads must be targeted in advance at specific U.S. missiles, but it is the warhead types that are of concern here. A number of Soviet missiles of type j, $M_{j,USSR}$, is targeted at a number of U.S. missiles of type k, $M_{k,US}$. Each Soviet missile launches $W_{j,USSR}$ warheads, so that the attack multiplicity is $M_{j,USSR} W_{j,USSR}/M_{k,US}$. There is no significant loss of generality if we assume that missiles $M_{k,US}$ are attacked only by the $M_{j,USSR} W_{j,USSR}$ warheads. If necessary, the quantities j and k can be defined to facilitate this assumption by appropriate subdivision of the missile sets ("arsenals") on each side.

Given that there are few ABMs on either side (see assumption A6, on ABM deployments) there is a good chance that the $M_{k,US}$ missiles will be undefended. If they <u>are</u> defended, the index k can be defined so that they are <u>all</u> defended, without any loss of generality. ABMs will be assumed to defend their assigned set of missiles until exhausted or until attack ceases. We can then determine an expected number of surviving Soviet warheads that will actually attack the $M_{k,US}$ missiles and the fraction of those missiles expected to survive. The GSF must thus be used twice,

---

*The reader is referred to Table 13.1 for a summary of symbols used in this section.

TABLE 13.1

Summary of Symbols Used in the Nuclear Exchange Model DETER/YIELD

Symbol	Name or Description	Character*
I. General symbols		F
ECVS	Expected Countervalue (attack) Survivability	
ECVR	Expected Countervalue Retaliation = 1 − ECVS	F
$f(a,b,)$	General Survivability Function (GSF)	F
a	Attack multiplicity (ratio of attackers to targets)	
b	Kill probability for a single attacker directed against a single target	F
ECFS	Expected Counterforce Survivability (fraction of missiles surviving a first strike)	F
US; USSR	Subscripts used to denote "ownership" of a missile or a target. For each symbol listed below there is an analogue with the subscripts US and USSR interchanged	
II. Variables needed to express U.S. initial strength		
M_{US}	Number of launchable U.S. missiles	I
W_{US}	Number of warheads per U.S. missile	I
III. Additional variables needed to express U.S. survivability when attacked first by a USSR CF strike		
ABM_{US}	Number of U.S. ABMs protecting M_{US}	I
K^{ABM-US}_{W-USSR}	U.S. kill probability against one of the $M_{USSR}W_{USSR}$ incoming warheads	F
b_{jk}	Kill probability of the surviving USSR warheads against M_{US}; calculated according to equation 13.14	F
IV. Additional variables needed to express USSR survivability in the retaliatory phase of war		
ABC_{USSR}	Number of USSR ABMs protecting value targets, V_{USSR}	I
V_{USSR}	Number of value targets in the USSR	I
$K^{ABC-USSR}_{W-US}$	USSR kill probability against one of the $M_{US}W_{US}ECFS_{US}$ incoming warheads	F
b_{kv}	Kill probability of the surviving U.S. warheads against V_{USSR}; calculated according to equation 13.14	F

*The specification "character," listed where appropriate, has the following meanings: I, integer variable; F, fractional variable, bounded such that $0 \leq F \leq 1$.

first to determine the fraction of incoming warheads surviving the ABM defense, and then to determine the fraction of missiles surviving the attack. The GSF functional form for this first use will then appear "inside" the GSF for the second use.

In the first (CF) strike, the Soviet warheads, $W_{j,\text{USSR}}$, must first penetrate the U.S. defense of ABMs protecting missiles, $\text{ABM}_{k,\text{US}}$. Although by assumption A6 there is only a single ABM type on either side, the subscript k here denotes ABMs assigned to protect the $M_{k,\text{US}}$ missiles of type k. If the U.S. missiles of type k are protected, then $\text{ABM}_{k,\text{US}}$ will be nonzero, while if they are unprotected, we simply have $\text{ABM}_{k,\text{US}} = 0$. The expected survival rate for the Soviet warheads undergoing a U.S. ABM defense will be given by the GSF, with the ABMs as attackers and the warheads as targets. Assuming that the reentry vehicles are not attacked by the ABMs until after separation from their launch vehicles, we have the following:

$$a = \text{attack multiplicity} = \text{ABM}_{k,\text{US}} / M_{j,\text{USSR}} W_{j,\text{USSR}} \quad (13.3)$$

that is, a equals the ratio of ABMs defending missiles of type k to the total number of warheads incoming at that set of missiles.

Also,

$$b = \text{kill probability} = K^{\text{ABM-US}}_{\text{W-USSR}} \quad (13.4)$$

Note that by assumption A12 the U.S. ABMs are of uniform effectiveness against any type of incoming warhead, which implies no need of subscripts for warhead type in equation 13.4. The GSF for this case is then as follows:

$$f(a,b) = f\left[(\text{ABM}_{k,\text{US}} / M_{j,\text{USSR}} W_{j,\text{USSR}}), K^{\text{ABM-US}}_{\text{W-USSR}}\right] \quad (13.5)$$

which gives the survival probability for a single warhead. The total number of USSR warheads of type j expected to penetrate U.S. defenses and attack U.S. missiles of type k is then the number of warheads launched times the survival fraction given in expression 13.5:

$$M_{j,\text{USSR}} W_{j,\text{USSR}} \, f\left[(\text{ABM}_{k,\text{US}} / M_{j,\text{USSR}} W_{j,\text{USSR}}), K^{\text{ABM-US}}_{\text{W-USSR}}\right] \quad (13.6)$$

Note that when there is no ABM defense, attack multiplicity is zero, $f(a,b) = 1$ in expression 13.6, and all $M_{j,\text{USSR}} W_{j,\text{USSR}}$ warheads are expected to penetrate.

OPERATIONS ANALYSIS MODEL 289

When the surviving Soviet warheads of type j attack U.S. missiles of type k, the attack multiplicity will be expression 13.6 divided by the number of targeted missiles, $M_{k,US}$. If the kill probability of one such warhead against one such missile is taken as b_{jk}, the GSF yields the fraction of the $M_{k,US}$ missiles expected to survive. That fraction is the ECFS for the missiles of type k, and is expressed as follows:

$$ECFS_{k,US} = f\left\{(M_{j,USSR}W_{j,USSR}/M_{k,US})f\left[(ABM_{k,US}/M_{j,USSR}W_{j,USSR}),\, K_{W-USSR}^{ABM-US}\right],\, b_{jk}\right\} \quad (13.7)$$

Note that this expression requires a double or "nested" use of the GSF functional form, because the GSF is required at each attack stage and the number of Soviet warheads surviving ABM defense must be known before their attack against U.S. missiles can be calculated.

In principle, this expected surviving fraction will be different for each value of k—that is, for every combination of type j warheads and type k missiles. (Recall that j and k are defined so that the $M_{k,US}$ missiles are all attacked by the same type of warhead and are either all defended by ABMs or all undefended.) For certain purposes it will be clearly essential to know the number of each type of missile surviving attack. However, the overall figure of merit $ECFS_{US}$ is the fraction of all types of U.S. missiles surviving attack. It can be obtained as a simple weighted sum of missile quantities over types, using the $ECFS_{k,US}$ as the weighting factor. The overall figure of merit is thus obtained as follows:

$$ECFS_{US} = \sum_k M_{k,US}\, ECFS_{k,US}/M_{US}$$

$$= \sum_{\substack{\text{all jk} \\ \text{combi-} \\ \text{nations}}} (M_{k,US}/M_{US}) f\left\{(M_{j,USSR}W_{j,USSR}/M_{k,US})\right.$$

$$\left. f\left[(ABM_{k,US}/M_{j,USSR}W_{j,USSR}),\, K_{W-USSR}^{ABM-US}\right],\, b_{jk}\right\} \quad (13.8)$$

The detailed consideration of the structure of the kill probability terms, b_{jk}, will be deferred until after consideration of the second, retaliatory strike.

The Countervalue (Second) Strike

In the retaliatory phase of the war, the $M_{US}W_{US}ECFS_{US}$ surviving warheads are launched against the V_{USSR} value targets in the USSR, according to an allocation decided prior to the outbreak of war. As before, we begin by considering the allocation of a single type of missile and will later consider the aggregation of missile and target types. Thus, we begin with the $M_{k,US}W_{k,US}ECFS_{k,US}$ warheads launched by the surviving missiles of type k against some set of value targets selected from the V_{USSR}. Since a large city can be considered as several targets, it is not necessary to distinguish targets according to size. However, it is still necessary to recall that different warheads can cause different amounts of destruction, mainly because of different explosive yields. We would thus be expected to target larger, higher yield warheads against larger cities. Yet even this problem can be largely overcome by a suitable definition of the "number of targets" a city is to count, and without serious loss of generality we can treat the retaliatory strike as an attack by several types of warheads against a single type of target.

Before the retaliatory strike is completed, however, some of the incoming warheads must suffer a defense by ABMs assigned to city defense, ABC_{USSR}. As in the case of the ABM defense of missiles, the small number of ABMs expected implies that a small number of city targets (Moscow and environs) will be defended, and that the balance will be undefended. Again, we can define the index k so that the $M_{k,US}W_{k,US}ECFS_{k,US}$ warheads are all targeted at either defended or undefended cities. As in our treatment of the first strike, the attack multiplicity can be set to zero in those cases in which value targets are not defended by ABMs. We thus begin by considering what happens when there is an ABM defense.

The attack multiplicity of the defending ABMs against incoming U.S. warheads of type k is as follows:

$$a = ABC_{k,USSR} / M_{k,US}W_{k,US}ECFS_{k,US} \qquad (13.9)$$

The number of U.S. warheads of type k expected to penetrate Soviet defenses is thus

$$M_{k,US}W_{k,US}ECFS_{k,US} \, f\left[(ABC_{k,USSR}/M_{k,US}W_{k,US}ECFS_{k,US}), K_{W-US}^{ABC-USSR}\right] \qquad (13.10)$$

Here, as in equations 13.4 through 13.8, the kill probabilities of ABMs against warheads are designated as K, with superscripts

OPERATIONS ANALYSIS MODEL

indicating the attacker type and its nation, and subscripts indicating the target type and its nation.

The expression 13.10 indicates the number of warheads of type k expected to penetrate Soviet defenses. Yet, by the previous discussion, we can define value targets in such a way that they can all be considered as the same type. This means that in aggregating the results of the CV strike to obtain the figure of merit ECVR, we need only consider the type of the incoming warheads, and need not consider combinations of warhead type and target type. Thus, although each warhead type, k, will in principle have a different expected kill probability against one of the V_{USSR} targets, we need only know the number V_{USSR} and the number of warheads of each type expected to penetrate, as given by expression 13.10.

To see what happens to the GSF in this situation, begin by considering the survival probability (P_S) of targets of a single type subjected to multiple types of attackers. The survival probability of a single target struck by a_1 attackers, each of which has a kill probability b_1, will be $P_{S1} = (1 - b_1)^{a_1}$. If the same target were to be struck by a_2 attackers of another type, having a kill probability b_2 against that target, the target's survival probability from such attack would be $P_{S2} = (1 - b_2)^{a_2}$. Now suppose that the same target is subjected to both attacks. Since it must survive both attacks to survive at all, its P_S is given by the product $P_{S1} P_{S2}$, which is $(1 - b_1)^{a_1}(1 - b_2)^{a_2}$. Further, consider the case of one target subjected to attack by the a_1 while another target is attacked by the a_2; the probability that both targets survive attack is also given by the product $P_{S1} P_{S2} = (1 - b_1)^{a_1}(1 - b_2)^{a_2}$. Thus, whether one target is attacked by several types of warheads, or several targets are each attacked by one type of warhead, or some combination of these cases, the overall GSF will be a product of GSFs for each attacker type. (Recall that a product over individual targets of the same type is implicit in the attack multiplicity.)

Moreover, when attackers of several types are allocated to targets of a single type, the attack multiplicity for each type of attacker is simply the total of such attackers divided by the total number of targets. We thus have expression 13.10 divided by V_{USSR} as the attack multiplicity for the $M_{k,US} W_{k,US} ECFS_{k,US}$ warheads against value targets. If the kill probability of such warheads against value targets is denoted b_{kv}, the GSF for the CV attack by warheads of type k becomes the following:

$$ECVS_{k,USSR} = f \left\{ (M_{k,US} W_{k,US} ECFS_{k,US} / V_{USSR}) f \left[(ABC_{k,USSR} / M_{k,US} W_{k,US} ECFS_{k,US}), K_{W-US}^{ABC-USSR} \right], b_{kv} \right\}$$

(13.11)

The quantity ECVS is the fraction of value targets expected to survive the CV retaliation. Taking the product over all attacker types k,

$$ECVS_{USSR} = \Pi_k\, ECVS_{k, USSR}$$

$$= \Pi_k\, f\left\{(M_{k,US} W_{k,US} ECFS_{k,US}/V_{USSR})^f \left[(ABC_{k,USSR}/M_{k,US} W_{k,US} ECFS_{k,US}), K_{W-US}^{ABC-USSR}\right], b_{kv}\right\}$$

(13.12)

where the symbol Π_k indicates a product of terms for all the possible values of the index, k. While the ECVS is the fraction of value targets expected to survive the retaliation, the figure of merit ECVR is the fraction expected to be destroyed. Thus,

$$ECVR_{US} \underset{df.}{=} 1 - ECVS_{USSR}$$

$$= 1 - \Pi_k\, ECVS_{k, USSR}$$

$$= 1 - \Pi_k\, f\left\{(M_{k,US} W_{k,US} ECFS_{k,US}/V_{USSR})^f\right.$$

$$\left.\left[(ABC_{k,USSR}/M_{k,US} W_{k,US} ECFS_{k,US}), K_{W-US}^{ABC-USSR}\right], b_{kv}\right\}$$

(13.13)

Equations 13.13 for the $ECVR_{US}$, together with equation 13.8 for $ECFS_{US}$ and the GSF given by equations 13.1 and 13.2, comprise the basic form of the nuclear exchange model DETER/YIELD, and permit calculation of the figures of merit ECFS and ECVR in terms of the various parameters.

Kill Probabilities

Thus far, the development of the model has proceeded on the assumption that we could stipulate kill probabilities, whether those of ABMs against missile warheads, or those of warheads against missiles or value targets. We now turn to a more detailed treatment of the kill probabilities.

Since by assumption A6 there is only one ABM type on each side, and since by assumption A12 each nation's ABMs are uniformly effective against any type of incoming warhead, it is plausible to stipulate the values of the kill probability parameters, K_W^{ABM}. These probabilities may either be set to empirically determined values or varied over a range in order to permit sensitivity tests.

The kill probability of a warhead against a target, however, is a function of several parameters, as noted in assumptions A10 and A11. Those parameters include the accuracy of the missile (CEP), the explosive yield of the warhead (Yield), and the resistance of the target to destruction by overpressure (Hardness). Moreover, these parameters vary widely from one missile type to another and between the two sides in the U.S.-Soviet system. (At this writing the U.S. tends to have smaller but more accurate warheads.) Consequently, kill probabilities were calculated as follows:

$$b_{jk} = 1 - (0.5) \exp \frac{9 \text{Yield}_j^{2/3}}{H_k^{0.8} \text{CEP}_j^2} \qquad (13.14)$$

Here the subscripts j label warhead properties, and k labels a target parameter. This is a widely used unclassified formula.[9] It has been arrived at empirically and is intended to apply mainly to so-called hard point targets, such as missile silos.[10] It may also be applied to dispersed targets, such as cities, by entering a very low value for hardness—that is, indicating a very low resistance to destruction. In the calculations reported in this chapter, a hardness of ten pounds is assigned to value targets, as compared to values ranging from 300 to 1,000 pounds for missile silos.

Summary Expression of the Model in Mathematical Form

The set of equations below summarizes the nuclear exchange model, DETER/YIELD. Equation 13.8 expresses the fraction of U.S. missiles expected to survive a Soviet first strike, given the various parameters for weapons quantities and properties; equation 13.13 expresses the expected Soviet loss of value targets in retaliation for such an attack. Both equations have analogues in which the labels US and USSR are interchanged, to represent the case of an initial U.S. attack against the Soviet Union. Equation 13.14 gives the kill probability for missile warheads against their targets, as used here, and equation 13.2 plus the specifications 13.1 give the GSF needed to calculate the expected survival rate of a set of targets subjected to attack.

$$\text{ECFS}_{US} = \underset{\text{all jk combinations}}{\Sigma} (M_{k,US}/M_{US}) f \left\{ (M_{j,USSR} W_{j,USSR}/M_{k,US})^f \left[(ABM_{k,US}/M_{j,USSR} W_{j,USSR}), K^{ABM-US}_{W-USSR} \right], b_{jk} \right\} \quad (13.8)$$

$$\text{ECVR}_{US} = 1 - \Pi_k f \left\{ (M_{k,US} W_{k,US} \text{ECFS}_{k,US}/V_{USSR})^f \left[(ABC_{k,USSR}/M_{k,US} W_{k,US} \text{ECFS}_{k,US}), K^{ABC-USSR}_{W-US} \right], b_{kv} \right\} \quad (13.13)$$

$$b_{jk} = 1 - (0.5) \exp(9 \text{Yield}_j^{2/3}/H_k^{0.8} \text{CEP}_j^2) \quad (13.14)$$

$$f(a,b) = (1-b)^{\{a\}}(1-rb) \quad (13.2)$$

$a =_{df.}$ (Number of attackers)/(Number of targets) $=_{df.} \{a\} \div r$

$b =_{df.}$ kill probability for a single attacker directed against a single target

$\{a\} =_{df.}$ The greatest integer $\leq a$ $\quad (13.1)$

$r =_{df.}$ Fractional part of a; $r - a - \{a\}$

Interactive Computation Structure

The DETER/YIELD model requires numerical computation for several reasons. Since the GSF is not continuously differentiable, the model does not have analytic solutions, so maxima or minima of the figures of merit can be obtained only by calculating and comparing the values corresponding to many different sets of parameters. Hand calculation of the equations is extremely tedious even for a single type of missile, and numerical computation simplifies the taking of the various sums and products over different missile types or allocations to targets. Use of a high-speed computer program also greatly simplifies keeping track of the values of the many parameters in the model, displaying them for the analyst's convenience and simulating parameter changes over time. Perhaps most important, an interactive computation structure facilitates the rapid change of parameter values to determine their effects on the figures of merit, and thus expedites the use of the model as a tool for policy analysis.

DETER/YIELD has been programmed in FORTRAN for interactive use by an analyst working at a computer terminal. In the normal sequence of operation, the model and one or more "starting" data cases or sets of parameter values are stored as permanent files on magnetic disks. A case is read in, the complete set of initial and final parameter values is printed for reference, and the calculated figures of merit corresponding to the initial and final values are printed. The analyst is then given branching options to continue, with or without parameter changes (which may include increasing the number of "time" periods between the initial and final states); reading in a new case; printing out the set of parameter values as currently stored in core in order to allow a check of all parameter changes made from the starting case; or exiting from the program. A sample of the interactive output is shown in Figure 13.2. Having thus described how the model is translated into mathematical form and operationalized on the computer, we turn in the next section to some illustrative applications.

SAMPLE APPLICATIONS

The U.S.-Soviet Strategic Balance, Circa 1975

The first of the figure-of-merit lines in Figure 13.2 gives values for the United States and the Soviet Union circa 1975, assuming the two sides have the arsenals given under "Initial Missile Parameters" in Figure 13.2. As always, the accuracy of the calculated figures of merit depends on the accuracy of the parameters input to the model. In this case, those parameters were drawn from open-literature estimates generally recognized as informed, and extrapolated to January 1, 1975.[11] The calculated figures of merit are as follows:

FIGURE 13.2

A Representative Case of the Interactive Computer Output
from the DETER/YIELD Program, with Key

Nation 1 = U.S.
Nation 2 = USSR

General Parameters

Initial		Final	Key
1	NT		Number of "time" periods simulated
0.	AC1	0.	City-defense ABMs in nation 1
100.	AC2	100.	City-defense ABMs in nation 2
100.	AM1	100.	Missile-defense ABMs in nation 1
0.	AM2	0.	Missile-defense ABMs in nation 2
500.	C1	500.	Value targets in nation 1
500.	C2	500.	Value targets in nation 2
0.500	KC1	0.500	Effectiveness of the AC1 ABMs
0.500	KC2	0.500	Effectiveness of the AC2 ABMs
0.500	KM1	0.500	Effectiveness of the AM1 ABMs
0.500	KM2	0.500	Effectiveness of the AM2 ABMs

Type/Quantity		CEP	HF	HV	W	Y
Initial Missile Parameters						
M110 =	554.	0.300	300.0	10.0	1.	1.000
M120 =	500.	0.200	300.0	10.0	3.	0.200
M130 =	304.	0.500	5,000.0	10.0	3.	0.200
M140 =	352.	0.300	5,000.0	10.0	10.	0.050
M210 =	1,575.	1.000	1,000.0	10.0	1.	2.000
M220 =	0.	1.000	1,000.0	10.0	3.	5.000
M230 =	720.	1.000	5,000.0	10.0	1.	1.000
M240 =	0.	1.000	5,000.0	10.0	10.	0.050
Final Missile Parameters						
M11F =	0.	0.300	450.	10.		1.0000
M12F =	1,000.	0.200	450.	10.		0.2000
M13F =	390.	0.500	5,000.	10.		0.2000
M14F =	320.	0.300	5,000.	10.		0.0500
M21F =	255.	1.000	1,000	10.		2.0000
M22F =	1,320.	0.400	1,000.	10.		5.0000
M23F =	720.	1.000	5,000.	10.		1.0000
M24F =	0.	0.400	5,000.	10.		0.0500

PERIOD	ICBMSF1	SLBMSF1	ICBMSF2	SLBMSF2	ECFS1	ECFS2	ECVR1	ECVR2
0	0.9447	0.9925	0.4862	0.9395	9.9631	0.6284	1.0000	0.9651
1	0.1692	0.9931	0.4684	0.9407	0.5113	0.6166	1.0000	1.0000

Additional Key

Missile Type/Quantity: Mxyz
- x: Nation label.
- y: Type label. 1, 2 are ICBMs; 3, 4 are SLBMs.
- z: Period. 0 = initial, F = final.

CEP: Circular error probable; see assumption A10, on warhead properties.
HF: Hardness of a military target against which the missile might be directed; see assumption A11 on target properties.
HV: Hardness of a value target against which the missile might be directed.
W: Number of warheads per missile.
Y: Yield of a warhead in megatons of TNT; see assumption A10.

Figures of Merit
- ICBMSF: Fraction of ICBMs expected to survive the first (CF) strike.
- SLBMSF: Fraction of SLBMs expected to survive the first strike.
- ECFS: Expected Counterforce Survivability; fraction of all ICBMs and SLBMs expected to survive the first strike.
- ECVR: Expected Countervalue Retaliation.

ICBMSF1	SLBMSF1	ICBMSF2	SLBMSF2
0.9447	0.9925	0.4862	0.9395

ECFS1	ECFS2	ECVR1	ECVR2
0.9631	0.6284	1.00000	0.9651

These figures of merit indicate that "mutual assured destruction" presently holds in the U.S.-Soviet system. It would be foolish for either side to initiate strategic war, because a loss of almost all value targets would result; ECVR for each side is at least 96 percent. This high expected ability to retaliate results from the large number of missiles expected to survive the initial attack—more than 96 percent for the United States (ECFS1) and more than 62 percent for the Soviet Union (ECFS2). Soviet ICBMs are seen to be considerably more vulnerable than those of the United States; ICBMSF2 is barely more than half ICBMSF1. Study of the changes in these values caused by shifting some of the input parameters indicates that the much lower Soviet ICBMSF results mainly from the considerably higher accuracy (lower CEP) of U.S. missiles. Finally, we may note that SLBMs show a much higher expected survivability than ICBMs (SLBMSF > ICBMSF) for both sides, indicating that land-based missiles are considerably more vulnerable than submarine-launched missiles.

Concerning the relative vulnerability of ICBMs and SLBMs, the following remarks are in order. It is assumed in DETER/YIELD that in the CF (first) strike, ICBMs will be targeted at ICBMs, and SLBMs at SLBMs, an allocation strategy that would be expected to lead to a high probability of wiping out the more vulnerable, land-based ICBMs. In the calculations reported here, SLBMs were assigned a very high hardness, 5,000 pounds per square inch, to represent the greater difficulty of locating and destroying a ballistic-missile submarine (SSBN), as compared to an ICBM silo on land.

The model also contains an implicit assumption that each SLBM is independently attacked, even though we know that SLBMs are grouped in even numbers on SSBNs (16 for Polaris/Poseidon, 24 for the proposed Trident) and that a number of SLBMs would thus be destroyed in a single successful "hit." If the probability of destroying a single SLBM were b, its survival probability would be $(1 - b)$. Grouping $\underline{k}$ such missiles together on a submarine would imply an effective increase in the number of attackers by $\underline{k}$, so that the survival probability of the SSBN would be $(1 - b)^k$, and the probability of the submarine's being destroyed would be $1 - (1 - b)^k$.

Assuming CEP = 0.4 miles, yield = 0.05 megatons, and hardness = 5,000 pounds per square inch, the probability that one missile would be destroyed by one warhead is 0.0058, using equation 13.14. If there are 16 missiles per SSBN, ten warheads per SLBM, and the United States and the Soviet Union have equal numbers of such submarines, then each SLBM will be attacked by the equivalent of 160 warheads, so that the submarine's probability of being destroyed is 0.606. By assuming that each SLBM is separately attacked, we thus appear to be understating the probability that each SLBM will be destroyed in a CF strike. Yet this would be true only if the location of the submarine carrying the missiles were accurately known, as ICBM sites are known. The ratio of the "single-SLBM" and "grouped-SLBM" kill probabilities thus provides an estimate of the implicitly assumed probability of being able to locate an SSBN; in the case here, that probability is about 0.0096, roughly a 1 percent probability. Despite initial appearances, this is not an unreasonable assumption, since the official United States Navy position is that an SSBN is essentially unlocatable except at its port, and is thus almost invulnerable. The essential inability of detecting SSBNs at sea by present or expected technology has been confirmed by navy strategic analysts, thus validating the simplifying assumption made in the allocation of missiles to targets in the calculations reported here.[12]

The Vladivostok Accords of 1974

The Ford-Brezhnev 1974 summit meeting in Vladivostok yielded a set of accords that set broad guidelines for further arms-limitation agreements, including limits on the total numbers of strategic weapons and on the fraction of such weapons that could be MIRVed. Assume that the 1974 accords were implemented with no increase from 1975 missile quantities; that the Soviets reduced their bomber force to meet the limit of 2,400 bombers and missiles; that the United States exchanged its 54 Titan ICBMs for SLBMs; that both sides deployed MIRVs up to the limit of 1,320 MIRVed missiles, MIRVing ICBMs before SLBMs; and that the Soviet MIRVs began to approach the accuracy (CEP) of U.S. MIRVs. One would then obtain the projected arsenals for the period 1980-85 given under "Final Missile Parameters" in Figure 13.2, and the corresponding calculated figures of merit. Comparing those figures of merit with the figures for 1975 gives the following:

OPERATIONS ANALYSIS MODEL 299

PERIOD	ICBMSF1	SLBMSF1	ICBMSF2	SLBMSF2
ca. 1975	0.9447	0.9925	0.4862	0.9395
1980-85	0.1692	0.9931	0.4684	0.9407

PERIOD	ECFS1	ECFS2	ECVR1	ECVR2
ca. 1975	0.9631	0.6284	1.0000	0.9651
1980-85	0.5113	0.6166	1.0000	1.0000

Notably, most of the figures of merit are very little changed, even though major changes are made in the arsenals of the two sides. There is a dramatic reduction in survivability of U.S. ICBMs (ICBMSF1), leading to a reduction in ECFS1. Comparison with alternative cases indicates that this reduction is primarily the result of Soviet MIRVing (U.S. MIRVing already being far advanced in 1975) and accuracy improvements, combined with yields higher than those of U.S. warheads. Yet deterrence remains high, as reflected in the high or even increased ECVR levels. In the U.S. case, however, continued high ECVR1 can come only by means of a shift to the SLBM as primary deterrent weapon, as reflected in the continued very high value of SLBMSF1.

The ABM Contribution

As noted in assumption A6 on ABM deployments, the SALT I ABM Treaty of 1972 and the ABM Protocol of 1974 limit the two sides to 100 ABMs each. As shown under "General Parameters" in Figure 13.2, the above calculations are made assuming that beginning in 1975 the U.S. will have 100 ABMs defending missiles and the Soviet Union will have 100 ABMs defending value targets. What is the contribution of those ABMs to security levels on the two sides? By the shift of a few parameters we can compare the arsenals of Figure 13.2 with the equivalent case without ABMs:

1975	ICBMSF1	SLBMSF1	ICBMSF2	SLBMSF2
ABMs	0.9447	0.9925	0.4862	0.9395
NO ABMs	0.9430	0.9925	0.4862	0.9395

1975	ECFS1	ECFS2	ECVR1	ECVR2
ABMs	0.9631	0.6284	1.0000	0.9651
NO ABMs	0.9620	0.6284	1.0000	0.9651

It is immediately evident that the small numbers of ABMs allowed can contribute almost nothing to overall security levels of

300   MATHEMATICAL MODELS IN INTERNATIONAL RELATIONS

the two sides. With ABMs protecting some ICBMs, the United States cannot expect any change in SLBMSF1, but the change in ICBMSF1 is less than two-tenths of a percent, so that the change in ECFS1 is even smaller, ECVR1 is unaffected, remaining at 1.0, indicating that the large number of highly accurate U.S. warheads can easily overwhelm the Soviet city-defense ABM system.

How many ABMs would be required to have a substantial impact on the U.S.-Soviet strategic balance? For one interesting case, begin with the 1980-85 projection given in Figure 13.2 and examine the effect of increasing numbers of missile-defense ABMs (ABM1 and ABM2) on expected ICBM survivability.

Number of Missile-Defense ABMs	1980-85 Projections for	
	ICBMSF1	ICBMSF2
None	0.1649	0.4684
100	0.1692	0.4755
1,000	0.2086	0.5388
10,000	0.7047	0.9343

From Figure 13.2 it is seen that in this case there are 3,000 U.S. ICBM warheads targeted at 1,575 Soviet ICBMs, and 4,215 Soviet ICBM warheads targeted at 1,000 U.S. ICBMs. It is thus evident that ABMs that have a 50 percent chance of destroying an incoming warhead cannot have a major impact on the expected survivability of their assigned missiles until they outnumber the incoming warheads by two or three to one. Moreover, many technical arguments have been raised about the possibility of an ABM system ever achieving an overall effectiveness level of 50 percent, and about the expensiveness of adding more MIRV warheads to existing missiles, compared to that of building ABMs to defend against them.[13] Given all these arguments, it appears that the analysis of the nuclear-exchange model supports the technical arguments and indicates that the United States and the Soviet Union can use the ABM treaties of 1972 and 1974 to avoid a costly and ultimately fruitless ABM-vs.-MIRV race.

The Accuracy Race

How might a U.S.-Soviet race to develop more accurate warheads affect the strategic balance? We have already noted that predicted increases in Soviet warhead accuracy will lead to an ability nearly to destroy the U.S. ICBM force in a first strike. It has been proposed that the United States develop more accurate warheads that use "terminal guidance," the so-called maneuverable reentry vehicle (MARV), and it has been argued that such warheads would allow the United States to have the same destructive capabilities as the Soviets in the 1980s without increasing present explosive yields to match those of Soviet warheads.[14] Equation 13.14 indicates that an increase of, say, 50 percent in accuracy (decrease of CEP by half) would increase the kill probability much more than a comparable percentage increase in explosive yield or decrease in target hardness. Alternative formulations of the kill probability of a warhead against a hard-point target show the same effect.[15]

A 50 percent improvement in U.S. warhead accuracy (CEP12F) would have a very dramatic effect on projected Soviet ICBM survivability (ICBMSF2) in the 1980s:

U.S. Warhead Accuracy CEP12F, n. mi.	Soviet ICBM Survivability ICBMSF2
0.2	0.4684
0.1	0.0553

Given the larger yields and greater numbers projected for Soviet warheads, the USSR could achieve comparable effects with less-accurate warheads.

Soviet Warhead Accuracy CEP22F, n. mi.	U.S. ICBM Survivability ICBMSF1
0.4	0.1692
0.3	0.0435
0.25	0.0113
0.2	0.0000

It is evident from these sets of figures that accuracy improvements said to be achievable by 1985 could give both the United States and the Soviet Union the capability of wiping out the other side's land-based ICBM force in a first strike. Yet comparable accuracy improvements do not predict a comparable ability to destroy SLBMs, so one response to increased warhead accuracies might be to place greater reliance on SLBMs and perhaps even to phase out ICBMs. As in the case of ABMs, however, what is technologically feasible need not necessarily be deployed, or even tested, if the two sides can agree. Yet bans on the testing or deployment of MARVs would be extremely difficult to enforce.

NEW AVENUES FOR NUCLEAR-EXCHANGE MODEL APPLICATION AND DEVELOPMENT

Use of the nuclear exchange model DETER/YIELD to study some aspects of the contemporary U.S.-Soviet strategic ballistic-missile system yields some significant conclusions and predictions, as detailed in the previous section. Each side is seen to have an extremely high capability to absorb an initial attack and reply with devastating retaliation, and that capability is predicted to continue through the 1980s, regardless of any of the weapons-development programs examined. Soviet ICBMs are found to be more vulnerable than those of the United States in 1975, but that situation is predicted to be reversed by 1980-85 if the Vladivostok agreements of 1974 are implemented. That shift, in turn, could lead the United States to place greater relative emphasis on SLBMs as the primary strategic deterrent weapons system. It is seen that ABMs would be required in very great quantities to affect the strategic balance and that they might be offset by additional MIRVing at less cost. Finally, it appears that by 1980-85 each side can develop the ability virtually to destroy the opponent's land-based ICBMs in a first strike. Each of these findings or predictions has serious implications for alternative policy decisions regarding weapons development, arms limitations, and the evolution of strategic doctrine. We may then ask how these findings might be altered by changes or improvements in the DETER/YIELD model; and part of that answer lies in the nature of the ways open to us to test and validate nuclear-exchange models.

Nuclear-exchange models are suited mainly to working out the implications of particular policies, and thus to testing policy alternatives. The figures of merit calculated are values of physical quantities, sets of answers to the question, "If a war were fought according to a particular strategic doctrine, using particular arsenals of weapons, what would the _effects_ be?" The primary purpose of increasing the complexity of such models must be to make them more complete and realistic, and it is unclear at what point increasing complexity yields diminishing returns.

This lack of clarity results from the fundamental problem of testing and validating nuclear-exchange models. Without an actual nuclear exchange, we cannot make predictions that can be tested against referent world data. Presumably, it would not be difficult to obtain widespread agreement that it is desirable that nuclear exchanges remain strictly theoretical. Such "hard" data as do exist are thus only for tests of single weapons under peacetime "laboratory" conditions, and much of those data is not available in the open literature. How may we then test a nuclear-exchange model? How may we validate it to the referent world? And how may we distinguish a change that improves the model from one which merely adds to complexity?

Direct validation of such models is clearly not possible. In practice, many features will be adopted only because the consensus of analysts working in the field is that they are of value. In some cases, however, it is possible to compare two alternative forms for a model or part of a model, knowing that one form ought in theory to be more accurate. This was done in the comparison of the GSF for DETER/YIELD with a related functional form that is continuously differentiable but known to be only an approximation to the correct form. Since the GSF yielded significantly different results in some cases known to be important, it was reliably concluded that use of the more complicated form improved the model. Finally, sensitivity analysis to determine the parameters that affect the calculated figures of merit most strongly can tell us the points that are most sensitive to data inaccuracies.

Granting that the value of additional detail in nuclear-exchange models is difficult to assess, there remain a number of ways in which the DETER/YIELD model could be expanded and further developed, some of them extending it beyond the range of the nuclear-exchange models thus far discussed in the open literature. It seems clearly desirable to be able to represent more weapons types in order to improve the accuracy of the model. With only four missile types per side, it is not possible to distinguish all of the significant weapons types in the U.S.-Soviet strategic ballistic missile system, nor is it possible to have missiles of a specific type either all defended or all undefended by ABMs, as was assumed in the derivation. Moreover, it seems desirable to be able to include strategic manned bombers, which will apparently remain a major component of the U.S. deterrent force for some years to come. A more accurate formulation could be developed for the effect of a warhead upon a dispersed, "soft," value target, such as a city. While the model presently includes only blast effects of warheads, it is also possible to model radiation and fallout effects. A factor explicitly representing the grouping of SLBMs on nuclear-missile submarines could be included, as could a factor representing the percentage of such submarines on active patrol at any given time. Warhead allocations to targets could be optimized, probably to achieve maximum destruction, but possibly to achieve minimal cost.

The model could be extended to treat not just expected values of the figures of merit, but also their variances. This would require extending the limited form of simulation detailed here, in which parameter values are linearly extrapolated from initial to final values over a number of "time" periods set by the analyst, to a full dynamic simulation model with stochastic elements affecting such parameters as missile accuracies (CEPs). The model could also be used to examine the results of strategic doctrines other than the "mutual assured destruction" doctrine assumed under the Basic Deterrent Strategy (assumption A13). This could be done with relatively minor modifications, beginning with allowing for more than two attack stages in the war scenario. Finally, the nuclear-exchange model could be made part of a larger model, possibly one in which figures of merit would be optimized subject to constraints of budget or foreign policy variables. Given a model of the decision makers involved, we could also include a war threshold in such an expanded model. Clearly, such extended models incline toward total models of the strategic arms system as it interacts with domestic and foreign policy activities. In that light, by answering the question about the effects of particular types of wars under particular circumstances, nuclear-exchange models may help provide process laws for a larger theory.

NOTES

1. Thomas L. Saaty, Mathematical Models of Arms Control and Disarmament: Application of Mathematical Structures in Politics (New York: Wiley, 1968), pp. 22-25.

2. William H. Baugh, "Systemic Military Stability Among Nation-States: An Operations Analysis," Ph.D. dissertation, Indiana University, 1973; William H. Baugh, "An Operations Analysis of Systemic Stability in Ballistic Missile Systems: The U.S.-U.S.S.R. System After SALT I," paper delivered to the Annual Meetings of the International Studies Association, New York City, March, 1973.

3. William H. Baugh, "Arms Reduction Possibilities for the SALT II Negotiations and Beyond: An Operations Analysis," American Journal of Political Science forthcoming.

4. See Anthony Downs, An Economic Theory of Democracy (New York: Harper & Row, 1957), esp. p. 6.

5. Peter Osnos, "U.S., Soviets Sign Arms Limit Pacts," Washington Post, July 4, 1974, p. A1.

6. For further discussion on the basic deterrent strategy and the doctrine of mutual assured destruction, see Glenn H. Snyder, Deterrence and Defense (Princeton, N.J.: Princeton University Press, 1961); V. D. Sokolovski, Soviet Military Strategy (Englewood Cliffs, N.J.: Prentice-Hall, 1963), pp. 398-410.

7. See, for example, Michael Getler, "Installing of 50 MIRVS Halted," Washington Post, February 1, 1975, p. A8.

8. R. D. Specht, "The Nature of Models," in Systems Analysis and Policy Planning, eds. E. S. Quade and W. I. Boucher (New York: Elsevier, 1968), pp. 211-27. See especially pp. 214-15, where Specht discusses a model developed by RAND analyst T. F. Burke for the study of hard-point defense of missile sites. Specht takes the attack multiplicity as integral, though he states that "Burke did not make this simplifying assumption."

9. David Leestma of the Weapons Evaluation and Control Bureau, United States Arms Control and Disarmament Agency, personal interview, September 6, 1972.

10. See, for example, Lynn Etheridge Davis and Warner R. Schilling, "All You Ever Wanted to Know About MIRV and ICBM Calculations but Were Not Cleared to Ask," Journal of Conflict Resolution 17 (1973): 207-42.

11. Values estimated as of January 1, 1975, from International Institute for Strategic Studies, The Military Balance 1974-1975 (London: The Institute, 1974), p. 75, except for U.S. MIRV values taken from Getler, "Installing."

12. Personal conversation with Lieutenant Commander Richard Haskell, USN, engaged in SALT studies in the Naval Weapons Analysis Group, Center for Naval Analyses of the University of Rochester, Arlington, Virginia, February 21, 1975.

13. See Abram Chayes and Jerome B. Wiesner, ABM: An Evaluation of the Decision to Deploy an Antiballistic Missile System (New York: Harper & Row, 1969), esp. pp. 101-17.

14. See, for example, John W. Finney, "Maneuverable Warhead Being Developed by U.S.," New York Times, January 20, 1975, p. 1.

15. See, for example, Kosta Tsipis, "The Calculus of Nuclear Counterforce," Technology Review 77 (1974): 34-49; Kosta Tsipis, "Physics and Calculus of Countercity and Counterforce Nuclear Attacks," Science 187 (1975): 393-97; Davis and Schilling, "All You Ever Wanted to Know."

PART IV
DECISION-MAKING MODELS

CHAPTER

14

INTRODUCTION TO DECISION-MAKING MODELS
The Editors

The chapters in this part are all concerned with various decisions made by nations as actors in the international system. But it is not only this shared concern for national decision making that brings these chapters together into a group; in addition, they all employ the same paradigm for understanding decision making. This unifying paradigm is called "rational decision making" or simply "rationality." Each of the authors of the chapters assumes that actors (nations, alliances, coalitions of nations, and so forth) behave rationally. By rationality the authors mean that the actors (a) seek to maximize their utility by (b) following some set of decision rules or procedures so as to arrive at policy choices.* Although other assumptions may be combined with it, this rationality principle serves as the core assumption in rational decision-making models. No matter what the additional assumptions may be, the decision reached or the policy selected by the actors is the one that, following the decision rules, provides the greatest expected utility (benefits minus costs). This maximizing choice is often labeled the "optimal" choice or "best" alternative for the actor. Whatever happens to be the labeling of the selected alternative, the authors are referring to the same basic paradigmatic structure.

---

*The assumptions of rational choice decision making are laid out in rigorous detail in the following works: R. Duncan Luce and Howard Raiffa, Games and Decisions (New York: Wiley, 1957), Ch. 1 and 2; William H. Riker and Peter C. Ordeshook, An Introduction to Positive Political Theory (New York: Prentice-Hall, 1973), Ch. 2; Kenneth A. Shepsle, "Theories of Collective Choice," in Political Science Annual, vol. 5, ed. Cornelius P. Cotter (Indianapolis: Bobbs-Merrill, 1974), pp. 1-87.

Although the authors use the rationality assumption for differing purposes, the underlying assumptions of how decisions are made remain constant. For example, in Chapter 15 Ostrom uses the rationality assumption to develop the axioms for a model of an international balance of power system. In Chapter 16 Simowitz, on the other hand, critically assesses the use of collective goods theory (a theory that is derived from the rational-actor model) in international relations research. Still yet a different use of the rationality assumption is found in Sampson (Chapter 17) and in Bird and Sampson (Chapter 18). In these chapters the assumption of rational decision making is employed for the purposes of deriving conclusions from an axiomatic model. The underlying assumption remains the same across these four chapters: They all retain the common theoretical position that actors in the international system are rational. Taken together, the chapters in this part demonstrate the usefulness of the rationality assumption for addressing various research problems in international relations, constructing rigorous but yet empirically rich models of various applied decision problems in international affairs, and deriving propositions (theorems) about the policies that nations select, given various circumstances and conditions.

Before reviewing each of the chapters and noting the similarities and differences among them, the basic theoretical components of the rational-choice model need to be discussed. After this grounding has been laid, we will proceed with a discussion of the four chapters and how they interrelate.

ELEMENTS OF A RATIONAL DECISION-MAKING MODEL

Common to all models using rational decision making are a core set of elements. Each of these elements in applications can be elaborated in a variety of ways. But at least, in the abstract, these elements will appear in any rational decision-making model. In the applications provided in the following four chapters, some additional elements, beyond those that we will specify below as the core elements, are used, and in some instances the core elements mentioned less specifically than in others. Yet, upon examining the four chapters, the reader will quickly become convinced that all of the articles share the same paradigm.

The basic structure of rational decision-making models is rather simplistic. In the context of international relations, nations (or more precisely their decision-making representatives acting

INTRODUCTION

in the name of the nation) select from a basic set of alternatives those actions that "best" satisfy a set of goals or objectives. The set of goals or objectives are mapped onto a set of possible outcomes. The set of possible outcomes contains all the consequences from the basic set of alternatives (actions), and consequently for each alternative action there is a discrete outcome or set of outcomes (elements of the set of possible outcomes) evaluated by the set of goals or objectives. The evaluation of outcomes is a subjective matter. The outcomes evaluated as more beneficial are simply those the actor determines to be more beneficial.

Let A be the set of alternatives, $A = \{a_1, \ldots, a_n\}$, and let a_i be an action that an actor, say ego, can pursue as one possible alternative. For each ego there may be differing numbers of actions as well as differing actions. Ego's overall objective is to select an action that will best satisfy ego's goals or objectives. Let 0 be the set of goals or objectives, $0 = \{0_1, \ldots, 0_m\}$, where m is the number of goals or objectives. Each element of the set 0 tells ego the states of affairs that provide value. Goals or objectives are statements of desired ends that may never be achieved, but for which ego searches. For any given substantive decision there is a set of possible outcomes. Call this set X, $X = \{x, y, z, \ldots\}$. Actions lead to outcomes. By ordering the outcomes by the set 0, ego can select elements of A so as to arrive at those outcomes most highly valued by 0. The number of actions or outcomes need not be discrete and finite, but for the purposes of discussion here, we will proceed as if the number of actions and outcomes were discrete (each action or outcome being different from any other action or outcome and there being only one action that can be selected by the actor) and finite.

The rational decision maker desires to select some action so as to achieve a desired outcome. The desirability of the outcomes is determined by the set of goals or objectives. This evaluation is subjective, but certain decision-making rules or procedures must be followed. This set of decision-making rules or procedures is at the heart of any rational-decision-making model, including those in the following four chapters. Although examples using rational decision making may directly employ the axioms of utility theory, as do all of the models in this part, it is easier in a preliminary way to think of the decision-making rules as devices employed by the decision maker for constructing binary relations, R, defined on pairs of possible outcomes. These outcomes are best thought of as all candidate solutions to the decision maker's problem.

Using the set of goals or objectives, the binary relation on outcomes is defined such that (a) for any two outcomes, say x and y, it is the case that x R y (read: x is at least as preferred as y), y R x, or both, and (b) for any three elements of the set of possible outcomes, say x, y and z, if x R y and y R z, then x R z. In terms of utility, for each element in the set of outcomes the decision maker subjectively assigns some utility value. If x R y then U_x (read: utility for candidate outcome x) > U_y (read: utility for candidate outcome y). If x R y and y R x, then $U_x = U_y$. Now ego's task is to select, via the set of binary relations across all pairs of outcomes and their attached utility values, that candidate outcome or set of outcomes that is most preferred or has the greatest utility value (benefits minus costs). This set of most preferred outcomes is called the maximal set.

Now ego selects actions so as to arrive at the maximal set. To be more specific, there is an imputed binary preference relation, R^*, defined on all pairs of elements in A, such that $a_i R^* a_j$ (read: action a_i is imputed to be at least as preferred as action a_j, $i \neq j$) if and only if the outcome associated with a_j, say y; $a_i R^* a_j (i \neq j)$ if and only if x R y. This imputed binary relation maps the actions onto outcomes. By using this relation, ego can now order actions with respect to the binary ordering of outcomes. The imputed binary relation, R^*, must follow the same principles of ordering that follows.

Let us now take this rather technical discussion above and put it into more concrete terms with reference to international relations. In most instances the set of basic alternatives A is the set of policy alternatives available to a nation's decision makers. The decision that confronts the foreign policy makers is to select that policy that is "best" or "maximizing." The nation's goals (the set 0) are mapped onto the outcomes (the set X). The outcomes are ordered following the goals and objectives. Since policies lead to outcomes, the policies can also be ordered. The nation's decision makers now have a device to achieve their goals and objectives.

Policy in the above conceptualization is a means to achieving some end. It is an instrument rather than an end in itself. However, it is not necessary to perceive policy as a means. Rational-choice models can be employed for modeling any situation in which (a) there is a clear set of basic alternatives that are (b) linked to outcomes that (c) can be ordered by the binary relation R. In an application of rational decision making the outcomes may be policies, and the alternatives may be agendas. In such an application agendas are the means to policy ends.

Although the core elements of rational decision making have now been mentioned, a few additional properties of rational-choice modeling need to be introduced before we can turn to discussion of the four chapters.

INTRODUCTION

ADDITIONAL ASSUMPTIONS

Above we have been describing rational decision making as if the decision maker knows for certain the relations between actions and outcomes. Although certainty is a convenient assumption, it obviously does not describe many decisions in international relations. A decision under certainty is one in which each action is known to lead invariably to a specific outcome. The assumption of certainty is also commonly referred to as "complete information" or "perfect information." To reduce the poignancy of the assumption of certainty, we can employ models involving risk. A decision under risk is one in which each action leads to one of a set of possible specific outcomes, with each outcome occurring with a known probability. The probabilities are known to the decision maker. In actuality, certainty is a degenerate case of risk in which the probabilities assigned to the outcomes given a specific action sum to one and are all zero and one. The probabilities under risk sum to one but are not all zero and one.

To complete the set of possible information conditions we should mention decision making under uncertainty. Decisions under uncertainty are those in which the probabilities of outcomes as consequences of actions are unknown and not even meaningful. In other words the decision maker has no information on which to base a decision; the outcomes that flow from a specific action are unknown. It is difficult to deal analytically with decision making under uncertainty. Furthermore, it is not a very realistic view of international relations. If policy decisions are made under uncertainty, the selection of actions would be a random process. If policy making is a random process, then scientific understanding of policy choices would be a worthless exercise. But, alas, decision makers do seem to have at least some idea of the outcomes that flow from their actions. Although these ideas may be mistaken or the decision makers' information may be in error, foreign-policy decision makers still act as if they do have some level of information, and that the information is accurate. Consequently, the intended outcomes may not follow, but at the time of the decisions, those making the choice acted as if the intended outcomes would follow.

It is important to understand that by using rational-choice decision making the modeler is not claiming that in fact decision makers are rational and follow precisely the decision-theoretic scheme outlined above. The assumption made by the modeler is weaker. The modeler simply argues that the decision maker is behaving as if he is following the model. The "as if" assumption simply states that we can understand decisions reached in international affairs following this model. The actual causes may well lie in such factors as the attitudes, cognitions, personalities, and so on of decision makers and the decision making environment.

USES OF RATIONAL DECISION MAKING

The four chapters that follow provide examples of the use of rational decision making in international relations. The most elaborate uses are those of Sampson and of Bird and Sampson. The four chapters have been ordered from the most fundamental application to the most complex.

Chapter 15 applies rational decision making for the purposes of laying out the axioms of a model of the balance of power in the international system. Ostrom clearly assumes that actors—nations in his application—are rational. In Ostrom's formulation each actor has only six courses of action. Actors also share the same lexically ordered goals. These goals describe the states of affairs nations desire. Matched up against outcomes the nations' decision makers can select from the lexically ordered goals those outcomes that are preferred over others. To return to our earlier notation, the decision makers can construct the binary relation R across all pairs of outcomes using the lexically ordered set of goals. Given that actions yield outcomes, the nation's decision makers now have the basis for formulating the imputed binary relation R^* across their six alternative courses of action.

In Ostrom's formulation national decision makers can ask a series of questions so as to select the appropriate course of action. At first actions are chosen as if the decision maker is certain of the outcomes that flow from actions. Later, Ostrom revises his model to include probability estimates and considers decision making under risk.

Chapter 16 provides a different use of rational-choice modeling in international relations research. Simowitz's objective is to evaluate critically the theory of collective goods as it is used to explain alliance formation in the international system. To meet her objective Simowitz uses symbolic logic to assess the definition and reasoning involved in the theory of collective goods.

The theory of collective goods is based upon rational decision making. First, collective good is a good (product or service) that is jointly supplied to all members of some collective (alliance). Second, a collective good exhibits external economies. That is, if a collective good is produced and paid for by one member of the collective, then it can be consumed by other members of the collective; the good is an external economy to those who consume

INTRODUCTION 315

it without paying for its production by themselves. As Simowitz notes, some scholars choose to define collective goods by the property of exclusion (the goods are withheld from those who are not members of the alliance). However, using symbolic logic she clearly demonstrates that the exclusion property is a subset of the external economies property.

Understanding alliances from the perspective of collective goods theory yields what has become known as the "free-rider problem." All members of an alliance are rational. They have goals and objectives that they map onto outcomes. Certain actions imply outcomes. The outcomes are ordered by the binary relation R, and the actions are ordered by the imputed binary relation R*. Given the rational-choice model and the existence of collective goods, a nation may choose to join an alliance as a free rider. A free rider is one who gains the benefits of the alliance without having to pay for the good. Since the good is jointly supplied to all members of the alliance, it cannot be withheld from any member. The free rider enjoys the benefits of the alliance without paying the costs.

As Simowitz points out, the free-rider notion has been used by some scholars to explain the disproportionate cost sharing in alliances. It is empirically true that in the North Atlantic Treaty Organization and in the Warsaw Treaty Organization the major powers pay a disproportionately large share of the bill; smaller nations pay less than their share. Simowitz asks whether the theory of collective goods can explain this disproportionate cost sharing. Using careful logical analysis, Simowitz finds that the theory of collective goods provides a simple but sound argument explaining the occurrence of free riders. However, she also finds that the larger issue of why some nations find it in their interest to provide the good or bear a disproportionately greater share of the costs remains unanswered. In short, collective goods theory only answers part of the problem. It explains why small nations join alliances when they are not required to pay their share of the cost, but it does not explain why large nations join alliances knowing that they will have to pay greater costs than their share.

Chapter 17 offers yet a different example of the use of rational decision making. Sampson's effort is to examine the flexibility of U.S. policy with respect to arms shipments to Israel. To examine flexibility Sampson creates the concept of a "policy zone." The larger the policy zone, the greater the flexibility.

To identify the policy zone for the United States Sampson must do several things. First, Sampson stipulates the United States' policy objectives in the Middle East. These objectives comprise the set O, the set of goals or objectives. Second, Sampson needs to stipulate a set of what he terms "decision rules." Sampson's decision rules comprise a set of inequalities that interrelate U.S. arms shipments to Israel, Soviet arms shipments to Egypt, U.S. lobby-group contributions to the Israelis, and Arab oil shipped to the United States. These "decision rules" map out the desired relations among a host of variables. In essence, the decision rules are the relations that must be satisfied no matter what policy is selected. They comprise what Sampson later calls the "objective function."

Objective functions are best understood as an operational form of the set of goals or objectives. Policies that satisfy the objective function are those that are optimal. Suboptimal policies are those that do not satisfy the objective function. The decision maker's task is to select that policy that best satisfies the objective function.

However, as Sampson notes, optimal solutions to objective functions can be found without difficulty. If a nation simply optimizes its objectives without being subject to constraints, unrealistic policy choices are the consequence. Consequently, Sampson introduces "constraints." Whereas the objective function serves as the judge of the desirability of outcomes, the constraints tell us which actions are feasible. Constraints serve to reduce the set of all possible actions to a set of feasible actions. Using linear programming, the appropriate mathematical technique for Sampson's problem, Sampson derives from the objective function and the constraints a mathematical expression that describes the optimal policy—that is, the policy that best satisfies the objective function.

Sampson's analysis continues by slightly altering parameter values. By altering the parameters, Sampson obtains an idea of the degree to which the policy zone is sensitive to slight perturbations. The policy zone establishes, first, whether the objectives are contradictory and, second, whether new policies will have to be pursued if there are slight changes in parameter values. Sampson finds that given the behavior of other nations as of 1972, the United States' policy toward Israel is consistent with U.S. objectives and that the United States has followed an optimal policy choice. He further finds that U.S. policy can cope with increased inputs from other nations up to a specified level.

Chapter 18 presents a different and more elaborate application of rational-choice modeling in international relations. Bird and Sampson provide considerable elaboration on the basic rational-choice model. They are concerned with modeling the "oil situation" involving the nations of the Organization of Oil Exporting Countries (OPEC), the oil consumers, and the oil companies.

One of the major elaborations this chapter has to offer is that of incorporating a game into the rational-choice model. The particular formulation the authors use is of a cooperative game.

INTRODUCTION

In a cooperative game the actors can exchange information prior to the game's commencement. That is, the actors of the game can cooperate. Additionally, the game formulated by Bird and Sampson is not a two-person game. It is an N-person game that cannot be reduced to a two-person formulation.

Following the rational-choice model, Bird and Sampson stipulate the objectives of actors. They furthermore stipulate a set of "solution concepts." For Bird and Sampson the solution concepts are those rules that allow them to select the solutions to the game—that is, the outcomes that will follow, given that all nations playing the game are seeking to satisfy their own interests. Actors in the game select actions that are consistent with their objectives. The solution concepts not only describe the choices which actors make but also the choices of the n-tuple of actions going across all N-actors.

From their cooperative game formulation Bird and Sampson deduce a variety of fascinating theorems. Given their model, they find, for example, that even if there is no increase in oil consumption and given that no new oil is found, it is worthwhile for the OPEC nations to remain in their coalition. They also find that if an oil producer supplies less oil than the surplus available elsewhere, other actors can ignore that producer without violating their own objectives. The series of rich theorems deduced from the Bird and Sampson game theoretic model demonstrates the utility of this kind of thinking for solving applied problems in international relations research.

CONCLUDING COMMENT

Rational-choice modeling can be used for a variety of purposes in international relations research. Whereas the Ostrom model is concerned with the balance of power and Simowitz's chapter addresses problems of alliance formation, Sampson and Bird and Sampson address policy problems in international relations. We can use rational-choice modeling to evaluate policies (see Sampson), to build theories (see Ostrom), to evaluate theories critically (see Simowitz), and to derive the consequences of the "games" or interrelationships among nations (see Bird and Sampson). It is a rich area for the development of mathematical models. And as is demonstrated by the four following chapters, it does provide a solid and rigorous basis for reasoning about international affairs.

CHAPTER

15

BALANCE OF POWER AND THE MAINTENANCE OF "BALANCE": A RATIONAL-CHOICE MODEL WITH LEXICAL PREFERENCES

Charles W. Ostrom, Jr.

The primary goal of every nation in the anarchic international environment is survival; that is, in the war of all against all, each nation strives to remain sovereign.[1] While none of the methods that have thus far been suggested to solve the problems created by anarchy appears workable, it has been argued that there are a number of possible approaches to mitigating the anarchic situation.[2] Prominent among these is the institutionalization of a balance-of-power system in which no single nation is allowed to obtain a preponderance of the power. The hallmark of such a system, as Inis Claude notes, is that nations recognize that unbalanced power is dangerous and act to insure that sufficient power will be available in the system to neutralize any nation that aspires toward domination.[3] Because a "stronger power may succumb to the temptation to dominate, to oppress, to conquer, to destroy," it is clearly in the best interest of each nation to do its utmost to insure that no one nation possesses more than half the power in the international system.[4]

Two suggestions for maintaining balanced power over time have been made. Many writers have argued that the maintenance of a balance is essentially automatic, an occurrence brought on by the workings of an "invisible hand."[5] Others have argued that maintenance of balance requires a firm policy commitment on the part of each nation to opposing, potentially dominant actors.[6] The present inquiry will adopt the latter point of view, that balance is neither automatic nor inevitable and that it requires the conscious effort of every nation in the system.

No formal constraints are placed upon the behavior of the nations in a balance-of-power system (that is, there is no international police force); instead, several informal constraints result from limiting the range of admissible behavioral alternatives and the adoption of a hierarchy of goals. Recognizing that unbalanced power is dangerous, every nation restricts its set of admissible behaviors to those conducive to maintaining a balance. As an example, Kaplan argues that the formation of permanent alliances or supranational organizations will not be allowed.[7] Furthermore, nations in a balance-of-power system are not concerned solely with power maximization. They will identify and hierarchically order the following three goals: self-preservation, system maintenance, and self-improvement.[8] Because of the hierarchical ordering, all goals cannot be simultaneously satisfied. A nation will thus determine whether its own survival is in jeopardy, and if it finds that to be the case, a behavior relevant to self-preservation will be chosen. If there is no threat to survival, the nation will then ascertain whether there is a threat to the maintenance of a balance, and if that is the case, a behavior relevant to system preservation will be chosen. Finally, only if no threats to self and system survival exist will an alternative maximizing capability gain be chosen. Certain types of behavior are relevant only under certain circumstances. Thus, even if an actor wishes to become dominant, in order to insure its own survival it must first prevent other nations from accomplishing the same objective. Due to the restriction on the set of admissible alternatives and the hierarchy of goals, the balance will be maintained through an informal policing procedure.[9]

Since the institutionalization of a balance-of-power system is not a solution to the anarchic environment but only an attempt to mitigate its problems, there are two questions to which consideration must be given. First, under what conditions will the nations survive? Second, under what conditions will the balance of power be maintained? The present inquiry is designed to formalize a model of the balance-of-power system by postulating a number of behavioral axioms. That is, like the work of Kaplan and Claude, this inquiry defines a balance-of-power system in terms of the rules and policies that govern the behavior of the nations.[10] Unlike Kaplan and Claude, however, it will formalize those rules into a model of the balance-of-power system.[11] Having specified the formal model, we will give attention to the conditions under which individual nations will survive and to the maintenance of a balance from one point in time to the next. In the latter investigation we will discuss the extent to which the maintenance of a balance is automatic.

THE BALANCE-OF-POWER MODEL

This inquiry will concern itself with a set of actors, A, that consists of all nations. Let $A = [a_i: i = 1, 2, \ldots, N]$ where a_i is the ith actor in the international system and N is the total number of actors. Additionally, some measure of the capabilities of the actors is necessary. Although the capabilities of the actors can be regarded as synonymous with what is generally understood by power, a precise definition is not essential for the purpose of the development of the model. Let $K(A) = [k(a_i): i = 1, 2, \ldots, N]$ where $k(a_i)$ is the capability of the ith actor. Finally the capabilities of an actor are specific to a particular point in time. Therefore, $k(a_i)$ will be subscripted—that is, $k(a_i)_t$—to denote the point in time at which a_i is in possession of a given level of capabilities.

In addition to these primitive terms, a number of definitions are important to the development of the model:

D1. <u>Survival</u>: An actor, a_i, is said to survive if it has some capability under its control. That is, if $k(a_i)_t > 0$.

D2. <u>Dominant actor</u>: An actor, say a_1, is identified as a dominant actor if it has capabilities greater than the sum of the other actors, $a_2, a_3, \ldots, a_N$, in the system. That is, a_1 is dominant only if

$$k(a_1)_t > \sum_{i=2}^{N} k(a_i)_t$$

D3. <u>Time increment</u>: The time increment, Δt, is the length of time necessary to complete an action.

D4. <u>Outcome</u>: An outcome will be defined in terms of the capabilities possessed by the actors of the system. That is, an outcome is denoted by specifying $k(a_i)_t$ for all $a_i \in A$.

D5. <u>Balance</u>: An outcome is said to be balanced if no dominant actor exists.

D6. <u>Capability gain</u>: Actor a_i's capability gain, $\Delta k(a_i)$, is the difference between a_i's capability level at time $t+\Delta t$ and time t.

D7. <u>Threshold</u>: The threshold, Υ, is one half of the total capabilities in the system at $t+\Delta t$. That is,

$$\Upsilon = \frac{1}{2} \sum_{i=1}^{N} k(a_i)_{t+\Delta t}$$

D8. <u>Potentially dominant actor</u>: An actor, a_1, is said to be potentially dominant if its capability gain will make it a dominant actor. That is, a_1 will be identified as a potentially dominant actor only if

$$k(a_1)_t + \Delta k(a_1) > \Upsilon$$

D9. <u>Helping coalition</u>: A^* is a subset of A that contains all actors who come to the aid of an attacked actor. Let $A^* = [a_h: h = 1, 2, \ldots, M]$ where a_h is the hth actor in the helping coalition, and M is the number of helping actors. Furthermore, the capability level of the helping coalition, $k(A^*)_t$ will be defined as follows:

$$k(A^*)_t = \sum_{h=1}^{M} k(a_h)_t$$

D10. <u>Appeasement percentage</u>: The appeasement percentage, α, is the percentage of an actor's capabilities that it offers to the attacker to call off an attack.

D11. <u>Internal growth percentage</u>: The internal growth percentage, β, is the percentage by which an actor's capabilities will be increased if it does nothing in the foreign-policy sector.

D12. <u>Attack success percentage</u>: The attack success percentage, δ, is the percentage of the defeated actor's capabilities that the attacking actor obtains as a result of its success.

D13. <u>Attack defeat percentage</u>: The attack defeat percentage, ω, is the percentage of the attacking actor's capabilities that it must relinquish as a result of an unsuccessful attack.

D14. <u>Attack success (resistance failure)</u>: An attack is successful (resistance is failure) if the capability level of the attacker is greater than that of the helping coalition at $t+\Delta t$. On the other hand, if the capability level of the helping coalition is greater than or equal to that of the attacker, the resistance is successful (attack is failure).

D15. <u>Attack success probability</u>: Prior to t+∆ an actor will have a certain probability of the attack being successful, p. The helping coalition will have a probability, 1-p, resisting the attack.

The following axioms, which characterize the behavior of the actors in the balance-of-power system, will provide a basis for discussing actor survival and the maintenance of a balance. The first axiom concerns the motivation of the actors:

<u>Axiom 1.</u> Each actor is rational.[12]

Actors will thus choose alternatives that are admissible while maximizing expected utility.[13] Such action, of course, requires that each actor possess knowledge of its set of admissible actions. These are specified in the second behavioral axiom:

<u>Axiom 2.</u> At each point in time, t, six admissible courses of action are available to each actor a_i: (a) react to being attacked by resisting; (b) appease the attacker; (c) react to an attack on another actor by coalescing into a helping coalition; (d) react to an attack on another actor by not helping; (e) attack; (f) do nothing in the foreign-policy sector.[14]

Given the set of admissible courses of action, an actor must have a set of goals in order to obtain a preference ordering over the choice set. The relevant goals are specified in the third behavioral axiom:

<u>Axiom 3.</u> Each actor a_i possesses three lexically ordered goals: (a) minimization of its own capability losses; (b) opposition to potentially dominant actors; (c) maximization of its own capability increases.

The actors thus examine each situation on the basis of each criterion in turn until the final one is reached or one of the higher-ranking criteria is satisfied.[15] This results in a sequential screening procedure in which the actors consider higher-ranked goals before lesser-ranked goals. Within the context of axioms 2 and 3 the following sequential screening procedure will be used by each actor to determine which of the three goals is relevant:

1. Am I under attack?
2. Is another actor under attack by a potentially dominant actor?
3. How can I maximize capability gain?

BALANCE OF POWER AS RATIONAL CHOICE

An actor will first determine whether it faces a capability loss through an attack, in which case a behavior relevant to minimizing that loss will be chosen. If there are no direct attacks on an actor, it will then determine whether any other actors are under attack by a potentially dominant actor; if such is the case, an actor will choose a behavior relevant to opposing the potentially dominant actor. Finally, if there is no threat of capability loss or imbalance, the actor will choose that alternative that maximizes its own expected capability gain. Thus, on the basis of the screening procedure, consideration will be given to a subset of the total choice set at a given time. Specifically, the set of admissible actions will be partitioned into three two-element choice subsets. This can be seen from Figure 16.1, diagramming the decision-making process.

If an actor is being attacked, it is appropriate either to resist or to appease. If an actor is not being attacked, but another actor is, the former will decide to help or not help depending upon whether the attacking actor is potentially dominant. Finally, if there are no attacks underway, an actor will seek to maximize its

FIGURE 16.1

Sequential Screening Procedure for Decision Making in the Balance-of-Power System

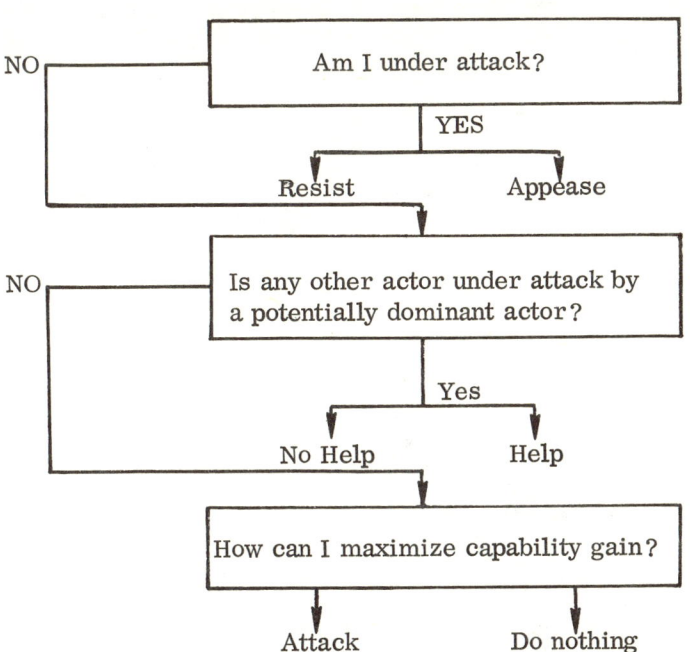

capability gain either by attacking or by doing nothing. Thus, the answers to the questions in the sequential screening procedure identify which of the three choice subsets is relevant (that is, resist or appease, help or not help, attack or do nothing). As a result, each actor in a balance-of-power system will maximize utility over a constrained choice set imposed by the lexical ordering of the goals.

Given the relevant two-member choice subset, an actor must have knowledge of the consequences of each alternative in order to determine which has the highest expected utility. The consequences of each action posited in axiom 2 are presented in the following behavioral axiom:

Axiom 4. The consequences of each alternative are specified in terms of the capability levels of each actor at $t+\Delta t$.

1. <u>Appease or resist</u>. If an actor a_i is under attack by another actor, say a_j, it can either appease or resist. Choosing to appease, a_i gives a_j a percentage of its capabilities, α, to call off the attack. As a result of appeasement,

$$k(a_i)_{t+\Delta t} = (1 - \alpha)k(a_i)_t$$

If, on the other hand, a_i chooses to resist a_j, it will either lose a proportion, δ, of its capabilities if the attack is successful, in which case

$$k(a_i)_{t+\Delta t} = (1 - \delta)k(a_i)_t$$

or it will obtain a percentage, ω/M, of a_j's capabilities if the attack is resisted, in which case

$$k(a_i)_{t+\Delta t} = k(a_i)_t + \omega/M[k(a_j)_t]$$

2. <u>Help or not help</u>. If a_i comes to the aid of an actor, say a_k, that is under attack by a_j, the consequences depend upon whether the attack is successfully resisted. If the attack is resisted, then a_i will receive a proportion, ω/M, of the attack-defeat percentage. As a result,

$$k(a_i)_{t+\Delta t} = k(a_i) + \omega/M[k(a_j)_t]$$

If the attack is successful, then a_i will neither gain nor lose capabilities; that is

$$k(a_i)_{t+\Delta t} = k(a_i)_t$$

By choosing the not-help option, a_i's capabilities will remain the same as they were during the previous time period.

3. <u>Attack or do nothing</u>. If a_i chooses to initiate an attack against another actor, say a_j, the consequences will depend upon whether the attack is successful or not. If the attack is resisted, a_i must forfeit a percentage of its capabilities, ω, to the helping coalition. As a result,

$$k(a_i)_{t+\Delta t} = (1 - \omega)k(a_i)_t$$

If the attack is successful, a_i will receive a proportion of a_j's capabilities, δ, in which case

$$k(a_i)_{t+\Delta t} = k(a_i)_t + \delta k(a_j)_t$$

In addition to success or resistance, a_i could accept appeasement from a_j and call off the attack, in which case

$$k(a_i)_{t+\Delta t} = k(a_i)_t + \alpha k(a_j)_t$$

On the other hand, if a_i chooses the do-nothing option, it will increase its capabilities by a percentage, β, through internal growth. As a result,

$$k(a_i)_{t+\Delta t} = (1 + \beta)k(a_i)_t$$

On the basis of these behavioral axioms it is possible to ask under what conditions an actor will continue to survive; that is, under what conditions will $k(a_i)_{t+\Delta t} > 0$? To fail to survive, an actor would have to lose all of its capabilities as a consequence of one of the actions posited in axiom 2. From axiom 4 an actor can lose capabilities through unsuccessful resistance, appeasement, or unsuccessful attacks. As long as α, δ, and ω are less than 1.0, each actor will lose only a proportion of its capabilities and hence will continue to survive. Since individual survival is a commonly made assumption in balance-of-power models,[16] it will be instituted in the present model as the fifth behavioral axiom:

Axiom 5. As a matter of policy no actors will be eliminated from the system; hence α, δ, and ω must be less than 1.0.

Capabilities will, however, change hands as a consequence of the admissible actions, and a critical question concerns the possibility that these "capability transactions" will result in the emergence of a dominant actor. Even though the individual actors continue to survive, the balance would not be maintained if one actor were to gain a preponderance of the capabilities. The conditions under which a balance can be maintained will be the focus of the following section.

MAINTAINING A BALANCE

Even though axiom 5 guarantees that each actor a_i will have a measure of capability under its control at each outcome, survival may not be guaranteed in the long run. If, through capability transactions, a dominant actor were to emerge, there would not be sufficient capability to deter that actor from doing as it pleases. A dominant actor would be able to maximize capabilities as it wished, since it would no longer have to be concerned with self-preservation (since no actor is larger) or system preservation (since it is no longer an issue). Attention will be given, therefore, to the conditions under which capability transactions take place but a dominant actor fails to emerge.

From axiom 4 there are a number of ways in which capabilities can be increased by an actor: successfully resisting an attack, helping to resist an attack successfully, launching a successful attack, and internal growth. Whether any of these increases will be large enough to allow an actor to attain dominant-actor status is an empirical question that makes it impossible to assert that dominant actors can always be deterred. The best that can be accomplished is a discussion of the conditions that are favorable to the maintenance of a balance. It can be argued that, in the short run, capabilities gained from resisting an attack and internal growth will not be of sufficient magnitude to allow an actor to emerge as dominant. Instead, only through the successful completion of an attack will an actor be able to gain the necessary capability increase at time t to make it dominant at t+Δt. The discussion of the maintenance of a balance will thus concentrate on the decision to help an actor that is being attacked by a potentially dominant actor, since this is the decision that will determine whether a dominant actor will emerge.

Provided that a balance-of-power system as defined in the previous section is balanced at time t, there will always be sufficient countervailing capability to resist any potentially dominant actor. This does not mean, however, that the maintenance of a balance is in any sense automatic. It should be clear that maintaining a balance requires that each actor locate the appropriate choice subset and then choose the correct alternative from that subset. Hence, maintaining a balance depends heavily on the decision rules employed by each of the actors (that is, the means by which one of the elements of the choice subset is shown to have a greater expected utility than the other).

Two factors will effect the decision rules of the actors: certainty and information accuracy. First, with respect to certainty, each actor will have only probabilistic knowledge of attack success; that is, unless $p = 1$ or $p = 0$, the outcome of the attack at $t+\Delta t$ is only known probabilistically. However, since it is the only information available, actors will use the attack-success probability to compute the expected value of attacking as well as that of resisting. The resulting expected value will then be used as a certainty equivalent to determine which action will yield the highest utility.[17] While the certainty equivalents are useful, they are not infallible, since $p > 0.5$ only means the attack is more likely to be successful than unsuccessful.

A second important factor in the decision rules of the actors is information that relates to the consequences of certain actions at $t+\Delta t$—that is, α, β, δ, ω, p, and Υ. The information requirements for making the necessary decisions are therefore extensive: Not only must each actor have information concerning the past and the present, but it must have considerable information relating to $t+\Delta t$. Some consideration must be given to the information that each actor possesses.

<u>Axiom 6.</u> Each actor a_i has accurate information relating to the past and present capability levels and decisions of all actors in the system. Information that relates to the future must be subjectively estimated.

As a result of axiom 6, a caret ($\hat{}$) will be placed over the value of of each of the variables (for example, $\hat{p}$) to denote that it is a subjective estimate of the true value. Furthermore, subscripts must be added to signify the actor that is making the subjective estimate. For example, $\hat{p}_j$ would be a_j's estimate of the attack-success probability.

It is now possible to discuss the decision to help an attacked actor resist the attacker. The discussion will be facilitated by the introduction of the following arbitrary designations:

a_1: attacking actor
a_2: attacked actor
$a_3, a_4, \ldots, a_N$: remaining actors in the system

These designations are merely convention and will be altered at each time period to reflect changes in the status of the actors.

Given that a_1 has attacked a_2, the remaining actors in the balance-of-power system, $a_3, a_4, \ldots, a_N$, must decide whether to help a_2. To make this decision each actor a_j (j = 3, 4, ..., N) must determine whether a_1 is a potentially dominant actor. That is, it must decide whether

$$k(a_1)_t + \hat{p}_j [\hat{\delta}_j k(a_2)_t] - (1 - \hat{p}_j)[\hat{\omega}_j k(a_1)_t] > \hat{T}_j$$

The left-hand side of the inequality, the expected capability level of a_1, becomes the certainty equivalent for each a_j of a_1's capability level at $t+\Delta t$. This value will then be compared to the expected threshold value to determine whether a_1 is a potentially dominant actor. If so, a_j will join A^* to help a_2 resist a_1. The more a_j joining A^*, the greater the likelihood that a_1 will be successfully resisted. Assuming that the system is balanced at time t, there is sufficient countervailing capability to resist a_1; whether the system is balanced at $t+\Delta t$ will depend upon a sufficient number of a_j making the correct decisions.

There are thus two factors that will effect the correctness of a_j's decisions and ultimately the size of A^*: lack of certainty and inaccurate information. If the value of p is not equal to 0.0 or 1.0, then it is possible for decisions to be made incorrectly even with completely accurate information. On the other hand, even if the attack success probability were equal to 0.0 or 1.0, it is likely that inaccurate information could contribute to incorrect decisions being made, resulting in A^* not being sufficiently large to resist a_1. The critical factor in determining the role of inaccurate information is whether or not it is biased.[18]

D16. <u>Unbiased estimate</u>: An unbiased estimate is one that, on average, is accurate. $\hat{T}_j$ is an unbiased estimate of T if $E[\hat{T}_j] = T$. However, if $E[\hat{T}_j]$ is different from T, the estimate is biased. In fact, bias is defined as this difference. Bias = $E[\hat{T}_j] - T$.

Bias can either be positive or negative. If it is positive, the expected value will, on the average, exceed the true value; that is, there is a tendency for $\hat{T}_j$ to overestimate. If the bias is negative, it indicates that $\hat{T}_j$ on average underestimates the true value.

BALANCE OF POWER AS RATIONAL CHOICE

The direction of the bias (if any) is an important factor in determining the effect of inaccurate information upon the maintenance of the balance. Provided that the estimates are unbiased (and there is certainty), it can be expected that the decisions will be made correctly and a balance maintained. On the other hand, if they are overestimated or underestimated, the decisions could be made incorrectly. The effect of inaccurate information on the maintenance of a balance will depend upon the direction of the bias. For example, consider the decision to help. If the estimates, $\hat{T}_j$, are biased and the tendency is to underestimate, then helping will be very likely. Hence, an attacking actor is likely to face a helping coalition with sufficient capabilities. On the other hand, if $\hat{T}_j$ is biased and the tendency is to overestimate, helping will be less likely, since the actors will view the threshold as being higher than it actually is. As a result, an attacking actor is likely to face insufficient opposition. As a result of bias in the information used in the decision rules, the actors in a balance-of-power system may fail to maintain a balance.

Therefore, even if the actors behave in accordance with all the behavioral axioms, two factors mediate against the automatic maintenance of a balance: lack of certainty and biased information. Because of these factors, the actors may make decisions based on subjective estimates that are objectively incorrect. Since the impact of incorrect decisions on the maintenance of balance can be quite devastating, it must be concluded that the maintenance of balance is anything but automatic. Instead, the actors must adhere strictly to the behavioral axioms, and, furthermore, they must possess certainty and unbiased information. Otherwise, no matter what the actors do, the balance of power may not be maintained.

CONCLUSION

Within the rubric of balance of power, this inquiry has been directed toward two ends: the specification of a formal model of a balance-of-power system and an investigation of the factors that effect the maintenance of balance from one time period to the next. The model specification presents a formal representation of a balance-of-power system in terms of a number of behavioral axioms. The investigation of the maintenance of a balance considers the conditions that increase the likelihood of balance.

The balance-of-power system is composed of a number of actors, each with a given level of capabilities. According to axiom 1 the actors are rational: Each seeks to maximize its expected utility through the selection of one of the behavioral alternatives. The range of admissible alternatives is limited to six possibilities in axiom 2. This means that certain courses of action can be ruled out on an a priori basis. From axiom 3 each actor possesses a hierarchy of goals concerning self-preservation, system preservation, and self-improvement. Acting in accord with axiom 3 implies that each actor will first locate the relevant choice subset through the use of a sequential screening procedure. From axiom 4 the consequences of each action are posited in terms of the effect on the capabilities of each actor at the next time period. The decision alternative that is ultimately chosen will be that alternative from the two-element choice subset that maximizes expected utility. Given the range of behaviors in axiom 2 and their consequences from axiom 4, it is clear that there are a number of ways in which an actor can gain and lose capabilities. Axiom 5 insures that while capability levels will change from time period to time period, each actor will have some capabilities under its control. Thus, actors in a balance-of-power system are maximizing their expected utility under a set of constraints imposed upon them by the lexical nature of the ordering of their goals. This is the distinctive feature of choice behavior in a balance-of-power system: Even if an actor wishes to become dominant, it must prevent other actors from accomplishing a similar objective in order to insure its own survival.

Balance is important because it insures that no actor will be able to dictate actions unilaterally to other actors solely by virtue of its power. The second portion of the inquiry has been directed toward determining some of the factors that effect the maintenance of balance from one time period to the next. The importance of the decision rules employed by each of the actors is emphasized. The conclusion is reached that balance is not automatic, because not only must the individual actors adhere to the behavioral axioms, but there must be certainty and unbiased information. Without these ingredients it should be clear that no matter what the actors do, balance may not be maintained. Because of this feature of a balance-of-power system, it should be obvious why the balance of power is not a solution to the problems of anarchy but is instead an attempt to mitigate its consequences.

To be sure, this inquiry has not covered all conceivable contingencies nor investigated all possible factors in a balance-of-power system. Consideration of other ways by which an actor could increase its capability and their effects, if any, upon the balance is an obvious next step. It is hoped, however, that this inquiry might provide a useful base for further refinements and extensions of the basic issues surrounding the concept balance of power.

NOTES

1. For an extensive discussion of anarchy and a number of selections relating to its meaning, control, and consequences, see Robert J. Art and Robert Jervis, International Politics (Boston: Little, Brown, 1973), pp. 1-158.
2. Two such solutions are "harmony of interests" and "world government"; see Art and Jervis, International Politics, pp. 46-80. International law, diplomacy, balance of power, international organization, and regional organization are examples of the approaches at mitigating the situation; see ibid., pp. 81-158.
3. Inis Claude, Power and International Relations (New York: Random House, 1962), p. 18.
4. Ibid.
5. For example, see P. S. Mowrer, Our Foreign Affairs (New York: Dutton, 1924), p. 252; Claude O. Lerche, Principles of International Politics (London: Oxford University Press, 1956), p. 128; A. Wolfers, Discord and Collaboration (Baltimore: Johns Hopkins University, Press, 1962), p. 123; Claude, Power and International Relations, pp. 43-44. Claude quotes the following passage from Rosseau, which highlights this version: "The actual system of Europe has precisely the degree of solidarity which maintains it in a constant state of motion without upsetting it. The balance existing between the power of these diverse members of European society is more the work of nature than of art. It maintains itself without effort, in such a manner that if it sinks on one side, it reestablishes itself very soon on the other."
6. Morton Kaplan, System and Process in International Politics (New York: Wiley, 1957), pp. 22-36; Claude, Power and International Relations, pp. 11-39.
7. Kaplan, System and Process.
8. This set of goals is an attempt to characterize the six behavioral rules presented by ibid., p. 23.
9. This is the distinctive feature of a balance-of-power system as opposed to some of the more formal "solutions" offered by other authors. See ibid., pp. 29-30.
10. Ibid., pp. 22-36; Claude, Power and International Relations, pp. 11-39.
11. This is by no means the first effort to formalize a model of a balance-of-power system. For two excellent examples of this approach, see Partha Chatterjee, "The Classical Balance of Power Theory," Journal of Peace Research 9 (1972): 51-61; Dina A. Zinnes, Douglas E. Van Houweling, and Richard H. Van Atta, International System Structure and the Balance of Power Propositions: A Computer Simulation Study, NU/ARPA Project of Simulated

International Processes (Advanced Projects Research Agency, SD 260) (Evanston, Ill.: Northwestern University Press, 1972).

12. See Chatterjee, "The Classical Balance of Power Theory," p. 53. This axiom is similar to Chatterjee's first axiom and hence to the "positive-theory" approach he takes. The major difference between the two models lies in comparing axiom 2 in Chatterjee's model with axiom 3 of the present model; namely, it is a difference in the nature of the utility function.

13. This follows from the definition of rational: Among the set of alternative courses of action available to an actor, the actor will choose that action that maximizes its utility. See R. Duncan Luce and Howard Raiffa, eds., Games and Decisions (New York: Wiley, 1957).

14. See Zinnes, Van Houweling, Van Atta, International System Structure, p. 3, for a similar list of alternative actions. The differences between their model and that presented here lie in the incorporation into the present model of a rationality axiom and lexical preferences, in contrast to their assumption that nations are simply power maximizers.

15. For a presentation of lexical orderings, see Peter C. Fishburn, "Lexicographical Orders, Utilities, and Decision Rules: A Survey," Arlington, Va.: Office of Naval Research, Technical Report, no. 4; John S. Chipman, "On the Lexicographical Representation of Preference Orderings," in Preferences, Utility, and Demand, eds. John S. Chipman, Leonid Hurwicz, Marcel K. Richter, and Hugo F. Sonnenschein (New York: Harcourt, Brace, Jovanovich, 1971), pp. 276-88.

16. For example, see Kaplan, System and Process, p. 24.

17. Robert L. Winkler, Introduction to Bayesian Inference and Decision (New York: Holt, Rinehart and Winston, 1972), p. 270.

18. Ronald J. Wonnacott and Thomas H. Wonnacott, Econometrics (New York: Wiley, 1970), pp. 40-41.

CHAPTER

16

ALLIANCES AND THE THEORY OF COLLECTIVE GOODS: AN EVALUATION
Roslyn L. Simowitz

Several economists and political scientists have employed the theory of collective goods to explain the behavior of nations in international organizations and alliances.[1] The application of this theory to alliances has been extended and elaborated upon by Mancur Olson in <u>The Logic of Collective Action</u>. After claiming that alliances provide collective goods to their members, Olson argues that there will be a systematic tendency for "exploitation" of the greater by the smaller members:

> Since no one has an incentive to provide any more of the collective good once the member who has attached the largest value to the good has obtained the amount he wants, it is also true that the distribution of the burden of providing the collective good in a small group will not be in proportion to the benefits conferred by the collective good. The member who attaches the largest value to the good will bear a disproportionate share of the burden.[2]

He then proceeds to suggest that an argument of this kind could be used to explain the apparent tendency for large countries to bear a disproportionate share of the costs in multinational organizations. This tendency towards disproportionality results from the fact that smaller members find they have little or no incentive to provide

---

Support for this research was granted by the National Science Foundation, Grant GS-36806. I would like to thank Professors John V. Gillespie, Dina A. Zinnes, and James Pierson for their helpful suggestions in writing this chapter.

additional amounts of the collective good once the larger members have provided the amounts they want for themselves.

In an examination of the cost-sharing arrangements in the United Nations and North Atlantic Treaty Organization (NATO), Olson and Zeckhauser find that the smaller nations fail to meet their quotas while the larger nations assume a larger share of the costs. They argue that this is

> . . . due to the processes described in the model, rather than to some other cause. . . . [The] different levels of contribution are not due to different moral attitudes since the less than proportionate contribution of the smaller nations are securely grounded in their national interests (just as the disproportionately large contributions of the larger countries are solidly grounded in their national interests).[3]

This tendency for small nations to pay a less than proportionate share of the costs for the good, while the larger nations pay a more than proportionate share, is thus explained to be a logical consequence of rational, self-interested behavior.

The study by Olson and Zeckhauser had an impact on further analyses of international organizations and alliances. The goods provided by these organizations were conceptualized as collective goods, and the theory of collective goods was used to explain disproportionate cost-sharing arrangements in these organizations.[4] However, before the arguments and concepts of a theory can be used for explanatory purposes, the arguments must be checked for soundness,* and the concepts must be well defined. If the concepts used in the theory of collective goods are not well defined, or if its arguments are not sound, then this theory cannot be used for explanatory purposes.

In this chapter an analysis is undertaken to determine whether the definition of the concept, <u>collective good</u>, is redundant and/or tautologous. Obviously, a concept would be better defined if it lacked redundancies and tautologies in its definition. This analysis is undertaken in the second section. In the third section the soundness of the arguments used to explain disproportionate cost sharing in alliances and other multinational organizations will be examined. Since these arguments are used in explaining behavior in multi-

---

*An argument is sound if its assumptions necessarily imply its conclusion. If the assumptions of the argument are true, the conclusion must be true.

national organizations, their soundness must be examined rather than be assumed. As the analyses in the second and third sections employ symbolic logic, an interpretation of the logical notation and the rules of inference are provided in the first section.

LOGICAL NOTATION AND RULES OF INFERENCE

Logical Notation

The following is an interpretation of the symbolic notation to be used in this chapter.

$\rightarrow$	if . . . , then
$\leftrightarrow$	if and only if
&	and
v	either . . . or
-	not
$\subseteq$	is a subset of
ε	is an element of the set . . .
$\notin$	is not an element of the set . . .
=	is identical to
(x)	for all x . . .
($\exists$x)	there exists an x such that . . .
(y: . . .)	the set of all y such that . . .

Description of the Rules of Inference[5]

1. <u>Rule of Assumptions (A)</u>: Any statement can be introduced at any stage of a proof. To the left of the statement the number of the line itself is noted. To the right of the statement, the rule of inference employed—in this case, (A)—is noted.
2. <u>Modus Ponens (MP)</u>: Given A and A $\rightarrow$ B, one can derive B as the conclusion. The assumptions underlying B are those that underlie either A or A $\rightarrow$ B.
3. <u>Modus Tollens (MT)</u>: Given -B and A $\rightarrow$ B, one can derive -A as the conclusion. The assumptions underlying B are those that underlie either -B or A $\rightarrow$ B.
4. <u>Conditional Proof (CP)</u>: Given a proof of B from A, where A is one of the assumptions, one can derive A $\rightarrow$ B as the conclusion. A $\rightarrow$ B rests on the remaining assumptions used to derive B.
5. <u>&-Introduction (&I)</u>: Given A and B, one can derive A & B as the conclusion. The assumptions underlying A & B are those that underlie either A or B.

6. &-Elimination (&E): Given A & B, one can conclude either A or B separately. In either case, the conclusion depends on the same assumptions on which A & B depend.
7. v-Introduction (vI): Given either A or B separately, one can derive AvB as the conclusion. If AvB was derived from A, its assumptions are the same as those of A; if AvB was derived from B, its assumptions are the same as those of B.
8. v-Elimination (vE): One may derive C from AvB, if C can be derived from A, and if C can be derived from B as well. The assumptions underlying C are those that underlie AvB, or those that underlie C in its derivation from A (apart from A), or those that underlie C in its derivation from B (apart from B).
9. Reductio Ad Absurdum (RAA): Given a proof of B & -B from A as assumption, one may conclude -A. The assumptions underlying -A are those remaining assumptions used to prove B & -B.
10. Theorem Introduction (TI): Any theorem already proved can be introduced at any stage of a proof. To the right of the theorem, TI is noted. To the left of the theorem, no numbers appear, since theorems do not depend on any assumptions. (This rule also allows one to introduce a substitution instance of a theorem at any stage of a proof.)

A more detailed description of the reductio ad absurdum (RAA) rule (number 9 above) is given here since it is frequently employed in the analysis that follows.

Description of the Reductio Ad Absurdum Strategy[6]

This rule is very useful as a means of indirect proof. Say one desired to prove the proposition -A. Instead of attempting a direct proof of -A, one assumes the corresponding affirmative proposition, A, and aims to derive a contradiction. If a contradiction can be derived from proposition A, then A cannot be true, and thus its negation, -A, may be affirmed. Perhaps an example will make this strategy more apparent:

P stands for the proposition that there is fire.
Q stands for the proposition that there is smoke.
From the assumptions P → Q and P → -Q we may prove -P as conclusions as is demonstrated in the following proof:

Assumption Number	Line Number		Rule of Inference
1	(1)	$P \to Q$	A
2	(2)	$P \to -Q$	A
3	(3)	P	A
1,3	(4)	Q	1,3, MP
2,3	(5)	$-Q$	2,3 MP
1,2,3	(6)	$Q \& -Q$	4,5 &I
1,2	(7)	$-P$	3,6 RAA

This is a typical example of an RAA strategy. We want to establish -P; thus, we assume P (line 3) with the hope that P will lead to a contradiction. If it is possible to derive a contradiction from P, we can affirm -P by RAA. At line 6 we obtained the contradiction Q & -Q. Thus, we were able to conclude -P at line 7 by RAA.

Now that the logical notation has been interpretated and the rules of inference described, we can turn to our analysis.

THE CONCEPT OF COLLECTIVE GOOD

The clearest definition of a collective good is provided by Samuelson.[7] In essence, a collective good is any good that exhibits properties of jointness of supply and external economies (definition 16.1). A good is said to be in joint supply if additional consumption of it by one individual does not diminish the amount available to others (definition 16.2). In other words, once produced, the good can be made equally available to all.[8] An externality, on the other hand, implies that a person receives a benefit from the actions of another person. In securing this benefit, he may pay nothing for it (definition 16.3).[9] Definitions 16.2 and 16.3 may be represented by the following:

Set of goods exhibiting jointness of supply =

$$[y: (y)(x)(x \epsilon N \& C_i xy) \& (\exists z)(z \notin N \& C_i xy) \to -(\exists x)(x \epsilon N \& -C_i xy)]$$

(16.2.1)

where

$y \leftrightarrow (z: Pz)$ Pz: z is a good
$C_i xy$: x consumes y at level i
x N: X is a member of some group N

and

Set of goods exhibiting external economies =

$$\{y : (y)(\exists x)(z)[(C_i xy \ \& \ Axy \ \& \ x \neq z) \rightarrow C_\ell zy]\}_{\ell \leq i} \qquad (16.3.1)$$

where

Axy: x pays for the good, y.

Definition 16.2.1 is read as follows: If x is a member of some group, N, that consumes a good, y, at a given level i, and there is somebody, say z, who is not a member of this group and also consumes this good at level i, then we may conclude that there is not anybody from the original group N who does not consume y at level i (that is, it does not diminish the consumption of anyone in N). Definition 16.3.1 may be read as: If there is some person, x, who pays for the provision of a good, y, and consumes it, then someone other than x (say) z, also consumes y. The logical statements in definitions 16.2.1 and 16.3.1 are intended to convey the intent (meaning) of definitions 16.2 and 16.3 respectively.

In addition to Samuelson, Head, Buchanan, and Baumol define collective goods in terms of the properties described by definitions 16.2 and 16.3.[10] However, Olson defines the collective good referred to in his analysis as any good that exhibits properties of exclusion.[11] A good is said to be exclusive if, when any person x_i in a group $x_1, x_2, \ldots, x_i, \ldots, x_n$ consumes it, it cannot feasibly be withheld from the others in that group (definition 16.4). It is possible to state definition 16.4 symbolically, as follows:

Set of goods with the property of exclusion =

$$[y: (\exists z)(C_i zy) \rightarrow -(\exists x)-C_\ell xy]_{\ell \leq i} \qquad (16.4.1)$$

In words, definition 16.4.1 says that if someone consumes (a good) y, there is not anyone who is not consuming y (that is, everyone consumes y). Again, definition 16.4.1 is intended to convey the meaning of definition 16.4.

Although the properties of a collective good seem clearly defined there are several inherent difficulties. First, the definition of jointness turns out to be tautologous (that is, a logical truth) as the following proof will demonstrate:

THEORY OF COLLECTIVE GOODS

Assumption Number:	Line Number:		Rule of Inference:
1	(1)	$-\{y\varepsilon\ [y\colon (x)(x\varepsilon N \& C_i xy) \& (\exists z)(z \notin N \& C_i zy)] \to -(\exists x)(x\varepsilon N \&- C_i xy)\}$	A
1	(2)	$-[(x)(x\varepsilon N \& C_i xb) \& (\exists z)(z \notin N \& C_i zb) \to -(\exists x)(x\varepsilon N \&- C_i xb)]$	UE 1
1	(3)	$(x)(x\varepsilon N \& C_i xb) \& (\exists z)(z \notin N \& C_i zb) \& (\exists x)(x\varepsilon N \&- C_i xb)$	TI 2
1	(4)	$c \notin N \& C_i cb \& b\varepsilon N \&- C_i ab$	EE3, UE 3
1	(5)	$b\varepsilon N \& C_i ab$	EE 3
1	(6)	$C_i ab \&- C_i ab$	&I 4, 5
	(7)	$-$(assumption in line 1)	RAA 1, 6

Using the RAA strategy, we find that the definition of jointness is a logical truth. The significance of a tautologously defined concept lies in the fact that one can now show that all goods must be collective goods. In other words, because the property of jointness is defined so as to constitute a logical truth, we can show that private goods cannot exist. To prove this, we represent the set of collective goods as follows:

Set of collective goods =

$$\{y\colon E \to [(x)(x\varepsilon N \& Cxy) \& (\exists z)(z \notin N \& C\ zy) \to -(\exists x)(x\varepsilon N \&- C\ xy)]\} \quad (16.5.1)$$

where the antecedent, E, may represent exclusion (according to Olson) or external economies (according to Baumol, Buchanan, and Head), and the consequent represents goods that are characterized by joint supply (definition 16.2.1).

340   MATHEMATICAL MODELS IN INTERNATIONAL RELATIONS

We now assert that there is some good, say p, that is a private good. Therefore, p is not a member of the set of collective goods. This can be written as follows:

1 (1) $(\exists w) w \notin \{y: E \rightarrow [(x)(x \varepsilon N \& Cxy) \& (\exists z)(z \notin N \& Czy) \rightarrow$
       $-(\exists x)(x \varepsilon N \& -Cxy)]\}$ A

1 (2) $p \notin \{y: E \rightarrow [(x)(x \varepsilon N \& Cxy) \& (\exists z)(z \notin N \& Czy) \rightarrow$
       $-(\exists x)(x \varepsilon N \& -Cxy)]\}$

1 (3) $-\bigl(p \varepsilon \{y: E \rightarrow [(x)(x \varepsilon N \& Cxy) \& (\exists z)(z \notin N \& Czy) \rightarrow$
       $-(\exists x)(x \varepsilon N \& -Cxy)]\}\bigr)$

1 (4) $-\{E \rightarrow [(x)(x \varepsilon N \& Cxp) \& (\exists z)(z \notin N \& Czp) \rightarrow$
       $-(\exists x)(x \varepsilon N \& C-Cxp)]\}$

1 (5) $E \& -[(x)(x \varepsilon N \& Cxp) \& (\exists z)(z \notin N \& Czp) \rightarrow$
       $-(\exists x)(x \varepsilon N \& -Cxp)]$

1 (6) $E \& (x)(x \varepsilon N \& Cxp) \& (\exists z)(z \notin N \& Czp) \&$
       $(\exists x)(x \varepsilon N \& -Cxp)$

1 (7) $a \varepsilon N \& -Cap$ EE 6

1 (8) $a \varepsilon N \& -Cap$ UE 6

1 (9) $Cap \& -Cap$ &I 7, 8

  (10) $-\bigl((\exists w) w \notin \{y: E \rightarrow [(x)(x \varepsilon N \& Cxy) \&$
       $(\exists z)(z \notin N \& Czy) \rightarrow -(\exists x)(x \varepsilon N \& -Cxy)]\}\bigr)$ RAA 8, 1

  (11) $(w)\bigl(w \varepsilon \{y: E \rightarrow [(x)(x \varepsilon N \& Cxy) \& (\exists z)(z \notin N \& Czy) \rightarrow$
       $-(\exists x)(x \varepsilon N \& -Cxy)]\}\bigr)$

Thus, we have shown that when the property of joint supply is used as a defining characteristic of a collective good, we are led to the conclusion that all goods must be collective goods (or, equivalently, that no private goods exist). Since it is patent that private goods exist, we must assume that the difficulty lies in the use of the property of joint supply. Consequently, we will omit

THEORY OF COLLECTIVE GOODS   341

this part of the definition of collective goods. The properties of exclusion and external economies then remain as the only viable alternatives for defining the set of collective goods. However, we need to examine carefully the properties of exclusion and external economies for possible redundancies in these components of the definition.

On the intuitive level, the properties of exclusion and externalities do not appear to be redundant. However, Head has claimed that "complete impossibility of exclusion is a special and extreme case of the modern externalities concept."[12] It is possible to prove that goods that are characterized by exclusion are a subset of the goods that are characterized by external economies (that is, definition 16.4.1 $\subseteq$ definition 16.3.1). The proof is given below. Again, the method of proof is RAA.

1	(1)	$-\left[\left(\{y: (\exists z)[C_i zy \rightarrow -(\exists x)(C_\ell xy)]\}\right) \subseteq \left(\{y: (\exists x)(z)[(C_i xy \& Axy) \& (x \neq z) \rightarrow C_\ell zy]\}\right)\right]$	A
1	(2)	$-\left(y\varepsilon \{y: (\exists z)[C_i zy \rightarrow -(\exists x) -(C_\ell xy)\}] \rightarrow y\varepsilon \{y: (\exists x)(z)[(C_i xy \& Axy) \& (x \neq z) \rightarrow C_\ell zy)]\}\right)$	Def $\subseteq$ 1
1	(3)	$\{y\varepsilon [y: (\exists z) C_i zy \rightarrow -(\exists x) -C_\ell xy]\} \& -\{y\varepsilon [y: (\exists x)(z)(C_i xy \& Axy) \& (x \neq z) \rightarrow C_\ell zy]\}$	TI 2
1	(4)	$[(\exists z) C_i zy \rightarrow -(\exists x) - C_\ell xy)] \& \{(\exists x)(z)[(C_i xy \& Axy) \& -C_\ell zy]\}$	
1	(5)	$C_i ay \& Aay \& -C_\ell cy$	
1	(6)	$-(\exists z) C_i zy \vee -(\exists x) - C\ell xy$	TI 4
7	(7)	$-(\exists z) C_i zy$	A
7	(8)	$(z) - C_i zy$	TI 7

7	(9)	$-Cay$	UQE* 8
1,7	(10)	$Cay \ \& \ -Cay$	& 5,9
7	(11)	$-$(assumption in line 1)	RAA 10,1
12	(12)	$-(\exists x)-C_\ell xy$	A
12	(13)	$(x)C_\ell xy$	TI 12
12	(14)	$C_\ell cy$	UQE* 13
1,12	(15)	$C_\ell cy \ \& \ -C_\ell cy$	& 5,14
12	(16)	$-$(assumption in line 1)	RAA 15,1
1	(17)	$-$(assumption in line 1)	vE 6,7,11,12,16
1	(18)	assumption in line 1 & $-$(assumption in line 1)	&I 1,17
	(19)	$-$(assumption in line 1)	RAA 1,18

*Universal quantifier elimination.

Having proved, then, that the set of goods that has the property of exclusion is a subset of the set of goods that exhibit external economies, we may propose a new definition for the set of collective goods. This definition is the following:

$$\{y: (\exists x)(z)[(C_i xy \& Axy) \& (x \neq z) \rightarrow C_\ell zy)]\}_{\ell \leq i} \qquad (16.6.1)$$

We now have an adequate definition of a collective good that we can employ in the analysis undertaken in the next section.

However, before turning to an analysis of the arguments used to explain disproportionate cost sharing, it is necessary to define two additional concepts that will be employed in the following section: "free rider" and "individual rationality." If an individual makes no donation to the good he values and would receive it if it were supplied, he attempts to be a free rider (definition 16.7). Definition 16.7 can be rewritten as follows:

$$\text{Set of free riders} = [x: (y)(C_\ell xy \& -Axy)]_{\ell \leq i} \qquad (16.7.1)$$

THEORY OF COLLECTIVE GOODS

Definition 16.7.1 states that anyone is a free rider who consumes a good and does not pay for it.

Individual rationality can be described as follows. If an individual can consume a good, y, and he has the option of either paying for it or not, then he will not pay for it (definition 16.8). This can be succinctly represented as follows:

$$\text{Set of rational actors} = \{x: (y)[C_\ell xy \ \&(Qxy \ v \ -Qxy) \rightarrow -Axy]\}_{\ell \leq i}$$
(16.8.1)

where Qxy:x has the option of paying for y.

Definition 16.8.1 is read in the same way that definition 16.8 is stated.

AN ANALYSIS OF THE ARGUMENTS USED TO EXPLAIN DISPROPORTIONATE COST SHARING IN ALLIANCES

Essentially, there are two distinct but related arguments that we used to explain disproportionate cost sharing in alliances and multinational organizations. The two arguments are related in the sense that they both maintain that a nation's actions are a logical consequence of rational self-interested behavior. The first argument concerns those nations that attempt to be free riders or to pay a disproportionately smaller share of the good's costs. The argument is often referred to in the literature on collective goods as the "free-rider problem."

The free-rider argument states that rational individuals (or nations) will become free riders in groups providing collective goods. It can be summarized as follows. Assume that a group exists that provides a collective good. Assume further that nations are rational and that they can consume the amount of the good they desire. Then these nations will be free riders. The following proof demonstrates the validity of this argument.

definition 16.3.1	(1)	$C_i ab \ \& \ Aab \ \& \ a \neq c \rightarrow C_\ell cb_{\ell \leq i}$	UE
2	(2)	$C_i ab \ \& \ Aab \ \& \ a \neq c$	A
2	(3)	$C_\ell cb$	MP 1,2
4	(4)	Qcb v–Qcb	TI

definition 16.8.1 (5) $C_\ell cb$ & Qcb v $-Qcb \rightarrow -Acb$ UE

2,4 (6) $-Acb$ MP 3,4,5

2,4 (7) $C_\ell cb$ & $-Acb$ &I 2,5

In essence, this argument is no more than a simple syllogism, but it does explain why nations that can consume a good without paying for it will be free riders. Once the good is provided for, the nature of the good is such that they cannot be prevented from consuming it (by definition 16.3).

The other argument used to explain disproportionate sharing concerns those nations who pay the full or a disproportionately higher share of the good's costs. This argument merely assumes that these nations are rational actors whose valuation of the good is greater. But this assumption does not allow one to deduce that they will pay the full or a disproportionately higher share of the good's costs.

How then do Olson and Zeckhauser claim that the theory of collective goods provides an explanation for the behavior of these nations? Their argument is as follows. It is in the national interests of larger nations to bear a disproportionately higher share of the costs. Larger nations are by definition those that place a higher absolute value on the good.[13] In their analysis Olson and Zeckhauser find that larger nations (as measured by GNP) do pay a disproportionately higher share of the good's costs.* They then explain this finding by claiming that it is in their national interests to do so because they value the good more. But this argument is circular and cannot serve as an explanation.

The theory of collective goods provides us with a simple but sound argument to explain the occurrence of free riders. However, the larger question of why some nations find it in their interests to provide the good or bear a disproportionately greater share of the costs remains unanswered.

IMPLICATIONS FOR INTERNATIONAL RELATIONS

At the beginning of this chapter we presented arguments given by collective-goods theorists for explaining behavior in international

---

*Olson and Zeckhauser define <u>larger</u> to mean a larger absolute value on the good. The fact that they then measure "large" by GNP and produce a significant correlation between GNP and cost sharing is inexplicable in terms of their model.

THEORY OF COLLECTIVE GOODS   345

organizations and alliances. A case was then made that before a theory can be employed for explanatory purposes, its concepts must be well defined and its arguments sound ones. If either the latter or the former is not the case, then the theory cannot be used for explanatory purposes.

In the second section it was demonstrated that the concept, collective good, was not a well-defined one. A collective good has been defined as having one or a combination of the following properties: jointness, exclusion, and external economies. The property of jointness was shown to be tautologous, while the property of exclusion was shown to be subsumed under external economies. In an attempt to eliminate the redundancy and tautologous quality from the definition of collective good, the latter was then defined in terms of external economies alone.

These findings have some serious implications for theorizing about international organizations and alliances. Specifically, when one describes the defense provided by a military alliance, such as NATO, the Warsaw Treaty Organization (WTO) or the health care provided by a multinational organization, such as the World Health Organization (WHO), as a collective good, it is necessary to specify the good's properties. All collective goods by definition must exhibit external economies. However, the set of goods having the property of exclusion is only a subset of the set of goods having external economies. Thus, if one finds for example, that health care or defense displays the property of externalities, one cannot assume that the good also has the property of exclusion.

The third property ascribed to a collective good has been jointness of supply. It is pointless to label a good a collective good merely because it exhibits jointness of supply, since every good can be shown to exhibit jointness. The property of joint supply must be eliminated from the definition of collective good if the latter concept is to be of any import in theorizing about international organizations and alliances.

In the third section we found that the free-rider argument provides a sound explanation of nations' attempts to become free riders in organizations providing collective goods. Assuming that the nation is a rational actor and can obtain the amount of the good it desires without having to pay for it, the nation will attempt to be a free rider. However, some nation(s) must first provide the good. The theory of collective goods explains why nations will be free riders once the collective good is provided, but it does not explain why some nations find it in their interests to provide the good. It is not an explanation to claim that nations that provide the collective good (or pay a disproportionately greater share of its costs) do so because they place a higher absolute value on the good. It is merely an assumption. Upon finding that some nations bear a disproportionately greater share of the costs in multinational organizations, one cannot claim (as Olson and Zeckhauser do) that they do so because their valuation of the good is higher. If one did so claim, one's argument would be circular and unsound.

Olson and Zeckhauser further claim that disproportionate cost sharing in alliances can <u>only</u> be explained by the arguments presented in the theory of collective goods. Not only is this statement incorrect in that the theory of collective goods provides only part of an explanation for disproportionate cost sharing in alliances, but it is also misleading. Because the argument is sound concerning those nations that attempt to be free riders, one can easily be misled into accepting the soundness of the argument concerning those who actually provide the collective good. In believing that the theory of collective goods provides sound arguments for disproportionate cost sharing, there will not be sufficient hesitation to use this theory in explaining disproportionate cost sharing in further analyses of multinational organizations. The theory of collective goods is thus far only of limited utility in explaining disproportionate cost sharing in alliances. It explains why some nations will attempt to be free riders. But the more interesting question as to why some nations will provide the good or pay a disproportionately greater share of its costs remains unexplained.

NOTES

1. See Mancur Olson, Jr., The Logic of Collective Action (Cambridge, Mass.: Harvard University Press, 1965); Mancur Olson, Jr., and Richard Zeckhauser, "An Economic Theory of Alliance," The Review of Economics and Statistics 48 (1966): 266-79; Mancur Olson, Jr., and Richard Zeckhauser, "Collective Goods, Comparative Advantage and Alliance Efficiency," in Issues in Defense Economics, ed. R. N. McKean (New York: Columbia University Press, 1967), pp. 25-58; Jacques M. van Ypersele de Strihore, "Sharing the Defense Burden Among Western Allies," Yale Economic Essays 8 (1968): 261-320; Philip M. Burgess and James A. Robinson, "Alliances and the Theory of Collective Action: A Simulation of Coalition Processes," Midwest Journal of Political Science 13 (1969): 194-218; John Gerald Ruggie, "Collective Goods and Future International Collaboration," American Political Science Review 66 (1972): 874-94; Harvey Starr, "Alliances and the Price of Primacy," in What Price Vigilance? ed. Bruce M. Russett (New Haven, Conn.: Yale University Press, 1970), pp. 91-127.

2. Olson, Logic, p. 29.
3. Olson and Zeckhauser, "An Economic Theory," p. 279.
4. Burgess and Robinson, "Alliances"; Ruggie, "Strategies and Structures"; Starr, "Alliances."
5. E. J. Lemmon, Beginning Logic (London: Thomas Nelson, 1965), pp. 9-14, 56-58.
6. Ibid., pp. 26-27.
7. Paul A. Samuelson, "The Pure Theory of Public Expenditure," Review of Economics and Statistics 36 (1954): 387-89; Paul A. Samuelson, "Diagrammatic Exposition of a Theory of Public Expenditure," Review of Economics and Statistics 37 (1955): 350-56.
8. John G. Head, "Public Goods and Public Policy," Public Finance 17 (1962), pp. 197-219.
9. James M. Buchanan, The Bases for Collective Action (New York: General Learning Press, 1971).
10. Samuelson, "The Pure Theory," pp. 387-89; Samuelson, "Diagrammatic," pp. 350-56; Head, "Public Goods"; Buchanan, Bases; James M. Buchanan, The Demand and Supply of Public Goods (Chicago: Rand McNally, 1968); William J. Baumol, Welfare Economics and the Theory of the State (Cambridge, Mass.: Harvard University Press, 1965).
11. Olson, Logic, p. 14.
12. Head, "Public Goods," p. 215.
13. Olson and Zeckhauser, "An Economic Theory," p. 269.

CHAPTER 17

POLICY ZONE: WHERE POLICIES WORK
Martin W. Sampson III

When will a policy become untenable? This chapter offers a mathematical concept of "policy zone" to address this problem and illustrates the policy zone with the case of U.S. arms shipments to Israel. The chapter opens with a definition of "policy" and a brief statement on the nature of the policy zone. It then discusses a policy, mathematically defines the policy zone with linear programming, and investigates the effects on the policy zone of various policy modifications.

A policy is here defined as a set of one or more decision rules. A decision rule is a predetermined response to an action by another actor that influences the policy. The Soviet Union, for instance, is such an actor. If the United States wants to send twice as much aid to Israel as the Soviet Union is sending to Egypt, the U.S. decision rule is (US) = 2(USSR). With only one decision rule this policy is unusually simple. Typically, a policy contains numerous decision rules.

Although decision rules could be equations as in the example above, it is preferable to model the decision rules as inequalities. Use of inequalities suggests that actors do not precisely respond to one another, and it allows for slippage that occurs in implementing a policy. Rules that are inequalities are therefore used in this chapter. An example is a decision rule that says the U.S. response will be at least twice the USSR's action: US $\geq$ 2(USSR).

Should two or more decision rules be contradictory, the policy is obviously unworkable. Less obvious is the possibility that certain levels of action by other nations can render a policy internally contradictory. Doubling whatever the Soviet Union does may be a viable U.S. policy as long as the Soviets do not do too much. At some level of Soviet activity this U.S. decision rule will conflict with other decision rules in the U.S. policy, such as budget limitations. Virtually any policy is vulnerable to such contradictions. This chapter is concerned with determining analytically where contradictions of decision rules will occur.

We will label an area in which all decision rules are workable the "policy zone." If the policy zone is large, then the actor who has formulated the policy is capable of responding to a large range of actions by other actors. A large policy zone suggests a fairly stable policy; it is unlikely that the actor will encounter contradictions in decision rules that force a reformulation of the policy. Conversely, with a small policy zone the actor may well be unable to respond to other actors without contradicting a decision rule. A small policy zone thus suggests a relatively unpredictable policy. Lack of a policy zone indicates that the policy is unworkable. The relationship of a policy zone to the decision rules that comprise a policy is discussed extensively in this chapter.

The first section of this chapter discusses components of a simple model of U.S. policy on shipment of arms to Israel. It uses recent data to obtain parameter values and is relevant to mid-1973. In the model the U.S. government is one of four actors. The other three actors are the USSR, Arab oil producing nations, and domestic pressure groups in the United States. Since these actors constrain U.S. options toward Israel, the chapter posits U.S. decision rules in response to them. It is a model from the U.S. government's point of view. It is also a hypothetical model; no State Department official has certified that its assumptions are identical with those made by the U.S. government. The form in which the decision rules are used and the process for identifying a policy zone might, however, be of use to an official who supplied his own assumptions.

The second section of this chapter discusses ways the policy zone is identified. Some attention is paid to linear programming in this section, but the main objective concerns questions about the policy zone. What is the zone for the U.S. government policy posited in the first section? Second, how does the policy zone change if the U.S. government modifies some of its decision rules? With the help of linear programming these questions are answered in the second section. The intended contribution of this chapter is the concept of the policy zone.

COMPONENTS OF THE MODEL

This section considers the U.S. government's relationship to the three other actors in the system. In its policy the U.S. government has two kinds of decision rules. One kind specifies how the U.S. government will act toward the three other actors. These rules can be changed by the U.S. government. The other kind of rule in the U.S. policy is what the United States assumes to be decision rules utilized by other actors in the system. This second kind of decision rule is essentially the U.S. government's view of how other actors relate to each other and to the United States. Since the United States does not control, for example, the response of the USSR to the United States, these rules cannot be changed by the U.S. government. They are, however, U.S. government assumptions about the system and are an important aspect of U.S. policy. These two kinds of decision rules are illustrated by the example that follows.

In providing arms to Israel the U.S. government has a number of interests that constrain the value of those arms. According to George Lenczowski, the major U.S. policy objectives in the area are (a) maintenance of U.S. political commitments in the area, (b) prevention of "a Soviet monopoly" of any Middle Eastern nation's policies, and (c) access to oil.[1] While Lenczowski specifies that political commitments include North Atlantic Treaty Organization (NATO) and Central Treaty Organization (CENTO) arrangements with Greece, Turkey, and Iran, clearly the most significant U.S. political commitment is to Israel. By the 1970s Israel has become almost exclusively dependent on the United States for foreign armaments, and, unlike the CENTO nations, it is chronically at war with its neighbors. Pursuing this U.S. interest by shipping arms as well as containing the Soviets and maintaining oil flows is complicated. The complexity is compounded by U.S. public opinion, which is more sensitive to U.S. government policy in the Middle East than it is to that in most areas. In this model the U.S. government has decision rules to accommodate its shipment of arms to Israel with these other considerations. These decision rules concern, in order of discussion below, the Soviet Union, domestic lobby groups in the United States, and Arab oil producers.

Decision Rules Toward the USSR

Until 1955 the Soviet Union virtually ignored the Arab countries. At the UN in the late 1940s the Soviets had asked for a mandate over Britain's part of Libya and had voted for establishment of Israel. These were anti-British actions that could not have pleased many Arabs. Even the 1952 coup in Egypt, which damaged British interests, received little attention from the USSR. Following Stalin's death in

1953, however, a shift in Soviet policy occurred. The Soviet Union became interested in non-communist, nonaligned nations and began to supply aid to them. "Antiimperialist" governments of any sort became suitable recipients of Soviet assistance. The Soviet/Egyptian arms deal of 1955 initiated a genuine U.S.-Soviet rivalry in the Middle East.

From 1955 through the mid 1960s there were numerous U.S. efforts in Arab countries to limit Soviet influence. Ostensibly because of aggression by a "Soviet puppet state" against Lebanon, the United States invoked the Eisenhower Doctrine and intervened militarily in Lebanon in 1958. Between 1959 and 1966 various sorts of U.S. aid flowed to Arab nations, including food for Egypt and weapons for some of the more anti-Soviet regimes. This aid totalled $907 million.[2] This was an era of superpower rivalry, not polarization in the Middle East. The USSR and the United States both maintained diplomatic and economic contacts with virtually all Arab nations and Israel.

Following the 1967 war, however, a polarization occurred. Nasser reportedly disliked increasing his reliance on the USSR but saw no alternative for rebuilding his army. Egypt as well as Syria, Iraq, the Sudan, and Algeria broke diplomatic relations with the United States. The USSR broke diplomatic relations with Israel. For the first time the superpowers were clearly on opposite sides of the Arab-Israeli struggle.

From 1967 to the early 1970s U.S. efforts to support Israel and to contain Soviet influence centered on arms supply to Israel. Essentially, the United States found no means of supporting Israel and balancing Soviet influence other than ensuring that Soviet efforts to reequip the Arabs militarily did not result in a genuine threat to the existence of Israel. The United States attempted to help Israel maintain the military edge it had won in 1967.

This U.S. supply of arms to Israel is here operationalized as the annual dollar value of the shipments. It is necessary to operationalize the influence of the Soviet Union on U.S. shipment of these arms. Since Egypt is the largest Arab nation, received 75 percent of Soviet military aid to Arab nations between 1965 and 1971,[3] has succeeded better than Syria or Iraq in providing some leadership for Arab nations as a whole, and is the most powerful of Israel's military adversaries, it seems reasonable to operationalize Soviet influence in the system as the annual dollar value of Soviet military shipments to Egypt.

Comparison of U.S. and Soviet arms shipments over the 1955-72 period unfortunately would show a peculiar trend. The dollar value of U.S. military support of Israel in the 1950s and most of the 1960s insufficiently reflects U.S. commitment to Israel prior to 1967.

During this time, France, Great Britain, and Germany were helping to further U.S. policy interests in this area by supplying arms to Israel. Likewise, the dollar value of shipments to Israel is not a good indicator of U.S. efforts prior to 1967 to reduce Soviet influence, since the United States was aiding Arab nations as well as Israel.

Following 1967, the situation changed drastically, and the U.S. became Israel's main supplier of weapons. U.S. government figures for Soviet and U.S. armament exports to Egypt and to Israel from 1967 to 1972 are given in Table 17.1.[4] The question, of course, is what would best describe the relationship between the shipments for a time period after 1972. There are numerous official U.S. statements about "maintaining the power balance"[5] that suggest that U.S. arms to Israel (designated I) is equal to or greater than Soviet arms to Egypt (designated E): $I \geq E$. In none of the years, however, does the value of U.S. assistance to Israel equal the value of Soviet assistance to Egypt.

During the years 1968-72 the value of U.S. military shipments to Israel ranged from 35 to 146 percent of Soviet shipments to Egypt. The average U.S. output to Israel was 60 percent of the Soviet contribution to Egypt. It is assumed here that this average figure is an acceptable description of U.S. government response to the Soviets. This equation is $I = 0.6E$. It is further assumed that this equation is a lower limit for U.S. response to the Soviets. Given some level of E, the U.S. response is thus equal to or greater than the value of this equation: $I \geq 0.6E$. In other words, the U.S.

TABLE 17.1

U.S. Armaments Shipments to Israel and
Soviet Armaments Shipments to Egypt, 1967-72
($U.S. millions)

Year	United States to Israel	USSR to Egypt
1967	23	204
1968	55	116
1969	163	112
1970	232	656
1971	257	360
1972	214	480

Source: U.S. Arms Control and Disarmament Agency, World Military Expenditures and Arms Trade, 1963-1973 (Washington, D.C.: The Agency, 1975), pp. 89, 97.

government will respond to the Soviets with arms shipments to Israel that are at least 0.6E.

Decision Rule Toward Domestic Influence in the United States

U.S. government support of Israel reflects more than a concern for the magnitude of Soviet weapons flowing into Egypt. To some extent the U.S. government policy is also a response to a domestic lobby of Americans deeply concerned about the well-being of Israel. This actor influences the U.S. government through voting strength and a few pressure groups that respond to the perceived well-being of Israel.

The most clear-cut example of this influence occurred between 1946 and 1948. Concerned that U.S. government support of Zionist objectives in the Middle East would provoke the Arabs into allying with the Soviet Union, the Defense Department and the State Department recommended to the White House that the United States not recognize a Jewish State. It seemed to these departments that recognition of Israel might cause the Arabs to shut off the oil that Europe desperately needed for its economic recovery. That would jeopardize the Marshall Plan and hamper U.S. efforts to contain the Soviet Union in Eastern Europe. Various government officials maneuvered to neutralize the pro-Israel lobby; Secretary of Defense James Forrestal even asked President Truman, Governor Dewey, some prominent Republican Senators, and the Democratic National Chairman whether the Palestine issue could be avoided in the 1948 presidential campaigns.[6] Reacting to the horror of Jewish experience in Nazi concentration camps, public opinion in the United States, however, generally favored strong U.S. support for Israel. President Truman decided to ignore the advice of the Defense and State Departments, and he recognized Israel within seconds of its founding in 1948.

This well-documented example of public opinion influencing U.S. foreign policy may be the zenith of pro-Israeli lobby influence on U.S. government decisions on the Middle East. The question is what effect various groups that constitute this lobby actually have on policy in the time period, mid-1973, for which this model is proposed. In other words, how strong is this actor?

The former Washington editor of the Jewish Telegraph Agency, Milton Friedman, remarked in 1972:

> The Israeli embassy is unlike any other embassy in that it has a constituency in the U.S. as well as in Israel. The U.S. government has to take into account the views

of Jews who have emotional ties with the Jewish state. When it talks to the embassy, the government also knows it is talking to a political force in the U.S.[7]

The executive vice-chairman of the American Israel Public Affairs Committee, J. S. Kenen, observes that the Israeli diplomats are "accredited not only to the U.S. government but also in a sense to the American Jewish Community."[8] With events such as the massacre of Israeli athletes at Munich it is not, however, necessary for Americans, Jewish and non-Jewish, to be told by the Israeli embassy what to think about U.S. policy toward Israel. Michael Brecher comments:

> Closer to the truth is the proposition that America's Jews know what Israel's basic foreign policy aims are, feel a deep community of interests with Israel and act independently to further these objectives. . . . [It] is autonomous behavior by sophisticated groups of American Zionists.[9]

It would seem accurate to say that various groups of this lobby simply try to coordinate efforts when they consider that Israeli interests are endangered. The upshot of these efforts is, in the words of a National Journal article, that "relationships between most Capitol Hill offices and the mainstream of U.S. Jewry remain exceedingly warm."[10]

This begs the question, however, of how much influence on U.S. government policy these pressures actually have. An anonymous Republican Senator has remarked:

> Whenever we've put on the heat, I've never seen an immediate favorable response from the White House. But I think it is fair to say . . . that every time there's a move in Congress for Phantoms for Israel, they get them 6 months later. There's a lag while the political pressures build up.[11]

In lieu of any further study of this relationship, it is here assumed that public opinion, expressed by individual voters and groups who feel strongly about U.S. interests regarding Israel, does influence U.S. shipment of weapons to Israel.

The pro-Israel lobby is an actor in the system because it influences U.S. government decision on the value of arms sent to Israel. Some variable is, therefore, needed to represent the strength of the lobby. One indication of increases and decreases in the lobby's concern about Israeli well-being is the level of dollar contributions to the United Jewish Appeal (UJA). These funds are raised primarily for Israeli purposes through annual campaigns in the United States. While no study has been made of the relationship of these annual private contributions to annual levels of threat directed against Israel when U.S. economic conditions are held constant, it is here assumed that a positive relationship exists. In 1967 UJA collections soared; in years of lesser violence, such as 1968, they diminish:[12]

Year	Contributions to UJA*
1967	$240 million
1968	145
1969	167
1970	197
1971	252

Thus, the lobby actor variable is operationalized as the dollar value of private U.S. transfers to Israel through the UJA. This variable is labeled L.

It is also assumed that the U.S. government wants to respond to the level of UJA contributions with at least a minimal arms shipment to Israel. Otherwise, the U.S. government incurs an unacceptable level of domestic pressure. Between 1967 and 1971 the average value for U.S. assistance to Israel as a percentage of UJA contributions was about 70 percent. It is assumed that the U.S. government in 1973 did not want to go below this figure. This decision rule is $I \geq 0.7L$.

Decision Rule Toward Arab Oil Producers

The third actor that U.S. policy is assumed to consider is the Arab petroleum producers. The advice to President Truman and his successors that U.S. support of Israel would jeopardize U.S. petroleum interests in Arab nations was 25 years premature. As James Akins argues in an aptly titled article, "The Oil Crisis: This Time the Wolf Is Here," in the 1970s Arab petroleum has rapidly become crucial to U.S. economic well-being. It has also become possible for Arab nations to levy serious economic retaliation against the U.S. for supporting Israel.[13]

---

*Regular fund plus Israeli emergency fund.

In 1967 a number of Arab states temporarily ceased producing oil to protest Western assistance to Israel. The results of this short boycott by Saudi Arabia, Kuwait, Algeria, Libya, and Iraq were less than sensational. After a three-week production halt, the Libyan government was so drained financially that it had difficulty meeting its payroll. The Saudi government reduced its expenditures because of similar problems. European oil supply was slightly affected, but since this boycott occurred in the summer, the effects of the embargo were not crucial. The United States easily found Western Hemisphere petroleum to replace Arab petroleum. The 1967 boycott hurt only the producing countries.

A new era has now begun. U.S. oil consumption is rising so dramatically that, according to Akins, by 1980 half the U.S. petroleum may be imported from the Middle East.[14] Similar consumption increases are occurring in Europe, Japan, and in the developing nations. The world is becoming more reliant on Middle Eastern oil and needs production increases in those nations.

With prices of oil consistently rising in the 1970s, nations such as Saudi Arabia have accumulated gold and foreign currency reserves that far outsoar what can be invested in their own economies. By 1980 the Saudi dollar savings may be as large as the worth of the U.S. stock market. With such cash reserves available, a three-month or even one-year oil boycott no longer has the domestic economic costs for these nations that it did in 1967.

The Arab oil nations are definitely an actor that can influence the size of U.S. weapons shipments to Israel. An appropriate variable that represents this actor is the annual dollar value of U.S. imports of Saudi Arabian oil. Saudi Arabia is chosen because U.S. companies have dominated its oil industry, it has had a more favorable policy toward the U.S. than other Arab oil nations, and its petroleum reserves are unrivaled. Saudi Arabia alone could supply all the foreign oil required by the United States.

It is assumed that the U.S. economy needs an annual level of $375 million worth of oil in the time period under consideration (mid-1973). This amount is a 75 percent increase over the 1972 U.S. import of Saudi Arabian oil.[15] Designating Saudi petroleum sent to the United States as S, this U.S. government decision rule is $S \geq 375$. In other words, the United States needs at least $375 million worth of Saudi oil.

There is no data base for even guessing the relationship between U.S. military shipments to Israel and Saudi inclination to stop supplying petroleum to the United States. This relationship is newly important. It is assumed that the United States expects that the Saudis will not cut their oil production as long as the value of U.S. government shipments to Israel does not exceed the value of oil imports by $50 million: $I - S \leq \$50$ million. The U.S. government decision rule here is to keep arms shipments to Israel within $50 million of Saudi oil imports. If, for example, oil imports are $400 million, then the United States will not supply more than $450 million of arms to the Israelis.

Having discussed the four U.S. government decision rules toward other actors in the system, it is now appropriate to consider what decision rules these actors might employ themselves. In this model the U.S. government does not control the other three actors: the Soviets, the Arabs, and the pro-Israeli lobby in the United States. Yet it does make judgments on what decision rules these actors have toward the U.S. government and toward one another. Four such policy assumptions are discussed below. Together with the four decision rules discussed above they constitute U.S. government policy.

Saudi Arabian Decision Rule Toward the United States

In the latter part of 1972 the Saudi Arabian government began to change its traditional policy of separating oil sales and politics. In April 1973 the Saudi oil minister, Ahmed Yamani, stated: "Saudi Arabia will not significantly expand its present oil production unless Washington changes its pro-Israeli stance in the Middle East."[16] Later in 1973, King Faisal announced that Saudi Arabia would not increase its oil production unless (a) it received U.S. assistance for industrialization programs and (b) a "suitable political atmosphere, hitherto disturbed by the Middle East crisis"[17] was attained. In other words, the Saudis were now willing to use their oil weapon.

By adding a possible 1973 level of U.S. government shipment of arms to Israel and a generous 1973 level of Saudi exports of oil to the United States, this Saudi Arabian policy can be represented as follows: $I + S \leq \$800$ million. Hence, the U.S. government believes that the Saudis do not adjust their oil exports to the U.S. unless $I + S = 800$. If a rise in I pushes this sum beyond 800, Saudi oil shipments to the United States drop. If the United States wants much more oil, it must lower its arms shipments to Israel. This inequality is assumed to represent Saudi decision rules toward the United States as perceived by the United States.

Soviet Decision Rule Toward the United States

Soviet policy in the Middle East has, according to A. L. Horelick, largely been "reactive":

> improvised in response to opportunities that presented themselves as a consequence of events over which the Soviet Union had little control, or as the unintended consequence of actions undertaken for other purposes.[18]

The obtuse Dulles policy of seeking Arab cooperation against an Arab nonfoe played into the Soviet's hands beyond Soviet expectations. Yet the Soviets have also faced dilemmas, including the possibility that too little military assistance will corrode Soviet influence in Arab nations and that too much assistance will trigger an undesirable war. The expulsion of Soviet advisors from Egypt in 1972 may illustrate both aspects of this dilemma. Disgusted with the low level of assistance from the USSR, Egypt asked that many Russians depart, yet arms kept flowing into Egypt, by mutual agreement of both nations. There is some minimal level below which the Soviet assistance cannot fall without generating permanent damage to Soviet influence in the region. There is also some level beyond which Soviet arms will not rise. In this model the U.S. government makes assumptions about both these levels.

It is assumed that the U.S. government considers that the Soviet maximum is the highest annual value for Soviet arms shipments to Egypt as a percentage of U.S. shipments to Israel between 1967 and 1972. This highest previous value is 2.8. Thus, $E \leq 2.8I$. It is also assumed here that the U.S. government considers that the Soviets will under no circumstances supply Egypt with less than what the United States is supplying Israel. Thus, the minimum is $E \geq 1.0I$.

U.S. Lobby Decision Rule Toward the USSR

Unlike Arab oil producers or the Soviets, the U.S. domestic pressure group does not have a policy vis-à-vis the U.S. government in this model. The reason is that this actor responds primarily to Israeli needs. Hence, it in a sense does have a policy toward the Soviet Union, which endangers Israel by arming Egypt. In this model the U.S. government assumes that there is a relationship between E and L. Between 1967 and 1971, the average level of UJA contributions as a percentage of Soviet arms to Egypt was 0.9.

POLICY ZONE 359

The E and L relationship is assumed to be L = 0.9E. It should be noted here that a rise in UJA contributions does not necessarily force a rise in Soviet military assistance to Egypt. U.S. domestic groups are not influencing Soviet actions in this model (the Soviets worry only about Phantoms). Soviet actions are likely, however, to affect domestic groups.

Summary of the Decision Rules

We can now pull together the four action rules of U.S. policy and the four U.S. assumptions about relationships in the system results in the following policy, where I = U.S. arms shipments to Israel; E = Soviet arms shipments to Egypt; L = U.S. lobby group contributions to the UJA; S = Saudi petroleum shipped to the United States:

$I \geq 0.6E$ $E \geq 1.0I$

$I \geq 0.9L$ $E \leq 2.8I$

$S \geq 350$ $L \geq 0.9E$

$I - S \leq 50$ $I + S \leq 800$

LINEAR PROGRAMMING AND THE MODEL

Three sorts of knowledge about the decision rules discussed above are important to a U.S. government decision maker. First, he needs to know, given U.S. government policy, what the optimum U.S. government response is to an action by another actor in the system. If, for instance, there is a Soviet input E = 329, the decision maker needs to know the optimum value of armaments that the U.S. government should send to Israel. Second, the decision maker needs to know under what conditions the policy becomes untenable. What kind of Soviet input exceeds the capability of the United States to respond, given the policy it has chosen? Stated differently, what is the policy zone within which the U.S. government decision rules are workable? Third, the decision maker needs to know how changes in U.S. policy would affect the policy zone. What, for example, is the implication of the U.S. government changing its decision rule vis-à-vis the Soviets from $I \geq 0.6E$ to a new rule, such as $I \geq 0.9E$. Does this new rule enlarge or contract the policy zone?

Linear programming is a useful technique for finding optimal answers to these three problems. It was developed in the 1940's by George Dantzig, has been used extensively in business management problems, and has recently become of interest to economists and political scientists.[19] Since it is a relatively new approach in political science, there follows a short discussion of the technique of linear programming. We will then apply linear programming to the decision rules stated earlier in this chapter. The result will be answers to the three questions of U.S. response, the location of the policy zone, and the implications of policy change.

Linear Programming

The task of linear programming is to find the optimal proportion of each variable, maximizing or minimizing the combination of variables given in a problem. Linear programming does this on the basis of four assumptions.

The first assumption of linear programming is that the variables are proportional; a certain quantity of one variable can replace part of another variable in a solution to a problem. Second, the variables must be additive; in other words, the optimal answer is a sum of the variables. Third, noninteger solutions must be acceptable; a value of 390.56 for a variable such as Soviet arms shipments must be meaningful to a person using linear programming. Fourth, it is assumed that all constants are known and are certain. The problem under consideration in this chapter has been formulated to meet these assumptions, but it might be noted that variations of linear programming have been devised for problems that violate some of these assumptions. An algorithm exists for finding optimal integer solutions, but it is not utilized in this chapter, because the unit of measurement, dollars, can be divided into parts smaller than one. There are methods of solving, under some circumstances, quadratic or other nonlinear problems, and there are techniques for problems in which constants are known within only a certain probability range, but none of these techniques is applied in this chapter or is required by the problem as it is formulated.

A linear programming problem has two parts: an objective function and constraints. An example of an objective function is $Z = 2X + Y$. Graphically, this objective function is shown in Figure 17.1. A point on any of the Z lines satisfies the objective function. If the problem is a maximization problem, in which Z is to be maximized by finding the largest sum of 2X and Y, then the optimal line is the one farthest from the origin. The graph above shows

FIGURE 17.1

Representation of Objective Function
$Z = 2X + Y$

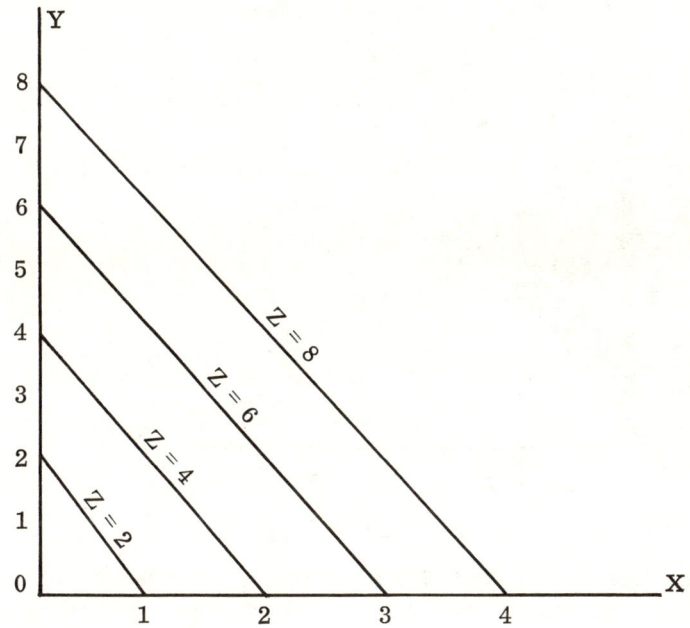

Note: This graph shows only four values of Z, but an infinite number of Z values is possible.

$Z = 8$ as the maximum value of the objective function can take, but this value can be any positive combination of 2X and Y.

This objective function might best be maximized by simply raising all the variables to infinity, except that the conditions of a linear programming problem typically preclude that. These conditions, called "constraints," constrain the variables within specified limits. They are the second part of any linear programming problem.

Examples of constraints are the following $X + Y \leq 6$; $2X - Y \leq 2$; $X, Y \geq 0$ (variables must be nonnegative). Graphed, these constraints are shown in Figure 17.2. The shaded area represents values of X and Y that are nonnegative and satisfy these two constraints. This area is a "feasible" zone; later in the chapter it is called a policy zone.

FIGURE 17.2

Representation of Constraints
$X + Y \leq 6$; $2X - Y \leq 2$; $X, Y \geq 0$

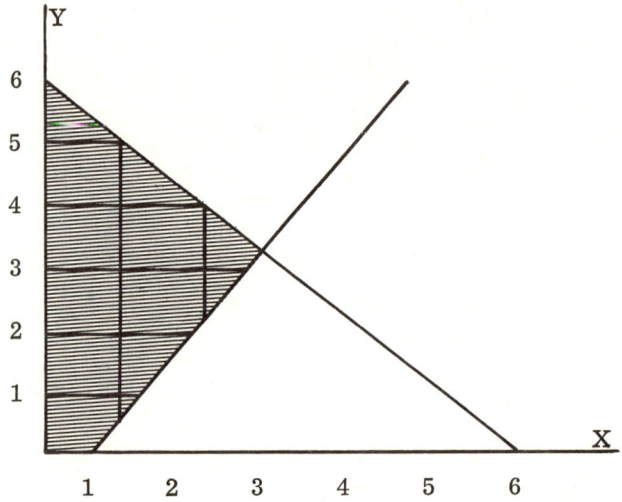

When Figures 17.1 and 17.2 are combined, the solution to the maximization problem is evident (see Figure 17.3). This solution occurs at the intersection, M, of a vertex of the feasibility zone and the largest objective function line that goes through the feasibility zone. A problem with only two variables can always be graphed in two-space and solved by looking for the intersection of a vertex and the optimum line. With more than three variables, however, an optimization problem becomes complicated. The mathematical theory of convex sets stipulates that for optimization problems in n-space (n = the number of variables) the optimal solution will always occur at one vertex of the feasible zone constructed in n-space. Linear programming is essentially a means of locating one such vertex. Linear programming can locate such a vertex in two-space or 300-space; it is applicable to problems with many more variables than the examples in this chapter.

The best-known algorithm for solving linear programming problems is the Simplex method. It finds the optimal vertex starting with suboptimal solutions (that is, at vertexes that are not the best solution). It actually starts at the origin and then efficiently jumps to other vertexes that are progressively closer to the optimal solution. When the optimal solution is obtained, the

POLICY ZONE

iteration procedure stops. Discussion of this method and the superior Revised Simplex method can be found in numerous introductory operations research texts.[20]

It should be emphasized that not all problems are amenable to optimization. Optimization problems do not work when there are contradictions in the constraints; if one constraint requires a variable to be larger than three and another constraint limits the variable to two, obviously no solution is possible. One indirect benefit then of applying linear programming to decision rules is to see whether they are workable.

A Linear Programming Model of U.S. Policy

There are various ways of constructing a linear programming model, and it should be noted that the model utilized here is unusual.

FIGURE 17.3

Solution to the Maximization Problem

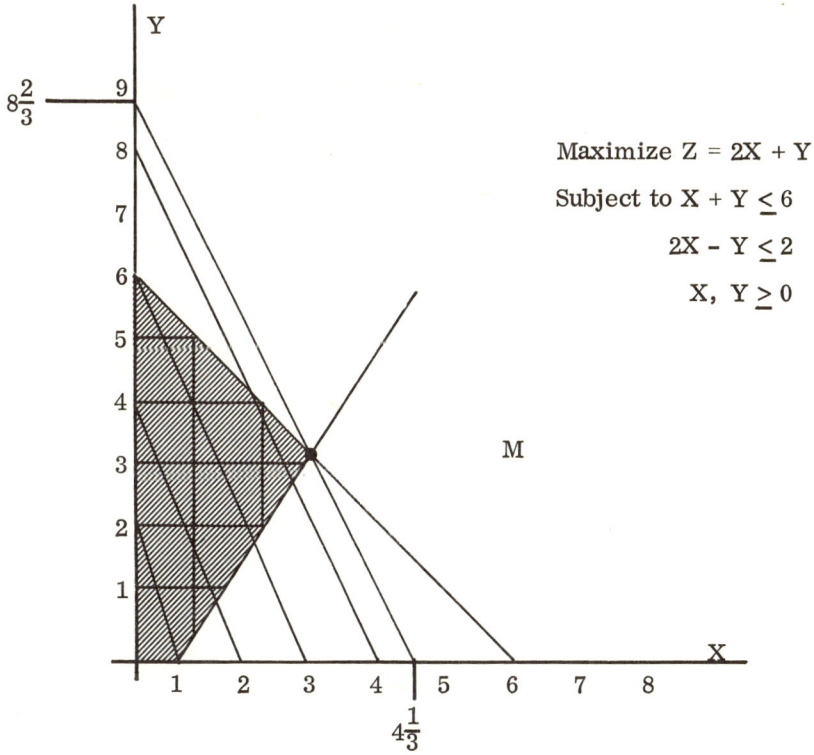

Typically, linear programming problems contain variables that are all controlled by whoever is optimizing the objective function. The objective function in most cases represents a combination of variables that the actor wishes to combine optimally for his own profit. For instance, the problem of determining what mix of U.S. weapons to send to Israel might have the following objective function: $Z = b_1$ (tanks) $+ b_2$ (planes) $+ b_3$ (guns). The b's here might represent unit costs of each item. Constraints in such a problem would refer to relative value and availability of each sort of weapon. Optimizing the objective function would here indicate what, on a dollar basis, is the best mix of weapons that the United States can send Israel.

This chapter uses a systemic objective function. That is, the U.S. government in this model does not control all the variables in the objective function. Maximizing (or minimizing) this objective function does not, therefore, indicate an ideal combination of factors that would add up to an optimal U.S. policy, as is true of the example in the preceding paragraph. Instead, optimizing this objective function indicates a maximum (or minimum) combined value that the system of the U.S. government, the USSR, the Saudis, and the lobby group can attain. If one considers that each actor is trying to maximize its own value or influence in the system, then the maximized objective function should be interpreted as the largest total amount of influence that the system can hold.

Specifically, the objective function of the model discussed in this chapter represents each actor in the system. Each variable in the objective function has a coefficient of 1, because the system contains one of each actor. The objective function for this model is, therefore, $Z = 1E + 1I - 1S + 1L$.

It is assumed that the U.S. government, Soviet Union, and U.S. domestic lobby actors maximize their impact on the system by maximizing their dollar input. In other words, the Soviet Union maximizes its impact on the system by sending a maximum dollar value of arms to the Egyptians. The U.S. domestic lobby maximizes its impact on the system by sending a maximum value of dollars to Israel. The U.S. government maximizes its impact on the system by sending a maximum dollar value of weapons to Israel. Accordingly, the coefficients for E, I, and L are positive; these actors wish to maximize their dollar input. The Saudi Arabian actor is assumed to be very different. Saudi Arabia influences the system by <u>lowering</u> its oil sales, which are badly needed by the United States. The Saudis, then, optimize their impact on the system by minimizing their oil shipments to the United States. The coefficient for S is, therefore, negative. Optimizing this objective function is a process of minimizing S and simultaneously maximizing I, E, and L. It should be stressed that optimizing this

POLICY ZONE 365

objective function replicates a situation in which each actor is trying to exert as much influence on the system as it possibly can, given its policy.

This objective function is combined with the U.S. government policy as summarized earlier to form a linear programming problem. Solving this linear programming problem is a process similar to what was demonstrated graphically, except that, for reasons not here discussed, this problem exists in 13-space instead of 2-space. Such a problem can be done by hand, but the computations for this chapter have been done with the assistance of a computer program entitled LP Driver. Accordingly, a number of questions about the mathematical implications of the U.S. policy modeled here can be answered very quickly.

Responses to Other Actors

Suppose the U.S. decision maker is advised that the Soviet Union is sending military assistance to Egypt at a level of $300 million per year. Applying linear programming to this model enables him to determine the maximum U.S. response, given a U.S. policy. By adding another constraint, E = 300, the decision maker can find the maximum level of U.S. arms for Israel by maximizing the resulting problem. The resulting answer is the most that the United States can do for Israel, given the constraints of its policy, in response to Soviet assistance to Egypt. The answer is in this case $300 million.

This procedure applies for any variable. By simply adding a value of one variable to the tableau then optimizing the entire set of equations, the decision maker can determine the optimal U.S. response. Given the U.S. policy specified in the first section of this chapter, the decision maker would obtain the following values in the following three examples:

Input	Maximum U.S. Response
L = $300 million	I = $333 million
E = 300	I = 300
E = 500	I = 425

It is assumed in this model that the U.S. government responds to whichever actor is requiring the United States under its policy to make the largest shipment to Israel. This point is illustrated by the following example. If L = 300 and E = 300, the decision maker obtains different results from optimizing the policy for each of these two inputs. The L input requires an I response, under U.S. policy, of $333 million. The E input requires an I response of $300 million. The decision maker focuses on L, ignores E, and responds with $333 million. This action is acceptable under the policy; under the policy $333 million is optimally responsive to the domestic lobby and more than satisfies the U.S. decision rule toward the Soviets. In other words, I = $333 million is an optimal answer, under these conditions, for all the decision rules of U.S. policy.

The possibility of a choice between what E requires and what L requires may suggest that the policy model is too simplistic. It might be nice to avoid this ambiguity by formulating a model that is a weighted combination of the E and L variables. Such precision would require knowing more about the relationship between E and L than the U.S. government does know in this model. Lack of such precise knowledge is, however, undoubtedly a typical situation for a decision maker; most policy models are imperfect and imprecise. Having a simplistic model does not, moreover, leave the decision maker unable to determine a feasible U.S. response, at least not in this example. The discrepancy between two inputs does not thwart the model, and the policy continues to be viable. The U.S. government can make a response to L = 300, E = 300 that is consistent with the decision rules of the policy.

The Policy Zone

There is, however, some level for each variable beyond which the U.S. government policy cannot offer a response that is consistent with the decision rules. If the E variable equals 2,000, there is no way that the United States can respond without exceeding the oil constraint: $I + P \leq 800$. That is an extreme situation. There undoubtedly is some lower level of E at which the U.S. policy is unworkable. The U.S. government decision maker needs to know the boundaries of his policy.

The policy zone in a linear programming model is exactly analogous to the feasibility zone of the graphs discussed earlier. Within this zone the decision maker can apply the policy to respond to any input. He cannot, however, respond to an input that is outside the zone.

The upper boundary of the policy zone is easily identified by maximizing the objective function given the constraints of the decision rules. This gives the maximum values that each variable can have according to the assumptions of the policy. The lower boundary of the policy zone is similarly identified by minimizing the objective function. For the policy modeled in this chapter the policy zone is located by performing these two operations:

Maximize $Z = E + I - S + L$
Minimize $Z = E + I - S + L$

Optimizing this objective function within the constraints specified earlier results in the following policy zone (minimized values on the left, maximized values on the right):

$$0 \leq E \leq 675$$

$$0 \leq I \leq 425$$

$$800 \geq S \geq 375$$

$$0 \leq L \leq 607$$

This policy zone indicates that Soviet armaments to Egypt cannot exceed $675 million. Saudi petroleum cannot go lower than $375 million nor higher than $800 million. UJA contributions cannot exceed $607 million. Finally, U.S. weapons to Israel cannot be greater than $425 million.*

What is meant here by "cannot" is that the U.S. government policy becomes unviable if one or more of the three actors does exceed these values. If, indeed, the Soviets send $750 million worth of weapons to Egypt, the United States must rethink its policy. According to the constraints of this model, a value of E that exceeds the policy zone requires that I become larger than 425. If I is larger than 425, then S must decrease from 375 because $I + S \leq 800$. However, the U.S. decision rule, $I - S \leq 50$, is then violated. Either the United States responds to the Soviets at a level lower than what is indicated by the U.S. decision rule, $I - 0.6E \leq 0$, or it follows this decision rule but breaks another, such as $I - S \leq 50$. In either case, it is a situation in which U.S. government policy has become unworkable: The policy zone has been exceeded, and the policy must be reformulated.

Obtaining this policy zone indicates some interesting things about U.S. policy as modeled here. It suggests, first, that the

---

*In these examples the lower boundary of the policy zone is zero for E, I, and L. Depending upon the constraints used, this lower boundary could have higher values, such as $E = 43$. The implication of such a lower boundary is that U.S. policy becomes unviable when E reaches some low level, as well as when it reaches some upper level.

policy is viable: There is in fact a zone, and the policy does not contain internal contradictions. Second, it suggests that the United States can respond to large increases in the E variable over the 1972 level of $303 million without reaching the constraint level imposed by the Saudis. Yet it also suggests that if Saudi oil shipments decrease sharply, the policy becomes obsolete. Events such as an oil embargo, where $S = 0$, or a war in which E doubles or triples and L expands rapidly, are wholly unmanageable under this U.S. policy. The model suggests, then, that the U.S. government policy for shipment of arms to Israel was viable in mid-1973 but could be rendered untenable, and the boundaries of the policy zone indicate where this happens.

Alternative Policies

Aware that a sharp decrease in Saudi oil exports to the United States or a very large increase in Soviet supply of arms to Egypt would exceed the zone of its policy, the U.S. government may wish to consider policy alternatives. The U.S. government may also wish to change some of the decision rules because of changed military or political conditions. With linear programming the mathematical implications of various policy reformulations can be easily determined. As examples, a few alternative policies are discussed below.

Since 1967 the U.S. government has provided Israel less arms, in dollar value, than the Soviet Union has provided Egypt. Because the Israeli military has a greater capacity than the Egyptian military to maintain and operate complex weapons, Israel needs fewer spare parts and less replacement equipment than Egypt. Moreover, the combination of Israeli air superiority and the Sinai buffer between Egypt and the Israeli populations means that a major Egyptian attack would suffer vast losses of equipment before threatening Israeli cities. For these reasons, and undoubtedly others, the U.S. government has been content to provide Israel with a lesser dollar value of arms than Egypt has received from the Soviet Union.

However decisive Egypt's defeat in 1967, it is possible that the level of Egyptian military effectiveness is consistently rising. The 1967 defeat resulted in leadership changes in the Egyptian army, in strategy reassessments, and in a new attitude for many Egyptians on the difficulties of fighting the Israelis. Also, after the 1968-70 "War of Attrition" along the Suez ended, Egyptian missiles remained in the canal area, bolstering Egypt's defense and representing what some Israelis have referred to as Israel's first major military failure in the Middle East.[21]

Aware of these two developments, better Egyptian air defenses and improved training in the Egyptian army, the U.S. government might reconsider its decision rule for responding to Soviet supply to Egypt. A revised U.S. policy might thus have a higher response coefficient to Soviet action in Egypt. Rethinking its policy, the U.S. government might decide that 0.6 is too low and substitute 0.9 for 0.6, changing the decision rule from $I \geq 0.6E$ to $I \geq 0.9E$.

The effect of this U.S. policy revision on the policy zone can be seen by maximizing the revised linear programming model. The new values are as follows:

Zone for Revised Policy 1

$$0 \leq E \leq 472$$
$$0 \leq I \leq 425$$
$$800 \geq P \geq 375$$
$$0 \leq L \leq 607$$

This policy is viable so long as Soviet assistance to the Egyptians does not exceed $472 million. There is a change here from the previous policy zone: Under the original policy, the United States could respond to Soviet actions to an upper limit of $675 million. Considering that in 1970 the Soviets actually supplied $656 million to Egypt, it seems unlikely that this revised policy would be viable for very long.

What is constraining the U.S. government in this revised policy? The maximum support the United States can give Israel is $425 million according to both this new policy and the original policy. A decision to maintain the original policy intact except for increasing the response to the USSR from 0.6E to 0.9E reduces the policy zone, but the United States still cannot give Israel more than $425 million. Somewhere else in the policy there is another constraint on the U.S. government's options.

That constraint is the U.S. decision rule on Saudi petroleum. Having decided that the United States needs at least $375 million worth of Saudi oil ($S \geq 375$) and having also decided that U.S. shipments to Israel will not exceed the level of oil by more than $50 million ($I - S \leq 50$), the U.S. government has tied its provision of weapons to Israel to its oil. Given the Saudi policy that its oil for the United States plus U.S. assistance to Israel cannot exceed $800 million ($I + S \leq 800$), there is an upper limit of $425 million on U.S. arms sales to Israel. If the United States exceeds this limit, then the Saudis reduce their oil exports below $375 million, and the United States receives less oil than it needs. The U.S. policy has then been violated.

In sum, revising the U.S. decision rule that responds to Soviet activity in Egypt from $I \geq 0.6E$ to $I \geq 0.9E$ yields a viable policy but a very much reduced policy zone. Since the United States cannot supply Israel more than $425 million of weapons, this policy becomes obsolete if the Soviets send Egypt more than $472 million. The United States would then have to modify its policy on petroleum imports, persuade the Saudis to change their policy, or change the decision rule on Soviet weapons again.

Convincing the Saudi Arabians to change their policy may be difficult because of the U.S. dependence on Saudi Arabian petroleum. Short of a U.S. military invasion of the oil-producing section of Saudi Arabia, the United States no longer has a great deal of leverage on Saudi Arabia. Military action against the Saudis would disrupt oil production, with serious economic consequences for the United States and Europe. It might also have catastrophic effects on U.S. business interests in Arab nations. In view of the rapidly increasing Arab dollar reserves garnered from U.S. purchases of Arab oil, the United States needs good business relationships with Arab countries. For these reasons, U.S. efforts to compel Saudi Arabia to change its policy from $I + P \leq 800$ to another figure, such as $I + P \leq 1,200$, would probably fail. It is here assumed that the United States cannot obtain a change in Saudi Arabian policy.

The U.S. government can, however, change its own policy on oil imports. While the implications of doing without Saudi Arabian oil may include unpopular items, such as gasoline rationing, paying extra for non-Arab oil, and abandoning pollution controls on coal, it is possible for the United States to reduce its reliance on Saudi oil.

Suppose that the U.S. government changes its two decision rules on imports of Saudi Arabian oil. The requirement for at least $375 million of Saudi oil is drastically cut to $50 million. The decision rule $S \geq 375$ becomes $S \geq 50$. Second, the U.S. government policy assumption that it is unwise for U.S. shipments to Israel to exceed petroleum imports from Saudi Arabia by more than $50 million ($I - S \leq 50$) is discarded.

The effect of these two changes on the original U.S. policy, in which the U.S. response to the USSR is $I \geq 0.6E$, is spectacular. By lessening its oil requirement from Saudi Arabia, the U.S. government's revised policy results in a greatly enlarged policy zone:

Zone for Revised Policy 2

$$0 \leq E \leq 1,190$$
$$0 \leq I \leq 750$$
$$800 \geq P \geq 50$$
$$0 \leq L \leq 1,071$$

With this policy the U.S. government can respond to any Soviet shipment to Egypt up to a level nearly $1.25 billion. Moreover, the U.S. government policy now enables it to supply Israel with up to $750 million of military assistance (depending on the actions of the other actors in the system). The activity of U.S. lobby groups as indexed by UJA contributions can, in this policy, reach a level of $1.071 billion. Retaining the $I \geq 0.6E$ rule but revising the U.S. decision rules on petroleum, $S \geq 350$ to $S \geq 50$, and dropping $I - S \leq 50$ dramatically enlarges the policy zone.

Revision 2 stems, however, from a lessening in U.S. dependence on Saudi oil, which is an unlikely possibility. Suppose the U.S. dependence on Saudi Arabian oil increases instead of decreases? In the view of Akins, Levy, and others, there is no easy or practicable alternative to an increase in U.S. oil imports from Saudi Arabia. These people argue that even construction of the Alaska pipeline and accelerated development of nuclear power will not prevent a rapidly increasing U.S. need this decade for Saudi Arabian oil. If this need for Saudi oil should rise, for instance, to a minimum of $550 million, the U.S. policy rule changes from $S \geq 375$ to $S \geq 550$. What is the effect of this modification, designated policy revision 3, on the policy zone? The new policy has a reduced zone:

Zone for Revised Policy 3

$$0 \leq E \leq 397$$
$$0 \leq I \leq 250$$
$$800 = S = 550$$
$$0 \geq L \geq 357$$

According to this policy, the United States must reduce its support for Israel below the amount it provided in 1971! It can, moreover, barely respond to Soviet inputs that are larger than the 1971 level. If there is a Soviet input $E = 400$, however, this policy becomes unworkable.

Other Policy Zones

We have thus far discussed U.S. government policy on arms shipments to Israel, delineated a policy zone given certain decision rules and assumptions that comprise that policy, and investigated the effects on the policy zone of modifying some U.S. government decision rules. Throughout, the discussion has focused on the U.S. government.

Were other actors' policies known in greater detail, defining a policy zone for each actor in the system would be similar to the exercise above. Extensive discussion of Soviet policy, for example, is outside the scope of this chapter, but that policy might be portrayed as containing five (or ten or 25) decision rules. Optimizing the systemic objective function $Z = E + I + L - S$ as constrained by the USSR decision rules would define the USSR policy zone. Similarly, the zone for Saudi Arabian policy could be determined by using Saudi decision rules as constraints and then optimizing the same systemic objective function. The procedure would be identical to that used for the United States, but for each actor the constraints on the objective function differ. It should be stressed that each actor's policy zone is an area in which that particular actor can act without contradicting any of its own decision rules or policy assumptions. In this sense, existence of a policy zone means that that actor's policy is viable.

Were policy zones defined for each actor in the system, a subsequent, more sophisticated, question can be answered. To what extent, if at all, do the policy zones of all actors overlap? In other words, is there a mathematical area in which the aggregate of all actors' policies is feasible? The existence of such an area can be determined easily with linear programming. Optimizing the systemic objective function, using as constraints the policies of all actors in the system, will produce such a feasible area, if it exists. Such an area is a "systemic policy zone." It is an area in which each actor can pursue its policy without contradicting its own decision rules or thwarting the policy of another actor. In other words, it is a policy zone that is much more precisely defined, because more knowledge is utilized, than the example of U.S. arms shipments presented in this chapter.

One should not equate a systemic policy zone with tranquility or lack of armed conflict, but the mathematical existence of a large zone would suggest that policies of actors would be highly predictable over time. With neither internal nor external contradictions, there is no compelling reason for any actor's policies to change. Conversely, the lack of a systemic policy zone suggests that at least one actor's policy must change and that even if the policies of some actors are viable, the policies of actors as a whole in the system are unstable. In that circumstance, how a systemic policy zone can be created or enlarged might be an interesting question. Are the constraints that obstruct a systemic policy zone the decision rules by which each actor responds to others, or are they the assumptions that each actor holds about others in the system? Expressed differently, to what extent is the systemic policy zone constricted by actors' misperception of other actors' decision rules?

CONCLUSION

This chapter has formulated a model of U.S. policy on armament shipments to Israel for mid-1973, then considered the mathematical implications of that policy. It has found that the decision rules of the policy are not contradictory. It has also found that the policy zone is larger than the input levels of the actors in 1972, and it has given examples of optimal U.S. responses to specific inputs. These examples indicate that the policy can cope with increased inputs into the system up to a certain level.

The chapter has also shown that a set of decision rules is not necessarily workable under all conditions. It has defined a policy zone concept to describe the range of numeric values in which a set of decision rules is noncontradictory and hence viable. Where policies of all actors in the system are known, the chapter has described how a systemic policy zone can be defined. Finally, the chapter has suggested that the size of the policy zone relates to the stability and hence predictability of the policy.

The chapter has also employed linear programming as a technique for efficiently finding the upper and lower limits of the policy zone. In the model formulated here there are eight decision rule inequalities with four variables, which are optimized with linear programming. It should be noted that linear programming is appropriate for linear optimization problems with a larger number of variables.

NOTES

1. George Lenczowski, United States Interests in the Middle East (Washington, D.C.: American Enterprise Institute for Public Policy Research, 1968), pp. 97-98.

2. Stockholm International Peace Research Institute, Yearbook: World Armaments-Disarmaments (New York: Humanities Press, 1972), p. 523.

3. Ibid., p. 299.

4. Various sources give different figures for this period, and usually the data are for a five-year period. See Stockholm International Peace Research Institute, Yearbook; Allan Solomorow, "Arms Crisis in the Middle East," Sane World (August/September 1974), cited in Fuad Jabber, "Curbing the Arab-Israeli Arms Race," The Link 7 (1974), p. 6. Since this model is constructed from the U.S. government's point of view, using published official U.S. figures seems justified. The figures are for total exports, which ought to be a reasonable approximation of U.S.-Soviet arms shipments. It would be preferable to have monthly rather than annual estimates; since the data are annual, the figures are not logged. Simplistic parameter estimation techniques are utilized in this chapter because only six data points exist.

5. Statement by Deputy Secretary Roger P. Davis to the Subcommittee on Foreign Operations of the United States Senate Committee on Appropriations, Department of State Bulletin 65 (August 23, 1971), p. 208.

6. Walter Millis, The Forrestal Diaries (New York: Viking Press, 1951), pp. 322-23, 344-48, 359-62.

7. Andrew Glas, "Foreign Policy Report: Nixon Gives Israel Massive Aid but Reaps No Political Harvest," National Journal 4 (1972): 67.

8. Ibid.

9. Michael Brecher, The Foreign Policy System of Israel (New Haven: Yale University Press, 1972), p. 501.

10. Glass, "Foreign Policy Report," p. 69.

11. Ibid., p. 62.

12. The American Jewish Yearbook 71 (1970): 267, 269-70; The American Jewish Yearbook 73 (1972): 247-49.

13. James Akins, "The Oil Crisis: This Time the Wolf Is Here," Foreign Affairs 51 (1973): 462-78.

14. Ibid., p. 468.

15. The World Almanac 1974 (New York: Newspaper Enterprise Association, 1973), p. 121.

16. Quoted in Fuad Itayim, "Arab Oil—The Political Dimension," Journal of Palestine Studies 3 (1974): 89.

17. Middle East Economic Digest 17 (1973): 1060. See also Middle East Economic Survey 16 (1973): 1-7.

18. A. S. Becher and A. L. Horelick, "Soviet Policy in the Middle East" (Santa Monica: Rand Corporation, 1970), p. 5.

19. George B. Dantzig, "Maximization of a Linear Function of Variables Subject to Linear Inequalities" in Activity Analysis in Production and Allocation, ed. T. C. Koopmans (New York: Wiley, 1951), pp. 339-47.

20. Two examples are Fredrick S. Hillier and Gerald Lieberman, Introduction to Operations Research (San Francisco: Holden-Day, 1972); Leon Cooper and David Steinberg, Introduction to Methods of Optimization (Philadelphia: Saunders, 1970).

21. See Walter Laqueur, Confrontation (New York: Bantam Books, 1974), pp. 98-99.

CHAPTER

18

**A GAME-THEORY MODEL
OF OPEC, OIL CONSUMERS,
AND OIL COMPANIES,
EMPHASIZING COALITION
FORMATIONS**
Charles Bird
Martin W. Sampson III

In no other commodity area has a group of developing nations succeeded in forming a coalition like that of the Organization of Petroleum Exporting Countries (OPEC). Not only has this coalition survived for 15 years, but it has managed to quadruple the prices it charges multinational companies for its commodity. This success has occurred despite substantial differences between the nations that belong to OPEC. For years Iran and Iraq have had border clashes; the Iranians and Saudis are competing for control of the Arabian/Persian Gulf; the Libyans dislike monarchies such as Saudi Arabia; and nations like Venezuela, Ecuador, and Nigeria want to ignore the politics of the Middle East in which these rivalries occur. Not only are there political and geographic distinctions in OPEC, but there are also economic differences. Venezuela, Algeria, Iran, Indonesia, Ecuador, and Nigeria have substantial populations relative to their oil income; consequently, they spend whatever they make from oil. Saudi Arabia, Libya, and Kuwait are unable to spend all their oil revenues and thus have different concerns about oil prices and a capability to reduce oil production. Over a decade and a half it might be expected that some nations would quit the OPEC coalition or that the coalition would be ineffective. Instead, OPEC thrived in the early 1970s, has weathered decreases in oil demand in the mid-1970s, and has not lost members.

In light of high oil prices it is unsurprising that officials of industrial nations are interested in ways of breaking up OPEC or limiting its power. Determining under what conditions OPEC is vulnerable to the actions of other nations is the basic question this chapter considers. Specifically, we are interested in conditions that would permit another coalition to control OPEC or conditions in which some of OPEC's members might decide to leave the OPEC coalition. Suggested measures have included formation of a consumers' coalition that would be powerful enough to keep OPEC from boosting prices. There are also examples of nations such as France attempting to arrange deals with specific OPEC nations in hopes of obtaining favorable and secure access to petroleum. It would be useful to describe the conditions under which such tactics could succeed.

This chapter discusses what we call "the oil situation" as a cooperative game, and it uses game-theory techniques to understand some of the processes that underlie the situation. In modeling the oil situation some specific assumptions have been made that should be stated at the outset. First, this is a game that involves numerous actors. Included are 12 full members of OPEC, at least seven multinational oil companies, and a host of oil-consuming nations. It is clearly not reducible to a two-person game, nor is it a game in which any solitary actor does better by refusing to cooperate with any other actors. Some cooperation is inherent in this situation. Second, it is assumed that actors in this game do not necessarily follow policies that yield the best possible benefit according to a single criterion, such as money or oil flow. Actors may have sluggish policy-making processes that prevent them from making their policies optimal. Their interests typically involve numerous considerations. Sorting out those considerations is a complicated and often incremental process, and the result is usually a preference to pursue previous policies unless forced to switch to new policies. It is therefore necessary that our model and its solutions allow for nonoptimal but feasible outcomes. Third, it is assumed that no actor will severely harm itself in order to harm another actor. This notion, discussed later in the chapter as "limited threat," means that actors do not calculate on the basis of the absolute worst that other actors could do to them. Oil nations, for instance, do not yield to the United States simply because U.S. nuclear missiles could annihilate them in 15 minutes. Likewise, according to this assumption, the United States does not fear that Iran will stop producing oil to impoverish itself voluntarily unless the United States agrees to Iranian demands. These events, of course, are possible, but a model based on limited threats seems more realistic and is therefore used in this chapter.

The solution concepts used in this chapter reflect these assumptions of the model. We apply some solution concepts that have not previously appeared in the political-science literature. These solutions (which are also relatively new in the mathematics literature) may be of interest to students of international relations, who study situations in which policies are rarely optimal according to a single criterion.

In sum, the chapter has two purposes: One is to present cooperative game theory as a viable tool for analyzing international relations; the other purpose is to use this tool to illuminate aspects of international cooperation in the oil situation. For the latter purpose we have constructed a model, then analyzed it to determine its mathematically qualitative properties. An appropriate subsequent task would be to gather data, make judgments about unavailable data, and then test the deductions of the model, which admittedly is not the most sophisticated model that could be used with the game-theoretic approach.

COOPERATIVE GAME THEORY

Characteristic Functions

There are several models for cooperative games, and each emphasizes certain aspects of the overall process. The model most often used focuses on the bargaining process and the allocation of payoffs among actors. This model is called the characteristic-function game.

A coalition of actors obtains something from participating in a game. It is useful to have an index that compares what various coalitions can obtain. The index for a specific coalition is called a characteristic function. In other words, the characteristic function is a measure of the power of a coalition. We use the characteristic-function game model for the oil situation because this model handles coalitions much more readily than do the other game-theoretic models.

A game has a set of players N and a set function V from each subset $S \subset N$ to the reals R. V(S) represents some index of the power of coalition S in terms of whatever is being divided up. V(N) is the total to be divided among all the players. The outcomes are vectors $X \in R^n$ with X_i being the amount each player i gets in an allocation:

$$\sum_{i=1}^{n} X_i = V(N)$$

The crux of formulating a characteristic function model lies in deciding how to evaluate the strength of coalitions. The best known and most widely used evaluation method in cooperative game theory is the Von Neumann-Morgenstern characteristic function.

This is derived by considering what each coalition can guarantee itself under any circumstance. In other words, this characteristic function reflects the worst outcome that can happen to the coalition. To determine what coalitions can guarantee we maximize over the strategies of the players in S, $\Phi(S)$, and minimize the strategies of the players not in S:

$$V(S) = \max_{\pi_s \in \Phi(S)} \min_{\pi_{n-s} \in \Phi(N-S)} r(S, \pi_s, \pi_{n-s})$$

$r(\cdot,)$ is the reward function for coalition S, given strategies π_s, π_{n-s}.

The value of coalition S, V(S), is derived from assuming that this coalition is playing a zero-sum game with all members not in the coalition. Clearly, this gives us a lower bound on the coalition power and indicates the worst that the actor can do.

In the context of the oil situation there are some difficulties with the Von Neumann-Morgenstern characteristic function. While it is possible for the United States to obliterate the Saudi Arabian oil fields, for the Saudis to refuse ever to sell oil to anyone, or for an industrial nation to cease importing oil, these extreme actions are unrepresentative of what the actors are likely to do. Even the U.S. threat to seize Saudi Arabian oil fields is dubious, according to an August 1975 Library of Congress report for the House of Representatives Committee on International Relations. That report states that seizing Saudi oil fields would require 80,000 people, and safely convoying tankers from Saudi Arabia to the tip of Southern Africa would tie up 76 percent of active navy destroyers and cruisers. Soviet activity in Angola since this report appeared suggests that convoying might have to continue west of South Africa, rendering the operation even more costly and difficult.[1] Presumably actions as costly as this are not what decision makers expect when dealing with other players in this game. Presumably, these are not the possibilities that decison makers typically have in mind when dealing with other players in this game (although in crisis situations those events might occur). To model the oil situation on the assumption that decision makers do not expect implementation of these extreme measures, some modification of the Von Neumann-Morgenstern characteristic function is made in this chapter.

We modify this characteristic function by assuming that each coalition has some level below which it is not willing to lower itself in order to drive another coalition down to the minimum guaranteed by its Von Neumann-Morgenstern characteristic function. For example, this would imply that all the oil companies are not willing to shut down all their foreign operations merely to damage the oil-producing and -consuming nations at the oil companies' expense.

Given a set of strategies by coalition S, and a reward function $r(S, \pi_s, \pi_{n-s})$, let R_0 be the minimum level of benefit to S. Then we assume that given the present strategy of its opponents $\pi_0 \in \Phi(N-S)$, coalition S will restrict its strategies to a subset $\Phi_L(S) = \{\pi \in T(S) \mid r(S, \pi, \pi_0) \geq R_0\}$. This means that given a present strategy by its opponents, coalition S will not select strategies that would make its position worse than a certain level with no change in the opponents' strategy. Note that this does not guarantee that $V(S) \geq R_0$ since N - S can play a strategy other than π_0. This merely assumes that S will not destroy its institutions unilaterally to create a threat. We call this the assumption of limited threats.

If we assume that all coalitions have some threshold below which they will not unilaterally go, then the modified Von Neumann-Morgenstern characteristic function with limited threats becomes the following:

$$V(S) = \max_{\pi_s \in \Phi(S)} \min_{\pi_{N-S} \in \Phi(N-S)} r(S, \pi_s, \pi_{n-s})$$

This characteristic function is more representative of the power of each coalition in most circumstances.

Solution Concepts

Having discussed some characteristic functions, we go into the second part of the model: choice of solution concepts. Solution concepts are mathematical methods for describing how coalitions bargain and reach outcomes. There are many plausible solution concepts; different solutions have various intuitive justifications.

Some solutions such as the bargaining set or the Von Neumann-Morgenstern solutions permit many outcomes. Others, such as the Nucleolus and the Shapley value, yield a single outcome.[2] In general, the more intuitively reasonable concepts have many outcomes, while the unique solutions rely on mathematical manipulation, sometimes at the expense of intuitiveness. Since the purpose of this chapter is to delineate general solutions rather than to pick out a unique outcome, we have chosen some of the more intuitive solutions: the core, core-stem, and level solutions.

The core is an older and better-known solution than the other two, which build from the core. The core rests on the idea of an objection. An objection to outcome occurs if some coalition can form that can obtain more than its allocation under the present outcome.

<u>Definition.</u> If X_O is an outcome, $\Sigma X_i = V(N)$. An objection to X by coalition S occurs if $V(S) > \Sigma_{i \in S} X_i$.

<u>Definition.</u> The core of a game V is the set of outcomes for which there are no objections by any coalition, $S \subset N$:

$$C(V) = \left\{ X \mid \sum_{i \in N} X_i = V(N), \sum_{i \in S} X_i \geq V(S), S \subset N \right\}$$

As one can see, the construction of the characteristic function is of importance in the use of the core. A coalition may bargain on the assumption that it can guarantee V(S) only to find that some other coalition T has a threat injurious to both S and T.

Consider the following example: $N = \{1, 2, 3\}$, $V(i) = 0$, $V(12) = 2$, $V(13) = 4$, $V(23) = 5$. A linear programming problem can be used to determine the smallest value for V(123) which will yield a core. A simple computation of the dual problem yields a value of 5.5.[3] Thus, if $V(1,2,3) \geq 5.5$ there will be a core, and if it is less than 5.5 there will not be. At $V(N) = 5.5$ there is a unique outcome (5.0, 1.5, 3.5).

The core is a very viable solution concept, but for a number of reasons it may not always be the most suitable solution concept. In a game that has numerous players and is played over a long period of time, actors may be slow in recognizing their best allies. The number of possible coalitions may be enormous; determining objections thus becomes a complicated process. There may be costs for actors in shifting coalitions that are difficult to model. Communication among actors may be very slow. There may also be noneconomic motivation that limits the coalition-forming behavior, so the core may not always be the most appropriate solution concept.

Martin Keane's example, called the BL[2] game, is a simple example of the core not necessarily being the most realistic solution concept.[4] In this game an individual has a heavy trunk to be carried from a railroad station. There are three men willing to do the job, which pays $1. None of the men can carry the trunk by himself, but the big man and either of the little men can carry it. The two little men cannot carry the trunk by themselves. The characteristic function is as follows:

$V(B) = V(L_1) = V(L_2) = 0 \quad V(BL_1) = 1 \quad V(BL_2) = 1$

$V(BL_1L_2) = 1 \quad V(L_1, L_2) = 0$

The core of the game is $1, 0, 0$, with the big man taking it all. While this is a plausible solution in some circumstances, other situations could also occur. Suppose that the two little men were to make an agreement not to be played-off against each other (a simple labor union). They could form a coalition and play as a unit against the big man. In the ensuing game both the big and the two little men would need the other's cooperation to divide the dollar. The core in this case is not the solution to the game.

This example illustrates the basic idea of two-solution concepts developed by Charnes and Sorenson: the level solution and the core-stem solution.[5] These related solutions arise from a sequential process that involves the formation of coalitions. This process describes a situation where a group of individuals form a coalition that is internally stable as measured by the core. They then agree to play as a unit in all further negotiations. Each coalition formation results in a level solution, with the players dividing up $V(S)$. The process of level solutions continues until one of two things happens: Either all has been divided up, and a core-stem solution occurs, or no further formations are possible. In this latter case there is a level solution that does not divide all of $V(N)$.

In our example the first-level solution occurred when L_1L_2 formed a coalition. The subgame was $V(L_1) = 0$, $V(L_2) = 0$, $V(L_1L_2) = 0$. Clearly, this game has a core. Then, after a level solution has formed, a partition game is played. The partition game results from the original game by deleting coalitions that are not unions of elements in the partition that arose from the level solution. In this case the level solution was $[(B_1), (L_1, L_2)]$ with $x_1, x_2, x_3 = 0$. The resulting partition games then had the coalitions $V(B) = 0 \quad V(L_1, L_2) = 0 \quad V(BL, L_2) = 1$. Notice that by agreeing to form a coalition and not to dissolve, L_1 and L_2 have neutralized the power of player B. The final core-stem solution results when the players divide up all of $V(N)$.

Now we state mathematically the definitions for core-stem and level solutions.

Definition. A partial outcome of a game is $\{X \mid X \in R^n \quad X_i \geq 0 \quad \Sigma_{i \in N} X_i \leq V(N)\}$

Definition. Let G be a set of coalitions, then a level solution $(\overline{X}, P)$ of (V, G, N) is a partial outcome $\overline{X}$ and partition P, such that $\forall S \in P\ \Sigma_{i \in S}\ X^i = V(S)$ and $\forall R \subset S\ \Sigma_{i \in T}\ X_i \geq V(T)$; $T \in G$.

Definition. A partition game of (V, G, N) is $[V\ G(P), N]$, where $G(P) = \{S \mid S \subset N \text{ and } S = \cup S_i, S_i \in P\}$. This means that the only coalitions allowed in a partition game are unions of the elements in the partition.

Definition. A core-stem sequence is a sequence of level solutions (X^k, P^k), such that (X^k, P^k) is a level solution to the game $(V, G(P_{k-1}), N)$ and $X_1^k \geq X_1^{k-1}$.

Definition. A core stem solution exists if there is a core-stem sequence $(X^k, P^k)_{k=1}^m$ and an m such that $\Sigma_{i \in N}\ X_i^m = V(N)$.

Theorem 6, 7. If for every partition P of N $\Sigma_{S \in P} V(S) \leq V(N)$, then (V, N) has a core-stem solution.[6]

Corollary. If V is superadditive—that is, $V(S) + V(T) \leq V(S \cup T)$ for $S \cap T = \emptyset$—then V has a core-stem solution and every coalition can form as a level solution.

This corollary indicates that if coalitions form by adding elements one at a time, they can eventually reach any size coalition they desire.

Although this theory was developed with the assumption that once a coalition formed it did not dissolve, this assumption can be relaxed with the introduction of some decision rules for coalition breakup. The rule we use will be that a member of a coalition will investigate the possibility of leaving if he should a get smaller outcome at time t than he received in a previous time period, t-1.

Most of the theoretical work on this concept has been concerned with the existence of core-stem solutions, but it is also clear that this concept is useful for modeling paths of coalition formation and for treating situations where coalitions have already formed. Thus, one can "look in" at the middle of a game without having to be concerned with how the present coalitions have formed. This can be of use when there are many players but only a few plausible coalitions that may form; this way the number of coalitions considered can be reduced to a workable number.

In the context of the oil situation, the level solution and core-stem solution seem akin to much of the recent history of oil companies and oil producers. For this reason, these solutions are applied to the model presented in the following section. Before discussing the model, however, it may be useful to illustrate these concepts with some events of recent oil history.

An example of a sequence of level solutions is the formation of OPEC. Each founding member had in 1960 no power over the multinational oil companies. Iraq and Venezuela were particularly interested in organizing a coalition that would be able to set production limits and at least keep companies from cutting prices as they had done in 1959. This coalition is a level solution. The addition of new members during the 1960s and 1970s, such as Libya, Algeria, Nigeria, and Ecuador, formed additional level solutions. It is probably untrue that all newcomers, such as Algeria, or even the founding members of OPEC are currently better off in OPEC than they would be in any other possible coalition. Undoubtedly, there is somewhere a case where the producer could do better by coalescing with a company and a consuming nation than it does in the OPEC coalition. Using the core for a solution concept, it would be necessary to argue that each actor belongs to the best possible coalition (considering all combinations of consuming nations, companies, and producing nations). That is a very restrictive concept, and it would probably lead to a conclusion that OPEC has always been an unviable organization, despite its 15 years of persistent existence. Instead, using a level-solution concept, the criterion is simply that the OPEC coalition have a core. That would seem to be the case. If OPEC does have a core, then the OPEC coalition would be expected to persist, even if the game as a whole should lack a core, until the benefit to some members of the coalition should substantially decrease. This is the idea of a level solution.

The difference between a level solution and a core-stem solution may be illustrated by a hypothetical future for the OPEC case. Clearly, OPEC alone does not divide up the entire value of the game; OPEC is only a subset of actors and is a level solution. Were the sequence of level solutions to continue, however, a core-stem solution might result. Other producing nations, such as Syria, Mexico, Canada, and China, would have to join the coalition. All consuming nations and companies would also have to join. The resulting global agreement would divide the entire value of the game and would be a core-stem solution.

It is interesting to note examples of level solutions between companies and producers. By 1973 oil revenues were so great for some Arab countries with small populations that they could cut production for noneconomic goals without violating their limited-threat constraint. This Arab boycott also enabled non-Arab OPEC nations to raise the price of their oil. The oil companies did not retaliate; cutting off production would have violated their own constraints. Instead, they joined in a virtual coalition with the oil-exporting countries and reaped high profits. Thus, a level solution formed between countries and companies.

As the present situation stands, the oil-producing companies and nations are in a coalition that is reaping high profits. OPEC is the dominant power group in this coalition. Perhaps it has enough wealth to nationalize all the oil companies' property and even to market oil, if the importing country will allow. Thus, the oil companies' characteristic function for revenue from oil is greatly diminished. They do still yield something to the coalition because of the cost that would be entailed if OPEC attempted to market oil itself. This is especially true since OPEC nations cannot obtain control of all "downstream" facilities without the host government's approval.

The oil-importing nations also have the opportunity of forming a coalition. Since there is an uneven distribution of oil-consuming nations, side payments would be necessary to keep the coalition together. Japan has a minimal amount of oil, while the United States has a great deal more, yet both need oil for their economies. Thus, the characteristic function for the oil consumers would have to reflect a rearrangement of oil so that the impact of a cut-off or increase in price would be minimized. This is likely to meet objection by the U.S. populace, for it is their oil that would no doubt be shipped to Japan to keep Japan in the coalition. The coalition may have a core, but it would no doubt have to be through side payments compensating the United States for its oil distribution. Whether such a level solution can be formed would depend on the side payment made to the United States.

Thus, it is possible that the oil-consuming nations could form a coalition. Then their characteristic function would be what they can do with an embargo by those nations in OPEC that can afford to embargo their oil. The OPEC characteristic function would be reduced by the quotas and tariffs imposed by the oil-consuming nations, again subject to their limited-threat constraint. The consumers best hope would be that some of the nations in OPEC would suffer decreased revenues, break ranks, and join in an agreement to supply oil at a lower price and higher quantity.

The key question here, using the level solutions, would be whether the subgame in OPEC has a core, or would have a core at reduced demands. If it does have a core in the side-payment case, then the OPEC coalition could hold simply by making a transfer payment from, say, Saudi Arabia to Indonesia. Alternatively, OPEC nations could coordinate production levels. If the producers' coalition does not have a core, it cannot stay together, according to the level-solution approach.

This discussion illustrates the level-solution concept in an informal manner. The solution concept is appealing because it seems to handle a number of things that have occurred in the oil situation. It is also appealing as a tool for looking in a more mathematical fashion at the conditions needed for successful formation of a consumers' coalition in the future. It is applied to the mathematical model that follows.

CONSTRUCTION OF THE CHARACTERISTIC-FUNCTION GAME

An illustration of the game-theoretic ideas of this chapter is an oil distribution and pricing system in a cooperative game framework. To model this we will construct characteristic functions for some of the important coalitions. (Here also an advantage of the core-stem solution appears: One need not construct all possible coalitions, since all possible coalitions need not form.) We will construct a plausible characteristic function by assuming that the various players set controls on production, and that then the pricing mechanism determines the revenue for the participants. First, we will give some definitions.

Index the oil producing nations by i, the multinational oil companies by j, and the oil consuming nations by k:

O_k = annual oil consumption by nation k
O_j = oil production from nondomestic sources by company j
O_i = oil production by country i
O_{ij} = oil production in country i by company j
O_{jk} = oil consumption by country k supplied by company j
O_{ik} = oil produced in country i and consumed in country k
O_{kk} = domestic oil production in country k
P_k = average price per barrel paid by country k
P_j = average price per barrel received by company j
P_i = average price per barrel received by country i
P_{kk} = average price per barrel of domestic oil
GNP_k = GNP of country k
PR_j = profit received by company j from production and supply of crude oil
Q_{ki} = quota on exported oil from nation i imported by nation k
T_k = tariff on imported oil
R_i = oil reserves in country i
M_{ri} = monetary reserves of country i
M_{ni} = monetary needs of country i
C_{uij} = upper limit on the annual production of crude oil in country i by company j

GAME THEORY MODEL

n_j = mark-up on a barrel of oil by company j
H_i = horizon of country j for oil (that is, the number of years from which it expects substantial income from oil)

The basic supply-and-demand equations are as follows:

$$O_k = \sum_{j \in J} O_{jk} + O_{kk} \tag{18.1}$$

$$O_j = \sum_{i \in I} O_{ij} \tag{18.2}$$

$$O_i = \sum_{j \in J} O_{ij} \tag{18.3}$$

$$\sum_{i \in I} O_{ik} = \sum_{j \in J} O_{jk} \tag{18.4}$$

$$O_{ij} \leq C_{uij} \tag{18.5}$$

$$\sum Cu_{ij} \leq Cu_i \tag{18.6}$$

$$P_j = (1 + n_j)(\sum_{i \in I} W_i P_i) \text{ with } \sum_{i \in I} W_i = 1, W_i \geq 0 \tag{18.7}$$

$$P_k = \sum W_j P_j + W_k P_{kk'} \text{ with } \sum W_j + W_k = 1, W_i \geq 0 \tag{18.8}$$

$$O_k = a_k P_k + a_k T_k + P_o \tag{18.9}$$

The first four equations are identities that ensure that all the oil produced is consumed. Equations 18.5 and 18.6 are constraints imposed by exporting countries on the amount of oil that is produced. Equation 18.7 is a weighted average of the price of the oil that then marks up this price by n_j before charging the consumers. Equation 18.8 is a weighted average of imported and domestic oil prices; W is the proportion of oil drawn from the sources. Equation 18.9 is the demand equation that says that consumption will be affected linearly by price and tariffs.

$$PR_j = n_j \sum_{i \in I} O_{ij} P_i \tag{18.10}$$

$$GNP_k = m_k O_k + m_{ok} \tag{18.11}$$

Equation 18.10 gives the profit on imported crude oil by company j. Equation 18.11 is based on the assumption that GNP is a linear function of the amount of oil consumed.

$$Cu_i \leq R_i/H_i \tag{18.12}$$

This constraint reflects the idea that no country wants to deplete its reserves too quickly; thus, each limits total output to some amount that is less than the reserves divided by the time period if it expects to rely on oil as a major source of revenue.

Notice that we have so far omitted profit-maximizing equations from the pricing mechanism. As we wish to allow the possibility of threats, we do not require that the oil-producing nations or oil companies always maximize profits. The optimizations will come in the construction of the characteristic function.

In employing a characteristic function we will use the limited-threat characteristic function to handle the possibility of threats. With the limited-threat characteristic function we still allow the possibility of threats but restrict the strategy set of each player so that any action they take does not unilaterally cause them to receive less than a certain minimum benefit.

Let us first look at the three major groups: oil producers, oil companies, and oil consumers. The limited-threat strategies for a set of oil-producing countries $S \subset I$ is as follows:

$$\Phi(S) = \{P_i \mid i \in S \sum [O_i P_i + M_{ri} \geq \sum M_{ni}]\}$$

This says that for fixed values of the decision variables for the other actors this group of producers will produce enough oil for their oil revenue plus a fraction of their monetary reserves to meet their essential monetary needs. Thus, a rich nation like Kuwait might be able to survive without oil revenue, while a poorer nation like Indonesia could not.

For a set of oil companies $T \subset J$ the limited threat strategy set is as follows:

$$\Phi(T) = \{O_j \mid j \in T \sum_{j \in T} PR_j \geq \sum_{j \in T} PR_{oj}\}$$

GAME THEORY MODEL

Again, this is with other actors' decision variables held constant. PR_{oj} is some profit level below which any company in T is not willing to go. In the case of a purely profit-maximizing firm, $PR_{oj} = PR_{opt}$, the optimal profit for that company.

For a set of oil consumers our limited threat strategy for $U \subset K$ is as follows:

$$\Phi(U) = \{T_k \mid k \in U \sum_{K \in U} GNP_k \geq \sum_{K \in U} GNP_{k_o} \}$$

Again, GNP_{k_o} is a level of GNP within the minimum acceptable level for country k, and, as before, this calculation is made with the other variables held constant.

For unions of producers and oil companies we can construct a similar limited-threat strategy. For other such unions, let $\Phi(S \cup T) = \Phi(S) \times \Phi(T)$. Then we can calculate the characteristic function of each coalition as follows.

For $U \subset K$, the oil consumers $V(U) =$

$$\max_{\pi \in \Phi(U)} \min_{\pi \in \Phi(N-U)} \sum_{k \in U} GNP_k$$

For $S \subset I$, the oil producers $V(S) =$

$$\max_{\pi \in \Phi(S)} \min_{\pi \in \Phi(N-S)} \sum_{i \in S} O_i P_i$$

For $T \subset I$, the oil companies $V(T) =$

$$\max_{\pi \in \Phi(T)} \min_{\pi \in \Phi(N-T)} \sum_{j \in T} PR_j$$

These characteristic functions reflect the notion of the best you can do subject to the worst your opponent can do, given that both of you are not willing to engage in very risky strategies that are precluded by the limited-threat strategy sets.

For coalitions that are unions of more than one type, such as oil producers and companies, we add the objective function and maximize over the joint-strategy set. This does not imply that V will be additive, since the oil producers and companies can set prices to maximize joint revenue subject to their limited-threat constraints. Definition V(S) is well-defined if

$$\min_{\pi_2 \in \Phi(N-S)} \max_{\pi_1 \in \Phi(S)} \sum_i r_i(\pi_1, \pi_2) = $$

$$\max_{\pi_1 \in \Phi(S)} \min_{\pi_2 \in \Phi(N-S)} \sum_{i \in S} r_i(\pi_1, \pi_2)$$

V is well-defined whenever the Von Neumann Minimax theorem is true.

Theorem. Let S, T be disjoint sets, if V(S) and V(T) are well-defined and the optimal strategies for s in problem V(S) and T for V(T) satisfy constraints 18.1 to 18.12 when coupled with the optimal strategy for N-S-T, and if $V(S) \geq \Sigma_{i \in S} r_{i0}$ $V(T) \geq \Sigma_{i \in T} r_{i0}$, then $V(S) + V(T) \leq V(S \cup T)$.

This theorem gives conditions under which a coalition can be formed and its members benefit. The well-defined condition means that both sides can play their optimal strategies and S can only benefit from a deviation by its opponent. The next condition is to insure that strategies available in separate coalitions are still playable in the union when one's opponent plays its optimal strategy. The final condition requires that the limited-threat levels be below the minimax value for the coalition; otherwise, situations could arise where a coalition would have no acceptable strategies. With these conditions S and T can join in a more powerful coalition.

Proof. Let π_0 be the initial strategy from which the limited-threat strategies are computed. Note that since π_0 is an acceptable strategy $\pi_S \in \Phi(S)$ for all $S \subset N$ where π_S denotes the S-tuple of strategies.

The individual objective functions $r_i(\pi)$ are additive, so that

$$V(S) = \max_{\pi_1 \in \Phi(S)} \min_{\pi_2 \in \Phi(N-S)} \sum_{i \in S} r_i(\pi_1, \pi_2)$$

Since V(S) is well-defined, the minimax property implies that V has the saddle-point property. That is if π_1', π_2' are the respective optimal strategies, then for any other π_1, π_2 the following holds:

$$\sum_{i \in S} r_i(\pi_1', \pi_2) \geq \sum_{i \in S} r_i(\pi_1', \pi_2') \geq \sum_{i \in S} r_i(\pi_1, \pi_2')$$

For disjoint coalitions S, T, let π_S', π_T'' be the optimal strategy for S and T in their respective problems. Then

$$\sum_{i \in S} r_i(\pi'_S, \pi''_T, \pi_{N-S-T}) \geq \sum_{i \in S} r_i(\pi'_S, \pi'_{N-S}) = V(S)$$

$$\sum_{i \in S} r_i(\pi'_S, \pi''_T, \pi_{N-S-T}) \geq \sum_{i \in S} r_i(\pi''_T, \pi''_{N-T}) = V(T)$$

This holds for all $\pi_{N-S-T} \in \Phi(N-S-T)$. So

$$\min_{\pi_{N-S-T} \in \Phi(N-S-T)} \sum_{i \in S \cup T} r_i(\pi'_S, \pi''_T, \pi_{N-S-T}) \geq V(S) + V(T)$$

Let π^m_{N-S-T} be the optimal strategy for N-S-T; then, by hypothesis $(\pi'_S, \pi''_T, \pi^m_{N-S-T})$ satisfies constraints 18.1 to 18.12, so we need only show that $\pi'_S \times \pi''_T \in \Phi(S \cup T)$. But $\pi_{ON-S-T} \in \Phi(N-S-T)$, so by the saddle-point property we have the following:

$$\sum r_i(\pi'_S, \pi''_T, \pi_{N-S-T}) \geq V(S) + V(T) \geq \sum_{i \in S} r_{i0} + \sum_{i \in S} r_{i0}$$

Therefore, the limited-threat constraint still holds and $\pi'_S \times \pi''_T \in \Phi(S \cup T)$. Thus

$$\max_{\pi(S \cup T) \in \Phi(S \cup T)} \min_{\pi_{N-S-T} \in \Phi(N-S-T)} \sum_{i \in S \cup T} r_i(\pi_{S \cup T}, \pi_{N-S-T})$$

$$\geq V(S) + V(T)$$

and V is superadditive on these coalitions. If $\Phi(S) \times \Phi(T) = \Phi(S \cup T)$, then this last requirement is met directly.

There are some important special cases to this theorem. First, if we are dealing with mixed strategies (randomized selection of decisions), then, because the objective functions are continuous and the decision variable can be bounded to place them in a compact convex set, one version of the minimax theorem guarantees that V(S) will be well-defined for all $S \subset N$.[7]

If on the other hand we use pure strategies (nonrandomized decisions), then for any coalition of players of the same type—companies or oil producers, or consumers—the objective functions are bilinear forms with a maximization over one set of variables and a minimization over the other. Again, by bounding the price and tariff variable by sufficiently large values, we will again have a convex compact set, and we can apply the minimax theorem as well, so that coalitions of oil producers, consumers, and companies are each well-defined.[8]

The interesting case occurs when we consider oil producers plus oil companies. In this case the objective function is quadratic in the maximization variables, so the minimax theorem may not apply. However, if S is purely oil producers and T is purely oil companies, then if the other conditions are met $V(S \cup T) \geq V(S) + V(T)$, even if $V(S \cup T)$ is not well-defined. Therefore, in many of the cases of interest pure strategy of the type contained in the limited-threat constraint will be sufficient for our purposes. The alternative is to use mixed strategies to get a well-defined characteristic function.

The second criterion of importance is feasibility. Again, we see that for any of the major types, feasibility is no problem. Oil producers can set their prices at any level and not violate equations 18.1 to 18.12. They must consider their limited threat constraints in setting P_i, but this is not at issue here. Similarly, the oil consumers can set their tariffs as they wish, still satisfying the first 12 equations.

The oil companies can produce up to their limit in each country and still satisfy these constraints. By adjusting their P_j, they can guarantee that the amount of oil they produce will balance with the demand equation. Similarly, unions of producers and oil companies can satisfy the feasibility constraints. Thus, we can say that, for unions of coalitions of one type, V is superadditive, if the limited-threat level $r_{i0} \leq V(i)$ for each player in that group. Likewise, if this condition is satisfied, then for consumers, producers, and oil companies V(S) is superadditive. Additionally, if S is a set of producers and T is a set of companies, then if the limited-threat levels are low enough, V is superadditive here as well.

FURTHER DEDUCTIVE OUTCOMES

This section discusses some specific outcomes of the model. It is useful to know whether the model allows for events that have happened, such as the formation of OPEC. It is also useful to consider various futures, such as formation of a coalition of consumers, producers, or companies, or conditions under which OPEC becomes of little worth to its members. Five simple results are presented and proved below. The first three theorems pertain to certain kinds of coalitions. The final two theorems are concerned with conditions for breaking up OPEC. The main implication of this section is that OPEC is in a strong position.

A first question to ask of the model and the solution concepts used here is whether a coalition of producing nations can form as a level solution. Theorem 1 below specifies conditions under which a coalition such as an OPEC can form:

Theorem 1. Let I be the set of oil producing countries. If $M_{ni} - M_{ri} \leq V(i)$ for all $i \in I$, the oil producers, then there is a level solution that divides up V(I) among all the players in I, and coalition I can form.

Proof. By the superadditivity theorem, if $r_{i0} \leq V(i)$ for all $i \in I$, the strategies are feasible, and V is well-defined, then V is superadditive. $M_{ni} - M_{ri} \leq V(i)$ implies that r_i is sufficiently low. The pricing strategies are feasible. Because the objective function is bilinear (linear in price variables and linear in oil variables controlled by the companies), the minimax theorem applies. Then, by the theorem on level solutions and the superadditivity of V on this set of coalitions, the existence of a level solution for all $i \in I$ is given. Additionally, coalition I can form from a series of smaller unions.

This result says that if the oil producers' needs minus their reserves are less than the amount they can guarantee themselves in dealing with the oil companies, then a coalition of producers can form.

One question that numerous observers of the oil situation discuss is the extent of cooperation between oil producers and multinational oil companies in raising oil prices. This chapter does not consider the empirical question of what sorts of cooperation have occurred, but a statement of conditions under which a level solution of producers and companies can form is given in Theorem 2:

Theorem 2. Let the producers and oil companies be in coalitions I, J. If $\Sigma_{i \in I} M_{ni} - M_{ri} \leq V(I)$, and if $\Sigma_{j \in J} Pr_{oj} \leq V(J)$, then there is a level solution between oil companies and oil producers which allows the formation of coalition I∪J.

Proof. This follows again from the same two theorems. V(I) and V(J) are well-defined since their objective functions are bilinear, and their joint strategies are feasible for the constraints as well. Thus, $V(I \cup J) \geq V(I) + V(J)$. Therefore, a level solution can form, with the excess profit $V(I \cup J) - V(I) - V(J)$ divided among the two groups.

This result says that if the producers have adequate reserves and if the oil companies' minimum profit level is below the maximum profit they can guarantee themselves under adverse circumstances, then both can benefit from this coalition. Thus in our model, at least, under some simple conditions it is possible for a coalition of oil producers and oil companies to form.

It is next appropriate to consider whether a coalition of oil consumers is viable, and, if so, whether a grand coalition of consumers, producers, and oil companies can form. Theorem 3 states that if the oil consumers wish to maximize their GNP their best strategy is to reduce tariffs to their lowest levels:

Theorem 3. If $a_k, a_k' < 0$ for all $k \in K$, then, given any strategy for oil producers, oil companies, and oil consumers $k \notin U$, the optimal strategy to maximize $V(U)$ is to reduce tariffs to their lowest levels.

Proof. To maximize GNP under our model is to maximize the amount of oil entering the country. Since $a_k < 0$, this maximization is accomplished by minimizing the price for oil. Clearly, this is accomplished by setting tariffs at the minimum feasible level. Thus, for any strategy undertaken by other consumers, producers, and companies the minimum tariff maximizes GNP.

One implication of this result is that for any strategy adopted by producers and companies, such as a joint revenue-maximizing strategy, the characteristic function for the oil consumers is additive, $V(K) = \Sigma_{k \in K} V(k)$. Thus, while nothing is lost by forming such a coalition to limit oil imports, any nation can do no better in the coalition than it can do alone. It is to the individual nation's benefit to have lower tariffs. If the coalition of producers and companies has adopted a strategy of maximizing profits, then this result suggests that the coalition of producers and companies discussed above is the final solution to the game. Since the consuming nations gain nothing by forming their own bloc, further coalitions would be extremely weak.

There are conditions, of course, under which the producers coalition is likely to become unviable. Theorem 4 states some conditions under which the value of the producers coalition would equal zero.

Theorem. Let $S \subset I$, the set of oil producing countries. If $P_i = P_j$ for all $i, j \in I$, and if $\Sigma_{i \in I-S} Cu_i \geq \Sigma_{i \in I} O_i$, then $V(S) = 0$.

Proof. If $\Sigma_{i \in I-S} Cu_i \geq \Sigma_{i \in I} O_i$, then the oil-producing companies can pump the oil from I-S and still pump out the same amount of oil at the same price, and then $Pr_j = Pr_{oj}$, the initial profit; therefore, this strategy does not violate the limited-threat constraint. Since the countries not in S are pumping out more oil at the same price, its revenues are not decreased. The oil consumers need take no action as they will still receive the same amount of oil. Note that lowering prices by S will not affect the value of V(S), since we assume the oil companies are not maximizing profit but merely exercising their limited threat strategy.

This statement simply means that if a producer supplies less oil than the surplus available elsewhere, other actors can ignore that country without violating their own limited-threat constraint. The theorem is simple but important.

Iran in 1951 is an example of a country lacking bargaining power because its production is less than the surplus available elsewhere. Annoyed by the hesitance of the foreign companies that controlled Iran's production to agree to more equitable financial arrangements, the Iranian government took over the oil industry. The multinational companies simply stepped up production in Kuwait, Iraq, and Saudi Arabia. Until a government shift in Iran and a subsequent agreement with the companies in 1954, Iran was unable to export oil. The effects on its economy were substantial.

A few years later five nations founded OPEC. During its early years OPEC had few important successes. Presumably, the conditions of theorem 4 still held. With the addition of other oil-producing nations in the 1960s, a rise in world oil consumption, and a rise in OPEC's share of the known world oil reserves, the strength of this coalition grew. The price rises OPEC effected in the 1970s suggest that theorem 4 no longer applies. Thus, we need another theorem that stipulates conditions under which the producers coalition has some power.

With theorem 5 it can be seen that the coalition of oil producers derives benefit from profit maximization policies of oil companies and from the current oil requirements of consuming nations.

Theorem 5. Assume each consuming nation has a limited-threat level which is equal to present value of GNP. If the present strategy of the oil companies is profit maximization, their limited threat level = $\Sigma_{j \in J}$, present profit level, and if $\Sigma_{i \in I-S} Cu_i < \Sigma_{i \in I} O_i$, $P_i = P_j$, then $V(S) > 0$, where S is a collection of oil countries.

Proof. If the oil companies pumped no oil from S, then their total amount of oil would drop. By the profit-maximization hypothesis this would result in a lower total profit. By the limited-threat constraint this strategy is not acceptable so long as tariffs remain at the same level. Since the oil companies cannot shut down the oil producers completely, this implies that a positive amount of oil will be pumped out of the nations in S.

Note that the theorem also holds if the oil companies are not profit maximizing, so long as the drop in production, $\Sigma_{i \in I-S} c u_i$, times the new price at this lower level is sufficient to meet the minimum profit level of that collection of companies. If coalition S controls a sufficiently large share of oil production, then the oil companies cannot make sufficient profits in the remaining countries not in the cartel.

Theorem 5 indicates (unless new oil is found) that, even with zero-growth policies (that is, zero increase in all forms of petroleum consumption) by the consumers, OPEC continues to provide benefit for its members. In other words, even if there is no increase in oil consumption in the rest of the world, it is worthwhile for the heterogeneous group of nations that comprise OPEC to remain in their coalition. Zero increase in petroleum consumption seems unlikely. A decrease in worldwide petroleum consumption in the near future is even more unlikely. Theorem 5 thus suggests that breaking up OPEC is no easy matter, whether companies are maximizing profits or not.

NOTES

1. U.S. Library of Congress, Congressional Research Service, "Oil Fields as Military Objectives: A Feasibility Study," prepared for the Special Subcommittee on International Relations (Washington, D.C.: Government Printing Office, 1975), pp. 62 and 66.

2. David Schmeidler, "On the Nucleolus of a Characteristic Function Game," SIAM Journal of Applied Mathematics 17 (1969): 1163-70; L. S. Shapley, "A Value for N-Person Games," in Contributions to the Theory of Game, vol. 2, ed. H. W. Kuhn and A. W. Tucker (Princeton, N.J.: Princeton University Press, 1953).

3. A. Charnes and K. Kortanek, "On Balanced Sets, Cores and Linear Programming," Cahiers du Centre d'Etudes de Recherche Operationnelle 9 (1967): 32-43.

4. Martin Keane, "Some Topics in N-Person Game Theory,"

5. A. Charnes and S. Sorensen, "Hierarchical Games," Research Report 61 (Austin: University of Texas, Center for Cybernetic Studies); S. Sorensen, "A Mathematical Theory of Coalitions and Competition in Resource Development," Ph.D. dissertation, University of Texas, 1972.

6. S. Sorensen, "Mathematical Theory of Coalitions," p. 107; Charles Bird, "Extension of Bargaining Concepts to Infinite Player Games," Ph.D. dissertation, Pittsburgh, Carnegie-Mellon University, 1973.

7. John Von Neumann and Oscar Morgenstern, Theory of Games and Economic Behavior (New York: Wiley, 1953).

8. Abraham Wald, "Foundations of a General Theory of Sequential Decisions Functions," Econometrica 15 (1947): 279-313.

ABOUT THE CONTRIBUTORS

William H. Baugh, Assistant Professor of Political Science, Michigan State University

Charles Bird, Assistant Professor of Mathematics, University of Georgia

George T. Duncan, Assistant Professor of Statistics, Carnegie-Mellon University

John A. Ferejohn, Associate Professor of Political Science, California Institute of Technology

John V. Gillespie, Associate Professor of Political Science and Director, Center for International Policy Studies, Indiana University

Brian L. Job, Assistant Professor of Political Science, University of Minnesota

Manus I. Midlarsky, Professor of Political Science, University of Colorado

Charles W. Ostrom, Jr., Assistant Professor of Political Science, Michigan State University

Anatol Rapoport, Professor of Psychology, University of Toronto

James N. Rosenau, Professor and Director, School of International Studies, University of Southern California

R. Michael Rubison, Fellow, Center for International Policy Studies and Department of Mathematics, Indiana University

Martin W. Sampson III, Research Associate, Social Studies Development Center, Indiana University

Philip A. Schrodt, Fellow, Center for International Policy Studies, Indiana University

Roslyn L. Simowitz, Research Associate, Center for International Policy Studies, Indiana University

Randolph M. Siverson, Assistant Professor of Political Science, University of California, Davis

Michael L. Squires, Research Associate, Center for Naval Analyses

Dina A. Zinnes, Professor, Department of Political Science and Center for International Policy Studies, Indiana University

RELATED TITLES
Published by
Praeger Special Studies

QUANTITATIVE INTERNATIONAL POLITICS:
An Appraisal
       Edited by Francis W. Hoole
       and Dina A. Zinnes

CONTROL THEORY AND INTERNATIONAL
RELATIONS RESEARCH
       Edited by John V. Gillespie
       and Dina A. Zinnes

QUANTITATIVE TECHNIQUES IN FOREIGN POLICY
ANALYSIS AND FORECASTING
       Michael K. O'Leary and
       William D. Coplin, with the
       assistance of Howard B. Shapiro

POLITICS OF DIVISION, PARTITION, AND
UNIFICATION
       Edited by Ray Edward Johnston

INTERNATIONAL ADMINISTRATION AND
GLOBAL PROBLEMS: An Analysis of the
World Food Conference
       Thomas G. Weiss and
       Robert S. Jordan